The Guns of August 2008
Russia's War in Georgia

Edited by Svante E. Cornell and S. Frederick Starr

Wars always give rise to a flood of self-justifications by the contending states and tendentious claims from other interested parties. The brief war between Russia and Georgia in August 2008 is no exception. Absent from all the polemics has been authoritative information on the actual course of events. This pioneering study by ten highly regarded experts traces the roots of the conflict back more than a decade. It details the intense preparations that preceded the war, the key moments of the fighting itself, and the broader consequences of the conflict to date.

This goes far toward establishing "what actually happened," which is precisely what the nineteenth-century German historian Leopold von Ranke considered the starting point for true understanding.

Studies of Central Asia and the Caucasus

Books in this series are published in association with the Central Asia–Caucasus Institute of the Johns Hopkins University's Paul H. Nitze School of Advanced International Studies, under the editorship of S. Frederick Starr.

THE
GUNS
OF AUGUST
2008
RUSSIA'S WAR
IN GEORGIA

SVANTE E. CORNELL & S. FREDERICK STARR
EDITORS

M.E.Sharpe
Armonk, New York
London, England

Library of Congress Cataloging-in-Publication Data

The guns of August 2008 : Russia's war in Georgia / edited by Svante E. Cornell and
S. Frederick Starr.
  p. cm. — (Studies of Central Asia and the Caucasus)
Includes bibliographical references and index.
ISBN 978-0-7656-2507-6 (cloth : alk. paper)— ISBN 978-0-7656-2508-3 (pbk. : alk. paper)
  1. Georgia (Republic)—Military relations—Russia (Federation) 2. Russia (Federation)—
Military relations—Georgia (Republic) 3. Georgia (Republic)—Foreign relations—Russia
(Federation) 4. Russia (Federation)—Foreign relations—Georgia (Republic) 5. South Ossetia
(Georgia)—History, Military—21st century. 6. Abkhazia (Georgia)—History, Military—21st
century. 7. Transcaucasia—History, Military—21st century. 8. Russia (Federation)—Foreign
relations—1991– 9. Russia (Federation)—Military policy. 10. National security—Europe—
Case studies. I. Cornell, Svante E. II. Starr, S. Frederick.

DK676.9.R8G86 2009
947.5808′62—dc22   2009019849

Printed in the United States of America

The paper used in this publication meets the minimum requirements of
American National Standard for Information Sciences
Permanence of Paper for Printed Library Materials,
ANSI Z 39.48-1984.

∞

| IBT (c) | 10 | 9 | 8 | 7 | 6 | 5 | 4 | 3 | 2 | 1 |
| VG (p) | 10 | 9 | 8 | 7 | 6 | 5 | 4 | 3 | 2 | 1 |

Contents

vi

List of Tables and Illustrative Materials

Maps

Leaflets

Tables

Boxes

Photographs

Photographs follow page xiv.

Photographs by Interpressnews (IPN)

List of Acronyms

BTC	Baku–Tbilisi–Ceyhan pipeline
CIS	Commonwealth of Independent States
CUG	Citizens' Union of Georgia
EU	European Union
FSB	Federal Security Service of the Russian Federation
GAF	Georgian Armed Forces
GRU	Foreign Military Intelligence Directorate of the General Staff of the Armed Forces of the Russian Federation
GTEP	Georgia Train and Equip Program
IDP	Internally Displaced Person
IMF	International Monetary Fund
ISFED	International Society for Fair Elections and Democracy
JCC	Joint Control Commission
MAP	Membership Action Plan
MFA	Ministry of Foreign Affairs
NATO	North Atlantic Treaty Organization
NCMD	North Caucasus Military District
NGO	Non-governmental Organization
ODIHR	Office for Democratic Institutions and Human Rights
OSCE	Organization for Security and Co-operation in Europe
PfP	Partnership for Peace
RFE/RL	Radio Free Europe/Radio Liberty
SSR	Soviet Socialist Republic
UAV	Unmanned Aerial Vehicle
UNOMIG	United Nations Observer Mission in Georgia
ZAKVO	Russian Transcaucasian Military District

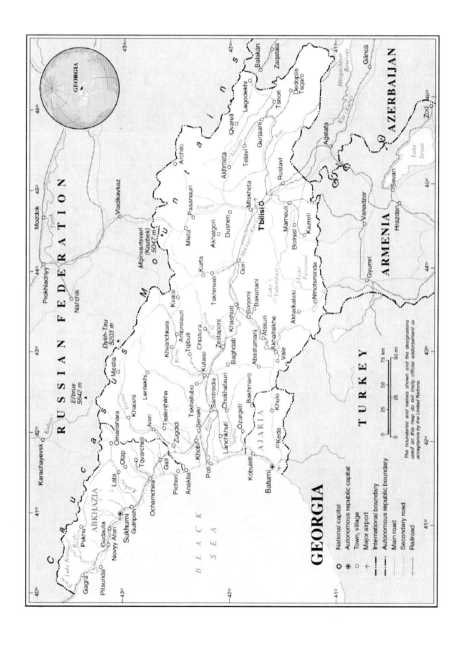

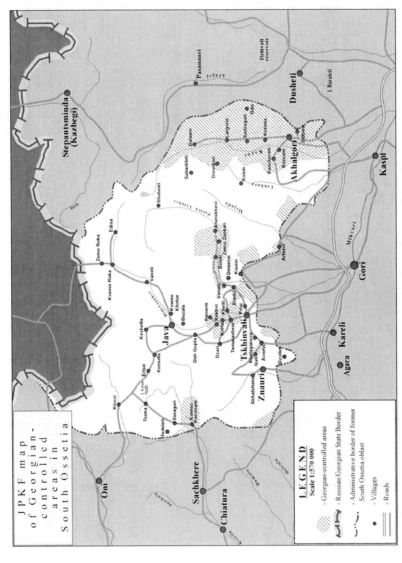

Joint Peace-Keeping Force map (International Crisis Group)

Leaflet distributed to Russian forces during Kavkaz-2008 military exercises in the North Caucasus, July 2008 (in Russian).

ВОИН, ЗНАЙ ВЕРОЯТНОГО ПРОТИВНИКА!

С 2001 года руководство Грузии резко изменило свой курс на добрососедские и дружественные отношения с Россией. Избрав направление на эскалацию отношений с нашим государством, руководство Грузии всяческими путями стремится вступить в состав НАТО, активно проводит милитаризацию страны.

Состав ВС Грузии: сухопутные войска, военно-воздушные силы и ПВО, военно-морские силы, национальная гвардия.

Численность ВС Грузии — 32 700 чел.

Бюджет министерства обороны на 2008 год — $970 млн.

Сухопутные войска

Численность 22 000 чел.

Сухопутные войска Грузии включают 5 бригад и 8 отд. батальонов

-1-я **пехотная бригада** (г. Гори). В 2002-2004гг. прошла обучение по американской программе GTEP, в 2005-2006гг. - частично по американской программе GSSOP.

-2-я **пехотная бригада** (н.п. Сенаки и г. Батуми). В 2005г. прошла обучение по американской программе GSSOP, в 2005-2006гг. прошла «обкатку» в Ираке.

-3-я **пехотная бригада** (г. Кутаиси и н.п. Ахалцихе). В 2006г. прошла обучение по американской программе GSSOP II, в 2006-2008гг. прошла «обкатку» в Ираке, 32-й батальон в 2007г. был в Косово.

-4-я **пехотная бригада** (г. Тбилиси и н.п. Мухровани). Сформирована из военнослужащих бывших внутренних войск.

-5-я **пехотная бригада** (г. Батуми и г. Поти).

На вооружении грузинской армии состоит:

танки:Т-72Б1, Т-72М Т-72АВ (по планам министерства обороны Грузии все 165 единиц Т-72 проходят модернизацию до уровня Т-72-SIM-1).

БМП: БМП-1, БМП-2, БТР-80, МТЛБ, БРДМ-2, бронеавтомобили Кобра.

Ствольная артиллерия: 203-мм 2С7 САУ "Пион", 152-мм 2С19 САУ Мста-С, 152-мм буксируемая гаубица 2А65 Мста-Б, 152-мм 2А36 буксируемая пушка Гиацинт-Б, 152-мм САУ DANA, 122-мм 2С3 САУ Акация, 22-мм буксируемая гаубица 2А18 Д-30, 100-мм буксируемая пушка МТ-12, 40 85-мм буксируемая пушка Д-44.

РСЗО: 262-мм М-87 РСЗО "Оркан", 122-мм-160-мм РСЗО Лар-160 "Град-лар", 122-мм РСЗО RM-70, 122-мм РСЗО БМ-21 Град, 128-мм М63 РСЗО "Пламен".

26 января 2008 года Грузия объявила об отказе от автоматов Калашникова в пользу автоматических винтовок М-4 американского производства.

Сильные стороны:

- подготовка многих подразделений сухопутных войск Грузии инструкторами НАТО;

- оснащение ВС Грузии современным американским, французским и турецким вооружением и техникой. Имеющиеся образцы вооружения и техники советского образца усовершенствуются или заменяются новейшими;

- финансирование подготовки войск США и НАТО;

- наличие боевого опыта подразделений 2-й и 3-й полевых бригад в Ираке, Косово в составе войск НАТО.

Слабые стороны:

- низкое состояние воинской дисциплины и морально-психологическое состояние военнослужащих. Имеются случаи дезертирства, проявления неуставных взаимоотношений, пьянства в подразделениях сухопутных войск;

- как показали опубликованные недавно опросы военнослужащих ВС Грузии, самой большой и светлой мечтой грузинского солдата является не претворение в жизнь агрессивно-милитаристских планов "саакашистов", а командировка в Ирак. По итогам такой поездки каждый грузинский воин может привезти домой около 10 тысяч долларов США и существенно поправить бедственное положение своей семьи;

- низкая обученность личного состава подразделений, в которых нет американских инструкторов.

Отпечатано в типографии газеты «Доблесть»   Зак. №4-08 xii

Soldier, know your probable enemy!

Starting in 2001, the government of Georgia abruptly changed its course towards neighborly and friendly relations with Russia. Choosing to exploit relations with our country, the Georgian government is using all possible means to enter the NATO club by actively increasing militarization of the country.

Composition of Georgian Armed Forces: ground troops, air force and air defense forces, navy forces, national guard.

Number of Georgian Armed Forces – 32,700 men.

The Defense Ministry budget for 2008 – $970 million.

Ground Troops

Size – 22,000 men.

The Armed Forces include five brigades and eight separate battalions.

1st infantry brigade (Gori city). In 2002–2004 underwent training based on American Georgia Train and Equip Program (GTEP). In 2005–2006 – partially [underwent] American Georgia Sustainment and Stability Operation Program (GSSOP).

2nd infantry brigade (Senaki town and Batumi city). In 2005 underwent training based on American GSSOP; 2005–2006 underwent "operation test" in Iraq.

3rd infantry brigade (Kutaisi city and Ahaltsihe town). In 2006 underwent training based on American GSSOP II; in 2006–2008 underwent "operation test" in Iraq; in 2007, was [part of] a special battalion in Kosovo.

4th infantry brigade (Tbilisi city and Muhrovani town). Composed of armed personnel formerly serving at the Interior Ministry.

5th infantry brigade (Batumi city and Poti town).

The Georgian Army forces include [the following armaments]:

Tanks: T-72B1, T-72M, T-72AB (according to plans of the Georgian Defense Ministry, all of 165 units of T-72 tanks are currently being upgraded to T-72-SIM-1).

Armored personnel carriers: APC-1, APC-2, APC-80, MT-LB multipurpose tracked vehicles, BRDM-2, armored car Cobra.

Bombardment artillery: 203 mm 2S7 "Pion" self-propelled artillery gun, 152 mm 2S19 MSTA-S self-propelled howitzer, 152 mm 2A65 Msta-B howitzer, 152 mm 2A36 "Giatsint-B" artillery gun, 152 mm ShKH Dana vz.77, 152-mm self-propelled howitzer 2S3 "Akatsiya," 22-mm howitzer 2A18 (D-30), 40 85-mm divisional gun D-44.

Multiple artillery rocket system: 262 mm M-87 "Orkan" MLRS, GRADLAR 122mm/160 mm, 122 mm RM-70, 122 mm Multiple Rocket Launcher BM-22 "Grad," 128 mm M-63 artillery rocket "Plamen."

On January 26, 2008 Georgia announced its refusal to purchase "Kalashnikov" machine guns in favor of M-4 machine guns produced by America.

Strengths:

- training of most of Georgian ground troops by NATO instructors; equipment of Georgian Armed Forces by modern American, French, and Turkish armament and technologies. Current armament and technologies of the Soviet production are being modernized or replaced by new units;

- training of troops is financed by the United States and NATO;

- combat experience of the 2nd and 3rd infantry brigades in Iraq and Kosovo as part of NATO forces.

Weaknesses:

- low level of discipline, military morale, and integrity among military personnel. Cases of desertion, hazing, and alcoholism are present across ground troops divisions;

- as recently published survey results of Georgian Armed Forces personnel show, the biggest and the brightest dream of a Georgian soldier is not execution of militaristic and aggressive plans of *saakashists*, but deployment to Iraq. After such a trip [to Iraq], every Georgian soldier is able to bring back home up to $10,000 and substantially improve his family's dire situation;

- low level of education among staff divisions that do not include NATO instructors.

Published by *Doblest'* newspaper's printing house.

Translated from Russian by Erica Marat.

Acknowledgments

This book is the product of an active collaboration among many persons. First, of course, comes the team of authors, who interrupted their busy schedules to produce chapters for the book. They performed like an orchestra of old pros who produce fine concerts with scarcely a rehearsal. We feel honored to have worked with such rigorous and principled colleagues. Scarcely less crucial to the project was the staff of the Joint Center, all of whom worked into the night to bring the book to fruition. Our particular thanks go to Mr. Alec Forss, the publications editor at the Joint Center's Stockholm office, as well as to two interns who ably assisted him, Mr. Andreas Mälarstedt and Ms. Tina Kavadze. We are especially grateful to Ms. Patricia Kolb and her hard-working colleagues at M.E. Sharpe, Inc., all of whom immediately grasped the importance of the topic and guided our enthusiasms into productive channels. We should also like to express our gratitude to InterpressNews (IPN) for kindly allowing us to use their photos of the war in this book. The bold and evocative cover is the work of Ms. Anna Starr Townsend. It features the Georgian five-cross flag, which dates back to the early middle ages and was adopted as the national flag by Georgia's Parliament in 2004. The cannon is from the time of Georgia's annexation by the Russian empire in the early nineteenth century, a fitting symbol for a war which seems to have fallen into our modern world directly from an earlier age of empire and territorially-based Realpolitik.

In the Caucasian Hills

On the Outskirts of Tskhinvali

Broken Russian Tank Outside Gori

Georgian Forces on the Road Toward Tskhinvali

Bombed Railway Bridge at Kaspi

Ossetian Militias at a Checkpoint in Gori

Georgian Soldiers in Gredvi

Bombed-out Building in Gori

Russian Forces establishing Positions at Igoeti

Courtesy of InterPressNews (IPN)

Bombed-out Building in Gori

Courtesy of InterPressNews (IPN)

Russian Forces at Igoeti

Courtesy of InterPressNews (IPN)

A Chechen Paramilitary

Russian Highway Checkpoint at Igoeti

Russian Forces in Poti

President Saakashvili at a Briefing

Saakashvili with East European Presidents in Tbilisi, 12 August

Saakashvili with U.S. Secretary of State Condoleezza Rice in Tbilisi

Saakashvili with President Nicolas Sarkozy of France

THE
GUNS
OF AUGUST
2008

1

Introduction

Svante E. Cornell and S. Frederick Starr

In the summer of 2008 an unprecedented event occurred. For the first time since 1979 the Russian military crossed national borders to attack a sovereign state. This attack followed a period of intensive and mainly negative developments in Russia's relations with Georgia and, more significantly, in Russia's relations with the West. What appeared to have begun in the breakaway Georgian territory of South Ossetia rapidly escalated to the most significant crisis in European security in a decade.

This war took the world by surprise. Yet over the preceding months those closely watching events in the Caucasus had been calling attention to the escalating conflict in the region. Steps taken by the Russian leadership following the Western recognition of Kosovo's independence in February 2008, and the NATO Bucharest Summit in April brought the situation in the Caucasus to an entirely new level. In spite of a mass of readily available information on the Russian arms buildup, however, Western governments were caught off guard when simmering tensions in the Georgian conflict zones exploded into full-scale war.

Few international events of this magnitude have been so quickly submerged under a cloud of polemics involving both spin and disinformation. The media coverage of the war during the crucial first few days largely reflected Russia's line. We now know part of the reason for this, namely, that the Russian government had flown some fifty Russian reporters to Tskhinvali days before the war began. In the West, the media's opinion-dominated news cycle from the outset prevailed over more authoritative reporting. Staff cutbacks in many news media left few qualified reporters available. Even though the region is readily accessible from Europe by air, scarcely any Western news media managed to post a professional war correspondent to the scene. The few Western reporters who went to the region faced belligerents who understood the need to disseminate their view of the events, which they each did in a predictably one-sided manner.

Thanks both to Russia's information initiative and the ineffectiveness of Western news media, initial opinions that had been hastily formed on the basis of incomplete or inaccurate information soon came to dominate the airwaves and print media. Rarely, if ever, were these opinions identified as such; in most cases they were offered as fact rather than as hypotheses. This in turn led to a climate in which it was possible, even likely, that policymakers in Western governments and civic organizations could make policy on the basis of premature judgments, erroneous information or, occasionally, very little information at all.

Months after the events, analysts have focused more on the consequences of the war than on the war itself and its antecedent events. But any analysis of the August war's consequences is inevitably shaped by the narrative one accepts on the events themselves, and particularly on their deeper historical context. In order to understand the war, one must understand the evolution of Russian-Georgian relations, as well as Georgia's and Russia's respective relations with the West, over the past two decades.

Should this confrontation be understood primarily as one between Russia and Georgia, or as the tailwind of Russia's relations with the West? The link between Russia's policies in Georgia and its relationship with the West is inescapable. Russian-Georgian relations had long since soured. Georgia was moving rapidly toward Euro-Atlantic integration, and at a time when an increasingly assertive Russian foreign policy was being shaped by sphere of influence-thinking. No less important, the escalation in the Caucasus came in the immediate aftermath of Western policy decisions on Kosovo and NATO enlargement. Indeed, Russian officials during the spring of 2008 explicitly cited these decisions to justify their actions in the months before the outbreak of war.

A number of Western officials and analysts followed this process with great concern. Among them was the Joint Center led by the two editors of this volume. Over the year preceding the outbreak of war, the Central Asia-Caucasus Institute & Silk Road Studies Program issued several publications on the acrimonious Russian-Georgian relationship. In the fall of 2007 the Center published a short monograph on Russia's missile attack at the Georgian village of Tsitelubani, which occurred on August 6—a year to the day before the start of the August war. The Joint Center then proceeded to issue four more policy papers on Georgian affairs, including one of the first analytical studies on the August war, which appeared less than three weeks after the start of fighting. Given this, it was a natural step to seek to bring together more detailed information on the events leading up to the war, on the war itself, and its likely implications for the future.

This volume draws on the expertise of ten Russian, Georgian, European, and American analysts and scholars. With backgrounds in academia, journalism, military affairs, administration, and diplomacy, they bring to the task a broad and diverse knowledge of the South Caucasus, Russian foreign policy, and international relations more generally. The book traces the origins of the conflagration beginning with the process of the dissolution of the Soviet Union in the late 1980s. It then follows the relationship between Georgia, its breakaway republics of Abkhazia and South Ossetia, and Russia over the sixteen years between the establishment of Georgian independence and the war.

Some readers may ask whether it is really necessary to dwell at length on events that took place long before August 2008. Yet the contributors to this volume had all come to the independent conclusion that the events of August 2008 were the culmination of a long preparatory period that began with the dissolution of the Soviet Union, if not earlier.

The war has already been given many names: the "War Over South Ossetia," or the "Five-Day War," etc. Most of these are misleading to the extent that they suggest that the war was only about South Ossetia or was limited in time. Russia's words and deeds made it clear from the outset that even though the war may have started in South Ossetia, it embraced all of Georgia, if not the South Caucasus. Contributors to this volume provide much evidence that the fighting in South Ossetia was only one theater of the broader Russian-Georgian conflict.

Even if one accepts that the war began on August 7, 2008 (though there are strong arguments to suggest it began days or even months earlier), it did not end with the cease-fire agreement signed on August 12. Russian military operations on Georgian territory continued long after that date. Even now, nearly a year later, Russia remains in violation of commitments it made in the cease-fire agreement.

This book is organized chronologically. It begins with an account of developments in Georgia during the transition to independence—a period marked by the rebirth of Georgian nationalism and a strong movement to secede from the Soviet Union. These years saw the rise and fall of Georgia's first nationalist president, Zviad Gamsakhurdia, the return to power of Georgia's Soviet-era leader, Eduard Shevardnadze, and the emergence of the conflicts in South Ossetia and Abkhazia. Thomas Goltz, who covered these events for leading American publications, provides a vivid picture of the chaotic time that led to Georgia's rebirth as a state; he also gives evidence of how Russia's interventions contributed to the overall weakening of this new Georgia as a state.

We turn then to the post-independence period dominated by the leadership of Boris Yeltsin in Russia and of Eduard Shevardnadze in Georgia. While more calm than either the preceding or subsequent periods, this era, as Thornike Gordadze shows, was more turbulent than it is generally thought to have been. On the one hand, Georgia sought to strengthen its independence. On the other, Russia worked to slow this process by intervening in its internal affairs, particularly in the conflict zones. Gordadze concludes that the rough treatment of Georgia by Yeltsin's Russia led Shevardnadze to orient Georgia increasingly toward the West, which in turn prompted a Russian reaction, which began in the last years of Yeltsin's rule but accelerated significantly after Vladimir Putin came to power in 1999.

The rise of Putin was accompanied by significant changes in Russia's attitude toward the former Soviet space. From the outset Georgia emerged as one of the Putin government's main targets. Former advisor to Vladimir Putin Andrei Illarionov, who resigned in 2005, presents a systematic overview of the measures affecting Georgia that began with Putin's ascent to power. His meticulous chronology reveals the steady march of premeditated actions that led to the escalation of tensions between Russia and Georgia since the fall of 1999. Readers will recall the widely disseminated view that the deterioration in Russian-Georgian relations traces to the "Rose Revolution" of 2003 and Mikheil Saakashvili's rise to power. But the evidence offered by Illarionov discredits that view, as well as its corollary that it was the rise of democracy in Georgia that brought the Russian army across the Russian-Georgia border. As Illarionov shows, the process had begun well before 2003 and unfolded inexorably thereafter.

This is by no means to say that the Rose Revolution was irrelevant. In his chapter Swedish researcher Niklas Nilsson details the transformation of the Georgian state from reactive and ineffective under Shevardnadze to proactive and demanding under Saakashvili. Nilsson shows how the Georgian government pushed relentlessly to change the status quo in Abkhazia and South Ossetia. Backing its position with numerous United Nations resolutions, the new government in Tbilisi refused to accept Putin's steadily mounting steps to control these territories and looked instead to the Euro-Atlantic community to back Georgia's claims to sovereignty.

These chapters bring the reader to the present day and to more focused questions on what transpired during 2008. The chapters that follow detail Western and Georgian reactions to Moscow's increasingly assertive policies, which reached a fever pitch following the Western recognition of Kosovo and the NATO Bucharest Summit in early 2008. In his analysis of European and American reactions, Stephen Blank lays bare the ineptitude of both the European and American reactions to Moscow's escalation in the Caucasus. He shows that Europe's rising profile in the region focused mainly on its own needs in the sphere of energy and its wishes in the sphere of governance. It conveniently ignored the region's own security requirements and the urgent need for conflict resolution there. By doing so the Europeans failed to devise a coherent response to Russian policies that threatened stability and Europe's own interests in the region. Meanwhile, the United States also failed to respond to what was clearly a growing threat to the sovereignty of states in the South Caucasus and to its own interests there. Inadequate intelligence and the diversion of attention to Iraq and Afghanistan reinforced this failure of policy.

David Smith focuses closely on Georgia's own reaction to the developments of 2008. His analysis finds that Saakashvili's government was increasingly aware of the likelihood of war, but also of its growing isolation and the probability that no one would come to Georgia's assistance if it were attacked. Smith shows how Georgia responded to Moscow with a series of tough-worded but diplomatic responses that reflected Tbilisi's unwillingness to bow to Putin's demands and, at the same time, its urgent appeals for the international community to rein Moscow in.

The three subsequent chapters assess the war itself. Johanna Popjanevski, who found herself on the ground in Georgia when the war erupted, provides a chronology of the events that triggered large-scale military action and discusses the most acrimonious questions that it raises. Popjanevski reviews the debate over responsibility for the war and details the mixture of political and legal arguments that both sides have advanced in their own defense. She shows how both sides have focused their arguments on the events of August 7, but suggests that these events are of lesser relevance to the issue of responsibility than Russia's military and other preparations over the weeks and months prior to that fateful date. In the next chapter the distinguished Russian military affairs analyst Pavel Felgenhauer draws the reader's attention to the full-scale invasion of Georgia by Russian land, air, and sea forces. Felgenhauer details the process by which a detailed plan for the assertion of military power was actually implemented. Even though planning and preparations had gone forward for months and even years, the Russian military encountered unexpected problems on the ground. For the Georgians the war presented staggering challenges at every turn. He concludes by outlining the important military lessons both sides have drawn from the conflict.

Closely paralleling the war on the battlefield was a war of information, which the contending parties both considered to be on almost the same level of importance as the actual military confrontation. The American expert on post-Soviet affairs, Paul Goble, details the process of the Russian-Georgian war in the arena of international opinion. He acknowledges Moscow's clear advantages in the media war arising from its vastly greater resources and institutional clout. Goble shows how a significant number of Western media borrowed the story disseminated by Moscow and blamed the fighting on reckless provocations by Mikheil Saakashvili. Certain Western political leaders, notably in Germany, also bought this "blame the victim" line, without testing or confirming the evidence on which it relies. Notwithstanding these notable achievements in the information war, Goble asserts that in the end Russia did not prevail. Citing intriguing evidence from bloggers, including many from within Russia itself, he shows how Russian claims were undermined by the contrary data and inconsistencies that Moscow itself had put out.

What, finally, are the broader implications of the war in August 2008? Obviously, a full answer to this question will require years, even decades. In the meanwhile, James Sherr, who heads the Russia and Eurasia program at Chatham House in London, shows how even before the war the West had failed to respond to Russia's revival of a classically modern, Realpolitik culture of security. The Georgia war simply brought this failure to the surface. It is too early to draw firm conclusions on the deeper implications of the war. But for now Sherr asserts that the post-war Western response remains inadequate, even counter-productive.

In this volume the editors endeavored to assemble a competent team of scholars and analysts in order to provide a comprehensive view of the war of August 2008. Aside from offering an initial outline, which itself evolved in the course of writing, the editors did not propose any organizing hypotheses, nor were they guided in their selection of authors by any expectation that they would adhere to one view or another. Indeed, it was assumed that the various writers would have different perspectives and that they might reach different conclusions. Rather than seek to iron out all of the resulting discrepancies, the editors chose to present them as submitted. After all, this is a first attempt at assembling a comprehensive picture of complex events extending over decades, not the last.

It is assumed that in coming years new evidence will come to light that will require revisions in the various conclusions that might be drawn from this volume. This is natural and desirable. But the dedicated analysts who participated in this volume have established one truth that is beyond dispute: vast amounts of information on the background, planning, preparation, and execution of the war of August 2008 is readily available in open sources. Anyone advancing new claims on the events leading up to the war or on the war itself will have to address these data, either discrediting them on rational grounds, embracing them, or showing how they in fact support different conclusions from those drawn to date.

At the very least, it will be all but impossible hereafter for anyone to deny that Russia had engaged in detailed planning for precisely the war that occurred, and that this planning had been underway for months, even years, prior to August 2008. Did Saakashvili fall into a trap? Maybe so, but Felgenhauer and Illarionov both suggest that even if he had not, a pretext would have been found to proceed with the campaign as it had been planned.

2

The Paradox of Living in Paradise: Georgia's Descent into Chaos

Thomas Goltz

Any telling of Georgia's complicated past ineluctably seems to start with the following myth, and then moves by fits and starts and leaps and bounds toward the equally complicated present: when God was dividing up the world between the nations, the Georgians missed their chance to select a homeland because they were sleeping off a festive drunk. When they awoke, everything was gone with the exception of that part of the world that the Almighty had been reserving for himself, which was, of course, literally heaven on earth.

"Where can we go?" wailed the Georgians. "And we were late only because we were toasting you and singing your praises!"

"Gosh," said a flattered God. "I guess I'll have to give you a piece of paradise."

Thus began, even in legend, the unique client status of the inhabitants of Georgia, who have been flattering Friends in High Places to achieve their ends, including ensuring their collective survival, since the theoretic beginning of time.

But being in possession of a little piece of paradise comes with costs, and Georgia has not only been coveted and conquered by outsiders since the dawn of time, but so beset by factional infighting among Georgians themselves, often in alliance with those same outside powers, that it has frequently disappeared from the map for decades or even centuries, only to reemerge in a modified and often severely divided guise.

The reason for this is rather simple. Along with neighboring Armenia to the south and Caucasian Albania (more or less today's Azerbaijan) to the east, Georgia has long served as a strategic transit corridor between East and West, as well as constituting the "cork in the bottle" down the North-South isthmus of land separating the Caspian and Black seas. This geographic position would be the curse the proto-Georgians would have to live with no matter who the great powers of the day might be: Achaemenid Iran versus Alexander the Great's Seleucids, the Parthian and then Sassanian Persian empires, the "New Roman" empire of Byzantium, the seventh century Muslim Arabs punching into the region from the south, Seljuks, the Mongols, competition between the Turkic Ottomans and the Iranian Safavids, and then the slow, piecemeal absorption of the entire Caucasus region in the eighteenth and nineteenth centuries by the new great power on the scene, Russia, which in turn had its claim to a near exclusive sphere of influence in the region challenged by imperial Britain, then Germany, and now, since the collapse of the Soviet Union in 1991, by the United States.

It has been a rough-ride down the historic highway for little Georgia, and it is again so today. Indeed, the geopolitical entity we think of today as Georgia has experienced the full spectrum of state existence over the centuries, from self-conscious mini-empire and overlord of others, to complete occlusion. The last time that happened was 1921, when the briefly existing Democratic Republic of Georgia, founded on May 26, 1918, was terminated by the Bolsheviks.

Some background is necessary at this point. By the time of the failed revolution of December 1905, the Marxist/Communist/Socialist movement in Russia had split into two basic groups, one that insisted on a top-down dictatorship of the working masses, and one that advocated the creation of a broad-based, working-class party from the bottom up. The former policy became known as "Bolshevism," or the policy of the "majority," as that is what *Bolshevik* means in Russian. The leader of this faction was Vladimir I. Lenin, who needs no introduction. The "minority" view, in turn, was known as "Menshevism," or the policy of the "minority," as that is what the word *Menshevik* means in Russian. The leader of this faction was Yuli Martov; his name does not even appear in the biographical entries of most comprehensive dictionaries.

In the South Caucasus, the "majority" view was defended by a former seminarian from the Georgian town of Gori, who was named Iosef Jughashvili, better known to history as Josef Stalin. His deep base in the region was the city of Baku, where he agitated among the thousands of oil-field workers who represented the ideal of an oppressed, "international" (multi-ethnic) industrialized proletariat ready to be radicalized. The "minority" view was defended by another Georgian, Noe Zhordania (Jordania), whose primary base of support was the local Georgian peasantry and small craftsmen inspired by local (Georgian) "nationalism." Seen from an underground Bolshevik perspective (including that of Stalin), Jordania's position was ideological anathema. Seen from a non-Bolshevik perspective, the evolving "Menshevik" government of "Georgia" was at the vanguard of new ideas, such as the combination of social democracy with an explicitly "national" state.

Then came the cold, hard reality of World War I, during which time the South Caucasus front became a notably obscure but nonetheless violent theater. Whole armies froze to death in the frigid wilds of the high Anatolian Plateau in winter, or died of scurvy in the broiling summers. Then came the February Revolution of 1917, the demise of the Romanovs, the establishment of the short-lived Provisional Government of Alexander Kerensky, and finally the Bolshevik putsch under Lenin and the removal of Russian forces from the war. Meanwhile, Ottoman Turkish forces were on the move to take advantage of Russia's collapse. First, under the provisions of the Brest-Litovsk Treaty, the Ottoman occupied the provinces of Kars, Ardahan, and Batumi that had been lost to Russia forty years earlier. Not satisfied with these gains, the Ottoman army (also called the Army of Islam following its inclusion of Azerbaijani Muslims in its push to the Caucasus) then began its long march across the Caucasus toward the greatest prize in the region—the oil fields around the city of Baku on the shores of the Caspian Sea. To legalize their eastward push, in early 1918 the triumvirate in power in Istanbul "helped" Caucasian Georgians, Armenians, and Azerbaijanis cobble together the ephemeral entity known as the Transcaucasus Democratic Republic, which self-dissolved when Noe Jordania's Georgian part of the troika declared its own independence under the secret sponsorship of the Kaiser's Germany.

Soviet Georgia

It was a confusing time that was made more confusing by the multiple territorial claims asserted by each of the three principal Caucasus states against the other two, the spillover of the civil war raging in Russia between the Reds and Whites, and the capitulation of the German war machine in November 1918. Adding to the confusion was the newly created League of Nations, which required all prospective member states to define their borders by several criteria, the primary ones being control of territory and the alleged consent of the governed. One ugly result was the arming of less-than-perfectly controlled militias by the new nationalist governments, who then sent their "armies" forth to stake out a maximalist vision of "traditional" lands of the new/ancient nation state, and ridding it of those elements who disagreed. State-sponsored "ethnic cleansing" is the modern term that comes to mind.

By the spring of 1920, the Red Army had turned the tide against Denikin's Whites and secured Bolshevik power in Moscow and most of Russia. It was time to reclaim lands lost during the dark days of the revolution. High on the list were the Transcaucasus republics of Azerbaijan, Armenia, and Georgia, which had represented such an essential part of Czarist Russia for over a century, but which had fallen under the sway of the imperialist British following German and Turkish collapse in November 1918. The first push was against the Democratic Republic of Azerbaijan. Next to go was the Armenian Dashnaktsutiun government in Yerevan in early December of that same year.

Surrounded and essentially friendless, the new British occupation forces that had replaced the Germans and Turks following the November Armistice would only guard the oil railway line from Baku to Batumi. Meanwhile, the Menshevik government of Noe Jordania waited alone for the inevitable invasion of Bolshevik forces. Jordania and his government fled the capital on February 25, 1921, boarded a ship in Batumi, and fled across the Black Sea and into exile. Georgia had just disappeared from history-again.

Following a ruthless purging of Mensheviks across the territory that had been independent Georgia, that entity entered the USSR at its creation in 1922 as a part of the newly created Transcaucasian Federated Soviet Socialist Republic, or TcFSSR, which also included Armenia and Azerbaijan (and Abkhazia).

The TcFSSR itself was a compromise solution bitterly opposed by Stalin and his fellow Bolshevik Georgian, Sergo Ordzhonikidze. Both advocated the complete assimilation of all the small national groups (and large ones, too, such as Ukrainians) into the new, Russian-speaking *Homo Sovieticus,* or Soviet Man. But in keeping with Lenin's policy of "national self-determination" for all the peoples of the new Soviet state, the three primary south Caucasus Soviet entities that made up the TcFSSR were encouraged to preserve elements of "national" culture. Simultaneously, they were also subjected to various levels of atomization that theoretically reflected the communal needs and aspirations of national minorities living among the three, titular new nations.

In the case of Georgia, these subnational territories included the "autonomous district" of South Ossetia as well as the "autonomous republic" of Abkhazia (the Abkhaz insist that they were "federated" with Georgia as an equal partner) and the "autonomous republic" of Adjara. The latter was unique in the lands of the USSR as being an autonomy designed to accommodate ethnic Georgian Muslims, who were not a nationality at all, but a religion-based community initially recognized by the officially atheistic state. The fact that all of these sub-states would become centers of communal confrontation and separatist strife when the house of cards known as the USSR collapsed in 1991 is seen, retroactively, as evidence of an initial, nefarious scheme of "divide and rule."

Georgia played a multifaceted role in this larger process, with Tbilisi serving as both the administrative center of the "Georgian" part of the TcFSSR as well as the capital of the entire TcFSSR from 1922 through 1936. That was the year of the next series of territorial and communal adjustments announced by Stalin and enshrined by the 1936 Soviet Constitution, which included provisions for Georgia, Armenia, and Azerbaijan to reemerge from the TcFSSR as separate and theoretically "independent" socialist states, but whose very first act of sovereignty was to ask to join the USSR. By that time, however, all three had been utterly transformed by the Soviet experience under the leadership of Georgia's most (in)famous native son, Joseph Stalin, and his equally (in)famous fellow Georgian henchman, Lavrenti Beria, until their almost simultaneous demise in 1953.

What is the connection between the de-Stalinization of the USSR (and the parallel de-Beriazation) and the inimical relationship between post-Soviet Georgia and the Russian Federation today? An intuitive sense suggests that the fulcrum moment happened when Georgians realized that they were no longer in theoretic control of the entire USSR and in fact being deeply resented by Russians—rightly or wrongly—for having been the place that gave birth to both Stalin and Beria. That dissatisfaction merged with an idealized ancient history—and a convenient amnesia of active Georgian compliance with Russian imperial ambitions in the nineteenth century—and resulted in the attitude that independence was preferable to getting downgraded to mere provincial status in a (newly) Great Russian-dominated USSR. How else does one quantify the 1956 riots in Tbilisi with those in Budapest that same year? But because the world saw the 1956 riots as a yearning by Georgians for Stalinist rule and not a yearning for the reestablishment of the independent, national (and Menshevik) state of 1918–21, all succor was dismissed and denied.

Throughout the deep Cold War years of the late 1950s, 60s, and 70s, Georgia appeared happy in "Socialist Heaven," and was best known as a vacation destination for Soviet citizens. The mixture of Black Sea beaches, the towering Caucasus mountains, and its reputation as the sybaritic wine-producing Sonoma Valley of the USSR resulted in the odd fact that the Georgian SSR had become arguably the wealthiest part of the entire USSR. If anyone outside the Soviet Union was watching, this was also the period that saw the rise of a certain Eduard Shevardnadze from obscure NKVD/KGB security bull to anti-corruption boss to leader of the Georgian Communist Party, and then non-voting member of the Politburo in Moscow before, of course, most famously becoming Soviet foreign minister under Mikhail Gorbachev. As for his attitude toward Georgia's place in the world, Shevardnadze once famously declared in a speech lauding the achievements of his mentor in Moscow, Leonid Brezhnev, that for Georgia "the sun rises not in the east, but in the north!"

This was not the attitude of many of his fellow citizens, however. Starting as early as 1954, two young dissidents by the names of Merab Kostava (a musician and poet) and Zviad Gamsakhurdia (a philologist, literary critic, and translator of everyone from Shakespeare to Oscar Wilde) began establishing underground human rights groups for which they spent time in KGB jails. The human rights that they were primarily interested in protecting were the right to remain Georgian, and not be wholly subsumed into that Communist ideal, the Russian-speaking Homo Sovieticus.

In Georgia, the most dramatic effort in that direction came in 1978, when the Kremlin declared Russian to be the sole official language of the country. It resulted in riots so severe that the Kremlin rescinded the decree. Another dramatic moment came in November 1983, when Soviet Georgia was gearing up to celebrate the 200th anniversary of the Georgievsk Treaty that established a Russian protectorate over Georgia and, at the same time, the anniversary of the Bolshevik Revolution of 1917. To spoil the party, seven Georgian youths hijacked an Aeroflot plane (on the ground at Tbilisi airport). A team of Special Forces pounced, killing two on board and bundling the others off to eventual execution—and the status, in death, of martyrs to the nationalist cause.

The most surprising thing about the nationalistic slow-broil (as it were) in Georgia is that so few outside observers were taking notice of events underway in "Stalin's home republic," and it was a shock when the citizens of the wealthy, seemingly quiescent SSR republic responded to Mikhail Gorbachev's mid-1980s call for glasnost and perestroika with a counter-call to once again re-establish the independent Republic of Georgia of 1918–21, and dissolve all connections with the USSR in any form.

That, sadly, is where the contemporary history of Georgia begins and almost ineluctably—and certainly unpleasantly—brings us up to the present day, when the children of God's piece of paradise decided to recast themselves as distant (and democratic) Europeans, when the rest of the world continued to regard them as a part of the Soviet state.

Independence and the Gamsakhurdia Era

The date was April 9, 1989, when a company of paratroopers waded into a sea of unarmed pro-independence protestors gathered around Kostava and Gamsakhurdia, and beat nineteen people to death with shovels. The April 9 Massacre became the most resonant day in the nationalist calendar and, after Kostava's death in a car crash (still a subject of conspiracy debate), sealed Gamsakhurdia's role as the leader of the independence movement. It also arguably marked the beginning of the downward trajectory of Georgia from its status as one of the most pleasant and prosperous places in the entire USSR, to becoming, within a decade, the very paradigm of a "failed state."

In October 1990 Gamsakhurdia's Roundtable/Free Georgia coalition won 155 of the 250 seats in the Supreme Council. But it is necessary to note that *all* 34 political parties (including the Communists) contesting the elections were in agreement on one point: complete independence; or at least the demand for independence was the public stance of all politicians when confronted by electors, who often seemed to have more in common with rowdy soccer fans (or street mobs) than practitioners of Robert's Rules of Parliamentary Order.

Further complicating the picture was Gamsakhurdia's rallying cry: the creation of a "Georgia for the Georgians." The problem with this seemingly sensible statement of purpose, of course, was that throughout its long history, Georgia had never been a unitary or mono-ethnic state. In addition to the basic East/West split of "core" Georgia between Kakheti/Imereti and further subdivision among Georgians into Karts, Laz, Mingrelians, Khevsurs, and Svans, as well as the Muslim Georgians of the Autonomous Republic of Adjara (and the odd Ahiska, regarded as Turkified Georgians by true believers), there were also Azerbaijanis in Marneuli in the southeast, the Armenians of Javakheti in the south, Chechens called Kists in Akhmeta in the northeast, Ossetians in their own autonomous district in the north-central mountains, and finally the Abkhazians of the Autonomous Republic of that same name on the northwest Black Sea shore, as well as a diverse number of Slavs, Germans, "Mountain Jews" called Tats, Kurdish-speaking Yezidis, Pontic Greeks, and Assyrians. A full thirty percent of the population of Georgia, in fact, regarded themselves as being less than full members of that state. Moreover, several minorities had enjoyed some manner of Soviet-style official self-determining status for the seventy-year experiment of the USSR, but were now watching it get stripped away by Gamsakhurdia's brand of glasnost-inspired street nationalism. In the unitary Georgia envisioned by Gamsakhurdia, the Soviet-style affirmative action enjoyed by the population of autonomous regions in the way of university placement, job quotas, and other perks enjoyed by officially recognized Soviet-style minorities would be swept away.

The first confrontation set the pattern for all to come, and the venue was the Autonomous Republic of Adjara on the Turkish frontier. While Gamsakhurdia did not send in an army, he made it clear to the mainly non-practicing Muslims of Adjara that they would not be accorded any special status.

"Adjarans! Remember that you are Georgians!" he famously declared in a 1988 rally in the Adjara capital city, Batumi. It logically followed that if the Adjarans were indeed just Georgians, then the "autonomous" nature of the province was redundant.

Tension continued to mount following Gamsakhurdia's election as Chairman of Georgia's Supreme Council (or Parliament) on November 14, 1990, and further expanded after the March 31, 1991, referendum on independence, when ninety percent of the population that voted demanded a departure from the USSR. The Adjarans, of course, were part of the ten percent who preferred the status quo. Then, on April 20, in murky circumstances, a local strongman and scion of a grand Muslim family by the name of Aslan Abashidze (or his guards) shot dead Gamsakhurdia's newly appointed administrator. Civil war threatened until the local (still Soviet) Russian military base commander outside the regional capital city (and oil terminal) of Batumi made it clear that his men would intervene on the side of Abashidze, who had been thoughtful enough to send bouquets of flowers to all garrison officers' wives on International Women's Day (and, presumably, a little local oil industry revenue to the officers, too). Almost instantly, Batumi departed from Tbilisi's even nominal control, with Abashidze declining to collect or send taxes to the central exchequer and waiving the obligation of local youth to serve in the new national army. This state of "armed autonomy" would remain in place until *Batono* (Lord/Protector) Abashidze's ouster more than a decade later in 2004.

The Autonomous District (as opposed to Republic) of South Ossetia presented Gamsakhurdia and his nationalists with a different type of problem. To begin with, the Ossetians (who call themselves Alans) were not ethnic Georgians, but regarded as Old Persian-speaking interlopers—if having arrived in the central Caucasus mountains over a thousand years (or perhaps a mere five or seven hundred) ago qualifies the Ossetians as being "newcomers" and thus less entitled to the claim of being as native as the indigenous Georgians, and despite centuries of marriage, both royal and ordinary, between the two peoples.

More to the point, the Ossetians had a long history of even greater fraternity with the Russians, both in Czarist and Soviet times (they had sided with the Bolsheviks in 1918), and had accordingly been rewarded with their own Autonomous Republic inside the Russian SSR, as well as their own Autonomous District inside the Georgian SSR.

The irony of the creation of this last territorial entity is that of the some 150,000 Ossetians living in Georgia, over half lived outside the Ossetian Autonomous area, which was itself populated by a roughly equal proportion of ethnic Ossets and ethnic Georgians—and it was among these erstwhile neighbors that Gamsakhurdia's nationalists began sowing the seeds of ethnic discord. The first step on the road to perdition came in the form of a 1989 proclamation that Georgian and not Russian (or Ossetian) would be the language of the land. The next was Georgia's banning of an Ossetian "Popular Front" organization following that organization's preemptive declaration of independence on September 20, 1990, that South Ossetia had become its own republic, and intended to remain inside the USSR no matter what Georgia did. Then, on December 11, 1990, Tbilisi stripped South Ossetia of its autonomous status altogether, resulting in escalating violence when Gamsakhurdia sent in armed militiamen to compel the wayward province back under Tbilisi's control.

The numbers killed in the first Caucasian "neighbors" war are hotly disputed, ranging from "mere" scores to more than a thousand. No effort will be made here to set that particular record straight. Suffice it to say that the main point posited here is that without overt and covert Russian military intervention it is difficult to imagine that the grossly-outgunned and outnumbered South Ossetians could have held their own against the Georgians. Tellingly, however, once the Kremlin made it clear that it would freeze the conflict into an OSCE-administered cease-fire in 1992, South Ossetia, and particularly its capital city, Tskhinvali, soon devolved into a smugglers' paradise and economic black-hole, with stolen cars, black-market booze, women, drugs, weapons, counterfeit dollars, and even a 100 gram sample of weapons grade uranium moving to or from North Ossetia via the Roki tunnel.

Meanwhile, back in Tbilisi, Gamsakhurdia's Round Table/Free Georgia Parliament was preparing for even bolder action. On the resonant day of April 9, 1991, evoking the theoretical right of secession by Lenin's 1922 USSR constitution, the Parliament of the Republic of Georgia declared that it had restored the independence that had been snatched away from it by the Bolsheviks in 1921.

Once again, few in the West took notice, as the world was still preoccupied with removing Saddam Hussein from Kuwait. Nor did many outsiders take notice when, on May 26, Zviad Gamsakhurdia was elected president of independent Georgia with 86 percent of the vote.

It was to be a remarkably short term of office, and saw a complete reversal in the way Gamsakhurdia was regarded almost everywhere in the world. From being a charismatic nationalist leader, he was soon being referred to in such unflattering terms as "messianic," "fascist," and, after stating that he believed that Mikhail Gorbachev had orchestrated the August 19, 1991, abortive putsch in Moscow against himself, "nuts," in the words of U.S. President George H. W. Bush.

More ominously, close allies at home not only began to desert Gamsakhurdia, but go into active and armed opposition against his government. These included Prime Minister Tengiz Sigua, who put a legalistic face on a budding troika-junta that also included the leader of the National Guard, Tengiz Kitovani, and the flamboyant criminal/playwright Jaba Ioseliani. The latter's "elitist" paramilitary organization called the *Mkhedrioni* (Knight Horsemen) soon became the terror of the country—or at least the terror of devoted supporters of Gamsakhurdia—and paved the way for the then return of former Soviet Foreign Minister Eduard Shevardnadze to power.

It was an oddly pivotal as well as turbulent time, and it needs to be noted that Georgia was not alone as it slid into chaos during the chaotic autumn of 1991. North of the border, a bitter and bloody conflict had erupted between North Ossetia and tiny Ingushetia over the status of the northern suburbs of the city of Vladikavkaz (known as Prigarodniy) which required Russian intervention (on the side of the Ossetians) to quell. The Ingush, meanwhile, had just been effectively divorced by their cousins the Chechens, who had declared not just independence from the Soviet Union but the Russian Federation itself. To the south, the dispute between Armenia and Azerbaijan over Mountainous (Nagorno) Karabakh was growing from being a "conflict" into open war—with plenty of evidence of a so-called "Russian hidden hand" stoking the fortunes of both combatants in the way of mercenaries, double agents, and conveniently arranged ceasefires ready to be dissolved at the drop of a hat (or sale of more arms). Far to the east, Tajikistan was engulfed in civil war, while far to the west separatists in the Moldovan SSR had seized a chunk of territory called Transnistria in order to maintain their association with Russia when Moldova became an independent state. Then there was the chaos and confusion in Russia itself, as Boris Yeltsin stripped Mikhail Gorbachev of all his authority, culminating in the announcement at Almaty of December 21, 1991, by fourteen of the fifteen member republics that made up the USSR that Gorbachev was the president of a historical footnote, and that the Union of Soviet Socialist Republics was no more.

The only erstwhile member of the union not in attendance was Georgia, which was on the cusp of a brutal civil war.

It began on December 22, when the National Guard and Mkhedrioni demanded that Gamsakhurdia resign. When he refused, they began firing on Parliament and the presidential apparatus building on Rustaveli Avenue in downtown Tbilisi from such close range that it soon took on the appropriate name of "The Hundred Meters War." It ended, more or less, on January 6, 1992, when President Zviad Gamsakhurdia fled into exile, first to Azerbaijan, then Armenia, and eventually to Chechnya, where he set up his government-in-exile as the guest of General Djohar Dudayev. An alternative date for the attenuated end might be March 8, 1992, when Shevardnadze returned to Tbilisi for the first time in eight years.

Zviad Gamsakhurdia's supporters, now called by the derogatory term "Zviadists," were either ruthlessly run to ground in Tbilisi or fled west to Mingrelia, the area from which Gamsakhurdia hailed, thus re-opening a centuries-old lingual-identity rift between eastern and western Georgians. There, the remnant leadership set up a "Position" government (that is, claiming they were the legitimate government, in opposition to the opposition) in the town of Zugdidi, until it too was overrun in late January, whereupon the "Positionists" took refuge in the neighboring Autonomous Republic of Abkhazia.

Although a natural choice for a last redoubt, the arrival of the Gamsakhurdia loyalists in the regional capital of Sukhumi was an unfortunate choice for everyone concerned because it added a new element to a time-bomb ready to explode, and with a fuse that could easily be traced back to Moscow. And when it did, the "War over the Red Riviera" would turn into the most vicious inter-ethnic war seen in the Caucasus since the Bolshevik take-over of Georgia in 1921.

Abkhazia

When God was dividing up the world between the nations, the Abkhaz missed their chance of selecting a homeland because they were sleeping off a festive drunk. When they awoke, everything was gone with the exception of that part of the world that the Almighty had been reserving for himself, which was, of course, literally heaven on earth.

Alas, the above is not a typo or a cut and paste job gone awry. The creation legend of Abkhazia and Georgia is identical, a sad fact that has not led to unity and fraternity between the two peoples, but rather to a belligerent disputation of basic history and the denial of the very humanity of the other group.

It was not always so. For much of the past two thousand years or so, Georgians and Abkhaz—who belong to the western Circassian language group that includes Adyge, Kabardin, and Shapsug—have intermingled, shared royalty, and possess a cultural heritage that includes architecture and food. But being situated on the fabulous Black Sea coastline exposed the residents of Abkhazia to outside influence and control in a way the inland Georgians were often spared. Seemingly everyone from the ancient Greeks to the Romans to the Khazars and even Genoese passed through and occupied the capital city and jewel of the region, Sukhumi.

The primary struggle, however, came in the form of the centuries-long rivalry between the Ottoman Empire and the emerging power of Czarist Russia, resulting in the mass, traumatic exodus of Muslim Abkhaz (along with other North Caucasus Muslim groups such as the Chechens, Ingush, and Ubykh) to Ottoman lands in the 1860s and then again following the Ottoman-Russian war of 1877, resulting in the large, self-conscious Circassian Diaspora communities in today's Turkey, Syria, and Jordan (the Hashemite palace guard in Amman are exclusively Circassian).

Another direct result of the mass migration (the word ethnic cleansing comes to mind) was the depopulation of much of Abkhazia of Abkhazians, and their replacement by Slavs, Germans, Armenians, and, especially following the Bolshevik take-over of Abkhazia along with Georgia in 1921, Mingrelian Georgians during the rise of Lavrenti Beria as the chief Bolshevik in the Transcaucasian SSR. A native of Abkhazia, he seems to have had a particularly vicious vendetta against the Abkhaz, and may have personally killed the Abkhaz Bolshevik leader Nestor Lakoba with his own hands during the Great Purges in 1936. Prior to this, Beria appears to have first convinced Stalin to lower Abkhazia's status to that of a mere autonomous republic within Georgia, and to have Georgian and not Abkhaz designated as the official language of the region. The demise of both Stalin and Beria in 1953 was a cause for great celebration in Abkhazia (at least among the minority Abkhaz if not the Georgians). At the time of the last Soviet-era census of 1989, the titular Abkhaz made up a mere seventeen percent of the total population of their own autonomous republic, with Georgians the largest single ethnic group, but still short of being an absolute majority. But de-Beriazation soon translated to the ending of outright repression of the Abkhaz and began a process wherein Soviet affirmative action policies led them to begin to enjoy disproportionate access to government positions and resources.

In Abkhazia, the so-called pleasure industry, and particularly the spas and sanatoria built for vacationing Soviet military officers in the 1960s and 70s, led to a curious alliance (and no doubt genuine affection) between the vacationing Soviet officer class and the Abkhaz leadership that would have serious implications in the future.

When the rest of Georgia boycotted Gorbachev's Union Treaty of March 11, 1991, the Abkhaz and other non-Georgians in Abkhazia voted for it by 52.3 percent, but in turn boycotted the March 31 referendum on Georgian independence from the USSR. With guns doing the talking in South Ossetia, Batono Abashidze's "armed autonomy" in Adjara and growing revolt among his ministers, Gamsakhurdia appears to have come to his senses and not risked greater chaos by picking a new fight with the Abkhaz (and their Russian military officer patrons and clients). Rather, he actually entered into a power-sharing arrangement with the Abkhaz leader and Hititologist scholar Vladislav Ardzinba, which increased the number of Abkhaz delegates in the Supreme Council and the number of men serving in local security forces. The irony is that this effectively turned Abkhazia into a relatively calm redoubt for the pro-Zviad "Position" government after his supporters fled Zugdidi to Sukhumi in January 1992. The violence that ensued in Abkhazia some months later can hence not be attributed to Gamsakhurdia.

Often accused by so-called Zviadists of having ousted Gamsakhurdia because of his pro-independence stance and their own putative pro-Russian policies, the members of the military junta in Tbilisi announced on February 21, 1992, that the Soviet-era constitution of Georgia was abolished and that of the 1918–21 Democratic Republic restored. This in turn was interpreted in Sukhumi as meaning the abolition of Abkhaz autonomy, and led on July 23 to the Abkhaz-dominated faction in the joint, power-sharing Abkhaz Parliament to declare the abolition of the late Soviet-era constitution of 1978, replacing it with that of 1925, it being the last legal document when Abkhazia had equal status with Georgia as part of the Transcaucasia SSR, which implicitly meant full Abkhaz independence. To give the declaration some teeth, Abkhaz police began physically removing ethnic Georgians (mainly Zviad supporters) from their various posts, and hoisted the flag of the Republic of Abkhazia over the government house.

The government in Tbilisi, now led by former Soviet Foreign Minister Eduard Shevardnadze, who had returned at the invitation of the junta in March, met in emergency session on July 25 and declared the Abkhaz move null and void, and invited Ardzinba to Tbilisi to join in a country-wide celebration marking (all of) newly independent Georgia's admission to the United Nations on August 7. Ardzinba initially accepted the invite, but then somehow managed to miss the plane from Sukhumi. For Abkhazia watchers, this seemed much less a mistake in Ardzinba's schedule than direct dictation from Moscow concerning the real limitations of Abkhaz "autonomy" in the new global context—i.e., even had Ardzinba wanted to attended the gala bash in Tbilisi, he would not have been allowed to do so because the Kremlin (or Ministry of Defense) had other plans, such as making war.

"They warned us, they warned us," a chief Shevardnadze aide told this author years later. "'Don't do anything rash or stupid or provocative,'" he quoted his Abkhaz interlocutor as admonishing him and everyone else in the Georgian leadership…"'Because if you do, the Russians will supply our (Abkhaz) provocateurs with any weapons they want, including aviation.'" But no-one was listening in Tbilisi. Then bandits interfering with road and train security (the precursors to such guerrilla groups as the Forest Brethren and White Legion that would so plague the Inguri River basin in later years) kidnapped the acting Minister of the Interior, and spirited him off to their hideout inside the crime-ridden sub-region of Abkhazia called Gali. In a national television address on August 11, Shevardnadze declared:

> I believe that evil has its limits, but now I am convinced that it has no bounds…we have demonstrated mercy and pardoned all our enemies [an amnesty had been declared for all Gamsakhurdia supporters who would lay down their arms] but now there will be no forgiveness!

On the night of August 13, a railway bridge was blown up over the Inguri River, presumably to block the rapid movement of Tengiz Kitovani's National Guard from mounting a punitive expedition into Gali to free the kidnapped minister. Shevardnadze called Ardzinba to tell him that Kitovani would be entering the next day by road, and that it was merely a cross-border police action and not an invasion of Abkhazia per se.

Ardzinba replied that if Georgian forces crossed the river, he would call on a full mobilization of Abkhaz men and resist to the death.

On the morning of August 14, Kitovani and some 3,000 guardsmen crossed into Gali, but did not stop there. After a three day orgy of killing and looting all the way up to Sukhumi and the Gumista River, Kitovani returned to Tbilisi in triumph, slapping a unique war trophy down in front of the other assembled members of the National Council/junta: the flag of the Republic of Abkhazia he had stripped from atop the government building in Sukhumi.

His triumphant men also started coming back with their own battle prizes: televisions, refrigerators, rugs, jewelry, and anything else of value they could find once the initial blast of killing was over.

But the war over the Red Riviera was not over; it had just been joined. The Abkhaz leadership under Ardzinba fled Sukhumi, and set up a provisional government and center of resistance at the resort town of Gudauta. It was a good choice, as the town hosted a Soviet (now Russian) airbase, and was thus protected from Georgian assault unless the Georgians chose to make war with the Kremlin.

This was not the case with the other famous resort towns named Gagra and Pitsunda. There, Georgian forces—primarily Jaba Ioseliani's Mkhedrioni—landed from the sea, burning and looting with virtual impunity until a new force entered the fray in September: Circassian volunteers from the Russian North Caucasus. These warriors called themselves the army of the Chechnya-based Confederation of Mountain Peoples, and swept out of the mountains, driving the Georgian forces and all Georgian residents of the resort communities into the sea, thus creating the first great wave of refugees of the Abkhaz war. The most infamous among the instigators of the exodus was Shamil Basayev, who would later be declared Public Enemy Number One in the Russian Federation thanks to his military and terrorist exploits in the upcoming catastrophe in Chechnya. While much has been written speculating about Basayev's early years, ranging from his having been "merely" a frustrated computer salesman looking for adventure and identity, to his having been a sleeper agent of the GRU/KGB/FSB all along and just waiting for the right war, a central fact remains: the future scourge of the Russian Federation first cut his teeth in Abkhazia. Even if not armed and trained by the Russian authorities (and there is reason to believe that he at least accepted their support), Basayev was certainly allowed to pass back and forth from the Russian North Caucasus to Sukhumi with minimal interference, and thus to mature in battle into the terror he was to become to the Russians themselves. Few better cases of "blowback" can be imagined.

Elsewhere, the Abkhaz and their Circassian cousins were not so effective in repulsing the Georgian forces, and fighting soon got bogged down in artillery duels and long-distance sniping across the Gumista River, five miles north of Sukhumi city center, punctuated by the occasional hecatomb offensive across the heavily-mined river banks to re-take the city, resulting in huge losses.

Whatever the merits of the original Georgian military action of August 14 and re-assertion of some manner of control over most of Abkhazia, one thing soon became apparent: Georgia was not only fighting the "Abkhaz," but rather, found itself fighting a strange coalition of local Abkhaz men (and women), Abkhaz and other Circassian volunteers both from the Russian North Caucasus and the wider Circassian Diaspora in Turkey and the Middle East, but also Cossack freebooters and other Slavic soldiers of fortune. Finally, and most ominously, it became clear that Georgia was also fighting against shadowy elements of the Russian military who supplied the motley Abkhaz forces with weapons, logistics, and even aviation.

The following is a reduction of a chapter from this author's book *Georgia Diary* about those sad times that deals with the indifference expressed by the international community when confronted with hard evidence of specific Russian involvement in the Abkhaz war. The events described below took place in March 1993.

> Sporadic sniper fire began at dusk, slowly swell[ed] into a constant snare-drum roll of heavy and light machine-gun fire as both sides put up a withering barrage designed to ensure that the other did not cross the river under cover of darkness. Then, around midnight, there came another sound: a monotonous drone, coming toward us from the north.
>
> Instantly, all candles were extinguished, and the commander insisted that all present put out their cigarettes...The droning sound of the jet engine came closer and closer, now directly overhead, seeking out its target while weaving a pattern of noisy, invisible circles in the night sky above the residential area of town called Novyi Raion (the New District). Then the plane began a long and almost languid swoop, wings slowly humming and then screaming out a two-second warning to whatever and whomever were below as it delivered its payload...
>
> After maybe five or six seconds that seemed like an eternity, a ball of fire erupted, illuminating an entire neighborhood. It was followed an instant later by first the sound and then the concussion of a tremendous blast that shook the earth...
>
> The phantom aircraft had just dropped a so-called vacuum bomb, a device that is technically known as an air-fuel explosive: 500 kilograms of liquid death and destruction explodes above the ground, thus maximizing the air-to-ground explosive impact. The plane continued to circle the site of the blast, now easily marked by flames on the ground as fires spread. Then it dove again, screaming down on the same area, strafing the streets with rocket and machine-gun fire before climbing back into the sky and banking west over the Black Sea.

In the morning, it didn't take long to find the area hit by the phantom fighter-bomber the night before. The 500-kilogram "vacuum" bomb had vaporized a two-story residential house and torn off the back half of four other houses surrounding it, with collateral damage spreading several hundred meters further. Miraculously, only one man—a local doctor—was killed outright, although his wife was said to have later died in a local hospital after she was brought in for treatment.

Traces of the strafing attack were equally easy to find. Football-sized divots defined the path of the rockets and cannon, while the accompanying machine-gun fire had ripped apart cars and fences along the street leading to the destroyed house, as if the pilot had intended to catch survivors or rescuers out of doors as they dug through the rubble of their friends' homes. That no one was killed in the strafing run was a miracle, although over a dozen people had been wounded.

The Abkhaz had no air force; the plane had flown in from the north through Russian Black Sea air defense space and returned more or less the same way. They were Russian planes, possibly piloted by freelance aviators or more likely by Russian air force men on 'loan' to terror-bomb civilians in Sukhumi.

[But] the government in Tbilisi was having a hard time convincing anyone outside the country about Russian involvement, too. Even when the Georgians managed to shoot down a MIG-29 and recover the body of the dead Russian pilot with all his papers, the Kremlin refused to admit any involvement. Confronted with the evidence, the Russian minister of defense, Pavel Grachev, denied that any Russian aircraft were operating anywhere near the theater—and then charged Georgia with terror-bombing its own citizens. When it was pointed out that the markings on the aircraft were distinctly Russian, Grachev blithely replied that the Georgians had painted his country's insignia on the plane in order to disguise it.

When the Georgians brought down a second 'mystery' aircraft, they invited a United Nations military observer to inspect both it and the papers of the dead pilot. The observer later said that although he was convinced that the dead man was indeed a professional Russian pilot flying a Russian MIG-29, he was unable to categorically state that the pilot was operating under orders from somewhere inside the Russian defense ministry.

"We need to see orders, written orders, and we need to see the pilots receive them, get in their planes, take off, bomb, and then return to fill out mission completion forms," the frustrated observer said. "We are never going to get all that..."

On September 27 of that same year, Sukhumi fell to the besieging coalition of Abkhaz militiamen, Chechen volunteers, and Russian mercenaries, forcing Eduard Shevardnadze to flee for his life. Some say that it was Yeltsin who intervened to save Shevardnadze's life, as a tacit thanks for Shevardnadze having backed Yeltsin during the summer of 1991; others suggest that his escape was almost a miracle, given the nearly pathological resentment held against the former Soviet foreign minister among Red Army brass who continued to condemn Shevardnadze for having "sold out" the USSR in Afghanistan and East Germany; still others dismiss all such stories and speculations and posit darkly that everything associated with Shevardnadze's return to Georgia was part of a much deeper, darker "Soviet" plot designed to lull the West into a sense of complacency before initiating a grand return of the Evil Empire to world dominance. The more likely scenario was and is much more prosaic. Having survived Sukhumi, where Shevardnadze had personally presided over the defense of the city, Shevardnadze was obliged to fly to Moscow to beg for Russian military support to fend off a bid by Zviad Gamsakhurdia to rally support among the war-exhausted and shocked population to restore him to power, and Yeltsin (and the top military brass) obligingly did so, thus graphically (if only temporarily) restoring a Russian sphere of influence in a break-away South Caucasus state.

The "Zviadists" were routed, and Gamsakhurdia himself either died of disease, was killed by his aides, or committed suicide in the mountains above Zugdidi on December 31, 1993—but not before some quarter of a million Georgians were forced to flee their homes as refugees.

The reason so few in the West heard of this mass ethnic cleansing was, presumably, because of parallel events in Bosnia which overshadowed those at play in the South Caucasus. A more cynical viewpoint was that when it came to Georgia, there was just too much "brutality overload," and with Russia's fledgling "democracy" suddenly threatened in Yeltsin's Moscow in the autumn of 1993, there was simply too much of "democratic Russia" to lose by delving more deeply into the Russian role in the catastrophe that Georgia had become.

The winter that year was as cold and brutal as anyone could remember. Tbilisi experienced only a sporadic supply electricity and gas, and was ruled by roving bands of Mkhedrioni thugs. In the countryside, meanwhile, almost 250,000 Georgian refugees who had been ethnically cleansed from Abkhazia suffered deprivations and bitter disillusionment with their three year-experiment with independence.

Indeed, if there is a period of recent Georgian history that could be labeled "rock bottom," it was the winter of 1993–94. The quest by Gamsakhurdia to restore a Georgia for the Georgians had resulted in Eduard Shevardnadze having inherited the makings of a failed state.

3

Georgian-Russian Relations in the 1990s

Thornike Gordadze

"Four centuries of resistance!"—so proclaimed thousands of leaflets distributed in Tbilisi by young Georgian activists during the August 2008 war with Russia. Analyzing Georgian-Russian relations solely in terms of resistance is understandable when Russian tanks were 40 km away from the country's capital, but a more balanced assessment requires a more nuanced understanding of the question. The relationship between a local polity and an external center of power attempting to establish its domination is by necessity more complex, definitely equivocal, and essentially unstable.

Throughout history, local rulers have made deals with empires, and their dependence has never been total. Phases of military conquest and crude repression have tended to be followed by a "hegemonic stage," in which the dominant power seeks to co-opt local elites. This has even been known to end in a growing dependence of the imperial power on the local ruler. An eagerness to control the Caucasus and its central country, Georgia, has been a *leitmotiv* of all Russian empires. It was in the Caucasus that imperial pride and dreams of greatness were nurtured, and where Russia took refuge in order to deflect frustration away from its continuous resentment vis-à-vis the West.

Today's Russia again considers itself something akin to an empire. After a short period of hesitation following the collapse of the Soviet Union, Russia, having failed to invent a new identity for itself, reverted to the old ideal of empire. But the modern Russian empire is strikingly more fragile than its predecessors, because it tries to carry out a rather difficult, if not impossible, task, namely to make a long abandoned political model viable in a totally new environment. As long as Russia sticks to this line, it will be condemned to great fragility, and as long as Russia is fragile, its relationship with the surrounding world—and especially with its immediate neighbors—will tend to be uneasy and troubled.

Being a hegemonic and nationality-based empire, the Soviet Union rehabilitated and in certain respects reinforced the role of local actors. The Soviet experience was formative for those who took on the ambivalent and dual role of acting simultaneously as community leaders and imperial servants. In the 1990s, during the era of Boris Yeltsin's Russia, Georgia was led by Eduard Shevardnadze, a former high-level Soviet official who had presided over Communist Georgia in the 1970s before being brought to Moscow by Mikhail Gorbachev, who made him Soviet foreign minister. Shevardnadze was a perfect example of a man who sought to reconcile in one life many different roles. Georgian-Russian relations under his presidency and that of Yeltsin in Russia vividly illustrate all the ambiguities and difficulties of a post-imperial conflict.

A Tumultuous Start: Georgian Independence without State and Russian Empire without Policy

The roughly two years spanning the fall of Zviad Gamsakhurdia and the end of the Abkhaz war, from January 1992 to September 1993, illustrate several core aspects of Russian-Georgian relations after the dissolution of the Soviet Union, indeed setting the stage for the coming decade. The West regarded with total indifference the overthrow of the radically anti-hegemonic regime of Zviad Gamsakhurdia. The main Western priority at the time was to guarantee stability on the territory of the dissolving nuclear empire. But once the shock of disintegration was over, both Russia and Georgia came back to their classical national projects: for Russia, the restoration of an empire or at the very least a zone of influence; for Georgia, the construction of a nation-state. Inevitably, their interests clashed again; the regime of Eduard Shevardnadze, presumed by many to be loyal to Moscow, turned out to be as attached to the idea of independence and sovereignty as its predecessor, the Gamsakhurdia regime, had been. Russia, in order to impose its hegemony, had somehow to punish this new regime. Yet during this period it became clear that no serious political force in Georgia would ever be so obedient to Moscow as to abandon its sovereignty and territorial integrity. In spite of the tense relations, it would be unfair to argue that Russia was unilaterally initiating all the processes that developed in Georgia and its breakaway territories. At least in the beginning of the 1990s, Russia was subjected to internal turmoil, which left it reacting to events in Georgia rather than initiating them. Even then, Russia was never unresponsive, because it had never, even in the worst times, abandoned the idea of maintaining a special influence outside its borders. Georgian opposition to Gamsakhurdia would certainly have existed even without Russia, yet Russia's role in his overthrow was by no means insignificant. Likewise, some sort of ethnic conflict in Abkhazia was probably unavoidable, but without Russian involvement the outcome of these events would in all likelihood have been very different.

There are now many indications that Russia backed the coup that ousted Zviad Gamsakhurdia from the presidency in December 1991–January 1992. Moscow viewed Gamsakhurdia as a Russophobe and as a danger to Russia's dominance over the entire Caucasus. Gamsakhurdia, whose term in office was characterized by serious mismanagement of both domestic and foreign affairs, was strongly attached to the idea of a "Common Caucasian Home." This was a rather utopian idea of a "United Caucasus" that would challenge Moscow's domination of the region. The first fruits of this idea were already apparent with the sealing of an alliance between Gamsakhurdia and Jokhar Dudayev's independent republic of Chechnya. Gamsakhurdia attended Dudayev's inauguration as president in 1991, and when Gamsakhurdia was overthrown, he chose Chechnya as his place of asylum. While he resided in Grozny, Gamsakhurdia also helped to organize the first "All-Caucasian Conference" which was attended by independent-minded groups from across the region.

The Georgian opposition to Gamsakhurdia was a strange alliance between defeated Communist apparatchiks, anti-Gamsakhurdia nationalists, and organized crime chiefs known as the "criminal authorities." Moscow supported this heterogeneous opposition both financially and technically, while the Russian military stationed in Georgia supplied it with weapons. Exiled former Georgian communist leaders, such as Akaki Mgeladze, had initiated the alliance between former communists, the outlawed Mkhedrioni militia, and some units of the National Guard under the command of Tengiz Kitovani. In his memoirs, published in 1999, Mkhedrioni chief Jaba Ioseliani described Kitovani's close relations with Russian generals.[1]

Once Gamsakhurdia was overthrown, power was vested in the Military Council made up of former Prime Minister Tengiz Sigua, Kitovani, and Ioseliani. The putschists used the anti-Gamsakhurdia nationalists such as the National Democratic Party, the Party of National Independence, and the Popular Front to provide some moral legitimacy for their coup but never offered them a share of power. They established a bizarre political assembly called the State Council (*Sakhelmtzipo Sabcho*), with representation of all existing political parties except Gamsakhurdia's followers. No elections were held until October 1992, and the Assembly, which was a simple agglomeration of existing parties, had neither a structure nor real power. Actual power rested in the hands of armed groups and militias under Ioseliani and Kitovani's authority. Even though the international community recognized Georgia's independence, Russia's military continued to act as an important guarantor of the new government.

All rulers seek a minimum of legitimacy. It is for this reason that the Military Council, which had become extremely unpopular for its brutal repression of the Zviadists, invited Eduard Shevardnadze to return to Georgia in March 1992.[2] Shortly thereafter, Shevardnadze joined Ioseliani, Sigua, and Kitovani to form the Presidium of the State Council. All four were given the power to veto decisions of the State Council. Parliamentary elections were held in October 1992, and Shevardnadze was elected Chairman of Parliament, which remained the highest position in the state until the adoption of a presidential constitution in 1995.

From the very beginning, a large portion of Georgian society was critical of Shevardnadze. Zviad Gamsakhurdia continued to enjoy substantial support, especially in the western part of the country, and Shevardnadze's past led to the firm belief that he was closely tied to Russia, some seeing him as nothing more than a Russian figurehead. This opinion was reinforced in June 1992, when Shevardnadze signed a cease-fire agreement on the South Ossetian conflict with Boris Yeltsin in the resort of Dagomys, close to Sochi in the Russian North Caucasus. Following the agreement, Georgian Forces that were in a dominant position in the Tskhinvali region and were blockading the secessionist stronghold there retreated, and joint Russian–Georgian-Ossetian peacekeeping battalions were set up to patrol the conflict zone. The agreement was clearly advantageous for Russia, given that Ossetian and Russian battalions were acting in concert, and it turned out to be very negative for Georgia. The document, officially called the "Agreement on Principles for the Settlement of the Georgian-Ossetian Conflict between Georgia and Russia," produced a quadrilateral Joint Control Commission (JCC), consisting of Russian, North Ossetian, South Ossetian, and Georgian sides tasked to supervise the implementation of the agreement. This four-sided body was by no means acceptable to Georgia. Besides the presence of Russia as a biased broker, it included *two* Ossetian delegations, while Georgia was represented only by its central government. Hence both the political representation and the peacekeeping structure ruled out any possibility of parity from the very beginning. Not surprisingly, Shevardnadze's critics considered this move as a betrayal of the national interests of Georgia in favor of Russia.

In fact, reality was much more complex. No doubt, Eduard Shevardnadze's entire political career had been connected with the Soviet Union.

He was a classically ambivalent figure, who knew how to take advantage of his local resources to gain a privileged place in an imperial system, but who also could use his imperial credentials to assert his power at the local level. As in many post-colonial transitions, he became the imperial servant who transformed himself into a post-imperial national leader. But in the beginning of the 1990s, Shevardnadze's Russian credentials were ambiguous. Earlier, he had been closely associated with Gorbachev's political team, but by 1992 this grouping had already been marginalized. The Soviet Union had collapsed, and Russia was ruled by factions, symbolized by Boris Yeltsin, that in the past had opposed Gorbachev. Moreover, Russia's orthodox Communists and the military and security communities hated Gorbachev and his circle even more than Yeltsin and his allies did, holding them responsible for "the loss of half of Europe," the "surrender of Afghanistan," and, finally, the destruction of the Empire. Shevardnadze himself had a small circle of allies in the Russian Ministry of Foreign Affairs, chiefly persons he had promoted when he was minister, men like Andrei Kozyrev and Igor Ivanov, who both ended up as ministers themselves. Yet most members of the new Russian political elite were hostile to Shevardnadze. Indeed, whatever political capital he may have accumulated as Minister of Foreign Affairs during perestroika was more exploitable in the West, where he had enjoyed the image of a liberal minister who was among those chiefly responsible for ending the Cold War.

Georgia was breaking the wall of international isolation that had surrounded the country under the successive rule of Gamsakhurdia and the Military Council. Yet Western interests in the region were still very limited compared to those of a weakened but still very visible Russia. Later claims by Russian officials and some Russian and Western analysts that Russia suffered a "severe humiliation" at the hands of the West in the beginning of the 1990s does not hold up to serious analysis. Indeed, events demonstrate that the West accepted almost everything Russia undertook in the Caucasus in the name of stability. The West strikingly lacked any willingness to get involved in the region. America's presence was very limited, and the administration of George H.W. Bush validated and even welcomed the creation of the Commonwealth of Independent States (CIS), which from the very beginning Russia defined as a zone of its own particular interest. It is revealing that the term "near abroad" emerged during the presidency of Yeltsin, not Putin.

Moscow had total freedom of maneuver during the wars in Abkhazia (August 1992–September 1993) and Mountainous Karabakh (from 1991 to May 1994).[3] Russia's conduct in these wars received no serious criticism or condemnation from Western countries. The West was happy that Russia was unable to intervene in the Balkans, one of the West's top priorities at that time, and was therefore disinclined to criticize Russia for its role in the ethnic cleansing and mass killings that occurred in Abkhazia in 1992–93, and which were committed either by Russian citizens involved as "volunteers" or by Abkhaz secessionists whom the Russian military had armed and trained.[4]

In April 1993, speaking to the Georgian Parliament, Shevardnadze had to recognize that in Abkhazia Georgia was in fact facing Russia.[5] By that time, the conflict in Abkhazia and Russia's growing involvement on the side of the Abkhaz had already nullified any hopes that may have existed of a partnership between the two countries. Georgians' distrust of Russia was even greater now than it had been during the Gamsakhurdia period.

Russia more and more actively involved itself in the war. Nevertheless, the first official reactions from the Kremlin and President Yeltsin's office were not anti-Georgian but conveyed rather benevolent neutrality. At the start of the Abkhaz war there was no consensus in Russia as to how it should be treated. Nor, for that matter, was there any consensus on the identity and orientation of the new Russian state. Those most opposed to Georgia were the military, conservative Communists, and nationalists, whose influence was steadily expanding.[6] In a manner that would recur during the war in Chechnya, Yeltsin decided to leave the issue of Abkhazia to those who with a "special interest" in it. Willing to confront neither the military nor an assortment of North Caucasian nationalists, pro-Soviet restorationists, and "red and brown" patriots, the Kremlin allowed itself to be dragged into a policy of active support for the Abkhaz secessionists. Abkhazia was Yeltsin's first significant concession to the conservatives; many similar steps were to follow, including the war in Chechnya and the rampant evolution towards authoritarianism. The Abkhazia war also signaled a return to imperial notions of regional politics.

Under the ideological and moral influence of its nationalists, Georgia decided not to join the CIS, even after the removal of Gamsakhurdia. But the significance of this move was more symbolic than real, since Russia's influence in Georgia was no less powerful than in any other CIS member state. Despite its financial and moral decay, the Russian army was still the most powerful military force in Georgia. It was the main supplier, both by smuggling and by legal transfers, of weapons to all belligerents and militias, including both Abkhaz and Ossetian separatists, as well as to the Georgian regular army. The headquarters of the Russian Transcaucasian Military District (ZAKVO) were still in Tbilisi, and Georgia's border with

NATO member Turkey was controlled by Russian border guards. In addition to Abkhazia and South Ossetia, Aslan Abashidze, the leader of the autonomous Black Sea province of Adjara, closed the administrative border with the rest of the country and with the help of Russian troops prevented the central government's forces from entering Adjaran territory. This established Abashidze's authoritarian, semi-separatist regime within the region, and created long-term problems between the regional government and the central authorities of Georgia. Near Batumi, Russia stationed a military contingent which for several years became a kind of private army for Abashidze. Many Adjaran youths served in the Russian army's border forces as a way of avoiding conscription into the new national army.

1993–95: Russian Hegemony and Pax Russica

By the end of the war in Abkhazia, Russian Foreign Minister Andrei Kozyrev declared at the UN General Assembly that "Russia realizes that no international organization or group of states can replace our peacekeeping efforts in this specific post-Soviet space."[7] This was a clear announcement, paradoxically expressed by the minister considered the most Western-oriented in Russia's recent history, that Russia's main priority was to restore its hegemony over the post-Soviet space. Lacking resources and facing internal chaos, Russia could fulfill its new doctrine only by sustaining its military bases and by supporting various separatist movements, especially in less loyal neighboring countries like Georgia, Moldova, Azerbaijan, and to some extent also, Ukraine. The objective of this support was not the independence of the rebellious provinces. Instead, by making itself the sole "peacekeeper" in the conflicts which Moscow had itself fuelled, Russia could dominate the newly independent states and prevent their rapprochement with the West. Thus, the strategy of "peacekeeping" in the post-Soviet space became a neo-Byzantine version of "piece keeping," in Paul Goble's words. Unfortunately for the independence of post-Soviet states, no international actor tried to impede this process. On the contrary, international organizations like the UN (in the case of Abkhazia) and the OSCE (in the case of South Ossetia and Karabakh) de facto endorsed the role Russia had arrogated to itself. Yet a relatively minor effort by the international community could have deterred Russia, which at this time depended on foreign funds for its survival.[8]

Georgia became the most striking manifestation of Russia's new interventionist policy in the post-Soviet space. In effect, Russia showcased its regional ambitions in Georgia, which in the 1990s was easier to do because of the Georgians' radical and often unrealistic approach to regional issues. Georgia's military defeat in Abkhazia resulted in the near total collapse of Georgian statehood. Civil war erupted in western Georgia, where a returning Gamsakhurdia and his followers achieved several victories in the fall of 1993, after which they started their advance towards the capital. Humiliated and defeated, or "on his knees" as Russian analysts and politicians liked to say, Shevardnadze was forced to accept the "aid" of Russian troops and of Russia's Black Sea Fleet. Only thanks to this was Georgia able to stop the Zviadists' progression and thereby retake control of the major communication arteries of their country.[9]

At the end of 1993, thus, Georgia had to swallow the bitter pill of Russia's peace terms. Despite fierce debates in the Georgian Parliament, Georgia entered the CIS on October 21, 1993, and in February 1994, even joined the Collective Security Treaty, the security organization that Moscow was building as a kind of post-Soviet version of the Warsaw Pact. Shevardnadze also had to sign a military agreement on "the status of the Russian troops in Georgia," according to which Russia was to maintain four military bases in the country. These were in Vaziani, just outside Tbilisi; in Akhalkalaki in southern Georgia; in Batumi; and in Gudauta, Abkhazia—in addition to the headquarters of the ZAKVO in Tbilisi and the border guards along the Turkish frontier. Boris Yeltsin visited Georgia in the beginning of February 1994, to this day the only visit of a Russian president to the sovereign Republic of Georgia. The visit resembled a review by a Roman Emperor of one of his newly subjected *limes*. Russia obtained not only the right to maintain its military bases in Georgia, but also acquired unprecedented influence over the appointment of the three "power ministers" in the Georgian government, that of Defense, Interior, and Security (the former KGB). On February 4, Yeltsin and Shevardnadze solemnized a treaty on Friendship and Cooperation which sealed Russia's de facto protectorate over Georgia. Regarding Abkhazia, Georgia had to endorse a humiliating "joint appeal" with Russia to the Council of the Heads of States of the CIS to send a peacekeeping force to Abkhazia.[10] Two months later, in April 1994, the Georgian and Abkhaz leaderships signed the Moscow Peace Agreement, entrusting to the Russian Federation the mandate for peacekeeping. The agreement also implied the return of more than 250,000 Georgian Internally Displaced Persons (IDPs) to their homes, but this point of the document was never implemented.

Georgia's subjection to Russia had a very negative impact on Georgia's already timid cooperation with the West. The only form of cooperation with the West that Russia initially permitted Georgia to pursue was humanitarian and financial aid.[11] Russia jealously supervised every move of the Georgian law enforcement and security forces and was careful to prevent links between them and their Western counterparts. Indeed, when an American Embassy employee, CIA officer Fred Woodruff, managed to establish close links with the Georgian president's security service in 1993, he was killed under circumstances that have yet to be clarified. Vardiko Nadibaidze, a Russian army general of Georgian origin and deputy commander of ZAKVO, was appointed Minister of Defense in February 1994.[12] Meanwhile, Igor Giorgadze, an experienced KGB officer and veteran of the Afghan war, became Minister of State Security and grew in influence thereafter. The third Russian protégé whose career leaped forward was Shota Kviraia, who was named Minister of Interior. Although a Russian nominee, he was a rival of Giorgadze's, thus extending into post-Soviet Georgia the traditional Soviet/Russian rivalry between the Ministry of Interior and the KGB.

With both its security and defense in the hands of Russian appointees, the Georgian government took no steps to move closer to NATO for several years. But despite this "good conduct," Georgia failed to receive any benefits from Russia in terms of steps toward the restoration of its territorial integrity. There were two direct meetings under Moscow's aegis between Shevardnadze and the leader of the Abkhaz secessionists, Vladislav Ardzinba: one meeting in Tbilisi mediated by Russian Minister of Defense Pavel Grachev, and one in Abkhazia arranged by Yevgeny Primakov, Russia's Minister for Foreign Affairs following Kozyrev's demise. Yet both ended in failure, officially because of Abkhaz intransigence.

As far as the rebuilding of Georgia's military was concerned, Russia offered some time-worn military equipment and promised to train Georgian officers in Russian military academies, but actually admitted only a small number. Russia even failed to deliver the twenty million rubles in aid (approximately $3 million at that time) promised in the 1994 treaty. In spite of all this, Georgia tried even harder to gain Russia's benevolence as a necessary step towards resolving its most significant problem—to reestablish its territorial integrity. But for various reasons having mainly to do with its domestic politics, Russia had no intention of abandoning Abkhazia. A bluntly anti-Western nationalism was gaining momentum in Moscow, and political leaders were disinclined to defy the military—which was emotionally and economically committed to keeping Abkhazia under its firm control.

Hoping that Russia, confronted with ethnic separatism on its own territory, would became more understanding of Georgia's separatist problems,

Shevardnadze publicly endorsed Russia's invasion of Chechnya in December 1994 and authorized Russian military jets to use Georgian airspace. The Georgian leadership naively believed that the active involvement of the Chechens in favor of the Abkhaz secession from Georgia would influence Russia's position on Abkhazia now that the Chechens had become Russia's bitter enemies.

Georgia's deferential behavior towards Moscow in these years sometimes verged on the absurd. One incident that comes to mind was the improvised baptism in Tbilisi of Russian Defense Minister Pavel Grachev, conducted in person by the *Catholicos* (Patriarch) of the Georgian Orthodox Church, with Vardiko Nadibaidze taking the role of a happy godfather.[13] Yet Grachev was the person most frequently accused of being the main culprit behind Georgia's defeat in Abkhazia. Indeed, Shevardnadze himself had stated on Georgian TV shortly after the defeat that "we lost the war to a Russian general, we lost the war to Pavel Grachev." Years later after losing power, Shevardnadze declared the following to the Russian newspaper *Argumenty i Fakty:* "Do you remember General Grachev? He called me and said, 'I'll help you. But I have to bring two more divisions into Abkhazia.' I believed him and agreed. My defense minister and security minister were right next to me. They resigned to protest my decision. And Grachev changed his mind later on: 'We can't leave Abkhazia, because then we'd lose the Black Sea.'"[14] Grachev also distinguished himself during the war in Abkhazia by accusing Georgians of painting their aircraft with Russian insignia and bombing their own cities.

This period of indenture to Russia was also marked by the absence of real stabilization, in spite of the often-heard claim that, thanks to the Russian protectorate, Georgia had at least gained peace and stability. If the main Zviadist armed groups were eliminated shortly after Gamsakhurdia's death, many smaller groups continued to threaten security in Mingrelia, which until 1995 was far from pacified. Only after Shevardnadze launched a campaign of national reconciliation did the situation improve in western Georgia, but the process of reconciliation was not completed until after Saakashvili came to power. In the rest of Georgia, political assassinations were frequent and many prominent politicians became victims of violent crime.[15] The newly reinforced ministries of State Security and Interior had marginalized the various militias, especially the Mkhedrioni, who lost ground in 1994–95. But these two ministries now became the major threat to the rule of law and respect for human rights. Police and KGB officials, working in close partnership with criminal groups, became deeply involved in international drug trafficking, racketeering, embezzlement, and other destabilizing forms of corruption.

1995–99: Drifting Apart

As early as 1995, Shevardnadze had realized that the evolution of Russian internal and external policies would exclude the possibility of a profitable partnership between Moscow and Georgia. Shevardnadze himself was increasingly under attack in Russia, perceived as one of the main gravediggers of the Soviet Union, an unpardonable sin for a Russian political elite increasingly dominated by revanchism. Hence the quasi-vassal relationship failed to bring any real benefit to Georgia. On the contrary, Russia kept trying to weaken Tbilisi through its continuous support for the secessionists and its numerous attempts to undermine Georgian sovereignty. Underscoring the fragility of the Georgian state, new centrifugal tendencies fuelled by Russia appeared in Adjara and Javakheti, with its large population of citizens of Armenian descent.

In this context, Georgia could only welcome the slow awakening of the West, chiefly of the United States, to their country and region. The Pax Russica of 1993–94 in the Caucasus had been a cold shower for decision-makers in Washington. The latter were becoming increasingly aware of the strategic importance of the Caucasus, as well as the importance of the energy resources of the Caspian Sea and Central Asia. Even if these resources were underexploited at the end of the Soviet era, or had fallen into disuse, the idea of a new east-west energy corridor that did not cross Russian territory was being formed. Moreover, such a corridor could itself provide timely support for the new sovereignties in the region.

Thus, the independence and stability of the countries situated between Turkey and China's western frontier was in the interest of the United States. But before 1995, American involvement in the region remained weak, as were forces in America advocating a more active U.S. engagement there. It will be recalled that President Clinton's first term was marked by a "Russia-first" strategy, while the peripheral countries of the post-Soviet area received much less attention.

Shevardnadze clearly understood this emerging opportunity. Although he had his hands tied by militias and Russian-controlled security services, he prudently started moving towards emancipating himself from Russian tutorship. Thus, he began promoting a group of young and promising Western-educated politicians inside the ruling Citizens' Union of Georgia (CUG). Within a few years, these became the most active and visible faction of the party. He also surrounded himself with overtly pro-Western advisors, and initiated the formation of parallel, and thereby competing, security services. A key example was his Presidential Guard, trained by American specialists.[16]

The failed assassination attempt against Shevardnadze on August 29, 1995, marked a turning point. Shevardnadze had already adopted a new constitution, which provided more substantial powers to the presidency as opposed to the nationalist-dominated Parliament. The Parliament, even though it symbolized Georgian democracy, nevertheless blocked the passage of many crucial laws and was constantly embroiled in making what amounted to rather childish accusations against the president. Shevardnadze gained considerable moral authority from having survived an attack on his life, which all agreed had been initiated from Moscow. For the first time he alluded in an interview directly to "some obscure forces in Russia"[17] that were trying to destabilize Georgia and derail the great energy project, that is, the Baku-Tbilisi-Ceyhan Pipeline (BTC)—in which Georgia was so actively participating. In a subsequent interview, Shevardnadze claimed that President Yeltsin himself had warned him of the "serious trouble" that could arise if he continued to support alternative ways of bringing Caspian oil to European markets.

The prime suspect in the attempt on Shevardnadze's life, Igor Giorgadze, precipitously left the country on a Russian jet chartered for the purpose, whereas Ioseliani was arrested and sentenced to ten years in prison. Only a few months earlier, Kitovani had been arrested on his way to Abkhazia, accompanied by a few hundred armed followers and a Russian colonel. The objectives of Kitovani's march remain unclear, but the maneuver was probably intended to use the hope of recovering Georgian control over Abkhazia as a means of plunging the country into a new round of instability.

American involvement became more active with the realization of the Baku-Tbilisi-Ceyhan pipeline project. Russia vehemently criticized BTC, but so did certain Western experts, who denounced it as being a solely political project designed to damage Russia and, at the same time, reinforce America's position in the region. As late as the late 1990s, many of these experts continued to write about the "absurdity" of the BTC project, referring to its purported lack of economic feasibility and the alleged absence of sufficient quantities of oil in the Caspian. Subsequent events have made it clear that this criticism was itself politically motivated, and far from disinterested. Moreover, it should not be forgotten that the idea of a pipeline stretching from the Caspian via Turkey to Western markets was very much supported by Ankara as well. Indeed, Süleyman Demirel brought up the idea as early as in spring 1992, and the first memorandum on what became the Baku-Ceyhan pipeline was signed in Ankara on March 9, 1993, in the midst of the fighting in Abkhazia and Karabakh. The final agreements were also signed in Turkey in October (Ankara) and November (Istanbul) of 1998. Thus, the independence of Georgia and Azerbaijan vis-à-vis Russia had become as crucial for Turkey as for the U.S. and the other BTC partners, including Azerbaijan, Norway, and Great Britain.

Another factor that fostered Shevardnadze's drift to the West was the weakening of Russia caused by the Chechen conflict. Despite the terrible cost in lives it inflicted and also paid itself to keep Chechnya under its control, Russia practically lost the first Chechen war of 1994–96. The disastrous war in Chechnya resulted in de facto Chechen independence, creating a quasi-state in Chechnya that was interested in a neighborly relationship with Georgia, its only link to the outside world. The pragmatic and moderate Chechen leader Aslan Maskhadov took steps to improve Georgian-Chechen relations, which had been significantly strained when Chechens had fought for the Abkhaz during the war in Abkhazia. Chechen Vice-President Vakha Arsanov, then Maskhadov himself, paid visits to Georgia. The latter publicly presented Chechen apologies for the events in Abkhazia, and made a commitment to severely punish any Chechen who would henceforth participate in any action against Georgia; the Chechen leadership was particularly interested in building a road from Chechnya to Georgia in order to end its isolation from the outside world. Georgians welcomed the initiative publicly, but did little, being worried that Chechen instability would spread south across the border.

Shevardnadze's pro-Western shift was far from a linear process. When Shevardnadze again narrowly survived an assassination attempt in February 1998, the process appeared threatened.[18] Then in October 1998 a military mutiny sprang up, during which rioters from the National Guard were clearly awaiting instructions from Moscow. Constant provocations were also taking place in Javakheti and Adjara. For example, in August 1998, several dozen armed local Armenians in Javakheti forced Georgian armed units to turn back from scheduled joint military drills with the Russian base at Akhalkalaki.

With the appointment of Boris Berezovsky as Executive Secretary of the CIS, Russia became more proactive in the region. Berezovsky promoted the idea of an alternative pipeline from the Caspian shores to Russia via Georgia and breakaway Abkhazia. To go forward this would require a resolution of the Abkhaz problem between Russia and Georgia. He also introduced some Russian companies into Georgia, in order to extend Russian influence there by means other than the military.[19] At the same time, there were further attempts to pull Georgia into a fresh Abkhaz trap. For example, during the May 1998 conflict in Gali, the southernmost part of Abkhazia, Georgian authorities were given guarantees concerning their probable recovery of the Gali region, but were again misled.[20]

1999–2003: A New Vicious Circle in the Georgia-Russia Relationship

At the end of 1990s and the beginning of the 2000s, Georgia's foreign relations presented a picture of extreme contrasts. On the one hand, the country had become among the leading beneficiaries of U.S. foreign aid per capita globally. On the other, its biggest neighbor and former overlord was vigorously trying to undermine Georgia's sovereignty through acts of destabilization and to extend its own influence there. One side was financing the formation of the country's military forces by an impressive influx of money and specialists—in 2001–2 American aid to the Georgian army represented two-thirds of the country's military budget. Meanwhile, the other side sought to prevent Georgian nationals and citizens living in Russia from sending their savings home to their families. In fact, there is a certain irony to this picture in that the former is a culturally and historically alien "Anglo-Saxon" superpower, while the latter supposedly a "spiritually and sentimentally" close Orthodox brother.

The second Chechen war began shortly after Yeltsin and his informal circle, known as "the Family," appointed a new prime minister, Vladimir Putin. Russia fought this war with no less cruelty than the first, but it presented a noticeable contrast to the first war in terms of the Russian government's motivation and determination. This time Moscow demanded that Georgia offer its airspace to the Russian air force and that it allow Russian border guards to control the Georgians' side of the Chechen-Georgian border. After asking for a day's delay for reflection, Shevardnadze refused Russia's request. He saw a serious risk that the Chechen conflict might be expanded onto Georgian territory. Besides, bitter experience had taught the Georgian leadership that additional Russian troops on Georgian territory could be used as a Trojan horse. Georgia's refusal infuriated the Russian leadership, and Georgia became the target of Russian verbal and, later, physical attacks as Russian jets bombed the Georgian side of the border. Moscow accused Georgia, moreover, of serving as a transit country for global Islamist networks that were sending forces into Chechnya, and also of supplying weapons to the Chechen rebels.

Russia never presented any credible evidence on Georgia's alleged involvement on the side of the Chechens. But the accusations served to exonerate the Russian army for its failures during the first year-and-a-half of the operation. It was also useful to Moscow to have tarnished Georgia's international reputation by endlessly representing it as at best a failed state that could not secure its borders, and at worst as a rogue state in league with terrorists. Russian accusations sometimes went to ludicrous extremes, as, for example, when Moscow claimed that Osama Bin Laden was hiding in the Pankisi Gorge.[21] Russian military spokesmen regularly announced the presence in the Pankisi Gorge of hundreds, if not thousands, of jihadi fighters, especially Taliban. Russian aircraft bombed several Georgian mountain villages, on one occasion causing casualties, and Russian civil authorities unilaterally redrew the Chechen portion of the Russian-Georgian border, advancing the line deeper into Georgian territory.[22]

Russian comparisons between the situation in Pankisi and Peshawar in the 1980s or Qandahar in the 1990s were hyperbole, but the situation in Pankisi was far from ideal. Among the 12,000 Chechen refugees in the valley, there were several hundred fighters and even some foreign Islamist combatants. However, their attitude was rather low-key. Criminal groups, some of them with combat experience in Chechnya, were a bigger problem. They were responsible for most of the abductions and drug trafficking that flourished in the valley. These groups were involved in a sort of criminal joint venture with corrupt Georgian interior ministry officials, and served as "subcontractors" for drug deals and the extraction of ransom money. The Ministry of Internal Affairs and its police pretended not to control the valley, blaming the "Chechen fighters" for the lawlessness there. In reality, the police were themselves involved in kidnappings and drug trafficking, with local bands acting as implementers. The senior police official in charge of the Ministry's anti-terrorist department was dismissed for such activities, revealing that complicity permeated the very top levels of government.

September 11, 2001, changed the game, as it enabled Russia to redefine the war in Chechnya as a struggle against international terrorism, and to ape America's military intervention in Afghanistan and then Iraq. In the process, Georgia became a vivid illustration of what Russia's revived ambitions as a great power meant in practice.[23] Not surprisingly, Moscow opposed Georgia's request to the OSCE to create a border monitoring mission on the Chechen portion of its border with Russia. This would not only have put a stop to Russian allegations but might also have proven that the goal of all such accusations was to justify some future military intervention on Georgian territory.

In the end, Moscow's exaggerated claims that the Pankisi valley had become one of the world's most dangerous centers of terrorism led to disastrous consequences not for Georgia but for Russia itself. By constantly alluding to the presence of Al-Qaeda or Taliban elements in Pankisi, Russian leaders aroused America's interest in this region. Foreseeing a Russian military intervention in Georgia "to bring order" and "fight terrorists," the U.S. in April 2002 pre-empted Russia by announcing a significant bilateral military cooperation program with Georgia, called the Georgia Train and Equip Program (GTEP). The State Department announced this $64 million project as a response "to the Government of Georgia's request for assistance to enhance its counter-terrorism capabilities and address the situation in the Pankisi Gorge." In the GTEP framework, between 150 and 200 American military trainers were supposed to arrive in Georgia. Russia could scarcely oppose a counter-terrorist operation directed against targets that were impeding its own war in Chechnya and for which it had itself been asking for some time, however much it resented the fact that a contingent of American military trainers would soon arrive in Georgia. In the end, Russia got what it least wanted: an American military presence close to its borders. These developments strongly reinforced the Russians' conclusion that Shevardnadze had become hopelessly pro-American, and consequently an arch-enemy of Russia.

Apart from the Chechen war, many other issues during Shevardnadze's last term in office contributed to the mounting tension in Russian–Georgian relations. Georgia's efforts to build an independent and sovereign state deeply irritated Moscow, as did the unresolved state of affairs in Abkhazia and South Ossetia, where Russia was unwilling to concede anything. Seeing no evolution in Russia's position, the Georgian leadership grew ever more dissatisfied with the conditions that Moscow had imposed on these areas in the early 1990s. In particular, Georgian leaders increasingly viewed Russia's military presence on Georgian soil as a destabilizing element. The long process of ridding the country of Russia's military presence began with the adoption, in April 1997, of a new law that called for Georgia to take full control of its national borders by the end of 1999. Russian maritime border guards were the first to leave, in the summer of 1998, and a year later Georgia took control of its border with Turkey. Critically important assistance from Turkey, Ukraine, and the United States enabled Georgia's Department of Border Control Forces to assume these responsibilities effectively.[24]

In 1999 Tbilisi for the first time mustered the courage to announce its intention to close the Russian military bases on its territory. To this end, Georgia first left the Russian-dominated Collective Security Treaty in April 1999. Then, in September 1999, Zurab Zhvania, the Chairman of Parliament and Shevardnadze's then heir apparent, declared that the day was close when Georgia would be free of the "foreign military presence." At the OSCE Summit in Istanbul two months later Russia was told to dismantle two of its military bases in Georgia and to find a solution for the remaining two before July 2001.[25] Long and difficult negotiations took place on the fate of the two remaining bases. Ten rounds and two years of negotiations later, Russia was still insisting on a period of fifteen years and on hundreds of millions of dollars in compensation to enable it to build accommodation for the evacuated military and their families. In parallel, Russia was pushing Javakheti Armenians and some local political groups close to Russia to support the continuance of the base in Akhalkalaki and to blackmail the Georgian government with possible revolts.[26]

In spite of these difficulties, the November 1999 OSCE Summit in Istanbul marked a high point in the diplomacy of the Shevardnadze era. The process that followed revealed clearly that Russia was less concerned with the preservation of its decaying and militarily ineffective bases in Georgia than with impeding Georgia's steady rapprochement with NATO. It was therefore no surprise that U.S. Secretary of Defense William Cohen's offer to cover part of the cost of removing the Russian bases was met in Moscow with silence.[27]

Most observers interpreted Georgia's decision to close Russian bases on its territory as a major blow to Moscow's interests in the Caucasus. Georgia's action would have ended nearly two centuries of Russian military presence there, broken only by the brief period of independence in 1918–21. Russia responded by requiring all Georgian citizens working in Russia or visiting there to get visas. Even though most jihadi fighters in Chechnya arrived via Central Asia and not Georgia, Moscow rationalized the visa regime as a step to keep out foreign terrorists. Had Russia really wanted to stop the inflow of foreign fighters, it would have had first to stamp out corruption in its own law enforcement bodies, which turned a blind eye to such movements—for a price. The decision on visas was part of a long-standing Russian plan to use the Georgian Diaspora in Russia as a tool for pressuring Tbilisi. It had been hatched by Sergey Ivanov, at the time head of Russia's National Security Council and a notorious hawk in regard to Georgia.[28] Ivanov in turn had picked up the idea from one Felix Stanevski, a former Russian ambassador in Georgia, who argued from the very beginning that Georgia was inevitably Russia's enemy, and that Georgian elites were, so far as almost genetically, Russophobes.[29]

The idea behind Russia's new visa law was that without the money sent by Georgian expatriates in Russia, Georgia would be driven to bankruptcy and Shevardnadze's government would collapse.[30] But it turned out that the entire project was based on erroneous data. The Russian political elite wrongly assumed that "millions of Georgians"[31] lived in Russia and that their remittances were supporting the rest of the Georgian population. In reality, only half a million Georgians lived in Russia; this represented barely one-third of the numbers of Armenians or Azerbaijanis. Also, the authors of the measure underestimated the readiness of their own corrupt lower officials to make deals to enable Georgians to stay in Russia. In the end, the visa law had only a modest impact on Georgia.

But Russia's visa legislation had one very damaging consequence for Georgia. For "humanitarian reasons," the visas were not required of residents of Georgia's secessionist provinces of Abkhazia and South Ossetia. By this move, the Kremlin was clearly challenging Georgia's territorial integrity.[32] Today, with hindsight, it is easy to identify this as the first step in Russia's effort to annex Abkhazia and South Ossetia. The next step was to be the broadside distribution of Russian passports in these regions.

Saving "Private Shevardnadze": Moscow's Paradoxical Attempt to Help the Kremlin's Foe to Keep Power during the Rose Revolution

It may appear illogical that in November 2003, when the Rose Revolution was on the lip of succeeding in unseating Shevardnadze, it was Russia that attempted to prop up his rule, even though Russians despised him for his role in the collapse of the USSR and his later apostasy to Georgia. But suddenly the preservation of Shevardnadze's presidency became Moscow's immediate priority in Georgia. Putin hurriedly sent to Tbilisi Minister of Foreign Affairs Igor Ivanov. His stated task was to resolve the crisis and preserve Shevardnadze's presidency. This erratic move suggests the great disarray in Russia's Caucasus policy at the time. With no larger strategy, Russia blindly supported the one person who might have been desperate enough to accept Russian backing. The Kremlin doubtless recalled the events of 1993, when the defeated Georgian army was fleeing Sukhumi. Shevardnadze, who was at the mercy of raiding secessionist and Zviadist bands, was rescued by the Russian military. Now, a decade later, a powerless Shevardnadze would have again been forced to accept Russian hegemony, abandon his pro-Western political orientation, forget about NATO and the EU, and appoint Russian nominees to key security positions.

It is worth noting parenthetically that Moscow has frequently chosen to back desperate losers. In 2004 and 2009 the Kremlin backed the besieged leader of the Moldovan Communists, Yuri Voronin, even though Voronin subsequently failed at times to play his assigned role of obedient vassal. Moscow also extended help to Uzbek President Islam Karimov after the brutal repression of a revolt in Andijan in 2005. Karimov had become an international pariah, so the tactic to offer support appeared expedient in binding Tashkent closer to Moscow. But Karimov, too, was quick to throw out the script that Moscow had assigned him, and seized the first opportunity that arose to once again diversify his foreign policy.[33]

Whatever Moscow's doubts about Shevardnadze, they paled to insignificance compared with its loathing of what have come to be known as "color revolutions." One of the main theses of Putin's "sovereign democracy" and "vertical of power" is the ideological assertion that Western-style liberal democracy cannot work outside of the geographical zone where it arose. Such Kremlin ideologists as Vladislav Surkov and Gleb Pavlovsky invoke this argument to denigrate the chances of success for liberal democracy outside the Western world. According to their logic, any attempt to establish a democratic system beyond the borders of the Euro-Atlantic world cannot be "natural" and must therefore be the result of a Western conspiracy, and an intrusion into the natural order of things symbolized by Russia—in modern Russian political terminology, the ideology of "sovereign democracy" and "vertical of power."

Obviously, then, the *successful* grafting of democracy onto a post-Soviet country would pose a fundamental challenge to Moscow's worldview. No wonder that Russian leaders depicted the Rose Revolution not as an expression of popular will but as the playing out of an American plan for regime change. Russia's insistence on the American sponsorship of the Rose Revolution found some echo in the Western media, which greatly overestimated American support for Mikheil Saakashvili in November 2003.

Some circles in the U.S. supported the Rose Revolution from the very beginning, among them the Open Society Institute and the Project on Transitional Democracies. But the State Department clearly wanted Shevardnadze to continue in office until the end of his term. During the summer of 2003, former Secretary of State James Baker, a personal friend of Shevardnadze's, traveled to Georgia to persuade Shevardnadze to distance himself from a new political group, the alliance "For a New Georgia," which had been formed by some highly controversial figures from the worlds of government and business. The purpose of Baker's mission was to avoid the instability that could result from a rigged victory by For New Georgia. Only later did the Americans come to support the Rose Revolution, when they effectively backed its efforts to fight corruption, restore the state's authority, and so forth. It was doubtless attractive for Washington to be able to speak of an "American-sponsored success story" but such support that occurred later was by no means forthcoming during the revolution itself.

The support Shevardnadze garnered from Russia and its regional allies, including his own former rival Aslan Abashidze, was not enough to maintain him in power. Neither the state power structures nor the president himself were prepared to use force to suppress the movement demanding Shevardnadze's resignation. The president resigned on November 23. Igor Ivanov subsequently tried to present himself as one of the architects of the peaceful solution to the crisis.

Conclusion

During the ten years of Shevardnadze's leadership, Georgia moved from a condition of quasi-domination by Russia to become one of the largest beneficiaries per capita of aid from the United States. The country paid a high price for its attachment to independence, however. Under Shevardnadze, Georgia lost control of Abkhazia and a significant part of South Ossetia. Two major assassination attempts threatened the president, while society was wrecked by two mutinies and countless plots to destabilize the government. Without underestimating the local dimensions of each of these crises, it is not difficult to discern the hand of Russia in all of them. Successively, Shevardnadze sought to reckon with this threat by engaging successfully in a policy of deference, then a policy of balance, and overall by taking a very cautious approach to Russia's interests. Yet all of these failed to avoid the effects of a Russian policy that can best be described as "all stick and no carrot."

All the problems relating to Russia that Georgia had to bear under Saakashvili's leadership were already present during the presidency of Shevardnadze. Clearly, the personality of any given Georgian leader is not the main determinant of bilateral relations between the two countries. Shevardnadze was lucky enough to face a relatively weak and chaotic Russia, but he also failed to build a strong and modern state. A more solid Georgia, free of a corrupt state administration, could have resisted Russian pressure more efficiently. The years that followed the Rose Revolution showed that a solid economy and a solid state structure helped Georgia resist even stronger pressures than those of the 1990s and the beginning of the 2000s. Russia's energy blackmail during the Shevardnadze era, probably the most effective weapon that Moscow could deploy against Georgia, would have been less devastating had the Georgian bureaucracy been less corrupt and had Georgian officials not themselves benefited from the situation. Georgia needed not only a wise and experienced leader who perfectly understood its adversary, but also a deep societal and cultural transformation.

4

The Russian Leadership's Preparation for War, 1999–2008

Andrei Illarionov

Three initial comments must be made at the beginning of this chapter. First, there is a substantial lack of important documents that are necessary for providing a full, objective, and balanced picture of the Russian leadership's preparations for war against Georgia. At this moment, researchers do not have access to many Russian documents that describe and outline the actions of key figures. Therefore, the author cannot claim to know every step the Russian authorities took, their motivations, their choices among available options, and important details of the implementation of their plans. As some elements are still missing, the whole picture must necessarily appear somewhat sketchy. What is possible to do now is to provide the reader with as full and thorough a sequence of events and description of the main developments as is possible at this point in time. Hopefully, they will speak for themselves and supply background information that can be used in the future to achieve a fuller account of how the Russian leadership prepared this war.

Second, this chapter makes no attempt to detail the Georgian government's responses to Russian actions, nor does it explain the Russian responses to the Georgian government's moves. It is undeniable that both parties—the Russian-Abkhazian-South Ossetian coalition, on the one hand, and Georgia, on the other—took steps toward a military solution of the crisis, or, more correctly, of the crises. Nevertheless, it is appears obvious that the initiative in most, if not all, of those steps lay with the Russian-Abkhazian-South Ossetian coalition. The role of the Georgian government, which is covered in other chapters of this book, was not exclusively passive. Nevertheless, much available evidence refutes the often-heard claim that the Georgian government under Mikheil Saakashvili played a crucial role in provoking the war.

The most important grounds for this conclusion is that the Russian leadership had in fact taken very important decisions that made war between

Russia and Georgia inevitable much earlier—between September 1999 and June 2003. Whatever the real or alleged contribution of Saakashvili's government to the worsening of Georgia's bilateral relations with Russia, neither he nor his colleagues occupied any position in the Georgian government structures before November 2003. As one can see, Russian authorities had been making serious preparations for war over the span of nearly one decade. Indeed, it is remarkable how detailed, precise, coordinated, and secretive was the Russian leadership's planning for the military actions that caught most of the world by surprise in August 2008.

Third, there is an ongoing debate regarding the hierarchy of specific reasons and factors that led the Russian leadership to launch the war against Georgia that itself is not covered in this chapter. However, an issue that deserves a special discussion is whether the Russian authorities took the decision to start the war in 2008 or earlier, even as early as in 1999–2001. In the latter case the actions that subsequently unfolded would represent merely the execution phase of a "Grand Plan" that had existed for years. In other words, the question is whether the Grand Plan to launch a war against Georgia existed from the very beginning or whether it emerged as a result of evolution, only after the failure of endless attempts by the Russian leadership to weaken, undermine, and destroy the Georgian side through non-military means?

If the latter is true, it is those failures which led to a steady escalation of Russian pressure on Georgia, a process that culminated in a full-scale war in the summer of 2008. The author does not pretend to be able to conclusively resolve this debate. Yet available facts point more to the conclusion that the Russian leadership's inclination to use pressure, coercion, and even violence in its bilateral relations with Georgia was fully evident as early as in 1999–2001. By 2002 the Russian leadership had brought about changes in the leadership of South Ossetia which in itself can be said to have made war with Georgia all but inevitable.

By supplying South Ossetia with heavy military equipment in February 2003, including twelve T-55 tanks, the Russian government deliberately chose a military solution to the conflict with Georgia. By providing the South Ossetian regime with seventy five additional T-72 battle tanks and huge stocks of weaponry and ammunition in May and June 2004, the Russian government further paved the way for future, even larger scale, military action. While it should be mentioned that the role of the Georgian authorities was far from passive in all this, it seems invariably that the Russian-Abkhaz-South Ossetian coalition in most cases made the first moves, to which the Georgians responded (see Table 4.1).

Moreover, even today, nearly a year after the August war, it should be mentioned that no one has put forth a policy that the Georgians might have pursued that would have offered a realistic chance of averting war with the coalition led by their mighty northern neighbor.

September 1999–December 2002: The First Series of Coercive Actions, Capture of the South Ossetian Presidency

The six-year period between October 1993 and August 1999 was a time of relative stability and peace in the relations between Russia and Georgia. This was also true to a certain extent of Georgia's relations with the de facto authorities in Abkhazia and South Ossetia. True, there were numerous difficulties, which are described in detail in Thornike Gordadze's chapter in this volume. However, this phase stands in distinct contrast to developments during the five years prior to this period—1988–1993—as well as to events thereafter, i.e., from September 1999 to the present. There may not have been a common will among all sides of the conflict to pursue cooperation and integration but, after several years of bloody conflicts, it did constitute a period of gradual build-up of trust between Georgia and Abkhazia; and especially between Georgia and South Ossetia, with the Russian government, if not fully neutral, markedly pursuing a less overtly interventionist policy than it had previously or would subsequently.

This period of relative calm came to an abrupt end in September 1999. A month after the appointment of Vladimir Putin as prime minister in August 1999, the Russian government (not the Russian president, who was according to the Russian Constitution in charge of international relations) took the first major step away from its earlier policies toward Georgia. It did this by unilaterally uplifting the ban against men of military age crossing the Abkhaz portion of the Russian-Georgian border, a ban that had been instituted by the combined presidents of the CIS countries at their summit on January 19, 1996.[1]

On November 9, 2000, the Russian government informed Georgia of its intention to implement a visa regime for Georgian citizens wishing to enter Russia. Over Georgian objections Russia quit the CIS pact that had abolished visas within the Commonwealth and promptly began demanding visas from all Georgian citizens entering Russia. By contrast, Russia set up a greatly simplified visa system for the inhabitants of Abkhazia, Adjara, and South Ossetia.[2]

In February 2001, an officer of the Russian secret service organized what was called a "Meeting of Four"—a meeting between himself and the three men considered to be the most radical South Ossetian leaders. These included the intellectual leader of the South Ossetian national movement, Alan Chochiev; former Communist official and by then twice South Ossetian prime minister, Gerasim (Rezo) Khugaev; and the former trade representative of South Ossetia in Moscow, Eduard Kokoity, who had a dubious reputation both as a businessman and professional wrestler. The goal of the meeting was to work out a strategy that would deny victory to the incumbent, Ludvig Chibirov, in the presidential election in the self-styled republic scheduled for late autumn of that year. Chibirov, a professor of Ossetian history by training, had been president of South Ossetia since 1996. He had voluntarily and sincerely cooperated with the Georgian authorities on a settlement of the bilateral conflict and was ready to accept a status of enhanced autonomy for South Ossetia within Georgia. In 1999, along with Eduard Shevardnadze, he signed the so-called Baden Document that could have opened the way for peaceful resolution of the Georgian-Ossetian conflict. The plan represented a highpoint in bilateral relations with substantial trust being built between the two communities after the skirmishes of the late 1980s and early 1990s. Clearly, for the new Russian leadership, this was not a desirable evolution in Georgian-Ossetian relations.

Soon after the Meeting of Four, it became clear that Chochiev would not perform the role defined for him by the Russian leadership, while Khugaev was unable to overcome registration barriers. Eduard Kokoity therefore remained the only aspirant whom the Russian authorities were prepared to support in the South Ossetian presidential election scheduled for late 2001. In the second round of that election held on December 6, 2001, Kokoity was elected president of the enclave with 53 percent of the vote. On January 9, 2002, he appointed Khugaev as his prime minister.

Several days later, Eduard Kokoity called a closed meeting of the South Ossetian elite in which around fifty of the most authoritative members of South Ossetian society participated. Kokoity revealed a plan to gain legal independence for South Ossetia by launching a war against Georgia. Most participants in that meeting found the proposed plan so odd that they dismissed it as nonsense. Over the following years most of those who disagreed with Kokoity at that meeting disappeared from the South Ossetian political scene. Some left the republic, others ended up in the Tskhinvali jail, and still others died under suspicious circumstances.

At Kokoity's urging, the South Ossetian Parliament, in March 2002, adopted a resolution requesting the Russian authorities to recognize the independence of the republic and to admit it into the Russian Federation.[3] The speaker of the South Ossetian Parliament, Stanislav Kochiev, traveled to Moscow to present the request. That same summer the Russian government began preparations for the mass distribution of Russian passports to the inhabitants of South Ossetia, Adjara, and Abkhazia. In June 2002, the Russian Parliament adopted the necessary amendments to the Russian Law on Citizenship, which evoked a strong protest from Georgian President Eduard Shevardnadze.[4] On June 23, 2002, Tskhinvali launched the registration of candidates for Russian citizenship.[5]

Meanwhile, Russian-Georgian tensions were rising as a result of Russian demands to use Georgia's airspace for Russian operations in Chechnya. On August 6, 2002, the Russian Air Force bombed Georgian territory in the Pankisi Gorge.[6] One civilian was killed and several others wounded. Georgia protested, but Russian authorities flatly denied that their planes had been active in the area.[7] The OSCE mission in Georgia, after a thorough investigation, confirmed that Russian aircraft had indeed bombed Georgian territory.

Moscow also encouraged greater coordination between Tskhinvali and the Abkhazian capital of Sukhumi. On September 7–8, 2002, Kokoity visited Sukhumi and signed a military union with Abkhazia against Georgia, based on Russian guidance and support.[8] A few days later, on the first anniversary of the September 11 terrorist attacks on the United States, Russian President Vladimir Putin issued an ultimatum to Georgia, which he characterized as a country "presenting a terrorist threat."[9] Putin announced his readiness to invoke Article 51 of the UN Charter in order to use military force against Georgia.[10] Six weeks later, on November 22, Shevardnadze responded to Russia's ultimatum. Speaking at the NATO summit in Prague, he declared Georgia's intentions to join NATO.[11]

The spiral of escalation continued. By the end of 2002, Kokoity began filling positions in the governmental bureaucracy of South Ossetia with representatives of the Russian power ministries (e.g., defense, security, and intelligence, etc.). And in spite of sharp Georgian protests, the Russian government on December 25 reopened the railway line between Russia and Abkhazia which the CIS presidents themselves had closed down back in 1996.[12]

Hence by the end of 2002, Russia had gradually ratcheted up pressure on Shevardnadze's government. It had taken steps that threatened Georgia's territorial integrity, going as far as to threaten military action—while working to smear Georgia's reputation internationally as a den of terrorism.

Sabre-Rattling and the Battle for Adjara, January 2003–April 2004

On January 15, 2003, Eduard Kokoity again asked Vladimir Putin to recognize the independence of South Ossetia. The Russian leadership responded on February 2, 2003, by sending significant military equipment, including twelve T-55 tanks, via the Roki tunnel to South Ossetia.[13] These were deployed near Java, in the northern parts of the territory, to which international observers did not have access. This delivery of modern heavy armaments from Russia to South Ossetia took place nine months before the Rose Revolution and Mikheil Saakashvili's ascent to power in November 2003.

The issue of Russian military bases was a major point of contention during this period, as the Russian government dragged its feet on implementing the commitments made at the 1999 OSCE Istanbul Summit. During bilateral negotiations on the withdrawal of the Russian bases from Georgia that took place on February 18–19, Tbilisi demanded that the process be completed within three years, in other words, by 2006. Moscow claimed it could not withdraw the bases before 2014. Moscow exerted further pressure on Tbilisi by refusing to attend a routine meeting of the Joint Control Commission (JCC) on the Georgian-Ossetian conflict scheduled for February 20–21, 2003, in Vienna.[14]

Later that year, in July, the Russian government broke the international embargo on Abkhazia that had been in place since 1992–93 by sending a tourist ship from Sukhumi to Sochi. In July 2003 the de facto South Ossetian authroities walked out from the earlier agreed documents.[15]

Moscow's threats directed at Georgia continued. On October 2, 2003, Russian Minister of Defense Sergey Ivanov declared that Moscow did not exclude the possibility of initiating military strikes in various regions of the world "for its own security."[16] Coming in the aftermath of the bombing of the Pankisi Gorge in August 2002, the statement was widely interpreted as a verbal preparation for another strike against Georgia—and as an attempt to benefit from a precedent set by the United States in Iraq.

Following the heavily rigged Georgian parliamentary elections of November 2, 2003, Shevardnadze sharply increased his telephone contact with Putin. Adjaran leader Aslan Abashidze communicated with his Russian colleagues not only over the phone, but also in person during several visits to Moscow, the first of which took place on November 13. On November 23, Russian Minister of Foreign Affairs Igor Ivanov, who had been sent by Putin as a mediator to Tbilisi, helped negotiate Shevardnadze's resignation.

That brought to power the triumvirate consisting of Mikheil Saakashvili, Zurab Zhvania, and Nino Burjanadze.

The Rose Revolution led to even closer consultations between Moscow and Georgia's secessionist regions. At a Moscow session on November 29, Igor Ivanov discussed strategy and tactics with Russia's proxies in Georgia: Eduard Kokoity from South Ossetia, Aslan Abashidze from Adjara, and Abkhazian Prime Minister Raul Khadjimba (Abkhazian President Vladislav Ardzinba was unable to attend for health reasons). One of the decisions taken at the meeting was to accelerate the process of granting Russian citizenship to residents of these three Georgian territories. On December 5, the Russian mass media reported that the Ministry of Foreign Affairs was preparing tens of thousands of blank passport for these regions. Four days later a new Russian visa regime, even more simplified than the existing one, was introduced in Adjara.[17] Abashidze himself continued to be a frequent visitor to Moscow, traveling to the Russian capital on January 14, February 7, and March 3, 2004, making a total of five official visits since mid-November 2003.

On February 11, 2004, the first meeting between Putin and the newly elected Saakashvili took place in Moscow. The Russian president made two requests of his Georgian colleague: first, to refrain from demanding the withdrawal of Russian military bases in Georgia, and second, "to take care of" (i.e., to keep in place) Georgia's Minister of State Security, Valery Khaburdzania.[18] Back in Tbilisi, five days later, on February 16, Saakashvili announced radical reforms of the Ministry of State Security, transferring Khaburdzania to the position of Deputy Prosecutor General. At the time of this chapter's writing, Khaburdzania was living in Moscow.

As Niklas Nilsson describes in his contribution to this volume, one of Saakashvili's first steps was to challenge Abashidze's semi-autonomous fiefdom in Adjara by orchestrating popular actions similar to those successfully employed during the Rose Revolution. Moscow reacted quickly. Once again Igor Ivanov was dispatched to Georgia to resolve the issue but he failed to pre-empt what became known as the "Adjara revolution." On May 6, 2004, Ivanov took Aslan Abashidze on board his plane and departed Batumi for Moscow. In a subsequent telephone conversation, Saakashvili boldly thanked Vladimir Putin for his contribution to the peaceful resolution of the crisis. Putin responded with the statement that: "Now remember, we did not intervene in Adjara, but you won't have any gifts from us in South Ossetia and Abkhazia."[19]

May 2004–April 2005: The Escalation of Tensions, Passports, Roads, Power Offensives, and the Battle for the Abkhaz Presidency

Following the Adjara crisis, Moscow further ratcheted up tensions with Tbilisi by expanding Russian military and administrative control over Abkhazia and South Ossetia and accelerating the distribution of Russian passports in the two territories. Henceforth it could rationalize its actions in these two regions by the claim that it was merely defending its "citizens." This period also saw growing violence in South Ossetia, as well as a botched Russian attempt to impose a new leader on Abkhazia, as it had done successfully in South Ossetia.

Only days following the Adjara crisis, the Russian president signed what appears to have been a secret decree outlining the Russian government's main goals in South Ossetia. These included the construction of military bases near Java (Iziugomi) and in Tskhinvali, opening a special department at the military academy in Vladikavkaz for cadets from South Ossetia, and sending several dozen Russian military instructors to the territory. Moreover, it included transferring Russian officers to South Ossetia for routine military service, as well as the appointment of Russians to head South Ossetia's ministries of defense, security, and law enforcement. The goal was to transform the badly organized, poorly equipped, and untrained South Ossetian militia into a 7,000-strong regular army.[20]

On May 25, the Russian Ministry of Foreign Affairs began distributing Russian passports to the South Ossetian population. On June 7, the South Ossetian Parliament asked the Russian Duma to recognize its independence and "to defend Russian citizens" living there.[21] Significantly, Andrey Kokoshin, Chairman of the Duma's committee for the CIS and compatriot affairs, now took up the cry that Russia was duty-bound to protect its new citizens.[22]

Tensions rose in South Ossetia following the Georgian anti-smuggling operations described in Niklas Nilsson's chapter to this volume. On June 2–6, Russia sent South Ossetia seventy five main battle T-72 tanks, twenty "Grad" multiple-launch rocket systems, thirty self-propelled artillery systems, and more than two-hundred "Igla" anti-aircraft weapons. Anatoly Barankevich, a Russian colonel with military experience in Afghanistan and Chechnya, was appointed Minister of Defense of South Ossetia.

On June 15, South Ossetian forces attempted to prevent the construction of a road connecting the Georgian village of Eredvi with the Georgian enclaves of Kurta and Tamarasheni, north of Tskhinvali. The next day, Russia cut the supply of electricity to Georgia. On July 8, Georgian authorities captured nine trucks loaded with armaments and ammunition sent from Russia to South Ossetia.[23] The following day, fifty Georgian peacekeepers were disarmed and humiliatingly forced to their knees in the center of Tskhinvali, a scene videotaped and broadcast on the main Russian television channels;[24] the same night, the Georgian-controlled villages of Tamarasheni and Kurta were shelled, as were Georgian checkpoints near the villages.[25] Moscow's infamous television anchor on the station ORT, Mikhail Leontiev, pronounced on air that "We've organized a trap for the Georgians. This time, it seems, they've walked into it."[26] The next day, the Russian Ministry of Foreign Affairs blamed Georgia for "organizing provocations" and promised to protect Russian citizens in South Ossetia. The same night, South Ossetian shelling wounded three more Georgian peacekeepers as well as one policeman. Exchanges of fire in South Ossetia continued until August 20, 2004, when Georgian troops left the region. By then nineteen Georgian soldiers and five Ossetians had been killed.[27]

The September 2004 terrorist attack on the school in Beslan in the North Caucasus had been used for further centralization within the Russian government and to increase pressure on Georgia. While the terrorists responsible for Beslan arrived there using a road from Ingushetia, some Georgian journalists traveling there used the Georgian Military Highway. On September 4, the Russian government closed the Georgian Military Highway at the Larsi checkpoint, claiming a "terrorist threat."[28] Three weeks later, while the Russian-Georgian border was still closed, Russia established a direct bus connection between the Russian city of Sochi and the Abkhaz capital of Sukhumi.[29] Tensions in South Ossetia receded but Russian threats of force did not. On September 8 and 12, respectively, the Head of the Russian General Staff Yuri Baluyevsky and Russian Minister of Defense Sergey Ivanov announced Moscow's readiness to undertake preventive strikes against targets outside Russia.

Events soon confirmed that these words were indeed intended for Georgian ears. Explosions on September 14 and 20 destroyed portions of the "Kartli-2" and "Kavkasioni" high voltage transmission lines on Georgian territory, cutting off electricity to large parts of Georgia. On October 9–10, more explosions severely damaged the "Kartli-2" and "Liakhvi" transmission lines and destroyed power lines in western Georgia. On October 20, Mikheil Saakashvili announced that Georgian special forces had neutralized a sabotage group from South Ossetia responsible for the explosions.[30]

Meanwhile, Abkhazia was moving toward presidential elections. In late August, Putin hosted Abkhaz Prime minister Khadjimba in his residence in Sochi. This brought a sharp rebuke from the Georgian government, but also indicated whom Moscow favored in the upcoming October 11 elections to choose a successor to the ailing Ardzinba. But his anointment by Putin failed to generate votes for Khadjimba, whom Sergey Bagapsh defeated handily. Moscow was so dissatisfied with this outcome that it rigged a standoff between the two contenders and their supporters, which continued until Putin summoned both candidates to Moscow on November 1.[31] The Russians demanded that Bagapsh give in but he refused, and he continued to claim victory. Moscow promptly punished the whole province for Bagapsh's temerity, closing the Abkhazian portion of the Russian-Georgian border (November 15), halting railway communication with Abkhazia (December 1), and banning the import of Abkhazian agricultural produce (December 2). A special delegation from the Russian power ministries then headed to Sukhumi. After tiresome negotiations, a Bagapsh-Khadjimba power-sharing agreement was achieved on December 6 with Putin's approval.[32] Moscow's failure to ensure the victory of its candidate indicated the limits to its powers and Abkhazia's relatively more independent-minded spirit, as compared with South Ossetia. Nonetheless, control over the defense and security sectors of the Abkhaz government was preserved.

Moscow also focused on filling all the key jobs in the power and law enforcement ministries in the regions with Russian officials. Similarly, Moscow named the head of the Federal Security Service's (FSB) office in the Russian Republic of Mordovia, Anatoly Yarovoy, as chairman of the South Ossetian KGB, still retaining its Soviet-era acronym. In March 2005, Lieutenant-General Anatoly Zaytsev, former deputy commander-in-chief of the Russian Trans-Baikal Military District, already Deputy Minister of Defense of Abkhazia, was also appointed Chief of the General Staff.[33] On April 25, the former Chief of Staff of the North Ossetian branch of the Russian Ministry of Interior, Mikhail Mindzaev, was appointed Minister of Interior of South Ossetia.[34] On July 4, 2005, Yuri Morozov, the commercial director of the Kursk fuel company in Russia and an old business partner of the South Ossetian leader, Kokoity, was named Prime Minister of South Ossetia. (For a full list of Russian officials in South Ossetia's government, see Box 4.1).

These appointments were accompanied by an increase in subversive activities by Russia in Georgia. In a remarkably brazen incident, an explosion on February 1, 2005, destroyed the police headquarters in the Georgian town of Gori, killing three policemen and wounding seventeen others. A five month-long investigation by the Georgian Ministry of Interior established that the explosion had been organized by the Russian military intelligence service (GRU).[35]

Paralleling this, Moscow's embrace of the secessionist territories became ever more visible. Russian Minister of Foreign Affairs Sergey Lavrov, during a visit to Tbilisi, refused to participate in a wreath laying ceremony at a monument to Georgians killed in the war in Abkhazia, while on April 3–4, 2005, in a very public manner, he received the foreign ministers of Abkhazia, South Ossetia, and Transnistria in Moscow as if they represented independent states. The next day Putin received Bagapsh and Kokoity at his residence in Sochi.

The personnel changes in Abkhazia and South Ossetia secured the Russian leadership's control over both secessionist provinces. From the beginning of 2005 it engaged the Russian telecom firm Megafon to build in South Ossetia a non-Georgian mobile communication system for use by the military and intelligence services.[36] Since 2004, moreover, the Russian government had substantially increased its economic support to both Georgian regions, gradually raising Russian subsidies. For example, South Ossetia's grew to almost 200 percent of its GDP in 2008. The main bulk of the subsidies in both regions went toward building-up their respective militaries, constituting up to 50 percent of Abkhazia's GDP and up to 150 percent of South Ossetia's GDP, probably setting a world record.[37]

The Deadline for the War is Set, Offensives on Wine and Mineral Water Fronts, May 2005–August 2006

On May 30, 2005, Georgian Minister of Foreign Affairs Salome Zurabashvili and her Russian counterpart, Sergey Lavrov, finally signed a joint communiqué on the timing and sequencing of the withdrawal of Russian military bases from Georgia. According to the document, Russian military personnel were to complete their withdrawal before the end of 2008. The decision was greeted with a sigh of relief on the Georgian side, and was considered a significant victory for Tbilisi in its efforts to secure the country's sovereignty. Virtually no one understood at the time that the deadline for the withdrawal of the Russian military bases from Batumi and Akhalkalaki was also the date the Russian leadership set for legalizing existing bases and establishing new ones in Abkhazia and South Ossetia.

In addition to the two existing Russian military bases in South Ossetia, Moscow in May 2006 began construction of a new military base in Elbachita, two kilometers northeast of the town of Java.[38] The base was designed to host 2,500 military personnel. The storing facilities in Ochamchira and Gali bases were designed for storing military equipment, armaments, and fuel for 100,000 people.[39]

By the beginning of 2006, Russian deliveries of military equipment to Abkhazia and South Ossetia reached such a level that the total amount of equipment, arms, and ammunition in these two regions, with a combined population of about 250,000, exceeded the total military capacity of Georgia, with a population of 4.5 million. By the beginning of 2008, the two breakaway regions had received at no cost more than twice the military equipment possessed by Georgia.[40] In February 2006, the Russian 58th Army of the North Caucasian Military district further conducted large-scale military exercises aimed at "providing immediate support to its peacekeepers battalion in South Ossetia," with different units being deployed along the Transkam highway in the immediate proximity of the Roki tunnel and the Russian-Georgian border.

The staff changes in South Ossetia continued: on March 3, 2006, Russian FSB colonel Nikolai Dolgopolov, former head of the FSB branch in the Republic of Mari El, replaced Anatoly Yarovoy as head of the South Ossetian KGB. The same month, Kokoity filed a request to the Constitutional Court of the Russian Federation for Russia to recognize South Ossetia's independence.[41]

Moscow also began to use its economic leverage more purposefully. In December 2005, the heads of Russian energy companies doing business in Georgia were summoned to the Presidential Administration in Moscow and asked whether it was possible to stop the supply of energy across the border. The businessmen replied in the negative, but the matter did not end there. Days later, on January 22, 2006, a series of simultaneous explosions in the Russian Republic of North Ossetia badly damaged two gas pipelines and a power transmission line that connected Russia with Georgia.[42] This deft move cut off the flow of Russian gas and electricity to Georgia (for which Georgia had paid) in the midst of one of the coldest winters of the decade. On January 26, another explosion destroyed high voltage transmission lines that provided electricity to eastern Georgia.

During 2006 Moscow worked persistently to inflict economic pain on Georgia in retaliation for Tbilisi's efforts to counteract Russian subversion on its territory. In late March, the Georgian authorities detained a Russian GRU officer involved in espionage activities. Georgia discretely deported the officer but without publicizing the event. Nonetheless, on March 29, the Russian government, in what seemed to be a riposte to this move, banned the import of Georgian wine, citing health concerns.[43] This in turn was followed in May by bans on the popular Georgian Borjomi and Nabeghlavi brands of bottled mineral water.[44] And lest the Georgians missed the point, Minister of Defense Sergey Ivanov proclaimed that "Russia always has the right to a preventive strike."[45]

As this was happening, Moscow's rhetoric on the secessionist territories grew more and more shrill. On January 31, 2006, during a conversation with journalists, Vladimir Putin noted that "if somebody assumes that Kosovo can achieve full state independence, then why should we refuse it to the Abkhaz and South Ossetians?" At the same time, the Russian president instructed Minister of Foreign Affairs Sergey Lavrov to come up with a universal legal formula on the independence of Kosovo that would be applicable in other similar cases.[46] In May, the Russian MFA began consultations with Abkhazia, South Ossetia, and Transnistria on the status of their territories. In March an aide to the Russian prime minister stated that a decision on the unification of the two Ossetian republics had been taken "in principle."[47]

At a June 14 summit in Sukhumi, the leaders of Abkhazia, South Ossetia, and Transnistria signed a Treaty on Friendship, Cooperation, and Mutual Support as well a Declaration on the Creation of a Commonwealth for Democracy and the Rights of Nations.[48] They agreed to provide military support to each other in case of an emergency, and to create joint peacekeeping troops in case Russian peacekeepers would leave their regions. They also proclaimed their loyalty to Moscow. Putin declared that the fate of those nations would be defined by the will of their peoples, based on their right of self-determination. Two weeks later, he stated that Russia would keep its peacekeeping troops in those regions "regardless of provocations."[49] And on July 7, the Russian Federation Council adopted a law allowing the Russian president to deploy the country's military forces outside Russian territory "to prevent international terrorist activity."[50] Shortly thereafter South Ossetia's Deputy Prime Minister Boris Chochiev announced that 98 percent of the region's population had already acquired Russian citizenship. Tensions over the secessionist areas grew worse as Tbilisi in July restored effective control over the Kodori Gorge, the only part of Abkhazia in which it exercised any authority after 1993 (see Niklas Nilsson's chapter for details).

The "Spy War," September–November 2006

A new phase in the escalation began on September 27, 2006, when Georgian Minister of Interior Vano Merabishvili announced the discovery of a spy network coordinated by GRU officers. As a result of the counterespionage operation, four Russian intelligence officers and eleven Georgian citizens were arrested.[51] The Russian MFA immediately summoned the Georgian ambassador to request an explanation. By way of response, Georgia's Ministry of Interior released audio and video recordings of five Georgian citizens confessing to having cooperated with Russian military intelligence, as well as footage showing Russian officers making cash deliveries to them. Former President Shevardnadze confirmed that the Georgian special services had long since accumulated evidence of Russian espionage activities on Georgian territory.

The Kremlin's reaction to the incident was nothing short of extraordinary: it demanded that the UN Security Council meet at once on the conflict in Abkhazia. At the same time, the Russian Embassy in Tbilisi stopped accepting visa applications from Georgian citizens; Russia recalled its ambassador in Tbilisi, Vyacheslav Kovalenko; and the Russian Ministry for Emergency Situations sent an airplane to Georgia to evacuate the families of Russian servicemen and diplomats. Russian Minister of Defense Sergey Ivanov called Georgia's actions "state banditry"[52] and the Ministry of Foreign Affairs darkly warned Russian citizens "not to visit Georgia." In response to all this, Georgia's parliamentary speaker Nino Burjanadze termed Russia's actions "political blackmail" while Saakashvili spoke of the Russian leadership's "hysteria."[53]

On September 29, a Tbilisi court handed down prison sentences to four Russian intelligence officers and ten Georgian citizens. Three more Russian officers were found guilty in absentia of espionage. Russia responded by evacuating all remaining Russian citizens from Tbilisi,[54] putting Russia's army bases in Georgia on the highest alert, and announcing that it would cease withdrawing troops from the bases in Akhalkalaki and Batumi. Militia units and OMON riot police surrounded the Georgian Embassy in Moscow, Russian forces in the North Caucasus were put on the highest alert and moved up to the Russian-Georgian border, and the Russian Black Sea Fleet initiated large-scale maneuvers along Georgia's coast. Increasing the economic pressure, the head of the Russian Migration Service, Vyacheslav Postavnin, promised to deport most Georgian migrant laborers and to set up strict controls over the few who remained.[55]

On October 2, Georgian authorities released the four Russian intelligence officers and sent them back to Russia. In a related move, they allowed Russian peacekeepers to patrol the Kodori Gorge, over which Georgian forces had only recently reasserted control. In what can be called a response to these concessions, Russia on October 3 unilaterally cut all communications with Georgia by air, sea, and rail, as well as the postal service—in violation of the Universal Postal Union's rules.[56] By these means Moscow subjected Georgia to a total embargo. In Moscow, meanwhile, troops encircled the Georgian Embassy with metal barriers and severely restricted access to it. Lavrov explained that it was "forbidden to insult Russia while thousands of Georgian citizens work on its territory." Police, tax, fire, and other inspection teams were sent to the cafés, restaurants, hotels, entertainment centers, and other enterprises belonging to ethnic Georgians in Russia. Scheduled Georgian cultural performances were cancelled. Taxi drivers were encouraged to request identification from their passengers and refuse service if they turned out to be Georgians. And a massive anti-Georgian propaganda campaign unfolded in the Russian mass media.[57]

By October 4 the anti-Georgian campaign had turned into a full-scale witch hunt. The State Duma adopted sanctions against Georgia, while the Federal Migration Service created a special "Georgian" department.[58] Georgians with multiple-entry visas who were already on Russian territory had their stays cut by half. The next day Putin instructed Prime Minister Mikhail Fradkov to set up quotas for foreigners by countries of origin, and the schools were ordered to compile lists of children with Georgian last names.[59] At the same time as Prosecutor General Yuriy Chaika was announcing that the actions against Georgian citizens were "not excessive,"[60] the Russian Ministry of Internal Affairs began checking into the income of the Georgian-born writer Boris Akunin (Georgiy Chkhartishvili), one of the best-loved contemporary Russian writers, while the Russian Accounting Chamber claimed to have found irregularities in the use of governmental funds by the Academy of Arts, headed by the Georgian-born Zurab Tsereteli. On October 17, during his deportation from Russia, 58-year old Georgian citizen Tengiz Togonidze died from an asthma attack at Moscow's Domodedovo airport, after having failed to receive medical assistance.[61] Russia began deporting Georgians from Russia on cargo aircraft while the Russian navy prevented foreign ships from entering Georgian ports.[62]

Russia's proxies followed suit: on October 12, the South Ossetian Parliament asked the leaderships of the Russian republics of North Ossetia, Karachaevo-Cherkessia, and Kabardino-Balkaria to recognize Georgia's "moral and political responsibility for the genocide of South Ossetians in 1920 and in 1989–1992." Not to be outdone, the Abkhaz Parliament again petitioned the Russian leadership to recognize its independence and to establish an association agreement between the two countries. The request stated that more than ninety percent of Abkhazia's population were Russian citizens. In the North Caucasus, meanwhile, Chechen President Alu

Alkhanov stated that Chechens were ready to intervene in Abkhazia and South Ossetia if war should break out there.[63]

At the CIS summit in Moscow on November 26, Saakashvili met three times with Putin. Based on their comments after the summit, they seemed to have made no progress on improving relations.

The Final Preparations for the Big War, December 2006–April 2008

By late 2006, it was becoming clear that none of the Russian leadership's many acts of pressure and intimidation were causing Georgia to abandon its course toward independent development, economic and legal reforms, as well as its efforts to restore its territorial integrity through peaceful means. Thus, in parallel with the re-election of Eduard Kokoity as President of South Ossetia on November 12, the Georgian government organized a rival presidential election in the part of South Ossetia that it controlled, that is, roughly half of the province. The victor was Dmitry Sanakoyev, an erstwhile leader of the separatist movement and a former Minister of Defense and Prime Minister of South Ossetia, who now sought a deal with the Georgian government.[64] The Russian State Duma responded by calling for the recognition of Abkhazia's and South Ossetia's independence,[65] while Russian General Andrey Laptev was appointed South Ossetia's Minister of Defense, replacing Anatoly Barankevich who became the head of South Ossetia's Security Council.

Events in Georgia were not occurring in isolation. As a part of the broader picture, Vladimir Putin delivered his now famous "Munich speech" at a conference on international security held in the Bavarian capital on February 10, 2007. His words were taken as a declaration of open confrontation with the West. Within two days Mikheil Saakashvili responded with the promise that Georgia would join NATO in 2009, to which Kokoity, on February 16, retorted that neither South Ossetia nor Abkhazia would ever join NATO. "Georgia may join NATO," he declared, "but without South Ossetia and Abkhazia."[66]

Close observers were now openly predicting that the Georgian-Russian confrontation could end in war. On February 27, 2007, the Russian newspaper *Segodnya* published an article by an "independent military analyst" with the Ossetian name of Zaur Alborov, entitled "Why Georgia will lose the coming war." In his article, Alborov described in detail the likely actions of Russian regular forces in a future war with Georgia over South Ossetia, a war which actually broke out only seventeen months later. On March 10, Alborov published another article in which he predicted that the independence of Abkhazia and South Ossetia would be recognized in response to the deployment of an anti-missile system in Georgia. In October 2006, the independent Russian military analyst Pavel Felgenhauer, a contributor to this volume, expressed his fear that a Russo-Georgian war was now "practically inevitable."[67]

While full-scale war would not happen for almost another one and a half years, the Russian leadership now crossed the line to direct military actions. On March 11, Russian military helicopters shelled Georgian administrative buildings in the Kodori Gorge in Upper Abkhazia.[68] During the whole of the next day Georgian villages in the Kodori Gorge were shelled from the Tkvarcheli district of Abkhazia, as well as from Russian helicopter gunships. This led to a rapid series of diplomatic moves. On March 13, the Georgian Parliament unanimously voted for Georgia's accession to NATO. Two days later, the U.S. Senate voted to support Georgia's and Ukraine's NATO membership (which was followed later by the U.S. Congress).[69] That same week Abkhazia's parliament again requested Russia to recognize its independence and to do so before Georgia joined NATO.

Efforts to improve the situation on the ground also came to nothing. On March 25, the co-chairs of the Joint Control Commission, at an informal meeting in Tskhinvali, agreed to hold an official meeting of the JCC in Tbilisi. After the meeting, a Georgian police car was ambushed, and two policemen killed. The investigation confirmed that the shelling came from the Ossetian side. The JCC meeting was cancelled. On March 29, the Russian MFA urged the Georgian government to drop its support for the alternative South Ossetian government of Dmitry Sanakoyev. On May 7, Kokoity announced the cessation of all negotiations with Georgia until Tbilisi ceased its contacts with Sanakoyev's administration in Kurta, only a few kilometers from Tskhinvali. Four days later, Kokoity declared the beginning of a full blockade of the Georgian villages of South Ossetia;[70] and on May 12, the Russian MFA accused Georgia of deploying prohibited anti-aircraft weapons in the conflict zone, an allegation that Georgia vehemently denied. Before an investigation could start, Ossetian trucks unloaded the weaponry and drove away.

By the summer of 2007 there were further signs that the Russian leadership had already decided to go to war. On June 27, Russia unexpectedly, and ahead of the agreed schedule, finished withdrawing its troops from its military base in Akhalkalaki. While it may seem counter-intuitive, it became clear in hindsight that Moscow wanted to avoid a situation in which Georgia could take Russian bases hostage. The next day Russian armored vehicles blocked the construction of a road leading to the Georgian enclave of Nikozi-Avnevi. The Russian special envoy in South Ossetia, Yuri Popov, demanded an urgent meeting of the JCC, while Kokoity left for Moscow.

On July 13, Vladimir Putin signed a decree terminating Russia's participation in the Treaty on Conventional Forces in Europe (CFE). He cited the U.S.'s plans for an anti-missile defense shield in Poland and the Czech Republic as the reason for his decision. No one at the time noted that the decision on such a deployment had *not* been taken, and no part of the shield had been built (nor has it yet). It took another year before the true motive of this move became clear, namely, that it removed all limits on the deployment of Russian troops and equipment in the North Caucasus in preparation for a war against Georgia. Two weeks later, on July 27, 2007, Russian Deputy Prime Minister Alexander Zhukov declared that Abkhazia would participate in the construction of the infrastructure for the Sochi 2014 Winter Games.

That same summer what could be called the "dress rehearsal" for the war took place. On August 6, while most Western leaders were vacationing, two Russian Su-25 aircraft violated Georgian air space and bombed a radar station near Tsitelubani, on the border of the South Ossetian conflict zone. However, the missile failed to detonate, which enabled Western experts to inspect it and confirm its Russian origin.[71] Georgia accused Russia over the incident while Russia brushed aside the charge, claiming that Georgia had staged the incident.

The escalation continued in Abkhazia as well. In violation of existing agreements Abkhazian troops held maneuvers in the lower part of the Kodori Gorge involving heavy equipment. The maneuvers, held on August 20–24, featured the Abkhaz army's expensive new military equipment, including planes and helicopters. During these maneuvers Russian aircraft repeatedly violated Georgian air space over Upper Abkhazia.[72]

In a spectacular lightning operation completed on November 15, Russia completed the withdrawal of its troops from the bases in Georgia.[73] Thus, an action which Russian authorities had repeatedly described as requiring at least eleven years was executed in less than five months. As a result of this, if war against Georgia were to be launched, there would be no Russian troops that could be surrounded or taken prisoner and no Russian military equipment on Georgian territory that Georgians might easily seize. On December 3, the law terminating Russia's compliance with the CFE Treaty entered into force. This removed all limits on the deployment of Russian heavy military equipment on the southern flank of the European theater.

Within a week Russia began deploying additional troops and military equipment in the Ochamchire district of Abkhazia.[74]

Early in February 2008, President Putin visited the Tsumadin district of Dagestan near the Mushak pass through the chief range of the Caucasus mountains. Russian TV aired a notable conversation that took place between Putin and his local host near a road that was under construction:

> Putin: Where does this road lead?
> Host: To Georgia.
> Putin: Good. You need to accelerate its construction. We need one more corridor [to] there.[75]

On February 21, 2008, just four days after Kosovo proclaimed its independence and with the process of its recognition proceeding at full speed, Vladimir Putin and Mikheil Saakashvili met for the last time as presidents. According to the Georgian president's account which he later made public, Putin told him that:

> As for the disputed territories of Abkhazia and South Ossetia, in this regard we shall respond not to you, but to the West—America and NATO, and in connection to Kosovo. You should not worry, it shouldn't bother you. What we do will not be directed against you but will be our response to them.[76]

In a further sign of the Russian leadership's preparation for war, Russian general Vasily Lunev, a former Deputy Commander-in-Chief of the army in the Siberian Military District and former Military Commissar of Russia's Perm region, was appointed Minister of Defense of South Ossetia on March 1, 2008. On March 11, Colonel-General Sergey Makarov, one of the most experienced Russian officers, was appointed head of staff of the North Caucasian Military District (NCMD), and on May 31 became the commander-in-chief of the NCMD.

On March 4, the South Ossetian Parliament, and on March 7 the Abkhaz Parliament called on Russia, the CIS, and the UN to recognize the independence of the breakaway regions. On March 6, Russia unilaterally withdrew from the sanctions regime against Abkhazia that had been imposed at the CIS summit in January 19, 1996. Henceforth Russia considered itself free to maintain economic, financial, trade, transportation, and military contacts with the de facto Abkhaz authorities. On March 13, 2008, the Russian State Duma, in a closed session, discussed a report prepared by the Russian secret services and MFA on a strategy for achieving the independence of Abkhazia and South Ossetia.[77] On March 21, 2008, it adopted a special resolution endorsing both requests for recognition. Konstantin Zatulin, Deputy Head of the Duma's committee on CIS affairs, declared that recognition of Abkhazia and South Ossetia should not be postponed, since "The window of opportunity opened by the recognition of Kosovo will not last forever."[78] On April 14, an anonymous Russian diplomat commented in *Nezavisimaya Gazeta* that, "The MFA recommended that the [Russian] President should recognize the independence of Abkhazia and South Ossetia under two circumstances: if Georgia seriously undertakes to join NATO and in the case of war."[79]

Meanwhile, at the NATO Bucharest Summit on April 3–5, German Chancellor Angela Merkel noted that countries with unresolved territorial conflicts could not join NATO. On the basis of this principle, which would have applied equally to West Germany at the time of its NATO accession, the summit denied both Georgia and Ukraine a Membership Action Plan. Twenty minutes after the Bucharest Communiqué was published, the Russian president issued a statement that, "We will provide effective assistance to South Ossetia and Abkhazia in return for NATO's decision."[80] The Head of the Russian Military Staff, for his part, added that "We will do everything [necessary] to prevent Georgia from joining NATO." A jubilant Putin sent letters to Bagapsh and Kokoity promising practical steps towards the removal of sanctions and the opening of diplomatic legal relations between Russia and the two republics.[81] On April 8, Lavrov reiterated that Russia "would do its utmost not to allow Georgia and Ukraine into NATO."[82]

The game changer came two days later. On April 16, the by then outgoing President Putin ordered the Russian government and Russian regional authorities to establish direct relations with the governments in Sukhumi and Tskhinvali. The specific type of relationship which he proposed was virtually identical to that which existed between Moscow and the federal territories within Russia proper. Georgia noted that Putin's order amounted to Russia's full annexation of the two Georgian regions.[83] The EU, OSCE, NATO, U.S., UK, France, and Germany all condemned Putin's order and urged him to retract it.[84] On April 17, meanwhile, 300 additional Russian servicemen with heavy equipment arrived at the military base in Ochamchire in Abkhazia.

The Low Intensity War, April 20–July 28, 2008

On April 20, a Russian MIG-29 jet took off from the airbase in the Abkhaz town of Gudauta, shot down an unarmed Georgian Unmanned Aerial Vehicle (UAV), and then withdrew northward into Russian airspace. A video camera mounted on the Georgian drone recorded the attack and managed to send footage to the control tower before it was destroyed. Georgia accused Russia of armed aggression while Russia denied the charge. But an investigation undertaken by the United Nations Observer Mission in Georgia (UNOMIG) confirmed that the attack had been carried out by a Russian jet.[85]

According to the UN General Assembly's resolution 3314 of December 14, 1974, this action constituted a clear and distinct act of aggression. From the moment of the shooting down of the drone, Russia and Georgia can be said to have been in a state of war, which remained at a relatively low intensity until July 28.

Over the week starting on May 4 Russian and Abkhazian forces shot down five more Georgian drones. On May 6, General Vladimir Shamanov, Chief of the Russian Armed Forces Main Combat Training and Troop Service Directorate, stated that the Russian military would no longer allow Georgian planes to fly over the zones of conflict.

In violation of the CIS's agreement on peacekeeping operations, Moscow deployed paratroopers from the Novorossiysk Airborne Division to Abkhazia beginning in April 2008. In early May these forces were equipped with three "Buk" anti-aircraft complexes, fourteen additional D-30 self-propelled cannons, ten 122mm BM-30 multi-rocket launchers, twenty anti-tank cannons, 120 anti-tank rockets, two helicopters, and 180 Russian technical specialists to service this equipment.[86] The Russian Black Sea Fleet performed eight military exercises focusing on infantry shore landings. On May 1, Russian troops set up additional unauthorized checkpoints within Abkhazia on roads in the Tkvarcheli and Ochamchire districts. A week later, Moscow confirmed an increase of its troop numbers in Abkhazia from 1,997 to 2,542. Georgian sources, on the other hand, claimed that the real number of Russian troops on their territory was 4,000. On May 14, Sergey Bagapsh asked Russia to establish a permanent military presence in Abkhazia.

Early in May the Russian Air Force sent out a nationwide call to active duty of all former military helicopter pilots who had experience flying in mountainous areas. By the middle of the month the Air Force began a seventeen-day exercise for some of these new call-ups in Nalchik in the North Caucasus. A key element of the preparations began on May 26, when a 400-strong corps of Russian Railroad Troops was deployed in Abkhazia to repair and rehabilitate the rail line connecting Sukhumi and Ochamchire in the immediate proximity to the Abkhaz-Georgian border.

At the Bombora air base, meanwhile, three new hangars for planes and ammunition were hastily constructed.

Several new Russian Su-25 and Su-27 fighter aircraft had landed at the air base in Gudauta by June 6 and, at the same time, the Zelenchuk Mountainous Infantry Brigade of the NCMD began a ten-day exercise "to perfect its actions on unknown territory and at a distance from its permanent base." Soon thereafter, Georgian authorities detained a group of Russian peacekeepers in the Zugdidi district on the Georgian side of the Georgian-Abkhaz boundary, confiscating twenty anti-tank missiles and other heavy armament prohibited in the zone of conflict. In response, the deputy head of the Russian General Staff, General Alexander Burutin, promised a bloodletting the next time Georgia confiscated Russian arms since, according to him, Russian "peacekeepers" had the right to open fire.[87]

On the last day of June, forces from the North Caucasus Military District, together with FSB troops, began week-long maneuvers in a forested mountain area adjoining the Georgian border. At the same time, Bagapsh closed the Abkhaz-Georgian border along the Inguri River, and a Russian military transport with 250 servicemen on board left the Russian city of Sochi for the port of Gagra in Abkhazia.

In June the de facto South Ossetian authorities set up an internet website called "Ossetian genocide." On July 2 and 8, the Ossetian information agency Osinform published articles by Zaur Alborov, in which he detailed the participation of units of the 58th Army *"in the future operation to force Georgia to peace."* On July 2, the Rosbalt information agency published an interview with Merab Kishmaria, the Abkhazian defense minister, in which he said that "his troops lacked neither arms, anti-aircraft guns, nor aviation…" and that "The Abkhaz army is being trained by Russian instructors… And this time I will get to Kutaisi."[88] On July 3, Abkhaz Minister of Foreign Affairs Sergey Shamba, in an interview with *Nezavisimaya Gazeta,* ominously announced that Abkhazia "cannot guarantee not to launch a war." On the very next day the website Kavkaz-center confidently predicted a Russian attack on Georgia during August 2008:

> Putin took the political decision to wage war against Georgia even before Medvdev's election as Russian president. Intensive preparations for the war have been under way already for several months.[89]

That same day, on July 4, Kokoity announced a total mobilization in South Ossetia, but then cancelled it the same afternoon. The next day the editor-in-chief of the Forum.msk.ru website, having paid a visit to the

North Caucasus, reported that the war against Georgia is incredibly close and the army "wants a war."[90]

On July 6, forces of the North Caucasus Military District started their "Caucasus-Border-2008" exercise. On July 7, exactly one month before the beginning of the war, both Russian peacekeeping battalions in Abkhazia and South Ossetia began simultaneously fortifying their positions.[91] Next day, returning from a 10-day visit to South Ossetia, Alexander Dugin, self-proclaimed specialist in geopolitics with extensive contacts in the Russian military and special services, announced: "Ossetians are waiting for war. The country is ready for war. All the adult male population is mobilized. All patriotic Russian youth should come to South Ossetia to fight with weapons in their hands against our global fundamental enemies—Americans, NATO."[92]

The same day, additional Russian anti-aircraft complexes and heavy armament were deployed in Abkhazia, while four Russian military jets violated Georgian air space over South Ossetia. In a remarkable move, Russia's Ministry of Foreign Affairs openly acknowledged the violation, explaining that it had been done "to cool hot heads."[93] On July 10, both Bagapsh and Kokoity were called to Moscow for consultations with the Russian authorities. The Commander-in-chief of the NCMD, General Sergey Makarov, promised further military support to the Russian peacekeepers on the territory of Georgia.

Throughout the summer, there were numerous proposals for bilateral and multilateral negotiations to seek a peaceful settlement of the conflicts. Among such proposals were those by Georgia (throughout July until August 7), by the U.S. (on July 8), by Germany (on July 14, again on July 18, July 25, July 30, and on July 31), by the EU (on July 19 and on July 22–24), and by the OSCE and Finland (on July 25, and on July 30). The Russian, South Ossetian, and Abkhaz leaders, however, brushed them all aside.

Just as these proposals were being made, on July 15 NCMD troops began large-scale military maneuvers—"Kavkaz-2008"—with the participation of 8,000 servicemen from the army, interior forces, and the FSB, including 700 armored units, and with support from the Air Force and the Black Sea Fleet. The goal of the exercises was to perform an "operation of peace enforcement."[94] Participants in the exercises were given a leaflet entitled "Soldier! Know your probable enemy!" with a description of the Georgian forces, which is reproduced among the illustrations in this book.

On July 18, the airborne storm-trooper regiment of the 76th Pskov Airborne Division took up positions on the Roki and Mamisson passes of the main Caucasian massif, while the airborne regiment of the Volgograd Infantry Division was deployed in Krasnodar Kray. On July 20, an infantry battalion with fourteen Armored Personnel Carriers entered the lower part of the Kodori Gorge, and three days later the 135th Infantry Regiment of the 19th Vladikavkaz Infantry Division replaced the Pskov paratroopers on the Roki pass. On July 25, a special medical detachment set up a field hospital named "Tarskoye" that could handle 300 wounded soldiers per day. "At the request of local authorities" the hospital remained in place after the exercises were completed "...in order to serve the local population," as the announcement claimed. Meanwhile, the construction of the Ugadangi base near Java was completed the following next day.

In a remarkably candid statement of Russia's intentions, Teimuraz Mamsurov, head of the region of North Ossetia in Russia, promised the readers of *Nezavisimaya Gazeta* on July 26 that Russian troops

> will enter Georgia to protect Russian citizens and help peacekeepers... There is armor, including tanks, at the northern gate of the Roki tunnel. They are deployed for demonstration purposes, but [their function is] not just to stand there...[95]

Two days later the magazine *Ogonyok* reported that between forty-five and fifty railway cars with tanks had reached the Gali district on the Abkhaz-Georgian border, and that echelons were moving day and night.[96] An otherwise unidentified colonel from the "peacekeeping forces" swaggeringly boasted that the quantity of armaments and ammunition in Abkhazia had reached the level "necessary to wage a conflict for several years. I feel that something will happen," he added.[97] Finally, on July 30, six days ahead of schedule, the Russian railway corps completed repairs to the Sukhumi-Ochamchire railway. The scene was now set for war. Now all that was necessary was the spark to start it.

Launching the Big War, July 28–August 6, 2008

On July 28, South Ossetian forces for the first time fired at the joint peacekeeping forces and OSCE observers. The next day, also for the first time, South Ossetian forces shelled villages with ethnically mixed populations that were under Georgian control.[98]

In the morning of August 1, a Georgian police truck was blown up, seriously wounding five policemen. Later an airplane loaded with Russian journalists ready and eager to report on a war that had not yet begun departed Moscow for Tskhinvali. Early the next morning, a second group of Russian journalists departed the Dagestani capital of Makhachkala for

South Ossetia. Foreign journalists, with the exception of only group from the Ukrainian TV channel Inter, were banned from entering South Ossetia. The Russian Ministry of Foreign Affairs claimed this was "due to problems with their documents." The Russian journalists began arriving in Tskhinvali in the morning of August 2. By August 7, their number had reached fifty (see Box 4.2).[99]

Ossetian and Georgian forces exchanged fire from the afternoon of August 1 until the next morning. For the first time since 2004, the South Ossetian side used the large-caliber artillery exceeding 100 mm which the CIS had prohibited from the zone of conflict.

On August 2, the North Caucasus military exercise "Kavkaz-2008" officially ended. But troops participating in the maneuvers did not leave their positions. Moreover, over the course of this day, several regular units began infiltrating the territory of South Ossetia. The Russian and Ossetian "peacekeeping" battalions were illegally increased from 530 to 850 servicemen each, but the Georgians' battalion remained at its level of 530 troops. South Ossetia now began moving civilians from Tskhinvali and the surrounding villages. By midnight of August 7, more than 20,000 civilians from South Ossetia had been evacuated to Russia. This number constituted more than ninety percent of the population of the future area of battle and about forty percent of the total population of South Ossetia, a proportion that almost exactly mirrored the one registered in Kosovo when Kosovars fled the Serb army in 1999.

On August 2, Sergey Mironov, Teimuraz Mamsurov, and Commander-in-Chief of the Russian Airborne Troops Valery Evtukhovich all simultaneously issued statements promising that Russian forces would intervene in Georgia "for the protection of Russian citizens and to help the peacekeepers." On August 3, the information agency Osinform published an article entitled "If war happens tomorrow," which assumed that the start of operations was imminent.

The same day, Russian Deputy Minister of Defense Nikolai Pankov, the Deputy Chief of Military Intelligence, and Commander-in-Chief of the 58th Army Anatoly Khrulev arrived in Tskhinvali, where they met with the military and political leadership of South Ossetia, including Kokoity, Morozov, Lunev, Mindzaev, Chochiev, Boris Attoev, as well as the commanders of the Russian and Ossetian peacekeepers Marat Kulakhmetov and Konstantin Friev. Georgian sources confirm that the purpose of the meeting was to finalize the plan of action for the 58th Army units in South Ossetia.[100] Simultaneously with this event, the Security Council of Abkhazia had been called to a meeting in Sukhumi as well.

Meanwhile, mobilization of "volunteers" and Cossacks started in the North Caucasus, with the first 300 mercenaries crossing the international Russian-Georgian border, arriving on August 4 in South Ossetia. As the Supreme Ataman of the Union of the Russian Cossacks, and at the same time deputy governor of the Rostov oblast, Victor Vodolatskiy explained, the mobilization of volunteers was centrally planned and officially performed via drafting stations at the regional and district military commissariats across Russia's North Caucasus. Most of volunteers were assigned to the 19th Infantry Division of the NCMD and to the North Ossetian peacekeeping battalion, while others signed direct contracts with the South Ossetia's Ministry of Defense (the existence of which, by the way, was also illegal according to the Dagomys or Sochi agreement).[101]

On August 4, NCMD troops moved to the immediate proximity of the international Russian-Georgian border, occupied Roki and Mamison passes, and deployed in the Zaramag area in order "to be able to immediately cross the border to provide assistance to the peacekeepers in South Ossetia."[102] The same day, medical and communications units of the 58th Army arrived in South Ossetia and eleven "Gvozdika" artillery gunships were relocated from Java to Tskhinvali. The number of Russian regular troops in South Ossetia had now reached approximately 1,200. AWACS-type military aircraft arrived at the Mozdok air base, and several Tu-22M3 heavy bombers were relocated from their permanent base near Novgorod to the southern region of Saratov.[103]

In the midst of these intensive preparations, *Nezavisimaya Gazeta* on August 4 published an article entitled "The Postponed War," while South Ossetia's Radio declared confidently that "the war could begin tomorrow."[104] In a seemingly coordinated move from Sukhumi, Sergey Bagapsh informed that if war broke out, Abkhazia "would not stand on the sidelines."[105]

On August 5, three days before the attack was launched, several more armored units, forty artillery systems, and an intelligence battalion of the 33rd Special Airborne Storm-trooper Brigade with full armaments and ammunition moved south across the Russian-Georgian border via the Roki tunnel into South Ossetia.[106] Thirty more artillery systems were transferred into Georgia via the Kodori Gorge.

It was becoming clear that the objectives of the Russian/Abkhaz/South Ossetian coalition in the looming war went far beyond the contested territories of South Ossetia and Abkhazia. South Ossetia's Minister of Interior Mikhail Mindzaev said that South Ossetia might claim terriotories in Georgia, including Borjomi and Bakuriani.[107] In an interview with *Nezavisi-*

maya Gazeta on August 5, Abkhaz Foreign Minister Shamba did not exclude a possibility of opening the second front against Georgia. An unidentified source in the Abkhaz intelligence services predicted that "specially trained diversionaries may blow up the Baku-Tbilisi-Ceyhan pipeline."[108] And indeed, in strict confirmation of that prediction, an explosion near the Turkish city of Erzincan temporarily closed the BTC pipeline the following morning.

By the evening of August 5, the following Russian units were deployed at the northern gate of the Roki tunnel: the 135th and 693rd Infantry Regiments of the 19th Division of the 58th Army, the 104th and 234th Airborne Assault Regiments of 76th Airborne Division, the 217th Airborne Regiment of the 96th Airborne Division, and the 31st Special Airborne Regiment. Altogether, these included 11,693 servicemen, 891 armored units, and 138 units of artillery.[109] The Tersk and Don Cossacks formed detachments and sent them to South Ossetia.

Beginning on August 6, all offices and shops in Tskhinvali were closed. The evacuation of civilians to Russia proceeded apace, while mercenaries and Russian journalists arrived from the opposite direction. That same day South Ossetian forces opened mortar fire on the villages of Eredvi, Prisi, Avnevi, Dwani, and Nuli. The following fire exchange led to the injuring of several people on both sides. *Izvestia* proudly stated that volunteers were arriving to South Ossetia from as far away as Moscow, while Radio Ossetia issued a special announcement saying that the war had begun.[110]

By the evening of August 6, the leadership of the NCMD was deployed to Java, while the leadership of the Leningrad Military District was deployed in the lower part of the Kodori Gorge.[111] The correspondent of the APN information agency reported from Vladikavkaz: "All the Republic… all people saw (beginning on the evening of August 6) the movement of a huge amount of troops in the direction of the [Roki] tunnel."[112]

The correspondent of *Nezavisimaya Gazeta*, rushing from Vladikavkaz to Tskhinvali in order not to miss the beginning of the unfolding war, reported what she saw with her own eyes:

> Russia is pulling serious military forces to the Georgian border. All Transkam from Alagir to Zaramag is full with military columns, trucks with servicemen, armor. The military still talk about military exercises, but there is no doubt that Russia demonstrates its decisiveness to defend its citizens in South Ossetia. Just up to performing of a peace enforcement operation.[113]

Georgian President Saakashvili requested an urgent telephone conversation with Russian President Dmitry Medvedev to discuss the dangerous turn of events in South Ossetia and in Russian-Georgian relations. The Russian Foreign Ministry responded with the following cold statement: "The situation is not yet ready for the Presidents to talk to each other. Let the Presidents speak later."[114]

Table 4.1

Who was first?

This comparison is constructed with the pure purpose to identify which side—the Russia-Abkhazia-South Ossetia Coalition or Georgia—was first in committing actions that can be considered an aggression based on the definition given by the UN General Assembly Resolution #3314 on December 14, 1974. Considering South Ossetia and Abkhazia as de facto actors allied with Russia is an observation of factual relations, which is unrelated to their international legal status.

Out of 46 actions that are believed to be acts of aggression, 45 were performed first by the Coalition (Russia, Abkhazia, and South Ossetia). One action was performed first by Georgia before the Coalition.

Actions performed by each party for the first time	Coalition (Russia, Abkhazia, and South Ossetia)	Georgia
• Air force bombing of the territory of another party	August 23, 2002	August 8, 2008
• Deployment of battle tanks on the territory of South Ossetia	February 3, 2003	August 7, 2008
• Building of military base on the territory of South Ossetia	May, 2004	Absent
• Artillery shelling of the territory of another party	March 12, 2007	August 1, 2008
• Exit from the Treaty on Conventional Armed Forces in Europe (CFE)	July 14, 2007	Absent
• Exit from the CIS regime of sanctions in relevance to Abkhazia	March 6, 2008	Absent
• De-facto recognition of the independence of Abkhazia and South Ossetia (establishment of direct contacts with the authorities of Abkhazia and South Ossetia)	April 16, 2008	Absent
• Shooting down of aircraft of another party	April 20, 2008	August 8, 2008
• Deployment in Abkhazia of the regular military forces not agreed with the other party	April 30, 2008	Absent

• Deployment in Abkhazia of military personnel in excess of the agreed limits	May 26, 2008	Absent
• Wounding a serviceman of another party since beginning of 2008	July 3, 2008	August 1, 2008
• Invasion of a group of aircrafts into the airspace of another party	July 9, 2008	August 8, 2008
• Obstruction of the activity of peace-keeping forces of another party	July 27, 2008	August 8, 2008
• Firing in the direction of the OSCE observers	July 28, 2008	August 8, 2008
• Artillery shelling of the territory of another party since beginning of 2008	July 29, 2008	August 1, 2008
• Casualty of a serviceman (law enforcement officer, or policeman) of another party since beginning of 2008	August 6, 2008	August 1, 2008
• Deployment of heavy weaponry in the zone of conflict in South Ossetia	August 1, 2008	August 7, 2008 9:00 P.M.
• Use of heavy weaponry prohibited in the zone of conflict and confirmed by observers	August 1-2, 2008	August 7, 2008, 11:50 P.M.
• Mass evacuation of civilians from the zone of conflict	August 2, 2008	August 7, 2008
• Mass arrival of journalists representing the media of the party into the zone of conflict	August 2, 2008	August 8, 2008
• Arrival of military commanders who would be leading the operation into the zone of conflict	August 3, 2008, morning	August 6, 2008
• Meeting of a security council (or similar type meeting) that would lead to the decision to launch military operations	August 3, 2008, morning	August 7, 2008, 1:00 P.M.
• Beginning of mass mobilization	August 3, 2008	August 8, 2008, 8:00 A.M.
• Confirmed arrival of mercenaries (volunteers) into the zone of conflict	August 4, 2008	Absent/No data
• Presence of regular military forces of Russia and Georgia on the territory of South Ossetia	No later than August 3, 2008	August 7, 2008, 9:00 P.M.

• Arrival of medical units and communication units of the regular military forces into the zone of conflict	August 4, 2008	August 7, 2008 9:00 P.M.
• Regular description of the situation by the media of the parties as a full-scale war	August 3, 2008	August 8, 2008
• Issue of order of a chief of military (or security) body to destroy (to raze down) a settlement (village) on the territory of another party	August 5, 2008	Absent
• Increase in the number of peacekeeping forces in South Ossetia in excess of agreed limits	No later than August 7, 2008	Absent /No data
• Confirmed crossing of Russian-Georgian international border by regular troops of the opposite party	August 7, 2008, 3:52 A.M.	Absent
• Public statement of a political leader of the party to "clean" the members of another ethnic group from the zone of conflict	August 7, 2008, 10:50 A.M.	Absent
• Order to put military forces on the highest alert	August 7, 2008, no later 11:00 A.M.	August 7, 2008, 2:00 P.M.
• Causing death to a civilian person of another party	August 7, 2008, 2:00 P.M.	August 8, 2008, 2:00 A.M.
• Causing death to a serviceman of peacekeeping forces of another party	August 7, 2008, 2:00 P.M.	August 8, 2008, 8:00 A.M.
• Implementation of unilateral cease-fire on August 7, 2008	Absent	August 7, 2008, 5:10 P.M.
• Announcement of unilateral cease-fire on August 7, 2008	Absent	August 7, 2008, 6:40 P.M.
• Shelling positions of another party after implementation of unilateral cease-fire on August 7, 2008	August 7, 2008, 8:40 P.M.	August 7, 2008, 11:50 P.M.
• Order to engage into military operations given to peacekeeping troops	August 8, 2008, 00:30 A.M.	Absent
• Fighting positions adopted by peacekeeping troops	August 8, 2008, 1:00 A.M.	Absent

• Engagement in military operations by peacekeeping troops	August 8, 2008, no later than 06:20 A.M.	Absent
• Use of tactical missile against the other party	August 8, 2008, 7:30 A.M.	Absent
• Announcement of cease-fire, its implementation, creation of a humanitarian corridor for transportation of wounded and civilians out of zone of action	Absent	August 8, 2008, 3.00-6.00 P.M.
• Blockade of maritime routes of the other party	August 8, 2008, 4:40 P.M.	Absent
• Implementation of ethnic cleansing of the opposite party	Since August 9, 2008	Absent
• Marine troops landing into the zone of conflict	August 10, 2008, 1:07 A.M.	Absent
• De jure recognition of the independence of Abkhazia and South Ossetia	August 26, 2008	Absent

Source: http://aillarionov.livejournal.com/70169.html

*Types, dates, and time of actions considered as acts of aggression according to the UN GA #3314 resolution performed by each party for the first time

Box 4.1

Russian Citizens in the Military and Political Leadership of South Ossetia, 2004–08

Barankevich, Anatoly Konstantinovich, lieutenant-general; Minister of Defense of South Ossetia, July 6, 2004–December 10, 2006; Secretary of Security Council of South Ossetia, December 11, 2006–October 3, 2008. Graduated from Ussuriysk Suvorov Military College, the Far East Military Command College, the Frunze Military Academy. Served in the Siberian Military District, the Group of Soviet Forces in Germany, in Volga and North Caucasus Military Districts. Participated in the Soviet war in Afghanistan, first and second Chechen wars. Was deputy military commissar in Chechnya, and in Stavropol kray.

Yarovoy, Anatoly, FSB major-general; Chairman of KGB of South Ossetia, January 17, 2005–March 2, 2006. Before his appointment to South Ossetia was a Head of the FSB Branch in the Republic of Mordovia, March 10, 2001–December 27, 2004.

Chebodarev, Oleg, FSB colonel, chief of the State Border Guard of South Ossetia since 2005.

Mindzaev, Michail, FSB lieutenant-general; Minister of Interior, April 26, 2005–August 18, 2008. Was a deputy chief of staff in the Ministry of Interior of the Republic of the North Ossetia – Alania. In 2004 in Beslan was commander of the Alpha Group's special forces of the Russian FSB.

Morozov, Yuri Ionovich, prime minister of South Ossetia, July 5, 2005 – August 18, 2008. Graduated from the Ufa Oil Institute. Before his appointment in the government of South Ossetia was a commercial director of Kursk fuel company.

Dolgopolov, Nikolai Vasiljevich, FSB major-general, Chairman of KGB of South Ossetia, March 3, 2006–November 8, 2006. Before his appointment in South Ossetia was a Chief of the FSB Branch in the Republic of Mari El.

Attoev, Boris Majitovich, FSB lieutenant-general, Chairman of KGB of South Ossetia since November 9, 2006. Before his appointment in South Ossetia was a Chief of FSB Branch in the Kabardino-Balkaria Republic, also senior fellow at the FSB central directorate in Moscow. Participated in the Soviet war in Afghanistan.

Laptev, Andrey Ivanovich, lieutenant-general, Minister of Defense of South Ossetia, December 11, 2006–February 28, 2008.

Kotoev, Vladimir Kuzmich, FSB colonel, Chairman of State Protection Guard, since 2007. Participated in wars in Chechnya and Bosnia.

Lunev, Vasily Vasiljevich, lieutenant-general, Minister of Defense of South Ossetia, March 1, 2008–August 18, 2008, from August 9 also Commander-in-chief of the 58th Army of the North Caucasian Military District. Graduated from the Moscow High Military College, the Frunze Military Academy, the Military Academy of the General Staff. Promoted from a platoon commander of an infantry regiment to the first deputy commander-in-chief of the army in the Siberian Military District. Served in the Far East, Siberia, Urals, also in Syria as a military adviser. Before his appointment in South Ossetia was a military commissar in Perm Krai.

Tanaev, Yury Anvarovich, major-general, Minister of Defense in South Ossetia since October 31. Graduated from the Minsk Suvorov Military College. Before his appointment to South Ossetia was a chief of the intelligence department of the staff in the Urals Military District.

Bulatsev, Aslanbek Soltanovich, FSB colonel, prime minister of South Ossetia since October 31, 2008. Before his appointment to South Ossetia was a chief of Federal Taxation Service in the Republic of North Ossetia - Alania, earlier was a chief of FSB Finance Department in the Republic of North Ossetia.

Bolshakov, Alexander Michailovich, Chief of the South Ossetia Presidential Administration since October 31, 2008. Graduated from the Vladimir State Pedagogical Institute. Over 15 years he occupied leading positions in the Party and executive bodies of the Vladimir oblast administration. Was a deputy director of OAO "Zavod Autopribor" (city Vladimir). Before his appointment to South Ossetia was a deputy governor, head of the Ulyanovsk oblast administration, a member of the ruling party United Russia. During the presidential election campaign, March 2, 2008, was a head of regional staff of the presidential candidate Dmitry Medvedev.

Box 4.2

Tskhinvali Pool of Russian Journalists

1) Said-Husein Tsarnaev, journalist with RIAN and Reuters:

"We've arrived in Tskhinvali three days prior to the attack on the city... We've got accommodations in the hotel "Alan." At once, I've noticed about fifty journalists of leading TV channels and newspapers gathered in the hotel. I have experience with two Chechen campaigns and such a crowd of colleagues at the headquarters of peacekeeping forces I took as a disturbing signal."

2) Irina Kuksenkova, journalist with Moskovsky Komsomolets:

"50 Russian journalists, stuck in the bunker of peacekeepers in Tskhinvali, on Friday [on August 8. – A.I.] have called international human rights protecting organizations, the Red Cross, OSCE and the United Nations with the request to organize a corridor for evacuation from the city. This request, as it is informed on the web-site of 'The Nezavisimaya Gazeta,' has been delivered to the secretary of Georgian Security Council, Kahi Lomaya".

3) The list of the Russian journalists present in Tskhinvali by 23.30 on August 7, 2008:

Arrived on August 2:
1. Olga Kiriy – correspondent, 1st TV channel, Southern Bureau
2. Olga Kuznetsova – operator, 1st TV channel, Southern Bureau
3. Anton Stepanenko – correspondent, 1st TV channel, Moscow
4. Kiril Butyrin – operator, 1st TV channel, Moscow.
5. Andrey Chistjakov – correspondent, TV channel "Rossiya"
6. Evgeniy Radaev, TV channel "Rossiya".
7. Damir Zakirov – video engineer, TV channel "Rossiya"
8. NN, TV channel "Rossiya"
9. NN, TV channel "Rossiya"
10. Ruslan Gusarov – correspondent, NTV
11. Vadim Goncharov – operator, NTV
12. Peter Gaseev – producer, NTV, resident of Tskhinvali

Arrived on August 5, replacing the previous group:
13. Evgeniy Poddubny – correspondent, TVTS
14. Alexey Komarov – operator, TVTS
15. Alexey Stepanov-Molodov, TVTS

Arrived on August 5:

16. Artem Vasnev – correspondent, Ren-TV

17. Roman Simbukhovskiy – operator, Ren-TV

18. Stanislav Hudiev – correspondent, MTRK "Mir"

19. Operator, MTRK "Mir".

20. Evgeniy Lukinov – correspondent, 5th channel

21. Operator, 5th channel

22. Alexey – technician on sound, 5th channel

23. Correspondent, Russia Today

24. Alexander – operator, Russia Today

25. Makhmud – correspondent of the Arab speaking version of Russia Today

26. Alan Bulkata (aka - Alan Tsorian) – correspondent, RIAN.

27. Said Tsarnaev – freelance photo correspondent, RIAN, also with "Reuters"

28. Sergey Uzakov – photo correspondent, ITAR-TASS.

30. Alexey Shtokal – correspondent, Interfax

31. Andrey Tadtaev – correspondent, Regnum

Arrived on August 6:

32. Ruslan Yarmolyuk – correspondent, TV "Inter" (Ukraine)

33. Jury Romanjuk – operator, TV "Inter" (Ukraine)

34. Marina Perevozkina – correspondent, Nezavisimaya Gazeta

35. Irina Kuksenkova – correspondent, Moskovskiy Komsomolets

35. Yuri Snegirev – correspondent, Izvestiya

36. Michael Romanov – correspondent, The New Times

Sources: Alexander Kovylkov, "War Notes. South Ossetia," Rostov Na Donu: Fenix, 2008, p. 56; Irina Kuksenkova, "Welcome to hell!" Moskovsky Komsomolets, www.mk.ru/blogs/idmk/2008/08/11/mk-daily/365829/; http://davnym-davno.livejournal.com/6488.html

5

Georgia's Rose Revolution:
The Break with the Past

Niklas Nilsson

The Rise of the "Young Reformers"

The political system established in Georgia under Eduard Shevardnadze rested on a sophisticated "balancing of interests," where former members of the Soviet elite were balanced against a faction of young, reform-oriented liberals, who had often worked or studied in the West. This system strengthened the president's position as an indispensable arbiter between various interest groups. At the same time, this provided for a slow and complicated decision-making process, avoiding tough decisions, which would risk alienating either faction. While these groupings were not clear-cut, the "young reformer" camp headed by Zurab Zhvania was a forthcoming faction in Shevardnadze's ruling party, the Citizens' Union of Georgia (CUG), and was active in recruiting Western-educated Georgians into government positions, one of whom was Mikheil Saakashvili, who joined the CUG in 1995, became Minister of Justice in 2000, but resigned in 2001.[1]

A crucial precondition for the Rose Revolution was the system of "weak authoritarianism" under Shevardnadze's presidency. This system allowed the "liberal" factions of the CUG to develop reform-oriented agendas. They could, furthermore, establish their own support platforms, and eventually defect from the CUG and form opposition parties of their own.[2] Mikheil Saakashvili thus formed the National Movement in 2001. Zurab Zhvania and Nino Burjanadze formed the United Democrats in November 2002, running in the 2003 elections in the bloc named the "Burjanadze-Democrats." The New Rights Party, which had left the parliamentary majority faction in 2000, and the Labor Party constituted fairly strong opposition forces in parallel with the former young reformist camp in the CUG government, while the Industrialists appeared a moderate force.[3] All these parties revolved around the strong personalities of their leaders. The political system under Shevardnadze provided for a fairly free media, where the

Rustavi-2 television channel, critical of the authorities, functioned as the mouthpiece of the opposition and allowed the opposition forces to communicate their agendas and voice strong criticism of Shevardnadze. Furthermore, a vibrant civil society had developed in Georgia during the 1990s, thanks to the large amounts of foreign aid provided for Georgia's democratization. Thus, professional watchdog NGOs such as the Georgian Young Lawyers Association and the International Society for Fair Elections and Democracy (ISFED) were able to conduct parallel vote tabulations and help uncover election fraud, while the Liberty Institute functioned as a think tank and helped to develop the political agenda of the reformist opposition. Student organizations at Georgian universities formed the youth organization *Khmara* (Enough), modeled on the organizations that had proven instrumental in the regime changes in Serbia and Slovakia. Especially Serbian Otpor activists provided inspiration for Khmara, training several of its activists in techniques of civil disobedience. These activities, as well as Khmara itself, received funding from George Soros's Open Society Institute. Khmara cooperated closely with other NGOs and segments of the reformist opposition, and in their protest actions against the Shevardnadze regime explicitly promoted a shift of power to the opposition.[4]

After 2001, the CUG became increasingly fragmented, with splinter factions setting up vocal opposition parties able to articulate an attractive agenda of reform, which was backed by important segments of civil society. The local elections in 2002 constituted the first significant event in the opposition parties' struggle to hasten the presidential succession, as well as a test of public support for the opposition parties. These elections signaled a significant weakening of the CUG, as the National Movement and Labor Party managed to defeat the CUG in Tbilisi, while the New Rights Party and the Industrialists were successful in several districts outside of Tbilisi. Saakashvili thus became the chairman of Tbilisi City Council.[5]

In these local elections, the various opposition parties demonstrated their strength as a force to be reckoned with in Georgian politics, achieving a significant shift of power from the CUG. Shevardnadze realized that he was becoming increasingly unpopular and that his party was falling apart, and sought to strengthen his position ahead of the 2003 parliamentary elections.

The Rose Revolution

Prior to the parliamentary elections of November 2, 2003, Shevardnadze formed the government bloc For New Georgia, consisting of the CUG and several minor parties, for which he was determined to secure a parliamentary majority. The elections were seen as a preparation for the presidential elections in 2005, where Shevardnadze's successor was to be elected. A poor result in parliamentary elections would have significantly undermined Shevardnadze's political camp ahead of the presidential elections. Simultaneously, Georgia's Western partners demanded that elections be conducted in a free and fair manner, and provided significant funding for securing proper election conduct.[6]

However, it soon appeared that Shevardnadze and the CUG were determined to stop power slipping from their hands. The OSCE/ODIHR final monitoring report disclosed election fraud to an extent unparalleled since Georgia's independence. It stated that the elections "demonstrated that the authorities lacked [the] political will to conduct a genuinely democratic process." Violations included highly flawed voter lists, extensive use of administrative resources, biased media reporting, and strong bias in both the composition and behavior of the election commissions at all levels. Violations were especially severe in Kvemo Kartli and Adjara. As voter lists were published, these turned out to be deeply flawed, excluding significant numbers of voters, among them Saakashvili himself, and including citizens who had been dead for years. The electoral commissions at all levels appeared committed to deliver Shevardnadze's party the victory it needed. Election day was chaotic, with large numbers of voters turned away from the polls and recurring instances of ballot stuffing and multiple voting. Several Precinct and District Electoral Commissions were directly involved in falsifying results during the tabulation of votes.[7]

As the Central Election Commission (CEC) began to publicize the preliminary results of the voting, it appeared that For New Georgia had won, which reduced the National Movement's seats in Parliament. The impression spread rapidly among voters and politicians in Tbilisi that the president's bloc was about to steal the elections. The announcement of parallel vote tabulations conducted by ISFED, funded and supported by the U.S. National Democratic Institute, and exit polls conducted by the U.S. firm Global Strategy Group, fuelled these suspicions. Both announced a victory for the National Movement and significantly lower support for Shevardnadze's bloc than in the official results.[8] In the official results, For New Georgia gained 21.3 percent, Revival Union 18.8 percent, and National Movement 18.1 percent. In the parallel vote tabulation, the same parties gained 18.9, 8.1, and 26.3 percent, respectively. In total, the official results showed a total of 40.1 percent of the vote for the government bloc and 46.7

percent for the opposition, while the Parallel Vote Tabulation (PVT) showed 27 percent for the former and 61.9 percent for the latter.[9]

As the magnitude of election fraud unfolded, the National Movement and the Burjanadze-Democrats joined forces and called for rallies in downtown Tbilisi. Their goal was to coerce the authorities into submitting the correct election results. The rallies rapidly grew in strength and spread throughout the country. While Saakashvili, Zhvania, and Burjanadze had been viewed heretofore as loosely allied reform-oriented opposition politicians, Saakashvili now emerged as the leader of the anti-government protests, due to his strong results in the elections and his leading role in the anti-government rallies.

The CEC announced the results from Adjara on November 6; Aslan Abashidze's Shevardnadze-allied Revival Union party purportedly received 95 percent of the Adjara votes—making it a leader in the official results on a par with For New Georgia.[10] Furthermore, Shevardnadze intensified his collaboration with Abashidze during the protests. Abashidze embarked on a tour to Yerevan, Baku, and Moscow, fuelling fears among the opposition that Shevardnadze intended to quell public unrest by activating Abashidze's Russian connections[11] and that a position in the new government was earmarked for him.[12] This blatant instance of election fraud involving the unpopular Abashidze intensified the protests in Tbilisi. As this occurred, supporters of Abashidze's party were bused to Tbilisi from Adjara in order to organize counter-demonstrations. Over the next three weeks a general uncertainty prevailed whether Shevardnadze would resort to violence to quell the protests and where the loyalty of Georgia's security forces would lie in the event of such a development. On November 20, the CEC announced the victory of Shevardnadze's bloc, with Abashidze's party winning a strong second place. This infuriated the opposition protesters, who increased their presence in downtown Tbilisi. Nearby a pro-government demonstration organized by Abashidze's supporters was also taking place. The two camps stood cheek by jowl outside Parliament.

On November 22, the Parliament convened. As Shevardnadze was delivering his opening speech, opposition supporters broke into the Parliament building holding roses in their hands. The security staff immediately evacuated Shevardnadze. Shevardnadze then declared a state of emergency. However, he failed to secure the support of the security forces, which either took a passive stance or joined the opposition protesters. Confronted by this situation, Shevardnadze resigned on November 23 and Nino Burjanadze, as Speaker of Parliament, assumed the interim presidency.

On January 4, 2004, an extraordinary presidential election was held, in which Saakashvili, running virtually uncontested, won 96 percent of the votes cast. OSCE/ODIHR observers judged this election to represent "notable progress over previous elections."[13] On March 28 of the same year, Georgia held repeat parliamentary elections for the proportional component and two majoritarian components, which the Georgian Supreme Court had declared invalid. Again, OSCE/ODIHR observers declared that these elections were a "notable improvement" over earlier ones and "the most democratic since independence."[14] The results provided a landslide victory for the now united parties of Saakashvili, Zhvania, and Burjanadze, lending them a constitutional majority in Parliament.

The Rose Revolution and its immediate aftermath released an immense wave of optimism in Georgian society. Nevertheless, once in power, the new government faced acute challenges. It inherited extremely weak and corrupt governmental institutions, poverty, and a lack of control over a significant portion of the country's territory. Saakashvili promised extraordinary measures to address these ills and proposed an extremely optimistic timeframe for implementing them. In so doing, he enjoyed immense public support for what was seen as a generational change in Georgian politics. The fact that heavyweight politicians in the "young reformer" camp like Nino Burjanadze or Zurab Zhvania took part in the revolution either as members of Saakashvili's National Movement or as close allies, signaled a strong political consensus on the need for reform and political change. Exceptions were the New Rights, Industrialist, and Labor parties, who opposed what they deemed the unconstitutional changes in government that the revolution had brought about. Even these remained mild in their criticism, however. In addition, the Republican and Conservative parties left the coalition shortly after the new leadership consolidated its control without them. Taken together, opposition to the revolution was very limited at the outset.

Georgia after the Revolution: The Reform Agenda

The new government set out with a strongly reform-oriented agenda that included economic liberalization, anti-corruption, and institution-building. As his top priority, Saakashvili called for the reestablishment of Georgia's territorial integrity. The reformists undertook an extensive liberalization of the economy that included some questionable privatizations, but which succeeded in attracting foreign direct investment and providing Georgia with a ranking among the top ten reforming countries in the World Bank's

"Doing Business" index. Between 2004 and 2008, Georgia achieved an average annual GDP growth of 10 percent which, combined with significant improvements in state revenues, allowed for investment in infrastructure and the expansion of health care and education.[15]

State institutions were successfully rebuilt and corruption reduced through mass redundancies, higher salaries, and new policies of "zero tolerance." Reforms to eliminate corruption in the public sector are vividly illustrated by the overhaul of the police force, the abolition of the traffic police, and a campaign to eliminate corruption in the universities. Over four years, Georgia's ranking in Transparency International's Corruption Perceptions Index rose from 133rd to 67th place among 180 countries listed.[16] The new government also managed to significantly increase revenues by simplifying the tax system. More controversial was the practice of arresting corrupt officials, sometimes on less than conclusive evidence, and offering their release if they repaid money they had taken from the state, a practice which initially secured significant contributions to a state budget that had been drained by the departing administration. All in all, the state budget increased threefold.[17]

During 2004, the government made several controversial changes to the constitution, significantly strengthening the powers of the president in relation to the Parliament and the judiciary. These measures were intended to provide the government with room to maneuver as it implemented its ambitious reform agenda. However, both independent analysts and opposition politicians pointed out that these reforms removed many of the checks and balances in the political system, and allowed for the president to rule by decree without the constraint of normal parliamentary processes. The government also introduced changes in the electoral system that increased the number of single mandate constituencies and favored winner-take-all practices in multimember constituencies. This had the effect of reinforcing the United National Movement's (UNM) dominance in the Parliament, leaving little room even for other major parties, and reducing severely the chance of smaller parties to gain proportional representation.[18] Critics decried what they saw as the arrogance of the new leadership in dealing with political opponents, charging that it was deaf to criticism, loath to debate the reforms they were carrying out, and failing to communicate to society the envisioned benefits of the harsh restructuring that was underway.

A Zeal for Territorial Integrity

The government's number one priority was the speedy reestablishment of Georgia's territorial integrity, to which Saakashvili made a deep personal commitment. Saakashvili asserted that the conflicts would be resolved in a non-violent fashion and according to principles of soft power. In January 2004, he argued that Georgia's economic development would significantly increase its attractiveness to the breakaway regions, which would in turn facilitate negotiations and the resolution of conflicts. His timetable for reintegrating these regions was extremely ambitious, calling for the process to be completed in Abkhazia, South Ossetia, and Adjara during his first term in office. The most immediate challenge was to restore Tbilisi's authority in Adjara. The government judged that public support for Abashidze's personal fiefdom was weak and that it would therefore be vulnerable to organized protest actions. These assumptions proved correct. Between January and May 2004, activists from Khmara and the "Our Adjara" organization launched a campaign within Adjara for Abashidze's resignation. This was accompanied by an economic embargo of the region and large military exercises just across the administrative border. Abashidze responded to this by blowing up the bridges connecting Adjara and Georgia proper. After several trips to Russia to secure support there, Abashidze eventually resigned on May 6 and left for Moscow. He was advised on this course of action by Igor Ivanov of the Russian Security Council, who had arrived in Batumi the day before.[19]

The reintegration of Adjara was a major success for the new government, and led naturally to the assumption that the same model could be successfully applied in South Ossetia, where it was felt the local leader, Eduard Kokoity, much like Abashidze, lacked legitimacy and where public support might easily be shifted from Tskhinvali to Tbilisi. Establishing control over South Ossetia was particularly desirable because large-scale contraband imports across the Russian border were draining large sums from the Georgian economy.[20]

Between December 2003 and May 2004, Tbilisi mounted a campaign to undermine the South Ossetian authorities through an anti-smuggling operation. Checkpoints along the administrative border were established, the Ergneti border market closed, and roads used for smuggling blown up. These efforts were aimed at fanning dissatisfaction with the de facto authorities and were combined with promises of humanitarian aid to win the hearts and minds of the local population. The strategy backfired, however, as the government apparently underestimated South Ossetian fears of

Georgian aggression. This enabled the Kokoity government to mobilize significant support. Violent confrontations between Georgian Ministry of Interior troops and Ossetian militias escalated from July onward, until Georgian troops withdrew in late August in order to avoid a full-blown military confrontation.[21]

The attempted reintegration of South Ossetia failed utterly. The government had not adequately understood the factors underpinning the conflict and had overestimated the role that economics could play in conflict resolution. Nevertheless, the 2004 events in Adjara and South Ossetia signaled the determination of the new Georgian government to reassert its authority in Georgian territories outside Tbilisi's control.

After the 2004 debacle, Tbilisi embarked on a campaign to draw international attention to the need for conflict resolution in both Abkhazia and South Ossetia, seeking EU participation to replace Russia's domination of negotiation and peacekeeping that had existed since the cease-fire agreements. Tbilisi became increasingly explicit in its criticism that the Russian mode of conflict resolution and its support for the separatist authorities had no other purpose than to keep the conflict alive and keep parts of Georgia under growing Russian control. Russia, in short, was a biased participant in the conflicts and had no interest in resolving them. Tbilisi believed that by bringing other external actors into the process of conflict resolution, Russia's evident bias in favor of the separatists could be neutralized.

In fact, Tbilisi increasingly saw the conflicts in the context of a broader Russian assault on Georgia's sovereignty. The urgency perceived in reintegrating the territories emerged in response to the heavy-handed Russian approach toward both Georgia and the regions from 2004 onward. Abkhazia and South Ossetia were increasingly treated as Russian subjects, and used as Russian bargaining chips in negotiations on Kosovo's independence. Tbilisi thus felt itself forced to act quickly, sometimes according to precarious strategies, lest it would risk losing the regions forever.

In order to secure active EU participation in the process of conflict resolution in Georgia, the government in Tbilisi embarked on a campaign to publicize the existence of unresolved conflicts in the immediate vicinity of the European Union's borders and the dangers they posed for the EU itself. Such pleading elicited no more than a lukewarm response from European capitals. It was probably naïve on Tbilisi's part to assume that EU governments would consider the security risks associated with Abkhazia and South Ossetia to be so serious as to warrant proactive steps to resolve them, especially when such steps might jeopardize key Russian interests in the Caucasus. Georgia was deeply frustrated with the Joint Control Commission in South Ossetia, which pitted Georgia against three obviously hostile parties: Russia, South Ossetia, and North Ossetia. In early 2008, Georgia withdrew from the Commission and proposed instead a new format including the EU that would allow Tbilisi to negotiate directly with South Ossetia's de facto government.[22]

Tbilisi also made efforts to change realities on the ground. Its chosen methods included proposals for ambitious peace plans and threats to use force if negotiations produced no steps forward. Tbilisi maintained the view that the conflict in South Ossetia was fuelled largely by the economic interests of local leaders and could be quickly solved through economic appeals that the Georgians could make directly to the population, over the heads of South Ossetian leaders who lacked legitimacy. Abkhazia, by contrast, was viewed as a much deeper conflict with strong ethnopolitical roots that could be addressed only through a prolonged process of reconciliation. The de facto governments of the two regions also differed in terms of both public support and dependence on Russia. The Abkhaz government had been able to assert a degree of integrity, not least through the election of Sergey Bagapsh in the presidential elections in 2005 over the Russian-favored candidate Raul Khadjimba. The South Ossetian government, however, was much more closely controlled by Russia. Russia nevertheless enjoyed a high degree of control over both regions, through the direct staffing of several key posts in the de facto governments with Russian security services officials and a strong military presence on the ground under the framework of the CIS peacekeeping missions.

Tbilisi energetically promoted peace plans for South Ossetia and Abkhazia from January 2005 onward. It envisioned far-reaching political and cultural autonomy for the two regions under a fairly loose federal framework, and secured OSCE support and funding for the outlined measures.[23] However, neither the separatist governments nor Russia saw much gain in such proposals. Georgia also made significant efforts to market these plans in international fora such as the UN Security Council, stirring criticism that they aimed to improve Georgia's international image and draw attention to Russia's role in the conflict zones, rather than provide realistic solutions.[24]

In July 2006 Georgia's efforts at altering the status quo again took a more assertive turn. The build-up of the Georgian military, largely conducted with U.S. financial support, provided Georgia with an army well trained for counter-insurgency operations, and with increasing numbers of soldiers who had served in Iraq. Under what was officially a law enforcement operation, Georgia re-established control over the Kodori Gorge in Abkhazia, previously run by a local warlord, and installed the Abkhaz government-in-exile there. In February the same year, then Defense Minister Irakli Okruashvili made hawkish remarks on how to reintegrate South Ossetia, threatening the use of military force and promising he would celebrate New Year's Eve in his native Tskhinvali. These actions, coinciding with a serious deterioration of the Georgian government's relationship to Moscow, unavoidably heightened fears on the Abkhaz and South Ossetian sides that Tbilisi was contemplating the use of force to reintegrate the two regions.

Tbilisi reinforced its charm offensive in South Ossetia in the spring of 2007. It introduced a "provisional administration" in the parts of South Ossetia it controlled, headed by Dmitry Sanakoyev, a leading former official in the de facto government. In order to demonstrate the prosperity awaiting Ossetians upon their return to Georgian jurisdiction, it then spent vast resources on rebuilding these areas. Russian aid to the separatist controlled part of region nevertheless countered Tbilisi's moves, initiating a fierce competition of aid programs for South Ossetia.[25]

Tbilisi's behavior toward its two breakaway regions after the Rose Revolution can indeed be termed ambiguous, in its mixing of peaceful and assertive messages. Nevertheless, Tbilisi's overarching strategy seems quite coherent in retrospect. Tbilisi's understanding was that the status quo prevailing since the early 1990s needed to be altered, should the conflicts ever approach solutions. Tbilisi viewed Russia's domination of the peacekeeping and negotiation formats, and its bias in favor of the breakaway regions, as the single most important obstacles to solutions. This dominance thus had to be altered through an internationalization of the formats. Realities on the ground needed to be addressed (primarily in South Ossetia) through alternative leaderships and economic improvements in order to increase Tbilisi's soft power. To provide new references in negotiations, Tbilisi offered the two regions what it viewed as the farthest-reaching autonomy possible within a federal framework of the Georgian state. At times, Tbilisi also sought to display changes on the ground in the balance of pure military power, thus contradicting the incentive of carrots with threats of using military force.

Overall, Georgia's post-revolutionary government displayed significant activity on all fronts in relation to its unresolved conflicts. It may be argued that set timeframes were overly optimistic and that strategies applied would have been well-served by better coherence, especially in refraining from their more assertive aspects. The fact remains, however, that Georgia's efforts at conflict resolution since 2004 were more active than had hitherto ever been the case. This was largely attributed to two factors: firstly, the strong resolve and public mandate the post-revolutionary government acquired for re-establishing territorial integrity. Secondly, the means for pursuing this goal obtained through the strengthening of the Georgian state and economy during this period.

The End of the Revolutionary Era

By 2006, the significant and for all practical purposes exaggerated hopes that Georgia would turn into a consolidated democracy in a few years started to fade, both domestically and internationally. The Saakashvili government's reforms had provided rapid and substantial progress in several of the areas considered the most problematic at the outset of the Rose Revolution. These changes may indeed be seen as paradoxical in their contradictions between state-building and democratization. The new government saw a need to strengthen the executive power in order push through difficult reforms and establish a functional state. However, it simultaneously removed many of the checks and balances in the political system and reinforced the dominance of the ruling party. This counteracted the long-term prospects for the development of a functional political party system and a constructive role for political opposition in Georgian politics. The dominance of the United National Movement in Parliament further reduced the room for public debate, implying that reforms of the electoral code remained insufficient.

In terms of deeper, systemic changes, the judiciary remained a weak institution, dependent on the government. Informal networks continually exercised undue influence over political decision-making, reducing transparency. The economic reforms, with all their benefits, also left large segments of society outside the economic development process. Media freedom was a contentious issue, with pressure being applied to journalists resulting in self-censorship, and large broadcasting networks, such as Rustavi-2, Mze, and the Georgian Public Broadcaster, termed as government-friendly. Until November 2007, Imedi and several minor TV and radio stations served as opposition mouthpieces—a role that the small, Tbilisi-based TV channels Kavkasia and Maestro took on from 2008 onward. Many observers, both domestically and internationally, have viewed such developments as steps away from the democratization process promised after the Rose Revolution, and have issued warnings of Georgia backsliding on its democratization promises.[26]

While the opposition in Georgia was extremely marginalized after the Rose Revolution, public disillusionment during 2005–6 gave way to the emergence of a more vocal group of opposition politicians, including former allies of Saakashvili. In the summer of 2007, ten opposition parties formed a coalition. This coalition united a quite diverse range of political actors, including former Saakashvili allies Salome Zurabashvili and Giorgi Khaindrava, radical opposition politicians such as Shalva Natelashvili and Koba Davitashvili, and moderate and liberal politicians such as David Usupashvili. The opposition coalition embarked on a set of protest actions at various locations in Georgia over the summer, yet failed to draw large crowds to the organized rallies. The coalition argued that the government had failed to deliver on the promises made after the revolution, and that Saakashvili's presidency had increasingly started to resemble that of an authoritarian ruler. It also voiced complaints of high-level corruption, seizures of private property, and demands for the release of alleged political prisoners.

In September the same year, the arrest of recently discharged Defense Minister Irakli Okruashvili on corruption charges sparked intensified activity in the opposition ranks. Okruashvili had shortly before his arrest gone public with serious allegations against President Saakashvili, and the arrest was understood in the opposition camp as the silencing of a critical voice from within the government. Government officials, however, made the case that an investigation into Okruashvili had been ongoing for some time, leading the latter to engage in false allegations. Okruashvili was later released and has set up an opposition party, which he runs from exile in France.

The opposition forces found a patron in the oligarch Badri Patarkatsishvili, who declared his ambition to remove the Saakashvili government from power and provided significant funding for the opposition's activities, allowing it to mobilize efficiently. Patarkatsishvili owned the Imedi television network, and began using it as a fierce mouthpiece of opposition to the government. The government viewed Patarkatsishvili's involvement in opposition activities as highly threatening. Such suspicions later seemed substantiated ahead of the 2008 presidential elections: Patarkatsishvili was, through a sting operation performed by Georgian secret services, caught on tape attempting to bribe a Ministry of Interior official to fabricate evidence of election fraud to justify a violent power takeover.[27]

The opposition started rallying in Tbilisi on November 2 to demand Saakashvili's resignation. Initially, at least 50,000 supporters gathered on Rustaveli Avenue outside Parliament, indicating the strength of public dissatisfaction. After five tense days, the demonstrations were broken up by riot police on November 7. A state of emergency was announced, lasting for ten days. The Imedi TV station, which had coordinated the opposition protests and provided their media outlet, was shut down on the grounds that it had encouraged attempts at unconstitutional change of government.[28]

The events of November 7 were a significant trauma in Georgian politics. They signaled the ultimate failure of political dialogue, radicalized the cleft between the country's political forces, and dramatically lowered public confidence in both the government and the overall political process.

The crackdown was a severe blow to Saakashvili's democratic credentials, which the government sought to remedy through announcing snap presidential elections and early parliamentary elections. Saakashvili won the presidential elections by 53 percent of the vote, according to the official tabulation, thus narrowly avoiding a runoff. While the elections were considered "consistent with most OSCE and Council of Europe standards" by international observers, several shortcomings were also noted.[29] The elections were characterized by a strong lack of trust between the political sides, as well as allegations on the opposition's part of intimidation of their activists and election fraud. Two large protest rallies were organized in Tbilisi in January to protest the election results, gathering over 200,000 protesters.[30] Ahead of the parliamentary elections on May 24, 2008, the electoral system was fiercely contested. The opposition argued that its entire design was aimed at maximizing the number of parliamentary seats for the ruling party through overrepresentation in electoral commissions and an increase in single mandate constituencies. The elections indeed led to a victory for the ruling party, which was able to use its name recognition and dominance in the outlying regions of the country to win almost all single-mandate constituencies. The opposition also performed poorly in both electoral campaigns, which helped the ruling party. For example, the opposition's main candidate in the presidential election campaigned chiefly on a promise to abolish the institution of the presidency. The elections were given a passing grade by international observers, who nevertheless pointed out several problems in Georgia's election system, among other issues.[31] After the elections, several opposition parties decided to boycott the parliament, leaving the newly formed Christian Democrats under former Imedi TV anchor Giorgi Targamadze and several minor parties represented in Parliament.

The events from 2006 onward can be termed as the end of the revolutionary era in Georgia. The gradual erosion of societal consensus over Georgia's reform process should be considered natural and expected. However, the circumstances under which these changes took place were most regrettable. These have provided for a strongly polarized and bitterly contested political climate in Georgia, with little trust or respect between the political factions. The domestic political contestation has reverberated in Georgia's international relations, affecting its prospects for achieving other important goals set out by the elite of the Rose Revolution. This relates especially to Georgia's integration with European and Transatlantic institutions.

The Revolution's International Dimension

Georgia's Western Vocation

The Rose Revolution and its aftermath had significant implications for Georgia's international standing and its relations with both Russia and the West. Georgia's orientation toward the West had begun long before the reformist opposition crowded Rustaveli Avenue in November 2003. Indeed, Shevardnadze at an early stage sought to build strong relations with the U.S. and EU, largely as an effect of his disillusionment with the nature of Russia's involvement in Abkhazia and South Ossetia. In relations with the West, he was able to capitalize on his credibility as USSR foreign minister during perestroika and his role in Germany's reunification. Shevardnadze thus secured an increasing flow of Western foreign aid and Western engagement with Georgia, not least through his promotion of the twin Baku-Tbilisi-Ceyhan (BTC) and South Caucasus pipeline projects, which secured a long-term strategic linkage between Georgia and the West.[32]

Nevertheless, Western hopes for Georgia's prospects of becoming a success story in the CIS in terms of reform and democratization gradually faded with the stagnation, corruption, and semi-authoritarianism during Shevardnadze's later years in power. Thus, the Rose Revolution was seen as a fresh start for the evolution of liberal democracies to Europe's east. It seemed to demonstrate that rapid political change was possible and that strong, Western-oriented governments were able to conduct fast and far reaching reform, even in the most troublesome of the post-Soviet states. As an effect, the Rose Revolution raised extremely high expectations in the new Georgian leadership. The new government was viewed as a partner with which it was possible to cooperate, as opposed to the previously corrupt government bodies. This resulted in a significant flow of development funding beginning to pour in, not only funding traditional development projects but directly aimed at assisting the building of state institutions, such as paying salaries for government officials.

The developments in Georgia also provided for strong Western optimism in the concept of "color revolutions," later replicated in Ukraine and to a much less successful extent in Kyrgyzstan. The events in Georgia were seen as evidence that support for reform-minded elites and strong civil societies could promote political change in a democratic and pro-Western direction. The U.S., in particular, invested heavily both politically and economically in Georgia's democratization and reform process. It also hailed Georgia's decision in 2004 to supply a large contingent to U.S. operations in Iraq. George W. Bush's visit in Tbilisi in May 2005 signified the reinforced strategic partnership between the two countries. Bush's declaration during the event that Georgia was a "beacon of democracy" was telling of the amount of U.S. political prestige invested in Georgia's democratization. To the new Georgian government, securing support in the West and reinforcing its ties with the U.S. and EU states were crucial in achieving its own goals, in terms of both reform and national security. Georgia's long declared ambitions to achieve membership in European and Transatlantic organizations—most importantly NATO and the EU—suddenly seemed realistic to Tbilisi, as the prospects for meeting the membership requirements of these organizations appeared within reach. The changes undertaken by the new government seemed to pay off rapidly as Georgia was granted an Individual Partnership Action Plan with NATO, and included in the EU's European Neighborhood Policy in 2004.

The strong connection between Georgia's reform process and its linkages with Western institutions is strongly pronounced in Georgia's National Security Concept, adopted in the summer of 2005:

> Georgia views NATO as an organization of collective defense that is the central mechanism for providing security and stability in the Euro-Atlantic area. Georgia's cooperation with NATO contributes to strengthening of democratic values in the country, accomplishment of democratic reforms, especially in the field of defense, as well as establishment of a secure and stable environment. Membership of NATO would not only endow Georgia with an unprecedented degree of military and political security, but would allow it to contribute to strengthening the security of Europe, particularly the Black Sea region. Georgia has already proved its readiness to share the responsibility of the collective security by sending its troops to Kosovo and Afghanistan.[33]

In relation to the EU, the concept reads:

> Georgia views the EU as a community of nations that ensures the peace and prosperity in Europe. Georgia's cooperation with EU contributes to the implementation of democratic reforms and to strengthening the market economy and security of the country. Values and objectives shared by the EU

are common to Georgia, which considers EU membership an important
guarantee for its economic and political development. Georgia's accession
to the EU will strengthen Europe by restoring the Black Sea region as a European trade and stability zone.[34]

It thus became crucial for Tbilisi to market the Rose Revolution in
Western capitals as a complete break with the past. It sought to retain the
image of a radically progressive government, ruthlessly doing away with
all previous aspects of state failure and framed Georgia's future within the
larger context of European security. The Georgian government made sure
to display EU flags next to Georgian ones on all possible occasions, in an
effort to underline Georgia's European identity. It also set extremely optimistic timeframes for reaching the membership requirements of both
NATO and the EU.

Under Saakashvili, Georgia has also sought to detach itself somewhat
from its regional belonging to the "South Caucasus" which—much like the
Balkans—suffers from negative connotations of conflict and authoritarianism. Instead, Saakashvili became active in underlining Georgia's belonging
to the Black Sea Region, parts of which are already included in the EU.
Georgia also reinforced its participation in regional cooperation frame-
works such as GUAM and Black Sea Economic Cooperation (BSEC); and
strengthened its relationship to Ukraine (for example in the establishment
of the short-lived Community of Democratic Choice), as well as with new
EU member states along what is envisioned as an axis between the Baltic
and Black Seas.[35]

The Georgian government thus built a strong connection between its
own state-building and democratization processes and its national security.
The support it sought to secure from the West and its prospects for membership in the Western security community were largely conditioned on
progressive domestic reform. Developments from 2007 onward have made
this connection increasingly obvious. Especially the government's crackdown on protesters in November 2007 and the growing allegations of less
than democratic practices on the government's part caused many Western
politicians to question whether the Rose Revolution had really brought
about the profound changes it promised. Was the substantial Western engagement with the country still motivated if Georgia deviated from its
democratic path? The dangers associated with the loss of credibility Georgia suffered in connection with these events underlined the strong connections between democratic development and security in Georgia's case.
Georgia's primary asset in its relations with the West, apart from being a
transit country for Caspian oil and gas as well as for troops to Iraq and

Afghanistan, was its image as a rapidly democratizing country in Europe's Eastern Neighborhood and the prospect of a success story of Western engagement in this region.

Russian Reactions

Russia proved less positive toward the developments in its backyard. While Georgia's relationship with Georgia had grown sour during Shevardnadze's time in office, the weakness of Georgia's statehood had never provided for any substantial progress either in conducting reform or in challenging Russia's political leverage over Georgia.

As a new government took office in Tbilisi, Russia initially sought to take an accommodating stance, hoping it would be able to establish a more cooperative relationship with Saakashvili's government than with Shevardnadze's. Russian mediation in convincing Abashidze, its key ally in Georgia, to leave Adjara without a fight is a case in point. However, it soon became obvious that Georgia under Saakashvili would embark on a much more decisive course toward the West than had ever been the case under Shevardnadze. As Georgia actively started undermining Russia's control over Georgia's breakaway regions, and Saakashvili employed harsh and uncompromising rhetoric condemning Russia's role in these, the relationship between the two states deteriorated rapidly.

In January 2006 a gas pipeline and an electricity line supplying Georgia were blown up on the Russian side of the border. Russia introduced a trade embargo on Georgia in the spring. In September 2006, six Russian citizens were expelled from Georgia on espionage charges, followed by the introduction of a complete Russian embargo on Georgia and the deportation of ethnic Georgians living in Russia. In 2007 Russia on two occasions bombed Georgian territory. Russian army helicopters shelled official buildings in the Kodori Gorge in March, and on August 6 a missile was dropped on Georgian territory close to South Ossetia.

Georgia's Western course and especially its prospects for integration into NATO were utterly incompatible with Russian designs for the region. Russia viewed these ambitions on the Georgian government's part as directly contradicting Russian interests, aimed at exercising an exclusive influence over the South Caucasus. Hence, Russia by all means available sought to apply pressure on the Saakashvili government to moderate its course. Levers applied have ranged from ones related to energy and trade, to exploiting its dominance over Georgia's separatist regions. As these had few effects, Russia resorted to military force through bombing Georgian territory, downing Georgian reconnaissance drones over Abkhazia, and ultimately through war in August 2008. From Moscow's perspective, the Rose Revolution did not constitute an expression of public discontent with a failing government. Rather, the events of November 2003 in Georgia were seen as a political shift orchestrated by the U.S. In this understanding, the U.S. simply replaced a CIS government that had fallen out of favor with Washington with a new one that would be more decisively under U.S. control, allowing for the enlargement of NATO into what Russia considered its "near abroad." These fears were further fuelled by the events in the fall of 2004 in Ukraine, leading on the part of Russia to the perception of "color revolutions" in the CIS as a coordinated U.S. bid to counteract Russia's effort to re-establish a sphere of influence over the former Soviet space.

After all, USAID had provided considerable financial support for the development of Georgia's party system and civil society, while American NGOs such as the National Democratic Institute had supported exit polls in the November elections. Not least, George Soros's Open Society Institute had supported Khmara and its contacts with Otpor. Russia understood these facts as evidence that the political shift in Georgia had been designed by the U.S. and that the changes brought about contradicted Russian interests.[36]

Conclusion

This chapter has sought to outline the changes the Rose Revolution brought to Georgian politics. The political shift provided by the Rose Revolution paved the way for the most rapid and profound set of reforms ever conducted in the CIS, comparable only to the reforms undertaken in the Baltic States a decade earlier. Reforms included the introduction of a very thorough package for getting Georgia's economy back on its feet and a ruthless campaign against corruption in public institutions. Georgia embarked on a determined struggle to re-establish its territorial integrity and to gain a place within European and Transatlantic institutions. The Saakashvili government's focus on building a strong Georgian state nevertheless put vital aspects of the democratization process on the back burner. This proved problematic, as it alienated significant proportions of the electorate and the political elite from developments in the country.

The strengthening of the Georgian state, in terms of both its mode of governance and its economy, provided Georgia with the means to tackle the most significant challenge of the post-revolutionary government—the reintegration of the separatist territories of Abkhazia and South Ossetia. The Georgian change of tactics toward the unresolved conflicts—for better or worse—is largely attributable to the abilities provided by the Rose Revolution. While the revolution did not signify any major shift in Tbilisi's objectives in relation to the conflicts, it made an enormous difference in the government's ability to act on these objectives. The Saakashvili government has been able to follow a comprehensive strategy for altering the status quo by different means, both on the ground and in the international setting.

The same ability for action complicated Georgia's international relations, and especially its relationship to Russia. Russia's gradually increased pressure on Georgia to fall back in line just made the Saakashvili government's attempts to undermine Russia's influence in the country more systematic, especially regarding Russia's control over Abkhazia and South Ossetia. The same Russian assertiveness only made Georgia more determined in its efforts to withdraw from Russia's orbit through closer integration with Western security structures. These dynamics fuelled the conflict between the two countries, which intensified rapidly after 2004. Russian foreign policy has been and remains a permanent challenge to Georgia as a reforming, as well as a sovereign, state.

In this regard, the promises and achievements brought by the Rose Revolution have increasingly become linked to Georgia's national security. Georgian strategy is in this regard closely tied to Western support for Georgian interests. This support is in turn linked to Georgia's ability to continue delivering on reform and democratization. Today, Georgia's chief challenges still revolve around these interconnected issues: maintaining international credibility and securing continued Western support in terms of both development and security, while safeguarding and advancing the achievements made after the Rose Revolution. The latter entails delivering on the promises of democratization, seeking reconciliation in Georgian politics, and providing for a truly pluralistic political system.

6

From Neglect to Duress:
The West and the Georgian Crisis
Before the 2008 War

Stephen Blank

The Russia-Georgia war of 2008 that ended in Georgia's defeat and territorial amputation was also a resounding strategic defeat for the West. The U.S. government, NATO, and the EU proved utterly powerless to do anything constructive on behalf of Georgia even though the war was clearly an act of provocation and ultimately aggression by Russia.[1] The consequences of that strategic failure are with us still. Indeed, Moscow still violates with impunity the accords on Georgia that it signed with the EU.[2] Thus Western policy towards Georgia and the Caucasus now exists under strategic constraints or duress imposed by Moscow. This is the logical consequence of more than a decade of Western neglect of the Caucasus and its frozen conflicts in general and of the Georgian conflict in particular.

Worse yet, it is clear that Europe still has not learned what is at stake when it attempts to opt out of international security challenges, whether in Afghanistan or in connection with Turkey's EU candidacy.[3] As Colin Gray has recently written:

> What is so dangerous about U.S.-Russian relations is that they have an explicitly continental military focus along, indeed across, a strategic frontier between NATO and Russia that is very much in live contention. Russia's spat with Georgia in September [actually August] 2008 needs to be regarded as a reliable sign of severe dangers to come.[4]

Sergey Markedonov, one of Russia's most insightful analysts of the Caucasus, observes that Russia, now operating in an internationalized negotiating format in Geneva, hopes to obtain a ratification of the new status quo that it created by force, but warned that:

At the same time, it is still hard to grasp that the two conflicts in question are not simply a matter of rivalry of ambitions and interests, but also an objective process. It is a question of the formation of nation-states after the destruction of imperial formations and the victory of the nationalist discourse. The breakup of the Soviet Union was not the end point in this process, it was a beginning. Such processes, by definition, are not completed quickly. A conflict of "imagined geographies," different mentalities, is in progress. And not only the conflict but the actual formation of political and even ethnic identities is not yet finished.[5]

Other observers similarly warn that the so called frozen conflicts along the peripheries of the former Soviet Union are now unfreezing and could incite further ethno-political conflicts there, if not elsewhere.[6]

Taken in their totality the consequences of this war are therefore of immense geopolitical and geo-economic significance. As a German study of the war's consequences concludes:

The escalation of the local conflict in South Ossetia into a European crisis has shown that the existing structures—NATO, EU, OSCE and CIS—are plainly unable to prevent conflict between hostile countries. Russia's elites, wanting to see their country regain its former role as a great power, ignore the normative framework the OSCE tries to establish, and disregard the CIS. Plainly neither organization is strong enough to structure a region extending from Europe through to Central Asia. NATO and the EU, on the other hand, are perceived as a threat by the Russian leadership, which makes them in their present form unsuited for integrating an expanded Europe. So the crisis has thrown up the medium-term task of redesigning the European order—to include Russia.[7]

Europe continues to believe that it can abstain from committing tangible resources to international security crises, and often seems to act as if it does not affect it. This can only lead to another major crisis, at which time it will learn what Russia and the U.S. know far too well, namely, that as Donald Kagan has written, "Peace does not preserve itself." At the same time, this neglect is astonishing for as early as 1995 it was clear that "Europe will never be entirely secure if the Caucasus is left out of Europe's security purview" and that the Caucasus was therefore fully part of Europe's security agenda.[8] Moreover, as discussed below, the geopolitical benefits to Europe from the post-Soviet status quo in the Caucasus were equally clear to observers. Without analyzing the history of missed opportunities and neglect it is impossible to come to terms with the more recent failures and present constraints.

Geostrategic Considerations for Europe and the U.S.

The timorousness and outright neglect which the international community showed towards the conflicts in South Ossetia and Abkhazia for a decade is all the more distressing in view of the fact that the consequences of failing to work more actively for a peace settlement were long recognized and clear to all. Writing in 1996, Dmitry Trenin observed that:

> Two years after the end of hostilities, the peace process has not yet begun and South Ossetia remains effectively outside Tbilisi's control. This decoupling of the military operation from the political peace process carries with it the real danger that the conflict in South Ossetia may reignite.[9]

By 2004 rumors of war abounded on both sides and intensified thereafter since both Georgia and Russia entertained the possibility of a forceful solution to their problems in Abkhazia and South Ossetia. Consequently crises multiplied and became deeper and longer in duration. The situation that emerged out of the Abkhaz and South Ossetian insurgencies of 1991–93 was initially frozen by the presence of Russian "peacekeepers." New factors like the importance of energy pipelines, the possibility of Georgian membership in NATO, and a general deterioration of East-West relations made a settlement more difficult to achieve, even as they made it all the more urgent. As Bruno Coppieters wrote:

> The issues of the oil wealth in the Caspian Sea and the routing of pipelines have dual consequences. On the one hand, they make the pacification of this region by international agreements more imperative, while at the same time, they increase destabilization by generating fierce international competition among those attempting to gain a foothold there.[10]

The Clinton administration's efforts to organize an international consensus for a Baku-Tbilisi-Ceyhan pipeline through Georgia to Turkey and thence to Europe should have been accompanied by an effort to mediate the conflicts around Georgia, but no such initiative took place. The consequences of this inaction for Georgia, Russia, and European security as a whole were becoming ever more visible to observers. In 2006 Lithuanian President Valdas Adamkus publicly stated that:

> 'Frozen' conflicts are obvious threats, which raise fear and impede economic development in entire regions. It is necessary to find fast and peaceful solutions to those conflicts, because the union of law and democracy cannot exist with conflicts and isolation. ... It is hard to imagine that democracy

would be established in regions where there is no cooperation of institutions or if they lack the essence of cooperation. The engine behind European and transatlantic cooperation should be cooperation, not competition.[11]

Simultaneously President Viktor Yushchenko of Ukraine noted that the so-called frozen conflicts along the Black Sea represented a major threat to stability, security, and democracy in a region where the spectrum of security challenges had grown.[12] Despite all this evidence of the costs of inaction, no Western state or security organization ever mounted an initiative to bring the parties to a serious negotiation and move the problem towards a solution, even one imposed from without by political means.

By 2004 it was clear that it was no longer possible (if it ever had been) to effectuate a solution without Russia, a condition that, given Georgia's central position as a bone of contention between East and West, required a focused dialogue with Russia, however difficult that may be.[13] Back then it would probably have been easier to reach a negotiated international settlement, since Russia's position was weaker than that of the West. Moreover, it was clear that the freezing of these conflicts was inimical to European objectives, and that the Russian forces which accomplished this were in violation of the Treaty on Conventional Forces in Europe (CFE) and the OSCE Istanbul Commitments of 1999. But once again, the will to act as an alliance was absent.[14]

Another factor contributing to the decline in the West's will or ability to transform the overall situation in the Caucasus or the particular one in Georgia was its neglect of Turkey, which consequently drifted toward a pro-Russian and anti-Western position. This problem was largely the result of Turkey's stalled application to the EU, the rise of the AKP party in Ankara, and the war in Iraq that eroded Turco-American relations. All these reduced Turkey's interest in playing a major pro-Western role in the Caucasus as a check to Russia. Instead, in important respects, Turkey grew closer to Moscow than it is to Brussels or Washington.[15] Analysts warned that if Turkey and the West failed to work together they would lose the ability to influence events in the Caucasus.[16] But such warnings went unheeded.

Developments in Russia were also ignored. The failure of democratization there had important implications for regional and international security. Also, Russia's initial activities in Georgia in 1992–94, where Moscow either ran guns to the Abkhazians or unilaterally imposed its forces as so called "peacekeepers" in the conflicts between Georgia and its rebellious provinces and forced Georgia to accept that verdict, revealed that during this period Russian armed forces were not fully under control and that the consequences of their operations in the Caucasus were unpredictable and dangerous. Every analysis of Russian policy at the time concluded that the main driver was the military, which acted largely on its own. Russian officers were motivated by their hatred for President Eduard Shevardnadze of Georgia (because they attributed to him the breakup, if not handover, of the Soviet empire), a longing to regain their Soviet era vacation homes in Abkhazia, and a desire to carve out an independent sphere for themselves in the making of Russian defense policy.[17] Yeltsin's failure to rein in the Russian military not only attested to the weakness of the Russian state at the time, but it showed that by 1993 key elements in Moscow welcomed efforts to establish some form of a Russian sphere of influence in the Caucasus. Boris Yeltsin himself made this point in a speech to the UN in 1993, when he formally demanded a sphere of influence in the CIS as a whole.[18]

Beyond exposing neo-imperial cravings, these episodes showed that the undemocratic nature of the relationship between the state and the unreformed defense establishment enabled the latter, along with complicit politicians, to engage in military adventurism without the likelihood of control by the political processes.[19] Not only does such a situation thwart the establishment of democracy in Russia—a principal security goal of the West—but it hinders the stabilization of the post-Soviet world. When these same Russian neo-imperial cravings were indulged in 2008, the other side produced no effective riposte, in spite of ample warnings. Back in 1997 Abram and Antonia Chayes wrote that:

> Russian meddling is not the only or even the main cause of ethnic and internal conflict in the former Soviet Union (FSU), and so Russian disengagement will not end it. [But] if there is no alternative method of resolving or at least containing these sources of instability on the Russian periphery, Russia will be inevitably drawn into it and ...the situation will slide toward Russian hegemony with all the negative consequences for both internal and external Russian politics.[20]

Such Russian meddling imperiled the development of more open political institutions in Russia and undermined hopes for reform of the defense establishment. It also rekindled the notion that Russia had an inborn right to such a sphere of influence. Indeed, the demand to divide Eurasia into spheres of influence, and the unrestrained right in the Caucasus to engage in "peacekeeping" or "peace support operations," to use U.S. parlance, eventually became bulwarks of Russia's formal policy. Russia, in short, seeks to freeze the process of European integration and replace it with a regional bipolarity. Reflecting this, when in 1999 Russia submitted its official strategy regarding the basis of discussions with the EU, then Prime Minister Vladimir Putin stated that:

> As a world power situated on two continents, Russia should retain its free-dom to determine and implement its foreign and domestic policies, its sta-tus and advantages of a Euro-Asian state and largest country of the CIS. The "development of partnership with the EU should contribute to consoli-dating Russia's role as the leading power in shaping a new system of inter-state political and economic relations in the CIS area" and thus, Russia would "oppose any attempts to hamper economic integration in the CIS (that may be made by the EU), including through 'special relations' with individual CIS member states to the detriment of Russia's interests."[21]

More recently, in December 2006 the then Defense Minister and now Deputy Prime Minister Sergey Ivanov advocated delimiting Eurasia be-tween NATO and the Russian-sponsored Collective Security Treaty Organ-ization (CSTO). At the December 1, 2006, meeting of the CIS and Baltic States Media Forum, Ivanov argued that:

> The next logical step on the path of reinforcing international security may be to develop a cooperation mechanism between NATO and the CSTO, fol-lowed by a clear division of spheres of responsibility. This approach offers the prospect of enabling us to possess a sufficiently reliable and effective leverage for taking joint action in crisis situations in various regions of the world.[22]

Beyond the danger which regional military operations pose to Russian democracy and foreign policy, they also impeded the rise of truly demo-cratic politics in Georgia. Indeed, even now, as is painfully clear from its current domestic crises, one cannot really call Georgia a stable democratic state that merits inclusion in NATO, let alone the EU.[23] This traces directly to Russia's military actions and the need to respond to them.

Russian pressure directed against former Soviet republics constitutes the latter's greatest security threat, which is widely recognized but publicly unacknowledged. The salience of such threats fosters the creation of milita-rized and centralized states and retards the evolution of democratic institu-tions. Georgia's trajectory confirms this reality.[24] While NATO is not con-ceived as a direct causal mechanism for democratization and/or democratic survival, ties to NATO tend to reduce external threats. States that make common cause with NATO are more likely to settle border disputes with other states vying for NATO membership, rather than allow them to des-cend into conflict. There is a greater expectation that NATO will honor and protect these states' independence and sovereignty. Thus, affiliation with NATO enhances chances for democratization by mitigating border disputes and external threats and can begin as soon as NATO demonstrates credible commitments to these states' survival.

The experience of the Baltic States exemplifies this process. Georgia and Ukraine, on the other hand, indicate what happens when the connection to NATO is either short-circuited or never gets off the ground.[25] And states in Central Asia that aligned with Russia to begin with and effectively excluded NATO, now must suffer the continual presence of Russian troops and of Russian political and economic influence in their policymaking.[26] Prominent Western analysts readily conceded the point that Georgia mattered by virtue of its location along key energy and strategic corridors and because of its visible aspirations towards democracy and Westernization.[27] Considered from the standpoint of energy:

> The South Caucasus forms the hub of an evolving geostrategic and geoeconomic system that stretches from NATO Europe to Central Asia and Afghanistan. It provides unique transit corridors for Caspian energy supplies and Central Asian commodities to the Euro-Atlantic community, as well as a direct access for allied forces to bases and operational theaters in the Greater Middle East and Central Asia. Thus the Black Sea and Caspian basins, with the South Caucasus uniting them, comprise a functional aggregate, now linked directly to the enlarged Euro-Atlantic alliance. Although located on the Euro-Atlantic world's outer edge, this region has already begun functioning as a rear area or staging ground in terms of projecting Western power and values along with security into Central Asia and the Greater Middle East. This function is likely to increase in significance as part of U.S. and NATO strategic initiatives. For all of the above reasons, security threats to the South Caucasus countries and the undermining of their sovereignty run counter to major Euro-Atlantic interests.[28]

Yet their governments plainly failed to act on these insights to their full extent. This was true even though the instruments for conflict resolution and greater Georgian integration with Europe were available to them. From the viewpoint of defense, former NATO Secretary-General Lord George Robertson observed that the Partnership for Peace is a "gold-dust asset" of NATO which must be utilized to bring Ukraine, the Caucasus, Central Asia, and the Mediterranean countries closer to the NATO coalition of common values and interests.[29]

The European Union

The European Union has been seeking a growing role on the international scene, and its presence in the Caucasus has grown in the past several years. It is, together with the United States, a major Western force in the region. As Victor Bojkoy observes:

> "Europeanization", understood as the conceptual framework linking transition and integration, is the practical embodiment of the drive to preserve and expand the [European] Union's international society in its geographical proximity. Its specific meaning materializes in a process of systemic transformation and structural accommodation based on a set of special requirements for full EU membership. The EU thus functions as a reference model for European states undergoing a transition towards law-governed, market-oriented, liberal democratic political and economic systems. The process leaves no space for the ways politics had been conducted and the economy and society managed during periods of authoritarian governance, which explains the number of references to a "return to the liberal family of Europe from which we were forcefully kept apart for more than 40 years" on the part of many of the Post-Communist East European leaders. Obviously, on the ideational level voluntary association with the international society of the Union necessarily implies dissociation from the previous integration models that are incompatible with it.[30]

Despite these supposedly strong geopolitical imperatives and the purportedly ambitious thrust of the EU's European Security Strategy of 2003,

> The EU played a rather marginal role as a political player during the 1990s. Although the EU provided technical assistance and aid to a noteworthy degree, the region had always been distant enough, geographically speaking, so that threats emerging from there were not perceived as immediate. Therefore European activities focused on *economic* transition-political dialogue remained more rhetoric than reality.[31]

Neither has the EU to date devised a viable strategy to counter Russian efforts to dominate European energy supplies. Its decision to become involved in reforming Ukraine's gas system represents at best a partial exception. In other words, the EU's initiatives to date in regard to the former Soviet Union as a whole are a case of too little too late. Georgia is not the exception here but the rule. As Pamela Jawad observed:

> The EU policies towards post-Soviet transformation countries have been nothing more than "exploitative, reactionary, and evolutionary steps" dur-

ing the 1990s. The EU has been reluctant to take an active political role in Russia's periphery due to special relations with Moscow at the (Member States') national level. The EU has been slow in differentiating the former Soviet Union—early instruments of assistance, such as TACIS, were aimed at the whole CIS area. The EU has clearly lacked a strategy towards the region "if by strategy we mean a coherent relationship between ends and means, there is no EU strategy in the Caucasus" and has rather been led by events.[32]

Not surprisingly, this EU failure has led to bitter disappointment in Georgia which, under President Saakashvili, consistently overestimated Europe's will and capability to stand up to Moscow and failed to grasp the full implications of Europe's actual lack of resolve and capacity.[33]

Worse yet, since the 2008 war the EU's ineptitude has continued, as it allowed Russia to break with impunity the terms of the truce which the EU itself had proudly negotiated with Moscow. It will be recalled that President Sarkozy of France seized the EU's lead role in these negotiations, despite warnings by President George W. Bush not to do so; Sarkozy later criticized Bush for not having been more active. Yet when Russia broke the cease-fire agreement, both Sarkozy and the EU sat passively. At a Washington meeting of the Council on Foreign Relations in November 2008, President Medvedev heaped ridicule on what Sarkozy and the EU had so laboriously fashioned.[34] Having failed to exact a price for the invasion of Georgia and with the palpably false rationale that Russia had "largely implemented" its cease-fire commitments,[35] the EU crawled back to Moscow for further negotiations. John Bolton, the U.S.'s former ambassador to the UN, noted:

> The European Union took the lead in diplomacy, with results approaching Neville Chamberlain's moment in the spotlight at Munich; a cease-fire that failed to mention Georgia's territorial integrity, and that all but gave Russia permission to continue its military operations as a "peacekeeping" force anywhere in Georgia. More troubling, over the long term was that the EU saw its task as being mediator—its favorite role in the world—between Georgia and Russia, rather than an advocate for the victim of aggression.[36]

Here it should also be noted that Russia never had any illusions about the EU's "active penetration" into the CIS, which it derided as a "virtual concept."[37] Likewise Moscow, thanks to its membership in the OSCE and the UN Security Council, used every opportunity to prevent these organizations from expanding their interest or activities in the region and from internationalizing the peacekeeping operations that Russia dominated, which was Georgia's understandable aim.[38] By successfully blocking OSCE and UN action, Moscow also knocked out the EU, the only other agency that could mediate the problem. The EU's appointment of a Special Representative for South Caucasus (EUSR) has so far failed to bring the EU a role in the conflict resolution process.

Brussels had decided not to get directly involved in the negotiation processes of the "frozen" conflicts in the South Caucasus region, and instead to leave these tasks to the UN mission and the OSCE.[39] This has been referred to as the "checkbook effect": the EU offers fast and consequential support, but only when the partner country is "ready," i.e., when a peace agreement has been reached.[40] This archetypal example of circular reasoning ensured that there would be no negotiations and that Russia would continue to dominate the situation as it became ever more explosive. As Pierre Jolicoeur bluntly put it, "Generally speaking, the EU is virtually absent from the peace processes."[41]

As long ago as 1998, Bruno Coppieters observed that the EU sees Georgia as a peripheral state to Europe or as part of the larger Caucasus bridge between Europe and Central Asia. Although that perspective has been somewhat modified over the last decade, it still holds largely true for the period leading up to the war. Thus,

> The European Union does not regard Georgia as belonging to Europe, but rather as part of a region bridging Europe and Asia. The European Union pursues neither specific Georgian policies nor a policy which acknowledges Georgia's image of itself as a European nation, but defends specific European economic interests and general ('universal') Western values throughout the Transcaucasus region. In this respect, its approach in the region is basically no different from that of the U.S. when it supports specific economic interests and universal Western values. The whole problem of a European identity, which has been so decisive both for the process of European integration before the fall of the Berlin Wall and for Georgia's policies of independence, is absent from the European Union's strategic approach to Georgia. Western European policies on Georgia can best be described as an attitude of benevolent indifference.[42]

The problem with this approach is that the revolutions of 1989–91 and the ensuing reorganization of the European status quo had as one of their underlying foundations the idea that European security was indivisible. To the extent that the EU or other security organizations erode that understanding in word or deed, new security vacuums are created, Russia will be tempted to undertake further adventures, and the door to renewed violence is reopened. The "benign" neglect of an entire region is in essence malign and gives rise to negative consequences for all, and especially the "neg-lected" states. Pamela Jawad's study of the EU in Georgia cited above makes this clear.[43]

Despite her frank recognition that Brussels has failed to live up to its promise, and in spite of asserting the importance of the EU's interests in Georgia, Jawad argues there was no chance of a genuine negotiation lead-ing to success because the conflicts were already frozen and would not change unless they escalated into hot wars. Therefore efforts to "unfreeze" them would be the wrong strategy. In any case, even though Europe was the largest donor to reconstruction efforts, other actors by 2006 were much more deeply directly involved in the issue, so that an EU intervention would have brought no value added. At any rate, it had more pressing is-sues on its agenda.[44]

Thus both Pamela Jawad and Dov Lynch, who authored another pene-trating study on "Why Georgia Matters" to the EU, concluded that EU ac-tivities in Georgia should be focused on infrastructural projects, economic reconstruction, and good governance. This would build a stronger Georgian state and enable the government to concentrate on humanitarian assistance and economic reconstruction rather than on the poisoned pawns of South Ossetia and Abkhazia.[45] Yet these gestures, however positive they may be, do not comport with the spirit or ambition of the EU's own Security Strate-gy of 2003.[46] Jawad in the end was voicing arguments prevalent in Brussels and other Western capitals. The problem is that they add up to an abdica-tion of responsibility. As such, they recall the Europe's passivity during the wars in former Yugoslavia in the 1990s, and, worse, the 1930s.

The EU's policy of keeping at arm's length post-Soviet states that wish to integrate with Europe generates as many tensions as it seeks to alleviate, and especially between the former and Russia and between Russia and the EU. As Arkady Moshes has written:

> Brussels cannot ignore a consolidated push of EU new member states to be more active on the eastern periphery. As long as it denies membership perspective for its neighbors, the policy of Wider Europe that it pursues, (however palliative it may look) nevertheless stimulates their search for al-ternatives to staying within the same geopolitical and geo-economic space as Russia. Moscow, in this situation, starts viewing the EU not so much as a partner, but rather as a systematic rival to its foreign policy goals in the Western NIS and the Caucasus; a revisionist power, it is instinctively in-clined to get involved in a "zero-sum game" type of relationship with the EU.[47]

Since Moscow's foreign policy derives in large measure from the nature of its political system, it rejects any concept of security in the Black Sea littoral or CIS other than one based on its exclusive domination of the CIS. After the 2008 war certain EU analysts drew the conclusion that there can be no security in the region against Russian wishes. This is precisely the wrong lesson for the EU.[48] It has long been apparent that conditionality of membership is the most powerful card in its deck.[49] Instead of exercising this in the Black Sea region, it has approached states there with a policy of half measures and hesitations that, in regard to the question of Russia, is bereft of strategic logic. This hesitation had led, by 2008, to spikes in energy prices, a gas war, division within Europe, the corruption of European political processes, and an overall retrocession from the hopes of 2004–5.

Joanna Kaminska writes that:

> The lack of strong response from the EU has proven to the Russian elites that any attempt at destabilizing the post-Soviet states will not meet any operationalized response from the EU side. Any kind of strong and assertive behaviors was left to the U.S. and NATO, showing the EU's impotence, or lack of will to react in such crisis situations. The lack of any kind of sanctions, or measures that might touch Russia or its elites, might encourage Russia to try to expand its presence again in Ukraine or any other former Soviet space members after the period of appeasement in Russian foreign policy.[50]

She concludes that the EU's lack of hard power limits its ability to be an actor in the Black Sea littoral and the CIS more generally, even as Russia's soft power deficit limits its capabilities. Worse yet, the EU appears to be unwilling to use its soft power to overcome its energy problems with Russia and strengthen Turkey's energy independence, as well as that of Georgia, Ukraine, and Azerbaijan. It remains utterly divided over the planning and finance of the Nabucco gas pipeline—the core project for ensuring its energy security against Russia.[51] As a result, Europe could be left to the tender mercies of Gazprom.[52]

Short of trying to redraw the map of influence in the Caucasus, the EU ignores Russia as an actor in the region, and refuses to devise a coherent response to Russian policy.[53] Russia, however, is determinedly active. Many authors have noted how robust and single-minded are its efforts to use its assets, mainly energy, to redraw the political map of Europe. This drive has attracted little attention and no real resistance from Europe.[54] Thus, for the Black Sea littoral we will have to rethink our basic concepts of security in today's world.[55] No longer can the West indulge in the kind of fatuous complacency and self satisfaction that the EU has demonstrated in Georgia, an approach which some observers have called "smug" and "wishy washy."[56]

Can anyone who seriously contemplates the consequences of the Russia–Georgia war truly accept the bizarre notion that, "All conflicts, however violent, however painful and costly in human lives and resources, are peripheral conflicts, fought on the margins of the international system."[57] Yet this is exactly how Alvaro Vasconcelos, the head of the EU's Institute for Security Studies, characterized the war's outcome. Doubtless, such thinking did not spring full-blown from Vasconcelos's mind on August 8, 2008.

The United States

The EU's abdication of its mandate and interests left the field open to the U.S., which Lynch characterizes as a revisionist power regarding Georgia, i.e., one that actively sought to prevent Georgia from failing by helping train its troops, mitigating tensions with Moscow, and advancing the democratizing trends of the Rose Revolution.[58] But the U.S. policy of supporting and strengthening Georgia and publicly attempting to expand the OSCE mandate for South Ossetia in conformity with Georgia's ambition to internationalize the peacekeeping regime there, also failed in every dimension. It was unable to offer coherent resistance to Russia's mounting pressure on Georgia, which culminated in the aggression of August 2008.[59] Washington supported Tbilisi to the extent of reversing itself early in 2008 to champion Georgia's aspiration for a NATO Membership Action Plan (MAP). This convinced Russia of the need to browbeat Georgia back into line and, failing that, attack it by force. Indeed, U.S. policy may have contributed to Georgia's misplaced belief that it would not be left in the lurch if it precipitated or was otherwise plunged into a crisis.

Moscow has repeatedly criticized Washington, Kiev, and others for supporting the Georgian attack on Tskhinvali on August 8, though it is safe to say that this is less intended to reveal the "truth" as it is to discredit those states in the eyes of Russia's domestic audience and foreign capitals. These verbal attacks are clearly part of the fundamental anti-Americanism that is now a permanent feature of Russian policy. As the Russian journalist Leonid Radzikhovsky has said, "The existential void of our politics has been filled entirely by anti-Americanism" and that to renounce this rhetoric "would be tantamount to destroying the foundations of the state ideology."[60] Indeed, it is quite inconceivable that, given U.S. policy, any respon-

sible policymaker in the Bush administration would have encouraged Tbilisi to believe that it could engage in such military activity and expect no
Russian reaction, or to succeed in so doing with impunity. Indeed, former
Secretary of State Condoleezza Rice recently stated that she had gone to
Tbilisi in July 2008 to explore the possibility of inducing Georgia to sign a
non-use of force pledge.[61] Furthermore, she added that the outbreak of hostilities did not surprise the U.S. government. Specifically, she said that, "I
wouldn't say it took us by surprise. The exact timing and exactly what
happened, of course, but the fact is that had been a really volatile region for
some time."[62]

That policy failure is wholly attributable to the numerous defects of U.S.
Georgia policy about which Rice, not surprisingly, was silent. Lincoln Mitchell and Alexander Cooley in a recent study point out the flaws in Washington's approach to Georgia, observing that "the United States supported
the Saakashvili government, rather than promoting broader Georgian democratic development," and that the "strong personalized ties that developed
between Washington and Tbilisi prevented the United States from using its
power and influence to credibly restrain the Saakashvili government."
Consequently, they argue, this "further emboldened Georgian hardliners."[63]
Thus the personalization of relationships between President Saakashvili
and President Bush, other Washington officials, and members of Congress
(including now Vice-President Biden) clouded U.S. policymaking. Georgia's adroit public relations campaign successfully argued that the core
problem in the region is that democratic Georgia is constantly menaced by
authoritarian Russia, and therefore deserves unconditional U.S. support and
aid. There is no doubt that Russia menaces Georgia, whose people over-
whelmingly want to join the West and integrate into Euro-Atlantic institutions, but the development of a strong political opposition in Georgia
against the bolstered constitutional powers that Saakashvili claimed after
the Rose Revolution and against the continued democratic deficits in the
country (not least in the media and the judiciary), suggests that Georgian
democracy is a work in progress, while it was portrayed as a beacon in the
region. Yet the Bush administration's lack of criticism of Georgia's devia-
tions from democratization may have led Saakashvili to overestimate
Washington's support for him.[64]

U.S. support for Georgia was not considered problematic, because official Washington did not expect Moscow to launch a war. True, threatening
actions by Moscow after April 16, 2008, were ominous: Russia opened
consular relations with Abkhazia and South Ossetia; prepositioned logistics
in Abkhazia; and built a railroad there to connect it to its own military and

logistic bases. All these measures pointed to the real threat of war, but Washington did not expect Moscow to take the final step. The escalation in Abkhazia almost led to the outbreak of war in May, but Saakashvili refused to be provoked, causing Moscow to reorient its plans to South Ossetia. Here a Russian-originated chain of escalating maneuvers and provocations ultimately did lead to war.

Saakashvili's regime has shown itself prone to provocative behavior— suffice it to recall Irakli Okruashvili's tenure as Minister of Defense—and there were also figures in the leadership who truly believed Russia would not act as it did.[65] Moreover, conversations with both Georgian officials and U.S. experts indicate that some among the Georgian leadership were convinced that they could somehow persuade South Ossetia and Abkhazia to rejoin the Georgian state under the most generous terms of autonomy, despite the fact that the elites and most people in both provinces—and especially Abkhazia—were resolutely against it.[66]

The truth is more complicated. Saakashvili's regime undoubtedly suffers from democracy deficits and was prone to behavior that needlessly provoked Moscow. But throughout this time, Washington advanced no plan to resolve the stalemates in the disputed provinces, did not publicly warn Moscow about the consequences, and was unable to organize a coherent Western response to Russian pressures, all failures that Moscow exploited to the hilt.

To be fair, the Bush administration repeatedly told the Georgians that they could not take U.S. support for granted and must not give in to Russian provocations. As Assistant Secretary of State for European and Eurasian Affairs Daniel Fried later testified:

> We had warned the Georgians many times in the previous days and weeks against using force, and on August 7 we warned them repeatedly not to take such a step. We pointed out that use of military force, even in the face of provocations, would lead to a disaster. We were blunt in conveying these points, not subtle. Our message was clear.[67]

However, there is no available evidence indicating that Moscow was ever warned that its behavior would have serious consequences. Indeed, given these warnings and Europe's obvious coolness towards Georgia's ambitions for European integration, it seems likely that by August, Georgian officials had worked themselves up to the point of anxiety that they might be left to face Russia alone. Georgian frustration with Europe, prevalent from 2007 onward, had by spring 2008 given way to a growing sense that the U.S.'s attention was also seriously lagging.[68] Indeed, by May 2008

Saakashvili told a visitor that neither Rice nor Fried was grasping the seriousness of the developments in the region. He specifically referred to Rice's pledge to travel to Georgia in July—more than two months later—as an indication of the lack of U.S. high-level attention to the issue.[69]

Beyond those failures, it is clear that U.S. policy broke down in regard to Russia. The inter-agency process that is supposed to govern the formulation and implementation of policy was in this case virtually nonexistent. Because of this, it can truthfully be said that the Bush administration had no single strategy for Russia, with each department of the government acting instead on its own, without detailed presidential guidance or high-level coordination.[70] Since there was no coherent policy on either Russia or Georgia, it is hardly surprising that the administration was both divided and caught flatfooted by the August crisis. Caught by surprise when the guns started firing in South Ossetia, the United States came up with an initial response that was unfocused and uncoordinated with its allies, who were long since divided amongst themselves.

In addition, one can point to another and equally consequential policy shortcoming that led to an intelligence failure as well.[71]

> U.S. officials acknowledge that there was a serious intelligence failure in the initial phase of the Caucasus crisis, when Georgian troops poured into the disputed enclave of South Ossetia and Russia responded with its own brutal invasion. Despite the presence of U.S. military trainers in Georgia and intelligence satellites overhead, the administration professes that it was shocked by the timing and scope of both actions. "It took us a few days to shift some assets and get a clear picture of what was actually going on," said one official who declined to elaborate.[72]

Under the circumstances the initial policy response reflected the same lack of coordination and coherence that had prevailed on the eve of the crisis. Indeed, *Washington Post* columnist Jim Hoagland observed how initial reports of Russian atrocities "fueled a sharp interagency debate in Washington." Accordingly, the State Department argued for rapid dispatch of U.S. ships and aircraft to signal American resolve, while the Pentagon and the Joint Chiefs of Staff "urged restraint until more reliable information became available."[73]

Although difficulties of this sort are inherent in the real world, it is amazing that American analysts and officials did not realize that Russia was intent on provoking a war to amputate Georgian sovereignty, if not more. This is even more astonishing if one credits Rice's statement above that a crisis was expected.[74] It should have been. After all, Russia's expanded military presence in and near the provinces, its issuance of Russian passports to Abkhazians and South Ossetians, its growing direct control over the territories and its new railroad linking Abkhazia and Russia were all widely reported in the press, let alone whatever information was gathered by intelligence agencies. So what turned out to be a strategically dislocating surprise was entirely avoidable. Unfortunately, this is not the first time such a failure occurred.[75] These circumstances left the U.S. President and administration incapable of a swift and cohesive response to both Georgian actions and the Russian invasion. This would likely have been the case even if President Bush had not been in Beijing attending the opening of the 2008 Olympics, though the president's absence is likely to have exacerbated the situation.

During its last month in office, the outgoing Bush administration reaffirmed U.S. support for Georgia in a charter signed in January 2009. Unless this policy is backed by credible action it could easily become a dead letter.[76] Russia appears to be intent on continuing its provocative behavior by demonstrations of military might and by the decision to base troops in Abkhazia and South Ossetia, in violation of all international rules including its own truce negotiated with the EU. In light of this, it is by no means inconceivable that another crisis might soon break out there.

Conclusions

The path to the Russia-Georgia war and its denouement underscore the West's failure to adequately exploit the strategic victory it won in 1989–91. As a result, both the security of the Caucasus and of Europe are now problematic in a way they have not been for over twenty years. Prominent NATO allies have already publicly questioned the value of Article V guarantees, which requires the alliance to come to the aid of partners in military need.[77] No wonder that Poland sought the U.S.-Polish agreements of August 2008 on missile defenses, signed as the guns were blazing in Georgia, which calls for direct and immediate U.S. assistance to Poland in case of an attack and provides for U.S. forces to be stationed in Poland to underscore this guarantee.[78] Thus, it is clear that the war in Georgia further aggravated the preexisting tensions that had divided NATO regarding relations with Russia and the future purpose and character of the alliance itself.[79] And, of course, it strengthened tensions between Poland and Russia. These and other episodes and possibilities illustrate the dangers to which Gray alluded in the citation above.[80]

The failure in the period 1992–94 to take the conflicts in the Caucasus with sufficient seriousness opened the path to Russian armed intervention. This occurred because the West had not been prepared to consolidate its victories in 1989–91 in such a way as to assure longer-term stability in the region. This failure lent credibility to Russia's belief that it alone should take responsibility for events in the CIS.[81] The subsequent course of events there confirmed the truth that if America or the West as a whole fails to shape the aftermath of wars in areas of vital interests, unfriendly powers will do so, and with dangerous consequences for the West.[82] Among the likely consequences of Russia's successful aggression in this instance are the likely permanent truncation of Georgia, its long-term exclusion from NATO, further divisions within NATO, and the emboldening of Russia to undertake further military actions in neighboring countries when it considers it necessary to do so. All this is possible because of a small war on the periphery of Europe that occurred when the West was preoccupied elsewhere and did not take the area seriously enough. The lessons of these crises and of their descent into war should be with us for a long time. But it is not clear that those charged with leading the West out of its strategic wilderness will learn these truths, or instead draw other, more dangerous, lessons from the experience.

7

The Saakashvili Administration's Reaction to Russian Policies Before the 2008 War

David J. Smith

Introduction

"Guts," said American author Ernest Hemingway "is grace under pressure."[1] Georgia was under severe Russian political, economic, and military pressure during the months before the August 2008 war, and it reacted with guts—grace under pressure. Georgia remained serene, diplomatic, and resolute in the western course it charted for itself.

It was that western course, born of genuine—not *de jure*—Georgian independence, that impelled Russia to attack Georgia in August 2008, a war long in the making. In retrospect, the warnings were evident, but the blinders of a twenty-first century diplomatic paradigm[2] prevented the West from reading the handwriting on the wall. No Western diplomatic establishment believed that a repeat of 1956 or 1968 was possible. NATO did not believe it possible. Consequently, as tension built, the West made demarches—many and some quite tough, too. Russia, following a nineteenth-century geopolitical paradigm, prepared its tanks for war.

Georgians, who had spent 187 years under the Russian yoke, instinctively understood that those Russian tanks could yet roll, but they had unequivocally chosen a western path. Moreover, they had their fingers burnt by Western criticism of a 2004 foray they had made into South Ossetia, the antics of then Defense Minister Irakli Okruashvili, and of their handling of civil disturbances in Tbilisi in November 2007.[3] These factors combined to produce an air of caution in Tbilisi that approached a suspension of belief in the possibility of wanton Russian aggression.

One explicit example of this is a comment made by Georgian Interior Minister Vano Merabishvili, often portrayed in the media as a "hawk." "The Russians are forcing the Abkhaz to prepare for war," Merabishvili told the Russian daily *Kommersant*, "to guarantee that Georgia does not get into NATO. If there is a war and there is a single shot from the Georgian side, Georgia will never become a member of NATO."[4] Even the Georgian government's *Threat Assessment Document* said, "The probability of direct large-scale military aggression against Georgia in the foreseeable future is relatively low; however, the potential consequences from direct aggression, should it occur, are severe."[5]

Essentially, if Georgia wanted to be welcomed into Western circles, it had to embrace the Western paradigm. And the Western paradigm missed both the big picture and the day-to-day indicators of approaching war. The big picture was—and is—that genuine Georgian independence irked, or indeed frightened, the Kremlin.

The prologue to Russia's August 2008 attack on Georgia is a tale of Russian escalation culminating in war. To view that escalation in context, one must step back from the months immediately preceding the assault. But when does the prologue begin? It can be said to have begun with the Soviet security services' attack on Georgian demonstrators demanding independence in 1989. Perhaps it can be traced to Georgia's renewed independence in 1991. From another perspective, confrontation may have become inevitable with the accession of Vladimir Putin to the Russian presidency in 1999.

At the latest, however, the prologue to the 2008 war began with the inauguration of Mikheil Saakashvili as President of Georgia on January 25, 2004. From that moment, Georgia followed a reasonably consistent independent policy, which can be summarized as consisting of the following elements:

- Commitment to reintegration of the Russian-backed separatist Georgian territories of Abkhazia and South Ossetia;
- Implementation of a Western-oriented security policy centered upon joining NATO;
- Exploitation of geography to establish Georgia as an energy transit state, coupled with an energy policy aimed at minimizing susceptibility to energy extortion;
- Liberalization of the economy; and
- Democratization underpinned by membership in Western-oriented international institutions, to culminate in NATO and European Union (EU) membership.

In the Western twenty-first century diplomatic paradigm, Georgia's path was normal and, therefore, unremarkable. In the Russian nineteenth-century geopolitical paradigm, all this added up to encroachment.[6] This sweeping observation raises the matter of at which level of analysis to consider the factors that led to the August 2008 war: the broad macro-level, or the micro-level of day-to-day developments? Both are necessary, of course, but the latter should amplify the former.

It will be important to devote considerable attention to day-to-day Georgian reactions to the mounting pressure during the spring of 2008. However, a few introductory remarks are essential to understanding the context. Indeed, the underlying dynamic was that Russia tried everything conceivable in its effort to derail Georgia's westward movement, particularly its bid to join NATO. And Georgia reacted by steadfastly trudging forward, even amplifying its quest for Euro-Atlantic integration.

Many in the conflict resolution community—diplomats, NGOs, journalists—choose to overlook all this because they dwell upon day-to-day developments in isolation. This is easier intellectually, because it does not challenge their paradigm; and also emotionally, because it skirts the necessity to look the Russian problem in the eye. Each time the rat-a-tat-tat of machine gun fire brings them scurrying to Georgia. With a few quiet days and some soothing words, they scurry home to write reports that few people will read beyond the executive summary.[7] The writing of punctilious reports that are even-handed to a fault becomes a cathartic object in itself. Conflict resolution devolves into a series of discrete incidents, "who-done-it" reports, and equivocal words—that is, conflict freezing.

Much of this work is important. Machine guns and mortars kill people, facts must be established, and the analysis of those facts can reveal movements at higher levels of analysis. However, concentration on day-to-day events readily combines with the prevalent Western predilection to view all conflicts as the result of mere misunderstanding and miscommunication. Such an approach prevents the formation of an accurate view of macro-level cause and effect. Active Russian propaganda compounds the problem.

In the case of Georgia, the West missed the forest for the trees with three disastrous consequences. First, in Serbia, the United States and the European Union blithely pressed for the independence of the province of Kosovo, basing their position more on local considerations than on international factors. Talks between Belgrade and Pristina were pointless and the West had grown weary of its role as Kosovo's foster parent. So America and the EU determined that Kosovan independence was the most expedient way out and, in the Balkans, they had sufficient power to make it happen. Little consideration was given to the likely wider geopolitical consequences.

"Kosovo cannot be seen as a precedent for any other situation in the world today," U.S. Secretary of State Condoleezza Rice said in a statement on February 18, 2008, less than six months before the Georgia war.[8] The West simply declared that Kosovo was no precedent for Abkhazia or South Ossetia—incidentally, a logical assertion—and moved on. Reasonably or unreasonably, Moscow fumed, and resolved to flex its muscle in an area that it considers its own sphere of influence. Yuri Baluyevsky, then Chief of the Russian General Staff, presaged Moscow's reaction a few months before Kosovo declared independence:

> If we cross the Rubicon and Kosovo gains independent status tomorrow, frankly speaking, I expect this independence to echo in other regions as well, including those close to Russia's borders. You perfectly understand what I mean – I mean Abkhazia, South Ossetia, and Transdniestria.[9]

Apparently the West did not perfectly understand what Baluyevsky meant.

Second, in Georgia, the West failed to see that Abkhazia and South Ossetia—each beset with serious issues, to be sure—were never the issue for Russia. The issue was Georgia's successful embarkation upon a westward path, and in particular its progress toward joining NATO. Russian officials said as much: "As soon as Georgia gets some kind of prospect from Washington of NATO membership," Dmitry Rogozin, the Russian envoy to NATO, told Reuters on March 11, "the next day the process of real secession of these two territories from Georgia will begin."[10] By failing to grasp this, the West permitted itself the delusion that it could dally in Georgia without safeguarding its own and Georgia's geopolitical interests.

During the Saakashvili years, despite its flaws, Georgia began looking increasingly like a Western democracy. Moreover, it attracted investment, offered an opening to landlocked Azerbaijan and the rest of Eurasia, bolstered its energy security, and became a candidate for NATO membership. Meanwhile, the oil and gas pipelines that would pry open an even broader East-West Corridor were built. "The implications of this 'moving to the West,'" writes University of Edinburgh Professor Emeritus John Erickson, "are consequently dire for those who insist doggedly that the post-Soviet 'space' in its entirety, encompassing the former states of the Soviet Union, is and must remain a closed Russian geopolitical preserve."[11]

Predictably, Putin's Russia seethed and, equally predictably, the West vacillated. When then U.S. President George W. Bush genuinely, almost pleadingly, said at the Bucharest Summit that "the Cold War is over. Russia is not our enemy," he betrayed his incomprehension of the Putin paradigm.[12]

The third consequence of missing the forest for the trees was the worst. Some Western countries convinced themselves that derailing a Membership Action Plan (MAP) for Georgia was not only expedient for NATO, but principled. When German Chancellor Angela Merkel told top German military officers on March 10, 2008, that "Countries that are enmeshed in regional and internal conflicts cannot become NATO members," she confused cause and effect.[13] Abkhazia and South Ossetia were pawns in Moscow's strategy to preclude any genuine Georgian independence, particularly its path to NATO membership. As long as the resolution to these conflicts was—officially or unofficially—prerequisite to Georgia's membership in the alliance, Russia was not going to allow the conflicts to be resolved. When Germany and France—with a few more countries hiding in their skirts—nixed MAP, they virtually waved the Russian tanks into Georgia and perpetuated indefinitely the conflicts over Abkhazia and South Ossetia.

The official statement of NATO's Bucharest Summit affirmed that "NATO welcomes Ukraine's and Georgia's Euro-Atlantic aspirations for membership in NATO. We agreed today that these countries will become members of NATO."[14] But because the summit did not provide for a mechanism to achieve this purpose, explicitly rejecting the Membership Action Plans that would fulfill this function, Putin read NATO's fudge for what it was. In other words, the West will continue its dalliance without seriousness of purpose.

Within twenty-four hours, Putin rejoined. "The emergence of a powerful military bloc at our borders will be seen as a direct threat to Russian security," Putin told his NATO hosts. "The efficiency of our cooperation will depend on whether NATO members take Russia's interests into account."[15] The West had missed the point.

For at least four years, Russia had been reacting negatively to what it considered Georgia's deliberately provocational pursuit of an independent policy, even though that policy did Russia no material harm. Or was Georgia reacting to the provocation of 187 years of Russian domination and Russia's continued occupation of Georgian territories? Here one encounters one of those cosmic chicken-and-egg dilemmas that the study of international politics so often presents. It is easily resolved with a common-sense value judgment: as a sovereign state, Georgia may chart its own course, subject only to the will of its people, harming Russia in no way.

The bigger picture acknowledges this but notes also that Moscow has steadily escalated with all manner of measures against Georgia, culminating in war. Whether one labels it as action or reaction, Georgia's behavior, viewed from the macro-level, was to follow a reasonably consistent westward direction reasonably consistently.

With the NATO Bucharest Summit, the die was cast. Moscow picked up the pace of its march toward war that began with Kosovan independence, perhaps earlier. Russian Foreign Minister Sergey Lavrov told Ekho Moskvy Radio on April 8, 2008, that "We will do everything possible to prevent the accession of Ukraine and Georgia to NATO."[16] And that is exactly what Russia did.

In Georgia, an artifact of the country's westward movement was Tbilisi's adoption—first by emulation, then by absorption—of Western ways. In particular, a day-by-day study of Georgian behavior from Kosovo's independence to Russia's attack on August 7, 2008, confirms that Tbilisi held steadily to the Western diplomatic paradigm. It made demarches while Russia prepared its tanks for war. That escalation is described elsewhere in this volume. Let us now move to analyze the conduct of Georgian foreign and reintegration policy from the time of the declaration of Kosovo's independence on February 18, 2008, down to the eve of the war with Russia. Because they constituted the focus of Georgia's actions, it is necessary to focus on formal proposals and diplomatic statements.

From Kosovo to Bucharest

During the seven weeks between Kosovo's independence and the NATO Summit in Bucharest, Georgian foreign policy faced a number of challenges. In seeking to handle these, Tbilisi

- Minimized the political fallout from Kosovan independence;
- Managed a meeting between Saakashvili and Putin;
- Proposed a new format for negotiating the South Ossetia dispute;
- Handled Russian withdrawal from the Commonwealth of Independent States (CIS) agreement for sanctions on separatist Abkhazia;
- Committed Georgian troops to missions in Iraq and Afghanistan; and
- Offered new proposals for resolving the conflict in Abkhazia.

Georgia's immediate diplomatic task was to contain the fallout from the Western-backed Kosovan declaration of independence. After all, on January 31, 2006, Putin intoned, "If someone thinks that Kosovo can be granted full independence, then why should we refuse this to the Abkhazians?" He had been growling about the so-called "Kosovo precedent" ever since. In November 2006, the Russian president told Saakashvili that if Kosovo were given independence, he would impose the "Cyprus model" on Abkhazia.[17]

The day after the Serbian province declared independence, Georgian Foreign Minister David Bakradze said, "We are trying our best to minimize all possible negative consequences." Russia sees Kosovan independence as "a challenge," he said. "The easiest way to respond, in the simple minds of some people in Moscow, is to undertake similar steps in the former Soviet space, just as the West has done in the Balkans. [This poses] a high degree of risk."

Chairperson of the Georgian Parliament Nino Burjanadze explained why Kosovo was not analogous to Abkhazia. "The major reason why it cannot serve as a precedent," she said, "is that there was genocide and ethnic cleansing in Kosovo. So comparing Kosovo and Abkhazia and South Ossetia is groundless and unacceptable."

Kote Gabashvili, Chairman of the Parliamentary Committee on Foreign Relations, drew the bottom line: "We will have a restrained position and we should rule out any recognition of Kosovo." Prominent Member of Parliament Giga Bokeria echoed Gabashvili: "Georgia has no plans to recognize Kosovo's independence."[18] After two years of Russian threats and innuendo on the "Kosovo precedent," Saakashvili offered some tough but diplomatic words:

> I have heard threats made in this context against Georgia's territorial integrity more than once in the last few years...I want our people, as well as the international community, to understand that we have the power to undertake effective action in response to the moves directed against Georgia in this context. We will meet any provocation and we will respond with appropriate measures. I do not advise anyone to poke their nose into this issue or escalate tension. We want to resolve all the issues peacefully – we do not need any unrest now – but Georgia will not step back.[19]

For a short time, at least on the rhetorical level, Georgia's handling of the Kosovo issue seemed to work. On February 21, Saakashvili and Putin met in Moscow. The two presidents agreed to resume air travel between their two countries, which had been suspended in the wake of Georgia's arrest of four alleged GRU spies in September 2006. "But for us the most important thing," Bakradze told reporters after the meeting, "was a commitment that we heard from Russia that the Russian side does not plan to recognize the independence of Georgia's territories."[20]

After a decent interval, Georgia announced that it would withdraw its 160 soldiers from the NATO-led peacekeeping operation in Kosovo. The move was billed as a decision to bolster Georgia's participation in the International Security Assistance Force in Afghanistan; however, the diplomatic message was clear.[21] For all its differences with Russia, Georgia wanted nothing to do with Kosovo's independence.

On March 31, 2008, Bakradze announced that Georgia would send 350 soldiers to Afghanistan in late August or early September. Earlier, on March 21, Georgian National Security Secretary Alexander Lomaia told Rustavi-2 Television that Georgia had agreed with the United States to extend its 2,000-strong deployment in Iraq for several more months. "Our American colleagues assess the presence of our troops in that important part [of Iraq] as very important for the success of the operation."[22] These are clear indications that as of the end of March, Tbilisi had no inkling that it might soon need Georgian troops on Georgian soil.

Nonetheless, Moscow's accelerating annexation of Abkhazia and South Ossetia was underway. On March 24, the Russian Duma called upon the Kremlin to consider the recognition of the two Georgian territories. However, even before this date the Kremlin had taken concrete steps toward annexing these territories. On March 6, it withdrew from the sanctions regime which the Commonwealth of Independent States (CIS) had imposed on the separatist authorities in Abkhazia in 1996. Apart from being a diplomatic slap in the face to Georgia, this move cleared the way for overt Russian arms shipments to the Abkhaz separatists. On March 11, Zalmay Khalilzad, the U.S. Ambassador to the United Nations, articulated this concern, saying, "Most alarming is the prospect that Russia's withdrawal from the sanctions could lead to arms transfers to the separatists."[23]

Having freed itself from the CIS sanctions, Russia abandoned even the pretense of respect for Georgian territorial integrity. The situation was now turning into a full-blown crisis. Nonetheless, Tbilisi continued to react diplomatically. "This is an immoral and very dangerous decision," Bakradze said. "This is immoral because thousands of people who were forced to leave Abkhazia are still unable to return to their homes. This is dangerous because by doing so, we are moving into a totally new phase." Burjanadze called for help from the international community. "[Russia's decision on Abkhazia] is totally unacceptable and alarming and I hope it will be followed by an appropriate response from our American and European friends."[24]

The following day, the Georgian Foreign Ministry issued a tough, but diplomatic and professional statement:

> The Ministry of Foreign Affairs of Georgia expresses its extreme concern over the Russian Federation's withdrawal from the 19 January 1996 Decision of the CIS Council of the Heads of State "On Measures Aimed at Settling the Conflict in Abkhazia, Georgia."...We seek to focus the international community's attention on the alarming fact that by withdrawing from the above-mentioned decision, Russia considers itself no longer bound by the obligation to prevent sale and supply to the Abkhazian side of all kinds of armaments, defence equipment and spare parts, ammunitions, armoured vehicles and equipment (paragraph 3); as well as to prevent the hiring of its own citizens and their enrolment in any armed group in the conflict zone (paragraph 5a)...

The Russian decision, the Foreign Ministry reasoned, undermined the entire legal framework under which the Russian peacekeepers operated in the conflict zone. Georgia, it concluded, retained "the right to undertake adequate actions under the Constitution, Georgian legislation, and international law to ensure the protection of its own national interests."[25]

Speaking the same day to a televised session of Georgia's National Security Council, Saakashvili offered characteristically tough remarks. A variety of Russians had been warning that Georgia would be the target of Russian retaliation for Kosovan independence, he said. Russian withdrawal from the CIS sanctions was, Saakashvili continued, an

> Extremely dangerous provocation aimed at destabilizing the region and entire Caucasus and at triggering totally uncontrolled developments. Georgia will spare no efforts to prevent this type of scenario...We are declaring a policy of zero tolerance towards deployment of armed forces, military hardware, military instructors and mercenaries in Abkhazia. We are declaring policy of zero tolerance towards militarization of Abkhazia...
>
> I want to reiterate that destabilization is not in the interests of Georgia and we are ready to openly work with the international community to prevent complications...I want to call for consolidation, calmness; I want to call for being organized and watchful.[26]

Three conclusions emerge from these statements. First, they reflect a palpable sense that a corner had been turned—a "new phase" entered, in Bakradze's words. Second, following from that, they appeal for help to Georgia's allies and friends. Third, they raise urgent questions concerning the legal status of the so-called Russian peacekeeping forces in the territories.

Speaking in Parliament, Gabashvili was explicit that one logical consequence of calling into question the agreements pertaining to the two Georgian territories would be to remove the legal basis for the presence of so-called Russian peacekeepers there. "The Russian decision unties our hands, enabling us unilaterally and without any prior notification to withdraw from the agreements related with the conflict zones."[27]

Gabashvili was raising an issue that recurred frequently in pre-war Georgian politics, according to the ebb and flow of Georgian-Russian relations. For example, in October 2005, Parliament unanimously passed a resolution instructing the government to take steps toward the withdrawal of the so-called Russian peacekeepers if their performance did not improve before February 2006 in South Ossetia and July 2006 in Abkhazia. In February 2006, at the behest of the government, which was carving out room for diplomatic maneuver, the Parliament failed to pass a resolution requiring immediate withdrawal of the Russian peacekeepers from South Ossetia. Instead, it approved a non-binding resolution recommending that the government seek Russian withdrawal.[28]

In 2008, even after Russia lifted the CIS sanctions on separatist Abkhazia, Gabashvili and his supporters deferred to those in the government seeking space for diplomatic maneuver. The matter popped up again in late May and June. By late June the balance in Tbilisi was shifting toward declaring the peacekeepers illegal. But even at that late date, Georgia demurred. "Our American and European colleagues asked us to give them the chance to work with the Russians," Lomaia told reporters.[29]

In the spring of 2008, Saakashvili still searched for a diplomatic path forward. On March 1, Tbilisi proposed abolishing the Joint Control Commission, established in South Ossetia by the 1992 Sochi Agreement. Represented on this Commission were Russia, Georgia, the de facto government of South Ossetia, and the Russian Autonomous Republic of North Ossetia. Stacked three-to-one against Georgia, the body was nothing more than the diplomatic freezer for a frozen conflict—in sixteen years it achieved nothing. State Minister for Reintegration Temuri Yakobashvili instead proposed a new formula, labeled "2+2+2." The proposal would have brought together the two interested states—Georgia and Russia—plus the two administrations in South Ossetia, that is, those of Moscow-backed Eduard Kokoity and Tbilisi-backed Dmitry Sanakoyev, as well as the two most respected and involved international institutions, the Organization for Security and Cooperation in Europe (OSCE) and the European Union.[30]

"Lightweight and superficial," responded Yuri Popov, the Russian chief negotiator on South Ossetia, within a week.[31] Nonetheless, Saakashvili persisted, next extending an olive branch to his fellow Georgian citizens living in Abkhazia. Speaking at the Georgian Foundation for Strategic and International Studies on March 28, the president unveiled a set of far-reaching proposals for Abkhazia:

- Free economic zones in Ochamchire and Gali;
- Abkhaz representation at all levels of the Georgian government, including the position of vice-president of Georgia;
- The right to veto any decision regarding Abkhazia's constitutional status;
- Gradual merger of de facto Abkhaz security structures with Georgian security structures;
- A joint customs-border space; and
- Full autonomy on the ground.

"We offer the Abkhazians immediately to resume talks over all these issues," said Saakashvili. He added, "I ask the Russian Federation to get involved in this process, although Russia is not a mediator today and is [in fact] a party in the conflict." However, he also urged all Georgians, including the Abkhazians, not to become victims in Russia's "great geopolitical game." He concluded saying that Georgia had never offered the Abkhazians "so much at an official level as we are offering now."[32]

The very next day, Sergey Bagapsh, the Abkhazian separatist leader, dismissed Tbilisi's proposals as "propaganda ahead of the NATO summit." He continued, "Georgia is trying to portray itself as a peace-loving nation in the eyes of the North-Atlantic alliance, which it wishes to join...Saakashvili's proposals are unacceptable for us and we reject them."[33] That is how things stood as Georgian officials departed for the NATO Summit in Bucharest.

From Bucharest to South Ossetia

After NATO's Bucharest Summit, at which the alliance shrank from offering MAPs to Ukraine and Georgia, Russia turned up the heat in and around Abkhazia and South Ossetia. Rhetoric and violent incidents intensified. Russian challenges to Georgia—people in the Caucasus love to call them provocations—reached a new level. There were major incidents like the April 20 shoot-down of an unarmed Georgian Unmanned Aerial Vehicle

(UAV) above the coast of Abkhazia. Well armed Russian troops poured into the Georgian territories.

Underlying it all was Moscow's gambit to annex the territories. The ink on the Bucharest Summit Declaration was barely dry when the Georgian Ministry of Justice received a letter from its Russian counterpart. Russia, the letter said, was dealing directly with the de facto government in Sukhumi to transfer prisoners holding Russian citizenship back to Russia. Apart from noting the letter's flagrant disregard for international law— states must deal only with other states on such matters—the response of the Georgian Foreign Ministry placed the letter in its political context:

> The Russian side has made a great number of provocative and aggressive steps with respect to Georgia's conflict regions in the last two months...Against such a background, the letter of the Russian Ministry of Justice must be seen as nothing more than a piece of the Russian Federation's destructive policy. The policy aims at achieving legitimization of the separatist regimes on the territory of Georgia and the conflict regions' full-fledged economic, legal and political integration with Russia. International law terms such policy the "creeping annexation of a sovereign state."[34]

As annexation crept, or, by April 2008, swept forward, Russian military forces positioned themselves on Georgian territory for what we now know was the coming war.[35] Naturally, Moscow screened its military buildup with vague utterances about a need to protect Russian citizens and with shrill denunciations of a supposed Georgian military buildup. "We do not plan anything of a military character," senior Russian Foreign Ministry official Valery Kenyaikin told an April 25 television audience, "but should military conflicts break out on one side or another, then the initiator of these conflicts should be assured that Russia will take all possible measures in order to defend the interests of its countrymen and its citizens."

Echoing claims made by de facto Abkhaz officials, the Russian Foreign Ministry on April 29 said that Georgia had amassed 1,500 troops in the Kodori Gorge, then a Georgian-controlled valley of Abkhazia. Lavrov handed visiting EU officials documents that he said proved that Georgia had "acquired a huge number of armaments." During his television appearance, Kenyaikin averred, "Matériel is being delivered practically every day, partly from Turkey."[36] Such misinformation challenges the author of a review like this to prove the negative, which is, of course, impossible. Moscow counts on the (sometimes naïve) objectivity of Western analysts, journalists, international organizations, NGOs, and government officials. Blowing smoke about faraway places with unpronounceable names is part of its technique.

In reality, as the UN mission in Georgia staunchly confirmed, there was no Georgian military buildup in the Kodori Gorge, in Mingrelia, or near South Ossetia. There were, to be sure, Georgian Armed Forces (GAF) units that were undergoing scheduled training in this period; the Joint Staff has provided a comprehensive list of training undertaken in those days.

To derive a militarily useful conclusion, let us disregard the activities of small military units such as platoons or companies and instead focus on the movements of battalions or larger formations. During the spring and summer of 2008, the only units of such size outside of regular garrisons were comprised of reservists performing their annual 18 day training—hardly the stuff of a military buildup. Inside regular garrisons—again, not the stuff of a buildup—there were five training activities involving units of battalion or greater size:

- In anticipation of its deployment to Iraq, the IVth Brigade underwent predeployment training for peacekeeping operations at the Vaziani GAF Base, near Tbilisi, June–August;
- Elements of the IVth Brigade participated in Exercise "Immediate Response 2008" at Vaziani, July 5–August 5;
- The so-called "Separate Battalion" participated in naval exercises in Batumi, on the Black Sea coast, near the Turkish border, May 12–June 25;
- The Medical Battalion held field hospital exercises in Kojori, near Tbilisi, during June; and
- The 53rd Battalion underwent basic training at the Krtsanisi Training Area, near Tbilisi from July 1.[37]

The bottom line is that, with the exception of summer training for reservists, GAF units of battalion or greater size were at their home bases performing scheduled training.

Moreover, many outsiders, including this author, visited the Kodori Gorge during that period. There were about 500 Ministry of Internal Affairs paramilitary police present. Moreover, the single road and rickety bridges of the steep, narrow Kodori Gorge did not afford a practical military route to anywhere. The Kodori Gorge is a place where light infantry can scramble over mountains; not a place where tanks can rumble into the rest of Abkhazia.

On the populated coastal plain, any significant buildup of Georgian forces would have been noticed on and around the Zugdidi-Gali Road. Near South Ossetia, any buildup would have been noticed on or around Georgia's main East-West road. No one—ordinary citizens, journalists, diplomats, or representatives of the UN, OSCE, or of diverse NGOs—saw any such thing. There simply was no Georgian buildup. Moreover, there were no accelerated deliveries of military equipment.

Consequently, like the preceding sub-section, the following analysis of the period between the NATO Bucharest Summit and the eve of war is mostly about proposals and diplomatic statements because these constituted the focus and stuff of Georgian actions. During the fourteen weeks between the Bucharest Summit and Russia's July 8 brazen overflight of Georgian territory, Tbilisi faced a number of challenges, which it continued to handle calmly and professionally, although the pitch of its calls for help became more elevated. In particular, Georgia

- Explained the outcome of the Bucharest Summit;
- Elaborated its proposals for Abkhazia;
- Responded to Putin's April 16 decree tantamount to annexation of Georgian territory;
- Responded to the April 20 Russian shoot-down of a Georgian UAV; and
- Responded to the steady Russian military buildup on Georgian territory.

Georgia's first task after the Bucharest Summit was to exercise some spin control on the Summit outcome. On the one hand, NATO had refused to take the next logical step with Georgia. On the other hand, it prejudged the eventual outcome by saying that Georgia would indeed become an alliance member. Saakashvili promptly characterized the outcome:

> The document, which was adopted here in Bucharest reads that 'NATO welcomes Ukraine's and Georgia's Euro-Atlantic aspirations for membership in NATO and we agreed today that these countries will become members of NATO.' Such a document had not been adopted even in respect of the Baltic States, Poland, the Czech Republic, Hungary or other candidate countries in the past...this is a direct commitment by NATO that Georgia and Ukraine will become members of the alliance. We have to pass this Rubicon. I am sure that we will become a NATO member before my presidential term expires.[38]

It is possible that Russia, too, concluded that Georgia was still headed for NATO membership.

Whatever the conclusion drawn in Moscow, the NATO Summit refocused Tbilisi's attention on restoring Georgia's territorial integrity. Merkel's argument that Georgia's protracted "regional and internal conflicts" barred its membership bid had taken a toll at the Summit, even though it would have applied equally to West Germany at the time it joined NATO. If there was any chance of NATO membership for Georgia before the expiration of Saakashvili's presidential term in 2013, progress on reintegration was needed. Accordingly, on April 12, Saakashvili raised the tempo of work on the Abkhazia peace plan that he had advanced on March 28.[39] The very next day, Bagapsh again peremptorily rejected the effort.[40]

Nonetheless, Saakashvili persisted with the idea of free trade zones on the Black Sea. In a speech inaugurating Ras al Khaimah's investment in the Poti Port, Saakashvili outlined his "major vision to turn Georgia into the Dubai and Singapore of this region." The launch of the Poti Free Economic Zone, he said, marked "the launch of a new golden age for Georgia."[41] Hyperbole aside, the Poti Free Economic Zone could prove a boon to Abkhazia and could readily be extended to include the inland cities of Zugdidi and Gali, as well as the port of Ochamchire.[42]

On the political side, Tbilisi worked toward a United Nations General Assembly resolution recognizing "the right of all refugees and Internally Displaced Persons and their descendants, regardless of ethnicity," to return to Abkhazia, which was approved on May 15, 2008.[43] Although hard work by Russian diplomats failed to defeat the resolution, it did lead to 105 abstentions. Russia clearly had other plans for Abkhazia: creeping annexation of the territory had turned to sweeping annexation with the Putin decree of April 16, which had the effect of turning Abkhazia into a quasi-autonomous republic of the Russian Federation. To this challenge, Georgia yet again responded diplomatically. On April 17, the Foreign Ministry released a stiffly worded statement:

> The Russian Federation has taken yet another very dangerous step, which aims to legalize the factual annexation of Abkhazia and the Tskhinvali region/South Ossetia...
>
> Russia seeks to justify its actions by 'the need to take care of the interests of population in the conflict regions, including Russian citizens living there'. These efforts bear a close resemblance to the most notorious developments of the 1930s when a number of sovereign countries were occupied by the totalitarian regimes under the same pretext...
>
> It is our deep belief that Russia's actions are motivated by its desire to prevent Georgia's integration with the North-Atlantic Alliance, which is

supported by an absolute majority of the citizens of Georgia, including the entire population of Abkhazia and the Tskhinvali region/South Ossetia.[44]

Again, Georgia appealed for help from the international community and it requested a session of the United Nations Security Council.

Saakashvili, speaking at a televised meeting of the Georgian National Security Council, said that "Nothing will hamper the process of the peaceful unification of our country. We will continue working with all our partners. We expect and demand that the Russian Federation revise all those decisions which breach Georgia's sovereignty and territorial integrity." To the international community, he said, "We need not only statements; we need serious diplomatic actions from our partners, our friends. We expect and hope that these actions will be made in the coming days and coming weeks."[45]

A week later, in a television address, Saakashvili resurfaced the idea of declaring the so-called Russian peacekeepers illegal. He called for "intensive consultations with [Georgia's] partners and friends over the expediency of the further presence of the Russian peacekeeping contingent."[46] Saakashvili said he would base his actions on two principles: "We will defend and not give up our territorial integrity...We will keep up maximum diplomatic efforts with our friends and allies to maintain our peaceful and democratic values in order to create guarantees for the protection of Georgia's security and protection of peace, and to force everyone to give up their aggressive and irresponsible policies towards Georgia." He added, "I have permanent contacts and conversations with the U.S. and European leaders" and "I have sent our Foreign Minister Davit Bakradze to meet with U.S. Secretary of State Condoleezza Rice and with other representatives of the U.S. administration."[47]

The television address was tough, to be sure, but well within the bounds of diplomacy. So was the Georgian government's April 29 decision to suspend World Trade Organization talks with Russia. That same day, Saakashvili again appeared on television, this time to try to speak directly to people living in Abkhazia and South Ossetia:

> Today's Georgia is offering you calm and protection, which you lack so much. Today's Georgia is offering you life without gangs and criminal authorities; today's Georgia is offering you life without corruption, wherein no one will ever be able to extort bribes from you, or shares from your businesses; today's Georgia is offering you opportunities for free and legal business activities, wherein no one will be able to restrict your initiative; we are offering you much better healthcare and education systems; today's Georgia is offering you real freedom of choice, wherein no one will force

you to accept citizenship of this or that country and where you will not be arrested because you want to elect your country's parliament and president; today's Georgia is offering an open economy and borders, law and order.

He urged them to unite against the "outrageous force of Russia."[48] Meanwhile, Russia had been using its outrageous force. On April 20, a Russian Su-27 or Mig-29 shot down a Georgian UAV. Showing newly achieved public relations acumen, Tbilisi sought to mobilize world opinion by releasing the UAV's videotape of its own destruction. Reuters news service flashed the video around the world—it can still be viewed on You-Tube.[49] When a May 26 UN investigation report found that Russia had indeed downed the Georgian UAV, Georgia requested a meeting of the UN Security Council.[50] The report also stated that, in the opinion of the United Nations Observer Mission in Georgia (UNOMIG), "overflight of the zone of conflict by surveillance aircraft constitutes a breach of the Moscow Agreement." In response, Georgian UN Representative Irakli Alasania told a May 30 New York press conference, "Since the report was issued, the Georgian side stopped overflights to honor the words of the current report. It doesn't mean that we will not use these military capabilities if the threat will recur in the region... But at this point ...we've stopped the over-flights."[51]

Until their cameras stopped whirring, the UAV observed a massive Russian military buildup in Abkhazia. First, Moscow dispatched heavily armed so-called peacekeepers to counter the mythical Georgian buildup in the Kodori Gorge and Mingrelia. Then, on May 31, the Russian Ministry of Defense announced that it was sending Railroad Troops in a "humanitarian" effort to rehabilitate the rail line between Sukhumi and Ocham-chire—though no peacekeeping mandate provided Moscow a right to send such forces to sovereign Georgian territory.[52]

On May 12, the Georgian Ministry of Internal Affairs released a May 8 video of Russian forces amassing in Abkhazia. "Our drones are conducting reconnaissance of the Abkhaz territory to identify where the Russian and Abkhaz armed forces and military hardware are concentrated," commented Shota Utiashvili, head of the Interior Ministry's Information and Analytical Department.[53]

Yakobashvili assessed that Georgia and Russia were very close to war "because we know Russians very well. We know what the signals are when you see propaganda waged against Georgia. We see Russian troops entering our territories on the basis of false information...We literally have to avert war."[54]

As customary, the Ministry of Foreign Affairs issued formal protests against Russia's expansion of its so-called peacekeeping contingent and its deployment of Railroad Troops. On the latter occasion, Deputy Foreign Minister Grigol Vashadze observed that:[55]

> Each citizen of Georgia understands very well that the annexation of Ab-khazia is underway in all directions, including trade, social, economic and legal ones. And now an extremely dangerous military component has been added to this process. Nobody needs to bring railway forces to the territory of another country if a military intervention is not being prepared. It is im-possible to assess it otherwise.[56]

Meanwhile Saakashvili's pleas for western help became more pointed. It was, he told Reuters on May 1, a "moment of truth." Europe needed to use "all its diplomatic arsenal to deter the aggressive instincts of some politi-cians in Moscow." He continued, "They clearly have said—and this was reiterated by Putin to me—that this is a response to the Kosovo precedent, that this is a response to the West's neglect of Russia's positions, and that this is a response to the perceived threat of NATO enlargement in this re-gion."[57]

"Georgia is not able to go to war with Russia and is not doing so," Saa-kashvili told Russian journalists visiting Batumi on May 8. "We have few combat units and NATO will not help us in this."[58] On May 12, the presi-dent appealed to a group of visiting EU foreign ministers: we "request the EU to study, investigate and react on illegal movement of Russian peace-keeping forces. We also want the EU's more active involvement in the conflict resolution process.[59]

"This is not a crisis only for Georgia," Saakashvili told journalists two days later.

> This is a very rough, outrageous and unprecedented attempt to revise the entire world order, which was established after the break-up of Commun-ism. This is a problem first of all for Georgia...But this is also a problem for France and Europe; this is a huge problem for the United States and other countries as well, including Russia itself.[60]

A meeting between Saakashvili and newly designated Russian President Dmitry Medvedev was arranged on the margins of a CIS Summit meeting in Saint Petersburg. "I want to try it with the new president of Russia," Saakashvili told a televised meeting of the National Security Council. "I think that it is in our interest, as well as in the interest of Russia and its new president. I hope that all necessary steps will be taken to defuse the current tension."[61]

The two met on June 6. Despite a meeting that was what Georgia's then Foreign Minister Eka Tkeshelashvili called "friendly in tone," there was no progress. "President Saakashvili conveyed to President Medvedev that Georgia aims to change the current peacekeeping format in Abkhazia," Tkeshelashvili said. "Our goal is to replace the Russian peacekeeping force, which operates under a CIS mandate, with a civil police force overseen by the European Union and the OSCE. We, of course, would welcome Russia's active and constructive participation in this effort." Before the meeting, Saakashvili had articulated three conditions to achieve progress:

- Withdrawal of additional Russian troops deployed in Abkhazia;
- Cessation of ongoing construction of military infrastructure in Abkhazia; and
- Reversal of the Russian April 16 decision to establish official ties with breakaway Abkhazia and South Ossetia.[62]

Debriefing reporters after the meeting, Lavrov said, "President Medvedev restated our strong interest in seeing those conflicts resolved…By the way," Lavrov added, "at least that is how I understood it—he [Saakashvili] understands that a course towards NATO membership is not the key to conflict resolution. We once again reiterated that it could not be achieved through artificially pushing Georgia into NATO, as it will lead to a new coil of confrontation."[63]

Rumors circulated that there would soon be another Saakashvili-Medvedev meeting, but it was not to be. A few days later, Lavrov told RIA Novosti, "I have no information, which would let me make such an announcement, that a new Russo-Georgian summit will be held in the near future."[64]

From then, things went from bad to worse. Violence—shellings, shootings, bombings, etc.—escalated dramatically. Russian rhetoric reached a feverish pitch. "The actions of Tbilisi," the Russian Foreign Ministry intoned, "show that an open act of aggression has been committed against South Ossetia, which is an internationally recognized party in the conflict."[65]

When Saakashvili and Medvedev met briefly at a celebration of the tenth anniversary of the Kazakhstani capital of Astana, a Kremlin statement said, "During the conversation with Mikheil Saakashvili, the Russian president turned attention to the unacceptability of inflaming conditions in the re-

gion, and underlined the need for continuing negotiations with all the parties involved."[66] On July 6, Russian Presidential Spokesman Sergey Prik-
hodko spoke to Interfax about Ukraine and Georgia in NATO. "For us this
is still a 'red line' for further development of relations with the Alliance
and with the United States in particular. I think that the Russian president
will reiterate this in talks with George Bush during the meeting in the
frame of the G8 summit."[67]

Rice planned to visit Tbilisi on July 9. Before arriving, she commented,
"Frankly, some of the things that Russia did over the last couple of months
added to tensions in the region...Georgia is an independent state. It has to
be treated like one. We have said that both Georgia and Russia need to
avoid provocative behavior."[68] That was tough diplomatic language, but it
did not matter. Moscow was not in a diplomatic mode. The die was cast.
Russia was about to invade Georgia. Tellingly, just before Rice's arrival in
Tbilisi, Russian fighter aircraft violated Georgian airspace on July 8. Unlike previous such instances, this time the Russian Foreign Ministry
claimed credit:

> On July 8, the situation in the South Ossetian conflict zone significantly es-
> calated. Information has been received, including from the command of the
> [Russian] peacekeeping force, about a possible incursion by Georgian
> forces under the pretext of releasing four [Georgian] servicemen who were
> detained by the South Ossetian law enforcement agencies. There was an ur-
> gent need to undertake tangible measures in order to prevent bloodshed. In
> order to clarify the situation, jets of the Russian Air Force conducted a brief
> flight over South Ossetian territory. As further developments have shown,
> this move cooled hot heads in Tbilisi and helped to prevent a forceful de-
> velopment of the scenario, which was more than real.[69]

Conclusion

The examination of the day-to-day performance of any government is
bound to reveal shortcomings. Reviewing the responses of the Georgian
government to Russian escalation between mid-February and July 2008,
one might see moments in which the Georgians might have been more accommodating and others at which they might have been tougher. At times,
they got the timing wrong; some presentations were not as polished as they
should have been. However, it is unlikely that changes in Tbilisi's day-to-
day conduct would have made much difference. The big picture is that after
Kosovo, Russia had decided to go to war in order to teach the West a les-

son and to stall Georgia's westward movement, particularly its approach to NATO membership.

Throughout the period, Georgia reacted with guts—grace under pressure. As some analysts have noted, there may have been hawks in and around the government counseling military solutions to Georgia's problems. But output is what counts in politics, and the Georgian government's output was consistently diplomatic. If there were such hawks, they were overruled and remarkably quiet. In any country, when senior advisers are consistently overruled they tend to grumble to the news media. The absence of much such grumbling in Georgia during this period strongly suggests that there was not much of a lobby for war. Hence, the Georgian hawk theory does not stand up to closer scrutiny.[70] It is likely the product of a few random public comments, of the Western penchant to find fault on all sides and, of course, of Russian propaganda.

The bottom line is that Georgia reacted to Russia's escalation as any Western democracy would have done, using diplomatic means to lodge protests at every step. It sought the help of friends. It used international organizations. It became savvier about public relations. It put forward peace proposals for the Georgian territories of Abkhazia and South Ossetia that should at least have been taken up as points of departure for negotiations.

The reality is that the August 2008 war was neither provoked nor a product of miscalculation. It was initiated and waged by Russia for well-articulated geopolitical reasons. Georgia behaved diplomatically—perhaps too long.

8

From Sukhumi to Tskhinvali:
The Path to War in Georgia

Johanna Popjanevski

Over the summer of 2008 tensions between Moscow and Tbilisi reached a peak, resulting in a full-scale war that rapidly expanded beyond South Ossetia and Abkhazia to include much of Georgia proper. The war was short but eventful, causing severe destruction to Georgia's military and economic infrastructure and resulting in the displacement from their homes of over 100,000 civilians. While the war took the world by surprise, developments over the spring and early summer of 2008 had strongly suggested that a confrontation in the Georgian conflict zones was becoming increasingly likely. It is therefore important to trace developments immediately preceding the war, and specifically the events leading up to August 7, 2008. Having done this, it is possible then to raise thematically the key contentious issues related to these events.

Overview: The Lead-Up to the Russia-Georgia War

In stark contrast to the escalation during the spring of 2008, the early months of 2008 witnessed what appeared to be the laying of groundwork for a rapprochement between Tbilisi and Moscow. In particular, Kosovo's declaration of independence in February 2008 proved to carry less immediate significance for Georgia than Tbilisi had originally feared. While Russia during 2006–7 had repeatedly warned the West that recognition of Kosovo would set a precedent for Abkhazia and South Ossetia, Russia in the early spring abstained from acting on that threat. Tbilisi, for its part, endured a deep domestic crisis in November–December 2007, which caused President Saakashvili to resign and hold snap elections. During the first months of 2008 the government appeared keen to adopt a more diplomatic approach toward Moscow. Following Saakashvili's re-election in January 2008, the newly appointed Minister for Reintegration, Temuri Yakobashvili, underlined the potentially important, albeit not exclusive, role that Moscow could play in the conflict resolution processes in Abkhazia and South Ossetia.[1] At a top-level meeting on February 21, Saakashvili and Russian President Vladimir Putin discussed the re-establishment of trade and air traffic links that had been cut in 2006.

Tbilisi's decision on March 4 to withdraw from the Joint Control Commission (JCC)[2] in South Ossetia caused, however, a setback in the Tbilisi-Moscow dialogue. Pursuing the government's long-term plea of reforming the negotiation and peacekeeping formats in Abkhazia and South Ossetia, Yakobashvili declared in late February that the JCC was outdated and proposed instead a new format in which North Ossetia would be replaced by the Tbilisi-backed South Ossetian administration[3] led by Dmitry Sanakoyev, and which would add the EU and the OSCE as parties to the negotiations. Moscow's response to Tbilisi's decision came without delay. On March 6, the Russian Ministry of Foreign Affairs announced its decision to lift its trade restrictions on Abkhazia, as imposed by the 1996 Sanctions Treaty, and called on other CIS countries to follow suit. Tbilisi, which only weeks before had urged Russia to stay true to the sanctions agreement, condemned the action, referring to the move as evidence of Russia being a party to and not an impartial mediator in the Abkhazia conflict.[4] On March 21, the Russian Duma, further sharpening its tone against Tbilisi, passed a resolution urging the Kremlin to step up efforts to protect Russian citizens in the Georgian conflict zones and to consider recognizing the independence of Abkhazia and South Ossetia.

Russia's suspension of the sanctions treaty, which paralleled discussions in Moscow regarding Sukhumi's potential role in the preparations for the 2014 winter Olympic Games in Sochi, led Tbilisi to speed up its efforts to resolve the conflict over Abkhazia. On March 28, Georgian President Mikheil Saakashvili outlined his new peace plan for Abkhazia. The plan put forward a number of offers to the Abkhaz administration, among them the establishment of free economic zones in the Ochamchire and Gali districts and substantial representation in the central administration that would include the post of vice-president.[5] Sukhumi's response to Tbilisi's offers was lukewarm: de facto Abkhaz President Sergey Bagapsh dismissed the initiative as a publicity stunt preceding the April 2008 NATO Summit in Bucharest.[6]

Abkhazia as the Setting for Provocations

Developments in April 2008, following the NATO summit, erased all doubts that the battle for Abkhazia had begun. The already tense situation worsened on April 16, when outgoing President Putin signed a presidential decree instructing Russian state agencies to establish official ties with the Abkhaz and South Ossetian de facto administrations; to institutionalize trade relations between Russia and the two entities; and to provide consular assistance to residents of the two regions. The move triggered a harsh reaction in Tbilisi, where it was viewed as a step towards recognition of the breakaway republics, or even their incorporation into the Russian Federation. It is notable that Putin's decree for the first time caused division among the Group of Friends,[7] with France, Germany, the U.S., and the UK issuing a joint statement urging Russia, its fellow member, to "revoke or not to implement" its decision.[8] In Sukhumi, the Abkhaz Parliament responded by criticizing the mediators for being biased in Georgia's favor and adopting a resolution urging Bagapsh to suspend Abkhaz participation in the UN-led talks.

Shortly thereafter, on April 20, a Georgian Unmanned Aerial Vehicle was shot down over the Gali district in Abkhazia. While the Abkhaz authorities assumed responsibility for the incident, the Georgian authorities released video footage of the shoot-down which suggested that the drone had been shot down by a Russian MIG-29 fighter plane, not part of the Abkhaz air arsenal. On May 26, the UN Observer Mission in Abkhazia (UNOMIG) issued an investigative report[9] confirming that Russia was responsible for the shoot-down, but neither the incident nor the report elicited a response from the West.

Controversies continued in late April, when Moscow accused Tbilisi of mobilizing its troops in the Kodori Gorge in preparation for an attack against Abkhazia. UNOMIG reported that it had noted no such military build-up in the conflict zone,[10] but Russia nonetheless used it as a pretext for increasing its number of peacekeepers in Abkhazia from 1,997 to 2,542 and for setting up new checkpoints along the Inguri River. Russia's move led Tbilisi to intensify its pleas for a revision of the peacekeeping format in Abkhazia, arguing that the Russian troop increase constituted a violation of the 1994 peacekeeping agreement and an illegal incursion into Georgian territory. Both the U.S. and the EU expressed concern over Moscow's actions[11] but refrained from taking any determined stance on Russia's future peacekeeping role in the region. Instead, on May 15, the UN General Assembly backed (albeit with a narrow margin) a Georgian-sponsored resolution[12] on the rights of Internally Displaced Persons to return to Abkhazia. Russia voted against the resolution, arguing that it presented an inaccurate picture of the conflict which potentially could destabilize ongoing efforts to resolve it. The majority of Western states abstained from voting, with the notable exceptions of the United States and Sweden, which endorsed it.[13]

In May developments in the Abkhaz conflict zone were temporarily overshadowed by the Georgian parliamentary elections, which were held early as a result of the domestic crisis that plagued the country throughout the winter of 2007–8. The elections, held on May 21, took place in a highly polarized political climate marked by lack of trust between political parties as a consequence of the November 2007 events, and by divisions caused by the increasingly tense Georgia-Russia relationship. Nonetheless, the elections, which all agreed were essential to Georgia's further democratic progress, suddenly and uncompromisingly thrust Georgia to the center of international attention.

Meanwhile, tensions in Abkhazia continued to mount. On May 31, the Russian Ministry of Defense announced the deployment of an additional 400 military personnel in Abkhazia, their task being to repair the railway infrastructure between Sukhumi and Ochamchire. Russia described the project as a part of Russia's mandate to provide humanitarian assistance to Abkhazia. Yet there was no justification in the peacekeeping mandate for such a military presence on Georgian territory. The Georgian authorities objected strongly, stating that reinforcement of the infrastructure in the conflict zone could only be viewed as a preparation for an armed intervention in Georgia.[14] While the U.S. only expressed its dismay over Russia's move, NATO Secretary General Jaap de Hoop Scheffer took a tougher stance, declaring it a violation of Georgia's territorial integrity and urging Russia to withdraw its forces.[15] In a notable resolution passed on June 5, the EU Parliament also called on Russia to withdraw its additional forces immediately. It went on to state that the Russian troops had "lost their role of neutral and impartial peacekeepers" and that the peacekeeping format must therefore be revised.[16]

In addition to the significant increase in the number of military servicemen in the conflict zone, the period from April to June saw a reinforcement of Russian military equipment in Abkhazia.[17] On June 17, Georgian authorities detained four Russian peacekeepers attempting to smuggle military hardware, including anti-tank missiles and aircraft rockets, from Abkhazia to a Russian peacekeeping base in the Zugdidi district. Georgian TV showed Georgian security officers forcing the four peacekeepers to abandon their vehicle and escorting them to Georgian police cars. Russia claimed that the soldiers were simply transporting ammunition to the base in Zugdidi.[18]

In June and July there were growing fears of a possible war in Abkhazia. In an interview with the Georgian newspaper *Rezonansi* on June 21, Russian military analyst Pavel Felgenhauer warned of the Kremlin's plans to launch a war in Georgia in the middle of August. According to Felgenhauer, hostilities would start in Abkhazia, spread to South Ossetia and then to the rest of Georgia. Similar information emerged in July, this time put forward by Kavkaz Center, the information hub of the North Caucasus Islamic Resistance. On July 5 it published an article[19] which, on the basis of North Ossetian intelligence sources, bluntly stated that a decision to launch a war against Georgia had been taken in Moscow months earlier. It alleged that the objective of the planned attack on Georgia was to invade the Kodori Gorge and then the rest of Georgia, with the ultimate aim of causing the disintegration of Georgia and the departure from office of President Saakashvili. Preparations for the war had been underway for several months, with the deployment of railway troops in Abkhazia being an important component of the campaign. According to Kavkaz Center, the war was to be launched in the period between August 20 and September 10.

The Shift from Abkhazia to South Ossetia

Indeed, toward the end of June, developments in Abkhazia seemed to be entering a dangerous stage. Following a series of explosions in the Abkhazian cities of Gagra and Sukhumi on June 29–30, injuring twelve persons, the Abkhaz authorities announced their decision to close the de facto border with Georgia. Another incident took place on July 6, when four persons were killed in an explosion at a café in the mainly Georgian town of Gali in southern Abkhazia. The Abkhaz authorities termed the attack as an act of terrorism by the Georgian side, and claimed its aim was to destabilize the situation in Abkhazia, and particularly to disrupt the tourism industry. Tbilisi, for its part, denounced Sukhumi's accusations, stating that the violence in Abkhazia was an attempt to justify the illegal presence of Russian troops in the conflict zone. On July 7, the Georgian authorities, in an attempt to prevent the situation from escalating further,[20] declared their readiness to establish a joint Georgian-Abkhaz police force under international supervision.

The unrest in Abkhazia caused growing unease among Western states. The French EU presidency and the U.S. both expressed their concern over the incidents, urging in typical language that the parties show "restraint" and resume dialogue.[21] Moreover, the U.S. called on Russia to "revoke its provocative actions in Abkhazia" and, notably, expressed support for Tbilisi's plea for an increased international presence in Abkhazia.[22]

Subsequently, a fresh wave of incidents during July in the South Ossetian conflict zone abruptly shifted the focus away from Abkhazia. On July 3, an explosion in the South Ossetian village of Dmenisi killed the local police chief, Nodar Bibilov. Later that day the head of the Provisional Administration, Dmitry Sanakoyev, hit a mine while traveling through the conflict zone en route to Batumi.[23] In a press statement on the following day, the Russian Ministry of Foreign Affairs accused the Georgian authorities of staging the attack to justify a military step-up in the conflict zone. The July 3 incidents triggered a stand-off between Georgian and South Ossetian military forces that continued through the night of July 4–5 and resulted in the deaths of two ethnic Ossetians. Tensions between Tskhinvali and Tbilisi intensified on July 7, when the Georgian authorities accused South Ossetia of kidnapping four Georgian police officers patrolling an area near the conflict zone. In a televised address to the Georgian National Security Council on July 8, President Saakashvili hinted at a possible armed operation to release the hostages. Following this threat the officers were promptly released. Raising a warning finger to Tbilisi, Russia on the next day sent four military aircraft into Georgian airspace over South Ossetia, an open violation of Georgian sovereignty. It is revealing that the Russian authorities did not deny their violation of Georgian airspace, which took place on the day of U.S. Secretary of State Condoleezza Rice's visit to Tbilisi. Instead, the Kremlin described them as an attempt to defuse tensions in the conflict zone.[24]

In mid-July, a yearly U.S.-led military exercise called "Immediate Response" took place at the Vaziani base outside Tbilisi, involving approximately 2,000 troops from Georgia, the U.S., Armenia, Azerbaijan, and Ukraine. Meanwhile, Russia announced the start of its own military exercise, Kavkaz-2008, in eleven regions near the Georgian-Russian border. The exercise officially involved approximately 8,000 Russian troops, although that number may have been intentionally understated. The assembled forces included the 58th Army, the Black Sea Fleet, and the Pskov Airborne Division. While Moscow officially referred to the exercise as a counter-terrorism operation, Sergey Makarov, the commander of Russia's North Caucasus Military District, revealed that it also aimed at providing assistance to Russian peacekeepers stationed in Abkhazia and South Ossetia, due to the recent unrest in the region. Again, the Georgian authorities vehemently objected. A press statement issued by the Georgian Ministry of Foreign Affairs on July 16 referred to Makarov's statement as an unconcealed threat of military intervention against Georgia.[25]

On July 30, a week before the outbreak of the August war, Russia announced the completion of the repairs to the 54-kilometer railway between Sukhumi and the southern region of Ochamchire. In connection with the pull-out of the Russian railway forces, a ceremony was held at the station in Drandra outside of Sukhumi. On the next day, the Abkhaz authorities reiterated their refusal to participate in German-brokered direct talks with Tbilisi, originally scheduled for July 30–31.[26]

Nonetheless, by the end of July, South Ossetia had replaced Abkhazia as the center of tensions between Tbilisi and Moscow. Over the first week of August tensions there escalated rapidly. Following a mine attack against a Georgian military vehicle on August 1, injuring five Georgian police officers, a new round of fire exchange between Georgian and South Ossetian military forces broke out. The South Ossetian side reported that Georgian sniper attacks on the night of August 2 had killed six and injured fifteen. Subsequently, the Georgian authorities announced that mortar attacks on Georgian villages had killed seven persons, including a Georgian police officer.[27] Following these incidents, the Commander of the Russian Airborne Troops, Valery Evtukhovich, confirmed Russia's readiness to provide military assistance to the Russian peacekeepers in South Ossetia if needed.[28] Georgia responded by accusing Russia of attempting to stage "an illusion of war" in order to undermine Georgia's efforts to bring about peace in South Ossetia and Abkhazia.[29]

It is important to note that over the next couple of days, numerous reporters from various Moscow-based media outlets started arriving in Tskhinvali. A Chechen freelance photographer with the Reuters news agency, Said Tsarnayev, travelled to the breakaway capital for a photography project on August 5. He reported to RFE/RL's North Caucasus service that he was surprised to discover that close to 50 Russian journalists were already staying at his hotel. According to Tsarnayev, the reporters had been sent to Tskhinvali days earlier, and were preparing to cover "something big."[30] Meanwhile, on August 3–5, the South Ossetian authorities announced that more than 800 ethnic Ossetians, mainly women and children, were being evacuated from the conflict zone to North Ossetia, presumably due to the likely resumption of hostilities. However, the North Ossetian administration went out of its way to deny that it was an evacuation, stating instead that the women and children were merely taking part in a pre-arranged summer camp program in North Ossetia.[31] These conflicting statements would appear to suggest that Vladikavkaz and Tskhinvali were receiving conflicting instructions.

In Tbilisi, the government requested direct negotiations with Tskhinvali. On August 5, the Georgian Ministry for Reintegration announced that the South Ossetian side had agreed to participate in bilateral talks between Georgian State minister Yakobashvili and South Ossetian negotiator Boris Chochiev on August 7, and that these would be facilitated by Russia's chief negotiator in South Ossetia, Yuri Popov. The Tskhinvali authorities immediately denied having agreed to the talks, stating it was only prepared to negotiate with Tbilisi within the JCC format.[32] Nonetheless, in the morning of August 6, Popov confirmed to ITAR-TASS that talks were to be held as planned on the next day in Tskhinvali. An ambiguous announcement by the South Ossetian Press and Information Committee stated that the South Ossetian side had discussed with Popov the possibility of participating in talks in preparation for a JCC session.[33]

Even in the late evening of August 6, it remained unclear whether or not talks would take place. But skirmishes in South Ossetia showed no sign of abating. In the morning of August 7, the South Ossetian authorities reported that overnight shelling against Tskhinvali and surrounding villages resulted in the injury of eighteen persons.[34] The head of the South Ossetian Security Council, Russian officer Anatoly Barankevich, announced that the South Ossetian army had requested assistance from North Ossetia, and that armed groups from North Ossetia were currently en route towards the conflict zone to assist the separatist army.

The Escalation to War

During the afternoon of August 7, it became increasingly clear that the situation in South Ossetia was on the verge of escalating into a serious confrontation. From 2:00 P.M. Tbilisi gradually reinforced its number of troops south of the conflict zone, ordering approximately 800 troops from their bases in Tbilisi and Gori to back up those already on the ground. Nonetheless, in Tbilisi, media speculation on possible talks with the South Ossetian side had not faded. In the early afternoon of August 7, Yakobashvili departed to Tskhinvali in an attempt to make contact with the South Ossetian side. Upon arrival in the breakaway capital, Yakobashvili was received by Russian peacekeeping commander Marat Kulakhmetov, who informed him that he was unable to reach the South Ossetian representatives. Information subsequently emerged that South Ossetian de facto leader Eduard Kokoity had already left Tskhinvali by this time, and that other representatives of the leadership had been moved to specially designed bunkers as a safety precaution.[35] Russian negotiator Popov also failed to show up, claiming that both of his office cars were inoperable due to flat tires. Kulakhmetov went on to inform Yakobashvili that with Georgian troops present at the border, the Russian peacekeeping contingent was no longer able to control the separatist army, and advised him to declare a unilateral cease-fire to allow Russia to defuse tensions.[36] Upon returning to Tbilisi, Yakobashvili announced on national television that the Georgian forces were holding their fire while the government attempted to establish contact with the South Ossetian side.[37] President Saakashvili formalized this cease-fire in an address to the nation that was broadcast by Georgian television at 7:10 P.M.

Shortly thereafter came the first media reports of troop movements through the Roki tunnel from North Ossetia. At approximately 8:00 P.M. on August 7, Moscow-controlled Rossiya TV showed Abkhaz leader Bagapsh addressing the Abkhaz National Security Council. In his address Bagapsh announced that a battalion from Russia's North Caucasus military district had entered South Ossetia. Bagapsh told the council that he had spoken to South Ossetian leader Kokoity, who had informed him that the situation in South Ossetia had stabilized following the arrival of the Russian convoy.[38]

Over the next few hours the Georgian side continued to hold fire, while reporting several incidents of shelling attacks against villages under Georgia's control.[39] According to Georgian officials, at approximately 11:00 P.M. President Saakashvili received intelligence information that another convoy consisting of more than 100 Russian military vehicles was already passing through the Roki tunnel. The Georgians passed this information to Western officials, who acknowledge having received it. Following reports that the police station in the village of Kurta, home to the Sanakoyev-led provisional administration, had been destroyed, Saakashvili at approximately 11:35 P.M. instructed the Ministry of Defense to order Georgian troops to advance towards Tskhinvali. The two stated goals of this advance were, first, to prevent the Russian convoy from advancing toward the separatist capital and, second, to put an end to the continuing shelling of Georgian villages by the separatist rebels. Tbilisi made official its decision to suspend the cease-fire shortly after midnight on August 8, when commander of the Georgian peacekeeping battalion in South Ossetia Mamuka Kurashvili announced on Georgian TV channel Rustavi-2 that Georgia had resolved to restore "constitutional order" in South Ossetia—a statement he was subsequently reprimanded for, as it had not been authorized by supe-riors.

During the night of August 8, Georgian ground forces launched a heavy artillery attack against Tskhinvali and positions located on higher ground around the separatist capital. At 1:00 A.M. the Georgian authorities re-ported that Georgian troops had managed to delay the advance of the Rus-sian convoy by shelling the road south of the Roki tunnel. Meanwhile, Georgian media continued to report on the advance of Russian troops to-ward Tskhinvali.[40] In a televised address to the nation on the morning of August 8, President Saakashvili announced that Georgian troops had taken control of the main territory of the conflict zone.

The War Spreads

At approximately 10:00 A.M. on August 8, the first Russian fighter plane entered Georgian airspace from South Ossetia. This marked the beginning of a full-scale Russian invasion of Georgian territory. Throughout the af-ternoon of August 8, Russian jets attacked targets in Georgia proper ex-tending to the area immediately around Tbilisi.[41] Meanwhile, the Russian side launched an advanced cyber-attack on Georgia, as discussed in Paul Goble's chapter. Numerous Georgian websites, vital to the distribution of information by governmental and independent media agencies, were ren-dered inaccessible during the first days of the war. This included the USA-ID-supported news site Civil Georgia, whose regular English language up-dates were frequently consulted by foreign media services.

During the evening of August 8, Russia expanded the scope of its bomb-ing campaign to western Georgia. Meanwhile, Russian air and ground forces, including large contingents of the 58th Army, launched a heavy counter-attack in South Ossetia, forcing Georgian troops out of Tskhinvali. Following several attempts to push their way back into the city's center, by the evening of August 8 the Georgians were forced to retreat to positions at the southern outskirts of the breakaway capital. While the Georgian side managed to hold the southern part of the city for another 15–20 hours, the steady increase of the number of Russian troops in the conflict zone forced the Georgian army to begin withdrawing towards Gori in the afternoon of August 9. By early morning on August 11, the retreat was completed.

As Pavel Felgenhauer discusses in his chapter, Russia rapidly expanded the scope of its invasion, bombing strategic targets throughout the territory of Georgia. In the afternoon of August 9, less than forty hours into the fighting, Russian opened a second front in Abkhazia. Assisted by Russian fighter jets, Abkhaz militia unleashed a heavy bombardment of the Kodori Gorge, home to the Tbilisi-backed Abkhazian government-in-exile. The bombardment drove more than 2,000 ethnic Georgians from their homes in the region. Russia subsequently deployed a total of 9,000 troops in Abkhazia by rail and sea. These units figured prominently in attacks against Kodori and the regions south of the conflict zones into Georgia proper. On August 10, the Georgian Ministry of Foreign Affairs passed to the Russian Embassy in Tbilisi a formal request for a cease-fire. In spite of this, Russia only intensified its assault, with continuous ground and air attacks across great expanses of Georgia, and which resulted in the capture of the cities of Gori, Senaki, and Zugdidi.[42] It also became clear that Russia was targeting not just Georgia's military infrastructure but vital elements of the Georgian economy as well. For days, Russian battleships completely blockaded the Georgian coast, preventing Georgian cargo ships from reaching Black Sea ports. The Russians also bombed the highway connecting eastern and western Georgia, on August 16 completely destroying the railway bridge at Kaspi, a lifeline to Georgia's economy. Moreover, on August 15–16, more than three full days *after* a cease-fire[43] had been reached, the Russian air force unleashed a series of air raids on Borjomi National Park, using fire bombs to inflict serious damage on what is regarded as a national treasure.

Analysis: The Question of Responsibility

The outbreak of the August 2008 war took the international community by surprise. In spite of the numerous warnings during spring and early summer, foreign governments and media were caught unprepared for the rapid escalation of events during July and August. It is therefore not surprising that widespread debate has arisen over the sources of the conflict, responsibility for the escalating tensions on its eve, and blame for the final outbreak of fighting. Such issues of culpability must in turn be considered in the context of recognized international law. In an attempt to clarify some of the complex questions at issue, let us look at three questions which, fairly or not, have been widely taken as essential to any attempt to allocate responsibility for the war.

Was the War Premeditated?

From the moment the war broke out, Moscow has insisted that its decision to attack Georgia was a reaction to Tbilisi's aggression in South Ossetia, which was in turn portrayed as the Georgian government's opportunistic attempt to regain control of South Ossetia. On August 10, Russia's Ambassador to the UN, Vitali Churkin, announced that Georgia's August 7–8 attack on Tskhinvali had killed as many as 2,000 civilians, and forced 40,000 people to flee the zone of conflict.[44] During the initial stage of the war, the international media appeared to accept Russia's claims of acting to protect its own citizens in the conflict zone against acts of "genocide" by the Georgian side. This was facilitated by Russia's well-prepared media offensive and the ongoing cyber-attacks against Georgian governmental and media websites, which hampered Tbilisi's ability to disseminate information during the first days of hostilities.

Soon, however, reports and analyses from independent human rights agencies established that Russia's claims were greatly exaggerated.[45] Researchers with Human Rights Watch, who travelled to the conflict zone on August 10, put the total number of deaths at less than one hundred. Indeed, Russia's own Prosecutor General later reported a total of 133 civilian deaths in South Ossetia.[46] Moreover, as events unfolded it became obvious to many that Russia's motives were more punitive than reactive. The fact that Russia met Georgia's retreat from South Ossetia and its request for a cease-fire with an expansion of the war and its extension to civilian and economic targets seemed to confirm this conclusion. Particularly telling in this regard was the failure of Russian forces to even try to put an end to the ethnic cleansing of Georgian-populated areas of South Ossetia after the end of major hostilities.

These considerations strongly imply that the August 2008 war directly served Russia's perceived interests and, more to the point, suggest that it was calculated by Moscow to do so. Numerous experts take this notion a step further, arguing that the war was the central element in the Kremlin's well-planned project to remove President Saakashvili from power.[47] Considerable evidence has accumulated indicating that the war was premeditated and carefully planned. It should be recalled that clear signs of preparations for a war were present throughout the spring and early summer of 2008. Tbilisi's publicly stated fears that the rehabilitation of the Sukhumi-Ochamchire railroad constituted a preparation for war proved valid, for this rail line, which Russian military engineering troops completed only days before the attack, found immediate service in deploying thousands of Russian troops into Abkhazia and western Georgia.

Particularly noteworthy is the fact that the Russian military had brought scores of Russian journalists to Tskhinvali days before the war, so they would be in place when the attack was launched. At the very least, one must be impressed at how exceptionally well prepared Moscow was for the precise time, type, and location of the confrontation that actually occurred.

However, up until July, most information at hand suggested that the most likely scene of a confrontation between Moscow and Tbilisi would be Abkhazia, not South Ossetia. Over the spring and summer of 2008 numerous provocations by Russia, starting with Putin's April decree and the gradual build-up of Russian troops in the conflict zone, suggested that Moscow was attempting to push Tbilisi toward a confrontation over Abkhazia. The gradual shift of the escalation to South Ossetia during July was in all likelihood a direct result of the restraint that Tbilisi showed, as discussed in David Smith's chapter. Moscow was unprepared for Saakashvili's refusal to meet its escalation in Abkhazia with counter-escalation; instead Tbilisi turned to the international community in repeated requests for international monitoring. Failing to mount a successful provocation in Abkhazia, Moscow turned its attention instead to South Ossetia.

While the lead-up to the August war was marked by confrontations initiated by both sides, not least with regard to continuous clashes between Georgian and South Ossetian forces, it should also be recalled that Russia did little or nothing to honor its official role as a "peacekeeper" in South Ossetia over the period leading up to the war. In light of its leverage over the separatist army—after all, South Ossetia's Minister of Defense was and is an ethnic Russian official seconded from the Russian Ministry of Defense—it can conclusively be argued that Russia effectively controlled the escalation of hostilities in early August. This further strengthens the notion that Moscow was not only anticipating, but also actively seeking and fomenting a confrontation with Tbilisi.

Who Fired the First Shot?

In spite of the clearly predetermined nature of Russia's attack, the prevailing Western view after August 2008 is that the Georgian government acted irresponsibly when sending troops into Tskhinvali late on August 7, as it provided Russia with a pretext for intervening. Georgian officials have persistently disputed this view, maintaining that its attack on South Ossetia was a response to a Russian intervention in South Ossetia that was already under way.

A key question is whether the Georgian government ordered its troops to advance towards Tskhinvali *before* or *after* Russia had attacked, and whether it did so offensively or in an attempt to prevent the Russian army from moving further into Georgian territory. A key question is therefore

centers on when Russian forces entered Georgian territory through the Roki tunnel. Russia, for its part, initially claimed that its troops did not pass
the Roki tunnel until sometime in the afternoon on August 8, but failed to
provide the exact time. Russian authorities later presented a timeline,[48]
putting the exact time for the advance of Russian tanks towards Tskhinvali
at shortly after 3:00 P.M. on August 8. However, a number of sources have
challenged Russia's claims regarding the timing of events on August 7–8.
A careful report by the International Crisis Group[49] published on August 22
and several articles in authoritative international media[50] suggested that
Georgia's attack against Tskhnivali, and the movement of Russian troops
through the Roki tunnel, virtually coincided. Since then, a body of evidence has come to light which suggests that Russian forces began their
approach towards Tskhinvali hours *before* the Georgian troops were ordered towards the separatist capital. Moreover, as Andrei Illarionov suggests in his chapter, Russia's military presence had been building in South
Ossetia for some time.

In September 2008 Georgian authorities presented telephone intercepts
indicating that Russian troops had already arrived in South Ossetia via the
Roki tunnel in the early hours of August 7.[51] While the Georgian government failed to present the tapes until a month after the war,[52] Western officials, technical experts, and media have deemed the recordings to be credible.[53] It is significant that Russia has not challenged the authenticity of this
evidence, claiming instead that the large-scale movement of troops and
materials was part of a routine rotation of Russian peacekeeping forces in
South Ossetia. However, according to the international agreement which
established Russia's role as a "peacekeeper" in South Ossetia, such a rotation would have required Russia to give prior notification to the Georgian
government and the OSCE, which it conspicuously failed to do. Moreover,
several reports in the press indicate clearly that troops of the Russian 58th
Army were relocated to the South Ossetian border several days before the
war began and, on August 7, to South Ossetia itself.[54] Among such reports
is an interview with Russian Armed Forces Captain Denis Sedristy published in the official newspaper of Russia's Ministry of Defense, *Krasnaya
Zvezda,* on September 3. In his interview, Sedristy described how his
troops were ordered towards the South Ossetian capital on August 7. Following inquiries by Western media, *Krasnya Zvezda* quickly altered the
dates in the story as it appeared on its website, changing August 7 to August 8.[55] Demeaning one of its own officers, *Krasnaya Zvezda* subsequently claimed that Sedristy had suffered injuries during the war and that this

was the cause of his confusion over the all-important date of the troop movement.[56]

The evidence of Russian troop movement on August 7 is compelling but for now circumstantial. However, several reports, most notably Sergey Bagapsh's televised statement on the evening of August 7 that a Russian battalion was *already present* in the conflict zone, substantiate an unauthorized Russian military presence there prior to the Georgian intervention on August 7. Russia, for its part, has focused less on the issue of who moved first and instead pursued its line of having acted in response to acts of ethnic cleansing in South Ossetia by the Georgian government. In doing so, it ignores the many instances of unauthorized Russian military activity on the territory of South Ossetia over several years. Instances such as the Russian army's construction of a tank refueling station in Java in 2006 indicate that the Ministry of Defense believed that its role as nominal peacekeeper gave it a free hand in South Ossetia long before the events of August 2008.

Importantly, however, the exact timing of troop movements on both sides on August 7–8 should not be treated as the sole determinant of who was responsible for unleashing the war. In particular, Georgian officials' preoccupation with the issue of "who moved first" overshadows two important points. Paradoxically, both of these neglected issues speak in Georgia's favor.

First, it is not necessary for Georgia to invoke the doctrine of self-defense in this instance because it did not breach a sovereign border in South Ossetia. Yet, legal scholars will argue that a country's actions to protect its territory do not require a prior attack by another state. It is enough that such an attack is imminent.[57] In this light, if on August 7 the Georgian government had sufficient reason to consider itself as under attack by Russia, the exact timing of events is of limited relevance. In truth, developments over the spring and early summer of 2008 gave the Georgian authorities good reason to believe that Moscow was making preparations for war on Georgian territory. The launch by Moscow of the Kavkaz-2008 military exercise in mid-July provided evidence that no responsible government could have ignored. Over the course of the exercise, 30 military aircraft and 700 combat vehicles were activated and underwent readiness checks. Adding to Tbilisi's suspicion that the exercise constituted a mere cover-up for Russian mobilization along the Georgian border, instead of returning to their bases the troops remained in their positions on the Georgian border even after the completion of the two-week exercise. In the days immediately before the war broke out, security arrangements undertaken by Tskhinvali, including the movement of civilians to North Ossetia and the Russian military build-up in the town of Java, all pointed in the direction of specific war-planning. Continuous reports of Russian troop movement toward South Ossetia on August 7 only fuelled fears in Tbilisi that an attack was forthcoming. On this basis, Georgia repeatedly and urgently gave public voice to its concerns that Russia was planning some kind of military action against it. It is for this reason that Georgia had for years pleaded with the international community to abolish Russia's peculiar monopoly as the sole international "peacekeeper" in Abkhazia and South Ossetia. Every time it advanced this point, Georgia pointed to attempts by Russia to aggravate, rather than defuse, tensions in the conflict zones. Thus, Georgia had good reason to believe it would in due course be the object of Russian military action, and had tried unsuccessfully to engage the international community to prevent it.

Secondly, while Tbilisi has actively sought to justify its intervention in the conflict zone on August 7, it is in fact Moscow that carries the burden of proof with regard to breaching Georgia's sovereign borders. Given this, it is the more striking that Russia has failed to present any credible legal arguments in defense of its intervention in Georgia. True, Moscow has claimed that it was motivated in its actions by humanitarian concerns. Whether or not this was the case (and it seems highly doubtful), when intervening on the territory of a sovereign state Moscow would have been bound by the principles of proportionality and just cause. The very concept of "Humanitarian Intervention" (or "Responsibility to Protect") is widely debated among legal scholars, as it contradicts the general principles of state sovereignty and non-intervention. While supporters of the principle argue that a state has the right to intervene in another state for the purpose of protecting civilians, it is widely accepted that this right should be interpreted restrictively and constitute a last resort.[58] Russia's excessive use of force across the entire territory of Georgia, which resulted in casualties well exceeding the number of deaths during the initial fighting and caused severe material destruction, thus discredits Russia's justification for its intervention. This applies also to Moscow's argument of seeking to protect its servicemen and citizens within the zone of conflict, since the endangerment of a state's citizens does not automatically create a basis for intervening militarily on another state's territory.[59] It is worth noting, finally, that Moscow's awarding of Russian passports to Georgian citizens living within the conflict zones in Abkhazia and South Ossetia directly contributed to the destabilization of those territories, where it supposedly served as a peacekeeper, and constituted an illegal intervention into Georgia's internal affairs. From the standpoint of international law, Russia's claims to have been protecting local residents and its own citizens thus constitute a thin and unconvincing defense of its war against Georgia.

Of course, in any operation aimed at protecting its territory, Georgia also had an obligation to protect civilians. Indeed, the indiscriminate shelling of Tskhinvali and surrounding villages by Georgian forces on August 7–8 are subject to the same questions posed above to Russia. Acknowledging this, no purported Georgian action gave Russia the right to launch a full-blown invasion of Georgian territory. To date, though, Russia has escaped accountability both for the use of excessive force and for the breach of Georgia's borders. Tbilisi has brought Russia before the International Court of Justice but that body lacks jurisdiction over border violations,[60] which reduces the case to one concerning possible racial discrimination by Russia.

Why Tskhinvali?

The conclusion that the Georgian government acted to protect its territorial integrity in South Ossetia leads to the final question: if the main aim of Georgia's operation on August 7–8 was to repel the Russian tanks approaching the conflict zone, why did the Georgian army extend its attack to include the shelling of Tskhinvali?

Before moving on to this important question, it should be noted that Tbilisi had little to gain from launching an attack on the South Ossetian capital. Contrary to common belief, the Georgian government had few illusions with regard to the support it would receive from the West for such an endeavor. In fact, its actions in South Ossetia exposed the Georgian government to international criticism that was harmful to its own aspirations with regard to integration with Western structures. Indeed, during the spring, one of the chief factors that conditioned Tbilisi's restraint in responding to Russian provocations in Abkhazia was not to damage its chances of joining NATO. Notably also, by attacking Tskhinvali—an operation that was sure to fail given Russia's role in the region—Tbilisi risked losing what constituted a far more valuable piece of territory, namely Abkhazia.

Thus, given the apparent risk of international exposure for such an endeavor, and, indeed, risks connected with Russia's potential response, the decision by the Georgian government to attempt to capture the separatist capital warrants close attention.

The answer may lie in Tskhinvali's geographic location. Situated at the foot of the mountainous zone connecting South Ossetia with North Ossetia, the city is a vital point of entry into Georgia proper. By pushing into the separatist capital, the Georgian troops made it significantly harder for the

Russian ground troops to enter Georgian-controlled territory, possibly holding up the larger invasion for forty-eight hours or more. With summer holidays in Europe, and the international media focusing on the opening of the Beijing Olympics, Tbilisi needed to stall the advance of the Russian attack long enough to gain the attention of its Western friends and allies. Nonetheless, Georgia's decision to advance towards Tskhinvali on August 7 likely constituted a grave miscalculation of the possible Russian response to such a move. Whether or not Tbilisi perceived itself as having no other choice but to order its troops towards Tskhinvali on August 7, its move provided Moscow with the pretext it needed to launch its invasion of Georgian territory.

Conclusions

On the basis of evidence currently at hand, Russia's invasion, whether premeditated or merely opportunistic, must be seen as the culmination of interventionist actions by Moscow which extended over months and even years before hostilities broke out; but which the international community failed either to acknowledge or act upon. The invasion of Georgia was the first armed attack by Russia on a neighboring state since the invasion of Afghanistan in 1979. It caught the West utterly unprepared and either unable or unwilling to deal credibly with a crisis whose importance extends far beyond the borders of South Ossetia or even of Georgia.

In the aftermath of the war, international observers have focused largely on the chain of events in the immediate lead-up to the war, seeking to attribute responsibility for the outbreak of hostilities. Notably, the Georgian government has been criticized for acting recklessly on August 7, provoking Russia into acting to protect its citizens in South Ossetia. As has been discussed above, this notion lacks full consideration of the facts at hand and, importantly, principles of recognized international law. While it is true that both sides are responsible for the escalation of hostilities in July and early August, two important points should be recalled. First, the events leading up to the war must be assessed against general trends in the region over an extended period of time. In particular, Russia's military build-up in the conflict zones over the spring and summer of 2008 suggested strongly that an attack by Russia on Georgia was forthcoming. On August 7, credible reports on Russian troop movement into South Ossetia provided valid reason to assume that an intervention by Russia was imminent, or—as South Ossetia is legally part of Georgian territory—already ongoing. Thus, Tbilisi's attack against Tskhinvali likely constituted (whether miscalculated or not) an attempt to protect its territory. Secondly, Tbilisi does not carry the burden of proof with regard to its intervention in the South Ossetian conflict zone. Instead, it is Russia that needs to present a justifiable basis for crossing into Georgian territory. The intensity and extent of Russia's intervention utterly violated the principle of proportionality as stipulated by international law, thus discrediting Russia's argument of intervening into Georgian territory based on humanitarian motives.

In sum, the events in early August, those on August 7 in particular, should not be treated as decisive with regard to the issue of accountability for the Russia-Georgia war. The five-day war in Georgia should instead be viewed in a broader context, with developments prior, during, and, indeed, since the war, all pointing to a premeditated violation by Russia of Georgia's sovereign borders. Moscow, taking note of the absence of any Western response to Georgia's recurring requests for support during the months preceding the war, believed that the international community would either ignore a Russian invasion of Georgia or excuse it as justified in order to prevent Georgian aggression against South Ossetia. Indeed, Russia has largely escaped responsibility for its actions, challenging not only the future stability of the South Caucasus region but also the upholding of international law.

9

After August 7: The Escalation of the Russia-Georgia War

Pavel Felgenhauer

The sequence of events that led to the Russia-Georgia war is a matter of political contention and shifting blame, even though there is broad agreement on the narrative of the subsequent combat per se. Of course, the fog of war continues to obscure many details; staff documents are still secret on both the Russian and Georgian sides, as are figures on the exact number of men, tanks, and warplanes that were involved. However, there are good estimates on numbers and on the moves made by both sides in a short but eventful war.

The Strategic Mismatch

The Russians and their separatist allies in Abkhazia and South Ossetia prepared and executed in August 2008 a war which the Georgians did not predict or expect. The Georgians, until they were plunged headlong into the fighting, appear to have prepared only for a replay of previous confrontations in the Abkhazia and South Ossetia regions in the early 1990s, which had resulted in a military standoff with the separatist forces, who were supported to some extent by the Russian military and by so-called North Caucasian volunteers and Cossacks. But this time, the Russian military staged an all-out invasion, planning to totally decimate and destroy the Georgian military—in effect, a full demilitarization of Georgia, as well as to overthrow the hated pro-Western regime led by President Mikheil Saakashvili. For this purpose, the Russian staffs mobilized and prepared for action tens of thousands of servicemen from the Navy, Air Force, and Army. The Russian war plans also envisaged a possible escalation of the conflict with Georgia to involve the U.S. and NATO.

In the actual fighting in August 2008, the separatist forces that the Georgians had seen as their main adversary played only a supporting role as a vanguard to the Russians, to engage and draw the Georgian forces into combat. Subsequently their role shifted to that of an auxiliary infantry. This strategic mismatch in perceptions and planning produced a disastrous result for Georgia and threw Western policy-makers into disarray and created utter uncertainty over what to expect from Russia in the Caucasus or elsewhere. This confusion persists to the present.

In public testimony before a parliamentary commission investigating the war with Russia, the Chief of Staff of the Georgian Armed Forces during the war, General Zaza Gogava, disclosed that "military and foreign intelligence information coming before August was not comprehensive enough to indicate that such a large-scale Russian military intervention was to be expected. We were not expecting what started on August 9 – a full-scale military intervention with the goal to take over the capital city, Tbilisi." Gogava, as well as other Georgian officials who testified before the commission, divided the Russian military intervention into two phases—the first from August 7–9, and the second starting from August 9, when Russia launched what the Georgians term a "full-scale aggression." The Georgian failure to predict the Russian intervention was attributable in part to intelligence failure. Indeed, Gogava complained ruefully that "In 2005 the intelligence unit in the Ministry of Defense had been disbanded."[1]

The secretary of Georgia's National Security Council during the war, Alexander Lomaia (appointed Georgian ambassador to the UN in December 2008), testified that Russia used about a third of its combat-capable land forces in the operation against Georgia ("over 80,000 Russian servicemen were involved in all operations") and that "neither we nor any foreign intelligence service had any information about Russia's expected full-scale invasion and occupation of a large part of our territory – it was a shock and a surprise." According to Lomaia, it was known that several thousand Russian troops deployed during the Kavkaz-2008 military exercises on Georgia's northern border and in the vicinity of South Ossetia in July 2008, began moving through the Roki tunnel into South Ossetia on August 7, but the Georgian leaders believed they had enough troops to deal with such a force. Apparently, the Georgians did not notice a statement by General Yuri Netkachev that the number of troops involved in the Kavkaz-2008 exercises (8,000) "was officially underestimated."[2] According to Lomaia:

> "We can suppose that a political decision [on full-scale military intervention] was made in Russia on August 9 when Prime Minister Vladimir Putin arrived in Vladikavkaz; it seems that he was informed about the heavy damage inflicted on the Russian forces [already fighting in South Ossetia]

and it seems that the decision was taken after that to put into operation the plan involving a full-scale intervention."[3]

Georgian leaders did not fully understand Russian intentions, and made staggeringly erroneous assessments that led to strategically disastrous decisions. Georgian foreign intelligence service chief Gela Bezhuashvili, a former defense and foreign minister, in public testimony before the parliamentary commission stated that:

> Our information suggested Russia was planning a military intervention. A decision was made in principle to carry out aggression against Georgia in the second half of 2007. Analysis of both open and secret sources indicated that provocations were being prepared in the conflict areas, involving training and arming of the separatists forces, as well as preparing Cossacks to intervene in the area of conflict. The mobilization of Russia's air force started at the Mozdok airbase in Russia's North Ossetian Republic. Russia's A-50 reconnaissance aircraft, which is an AWACS type spy-plane, landed in Mozdok on August 4 or 5th. It is capable of correcting [i.e. tracing] artillery fire.[4]

Bezhuashvili's assessment seems to be accurate, though some mistakes in it have never been corrected. For example, the old Russian A-50 AWACS is equipped with ancient electronics, cannot "see" anything on the ground, and cannot possibly "correct artillery fire." Such mistakes, apparently, led to disastrous misinterpretations. Bezhuashvili acknowledged that "an assessment of the expected scale of the aggression was not easy." As a result, according to Bezhuashvili, Georgian foreign intelligence did not foresee that war might break out in August. "We were expecting that Russia would escalate tensions in September, October or in November 2008." The Georgians did not foresee that Russia was planning an invasion on two fronts (Abkhazia and South Ossetia) at the same time. To quote Bezhuashvili again, "we had no intelligence information that Russia was planning to occupy western Georgia - including Poti, Senaki and Zugdidi."[5] Apparently, the Georgians did not take seriously a statement by Abkhazia's foreign minister, Sergey Shamba, made in May 2008, that "it will take us two days to go on the offensive into Western Georgia and create a security buffer zone."[6]

Georgia's defense minister during the August war, Davit Kezerashvili, told this author in Tbilisi in November 2008 that, "if we would have known the scale of the Russian invasion, we would have prepared defensive positions, trenches and dugouts." Several days later, Kezerashvili told the parliamentary commission that "Georgia's army was not prepared for conventional warfare, as its training was mainly focused on lower-scale military operations and anti-terrorist operations. In principle, we knew Russia might attack, but I was not sure it would until August 7. Friendly Western nations all told us that it is impossible that in the twenty-first century Russia might initiate a direct intervention. We could have built fortified defense positions, dugouts and bunkers from Gori to Tbilisi and from Abkhazia to Kutaisi, but this could have led to panic [of the civilian population]."[7] Therefore, nothing was built.

The massive Russian invasion caught the Georgians off guard and unprepared both strategically and tactically. Russia, led by former KGB agent Vladimir Putin, managed to hide its preparations and intentions not only from the Georgians, but also from Western governments and intelligence services. The Georgian military was ready for a mobile, mostly offensive war either in Abkhazia or South Ossetia, but not for simultaneous large-scale combat with superior, heavily armed, and air-supported enemy forces invading from Abkhazia and Ossetia, in other words, on both fronts at the same time. As Georgian forces pushed north into South Ossetia during August 8, they may have been prepared to fend off a limited Abkhaz assault against the heavily fortified upper Kodori Gorge, but a full-scale Russian invasion over the Inguri River to occupy western Georgia was surely a surprise. Because of this huge strategic blunder, from the very first shot in August 2008, the Georgians had no chance of successfully repelling the Russians. Political and military disaster was inevitable.

The Russian War Machine Goes into Action

Once the fighting was over, a Georgian parliamentary commission publicly scrutinized the events of the August war, though some of these proceedings in Tbilisi took place in secret. In Moscow, however, there were no public official hearings of any sort, or detailed official disclosures about the prewar plan of combat or the actual course of the war. Moscow wanted its military action in Georgia in August 2008 to be seen merely as a reaction to "Georgian aggression" against Tskhinvali, the capital of South Ossetia, and against Russian peacekeepers in the region. However, this official Russian position ignores the simple fact that an invasion of such a magnitude would require long-term preparations involving the entire Russian military, including the Army, Air Force, and Navy.

In December 2008 President Dmitry Medvedev told Russian TV how Russian Defense Minister Anatoly Serdyukov had reported that Georgian forces had begun an offensive in South Ossetia on August 7, and how he

(Medvedev) hesitated for several hours before giving orders to use force in response. According to Medvedev, the five-day campaign was effective, as it demonstrated the might of the Russian military and the valor of "our citizens and soldiers, who with minimal losses irreversibly crushed the Georgian war machine, restored peace and saved tens of thousands of people from extinction." Medvedev added that beforehand he had suspected that Saakashvili was planning military action, "so we prepared for that, and as a result of our preparations the operation was a success."[8]

Russia's top military commander, First Deputy Defense Minister and Chief of the General Staff General Nikolai Makarov, speaking to journalists in December 2008 about the need for urgent military reform, described some serious problems that had been encountered during the war in August. "Less than 20 percent of our units are battle-ready, while the rest have only officers without privates," stated Makarov, who went on to describe such skeleton or "cadre" units as "paper divisions." Officers who command each other have no experience in leading men and cannot command effectively on the battlefield in time of war. According to Makarov, during the war with Georgia, "We were forced to handpick colonels and generals from all over Russia, [men] who were able to command in battle; ...the commanders of the 'paper divisions', when they were given reinforcements of men and armaments... were confused and some [even] refused to obey orders."[9] It is obvious that this process of expanding cadre units and preparing them for action, and of seeking out able commanders all over Russia, could not have begun in the early hours of August 8 while Medvedev was considering whether to go to war or not. Thus, Medvedev himself provides crucial evidence that Russia's planning for the August war began long before August 8.

During the day of August 8, Georgian forces moved north through South Ossetia, bypassing pockets of resistance from Ossetian separatists and Russian peacekeepers, while columns of Russian armor, troops, and heavy guns were pouring south through the Roki tunnel to Tskhinvali to meet the Georgians. Two days of intermittent fighting in and around Tskhinvali followed. Russia deployed armored and mechanized regiments of the 58th Army of the North Caucasian Military District, the 19th Motor-Rifle Division based in Vladikavkaz, and the 42nd Motor-Rifle division from Chechnya, as well as a battalion of the 33rd Special Mountain Brigade. Regiments of the IS 76 Airborne Division from Pskov and the 98th Airborne Division from Ivanovo were sent into action, as were the 45th Airborne Special Forces regiment from Moscow. The 22nd GRU Special Forces Brigade of the North Caucasian Military District from Aksay near Rostov-on-Don, and pro-Moscow Chechen GRU battalions "West" and "East" (*Zapad* and *Vostok*) also saw action. Finally, heavy artillery and missile units of the 58th Army were deployed in South Ossetia, including a missile brigade armed with short and medium range Tochka-U (SS-21) and Iskander (SS-26) ballistic missiles.[10]

The Russian invasion was hampered by several factors. These included the single narrow road leading into South Ossetia from Russia, the movement of civilian refugees out of the battle zone, and the need to bring in supplies and take out the wounded. Old Russian tanks and armored battle vehicles often broke down, creating constant traffic jams south of the Roki tunnel.

The Russian military reported an almost total breakdown of military communication systems during the fighting in South Ossetia and that Russian commanders were using their personal mobile phones—which in South Ossetia were covered by Georgian mobile phone operators—in order to communicate with troops and commanders.[11] The Army chief General Vladimir Boldyrev who, from his headquarters in Vladikavkaz, directly commanded the joint forces that invaded Georgia, announced that the fighting revealed two main Russian military deficiencies: inadequate communications and a bad command system.[12] According to General Gogava, the Georgian side also had problems with communications: "We contracted [U.S. defense communications and information technology company] Harris Corp. in late 2006 to supply us with communications systems; we had a problem, since these systems need well-trained personnel."[13]

The skies were bright over Georgia in August 2008, allowing the Russian military to capitalize fully on its total superiority in the air. However, the outdated Russian Air Force is not equipped with aircraft capable of precise air support at night or in bad weather. August seems therefore to have been chosen as the time to invade because of its usually fine weather. This decision paid off. According to Gogava, "The largest casualties among the Georgian military were inflicted in the immediate vicinity of Tskhinvali as a result of air strikes."[14]

The Russian air offensive in Georgia was not without casualties. According to Gogava, the Russians lost 19 aircraft; according to Interior Minister Vano Merabishvili, the number was 15.[15] The Russian Defense Ministry officially acknowledged the loss of four aircraft, including one strategic supersonic Tu-22M3 (Backfire) bomber that was used to gather intelligence information and bomb the Georgians.[16] There exist Russian expert reports which claim that up to eight aircraft were lost.[17] According to the Defense Ministry's official spokesman, General Anatoly Nogovitsyn, the

Russian military were surprised by the Georgians' use of advanced BUK-M1 antiaircraft missiles; he also indicated that Russian aircraft suffered casualties mainly during the first day of fighting, when they were ambushed near Tskhinvali. According to Nogovitsyn, Russian military intelligence (GRU) had not reported that the Georgians had BUK-M1 and the Georgians did not switch on the BUK-M1 radars or otherwise reveal themselves until the Russian bombers were within strike distance.[18] Nogovitsyn's comments disclose a serious lapse of communication procedure within the Russian military, since Georgia itself had officially reported the purchase of BUK-M1 anti-aircraft systems from Ukraine, and the sale was much discussed on Internet sites prior to the August war.[19]

The Russian Air Force still has hundreds of jets, but the number of well-trained pilots is limited. The Air Force's losses during its short war with Georgia were painful. To save pilots' lives, the Air Force decided after the war to buy Israeli-made spy drones in what would be Russia's first purchase of military hardware from the Jewish state, and the first major official procurement of weapons from a "Western" nation since 1945. Israel had previously sold drones to Georgia, which it used successfully both before and during the August war. Meanwhile, Russia's defense industry has failed to produce modern drones. Deputy Defense Minister Vladimir Popovkin, in charge of procurement and armaments and negotiating the acquisition of a batch of different types of Israeli-made spy drones, told reporters in April 2009 that a firm contract had already been signed and further ones could follow. Popovkin ridiculed the performance of the newest Russian-made spy drone Typchak during the August war, saying that "its engine made a terrible noise that was audible 100 kilometers away." According to Popovkin, the noise of the Typchak scared both Georgians and Russians and the drone was badly damaged by friendly fire.[20]

In spite of the mishaps, Russian military and political leaders were playing it safe in August 2008. They acted in a way that was reminiscent of the second Chechen war in 1999–2001, in the sense that they wanted to leave little to chance and therefore deployed an overwhelming force. Still, the single narrow approach road leading from the Roki tunnel through South Ossetia to Georgia proper created problems and dangers. Russian troops moved into South Ossetia steadily, but slowly.

Georgia Counters Russian Onslaught with Military Improvisation

According to Gogava, at 11:35 P.M. on August 7, President Saakashvili speaking in his capacity as Commander-in-Chief, gave the military three orders. These were, first, to prevent all military vehicles from entering Georgia from Russia through the Roki tunnel; second, to suppress all positions that were attacking Georgian peacekeepers and Interior Ministry posts, or Georgian villages; and third, to protect the interests and security of the civilian population while implementing these orders. According to Lomaia, "the logic of our actions was to neutralize firing positions on the outskirts of Tskhinvali and try to advance closer to the Roki tunnel as soon as possible by circling around Tskhinvali."[21]

According to Kezerashvili, Russian infantry exceeding one battalion in size and more than 40 pieces of armor and heavy guns were deployed south of the Roki tunnel before August 7, while reinforcements were camped north of the tunnel, ready to be moved up. After the war, multiple reports and interviews given by Russian soldiers were published in different Russian newspapers, including the official Defense Ministry daily *Krasnaya Zvezda* (Red Star). These provided first-hand evidence that Russian troops indeed began the invasion of Georgia and actually crossed the border through the Roki tunnel before the Georgian troops attacked the Ossetian positions in the Tskhinvali region.[22]

Kezerashvili and his First Deputy Batu Kutelia (appointed Georgian ambassador in Washington in December 2008) told this author in Tbilisi, in November 2008, that on August 7 the Georgian military had a scout in position at the south end of the Roki tunnel who could not only monitor the movement of Russian troops and armor into South Ossetia, but also communicate the exact GPS coordinates of Russian tank columns that could be used to direct artillery fire using GPS targeting. Kutelia went on to say that the Georgians decided they could not miss this opportunity since they did not have such capabilities further south. The Georgian military swiftly moved up Czech-made Dana self-propelled howitzers and Israeli-made GRAD LAR long-range multiple rocket launcher systems. Bypassing Tskhinvali, these were moved instead to the Georgian-controlled enclave of Tamarasheni, north of Tskhinvali.

According to the "Timeline of Russian Aggression in Georgia," published by the Georgian government,[23] "At approximately 00:45 A.M. on August 8, Georgian forces fired artillery rounds at the invading Russian forces on roads being used by a Russian column already moving south of the Roki tunnel." According to intelligence information communicated to this author, the Georgian artillery and GRAD LAR armor-piercing cluster bomblets caused damage to advancing Russian armor. Indeed, the Russian military acknowledge that the Georgian artillery performed well during the

August war. However, the strategic goal of discouraging the Russians from continuing their overall onslaught was not achieved.

To fight in and around Tskhinvali the Georgians deployed their 4th Infantry Brigade, the Army Artillery Brigade, a separate tank battalion from Gori, the Gori-based Defense Ministry Special Forces Brigade, and Interior Ministry Special Forces. On August 8, after advancing into the conflict zone of South Ossetia, Georgian armed forces overtook a number of Ossetian villages around Tskhinvali. At approximately 11:00 A.M. on August 8, the Georgian forces secured the heights around Tskhinvali. Later, Defense Ministry forces and Interior Ministry Special Forces entered Tskhinvali, encountering resistance from Ossetian separatist and Russian peacekeeping forces. By midday on August 8, the first Russian reinforcements arrived into the Tskhinvali region from the north and west through the so-called Zara bypass road.

According to Gogava, "It was a mobile defense operation." There was no trench warfare. Russian and Georgian columns skirmished in and around Tskhinvali. Most casualties were inflicted by the Russian Air Force, and by Georgia's artillery and multiple rocket launcher systems. Ossetian forces supported by Russian peacekeepers continued to hold pockets of resistance inside Tskhinvali. On August 9, the commander of Russia's 58th Army, General Anatoly Khrulev, was wounded during hand-to-hand fighting that broke out when a column of troops he was traveling with was ambushed near Tskhinvali by Georgian forces.

The Ossetian fighters could not effectively resist the regular Georgian army and Special Forces. But the Georgians were increasingly overpowered and outgunned by the large numbers of Russian troops pouring into South Ossetia from the north. On August 8, Saakashvili declared a mobilization of the reserve National Guard. This turned out to be a total disaster. Reserve units clearly needed much additional training even to be used as auxiliary forces, but they were sent to the battle zone at Gori, south of Tskhinvali, which caused additional confusion. According to Kezerashvili, "The system of reserve forces failed and the command of the reserve troops and the National Guard failed; there was confusion and disorganization. One of the reasons was that the National Guard lacked experienced officers."[24] The 17,000-strong Georgian regular army was on its own, supported, according to Merabishvili, by up to 5,000 Georgian police officers with 70 armored vehicles.[25] Meanwhile, two thousand of the best-trained Georgian soldiers of the elite 1st Infantry Brigade were deployed in Iraq with U.S. troops. On August 10 and 11, U.S. transports flew them back to

Tbilisi, but by then the battle of Tskhinvali and the entire war had been lost.

Invasion from Abkhazia and Overall Georgian Defeat

By the end of August 9, the situation of the Georgian forces was fast becoming hopeless. High-ranking Georgian officials seem to believe that a turning point in fortunes happened after Putin arrived in Vladikavkaz and gave orders to begin a full-scale invasion. This notion is in all likelihood, however, an illusion. A massive pre-planned joint force operation was already in full swing, with tens of thousands of soldiers and thousands of pieces of heavy military equipment moving into battle along precarious mountain roads and no room to maneuver in that terrain. Additional Russian reinforcements could not have been rushed into Georgia, since the few invasion routes were already clogged up with traffic. Simply put, by the end of August 9, the Georgian leadership in Tbilisi could at last discern the original Russian plan for the invasion and, through the fog of war, could also more clearly see the war's likely outcome. All Putin could have done in Vladikavkaz on August 9 was to tell his generals to continue with the invasion, as they did.

The main mass of Russian troops that were designated to invade Georgia through South Ossetia had managed by August 10 to pass through the bottleneck of the Roki tunnel and was slowly closing in on Tskhinvali, mowing down the Georgians by overwhelming, though not very accurate, artillery and rocket fire, as well as aerial bombardment. Over 12,000 Russian troops with hundreds of tanks, armored battle vehicles, multiple rocket launchers, and heavy guns moved into South Ossetia and, beyond that, into Georgia proper. Several thousand armed Ossetians and other volunteer militias from the Russian-ruled North Caucasus supported the Russian forces as auxiliary infantry.

By August 10, the Georgian leadership received reliable intelligence that while Russian troops were pressing their way into the Tskhinvali area, an even bigger invasion force was rapidly assembling in Abkhazia, where there had not yet been any fighting. Moscow sent a diplomatic note to Tbilisi, announcing that from 4.00 P.M. on August 9, a naval task force had begun patrolling waters near Abkhazia, and declared a state of siege in regions of Abkhazia bordering Georgia.[26]

In July 2008 the Russian Black Sea Fleet task force had left Sevastopol, Crimea, to take part in the Kavkaz-2008 military exercises. The Fleet was led by its flagship missile cruiser *Moskva* and included frigates, missile boats, and large amphibious landing craft. An armored regiment of marines landed at the small Abkhazian port of Ochamchire, close to the border with Georgia. Infantry and armor of the 20th Motorized Rifle Division from Volgograd were moved into Abkhazia by means of the recently repaired railroad from Russia, and troops from the 7th Airborne Division were flown by transport jets from Novorossiysk to Sukhumi.[27] The sea landing and air transportation supplemented deployment by land routes, adding to their limited capacity and allowing a swifter aggregation of a credible assault force.

As discussed in detail elsewhere in this volume, Moscow had, on May 31, without warning sent a 400 man battalion of Railroad Troops into Abkhazia to repair railroad tracks and bridges from the Russian border clear to Ochamchire. The troops completed their task on July 30, 2008, just in time for the invasion.[28] Russian armor is traditionally moved in and out of battle zones mainly by railroad, and it is the task of special Railroad Troops to keep the tracks in repair and to organize makeshift armor battlefield disembarkment points. Russian highways are in poor condition, because during the Cold War they were seen as possible routes by which motorized Western armies could invade. There is still no highway connecting Moscow with the Pacific coast, for instance, but the railroads are in good condition and connect all strategic destinations. Because of railroad weight constraints, Russian tanks weigh less than 50 tons, their armor being thinner than that of their modern Western counterparts. In a war situation in Abkhazia, Russian tank columns would rapidly have destroyed the only coastal highway leading southward from the Russian border. The prior deployment of Railroad Troops and repairs of the tracks were an essential part of the overall preparations for serious armed action. In South Ossetia, Russian armor was forced to move from Vladikavkaz under its own steam. In the process it destroyed road surfaces and itself fell into disrepair, causing huge traffic jams.

Additional army, airborne, and marine troops reinforced the 3,000-strong peacekeeping force already in Abkhazia. In April 2008 the Russian Foreign Ministry accused Georgia of concentrating forces and weapons in the upper part of the Kodori Gorge in Abkhazia and of preparing an attack.[29] Several days later, the Russian Foreign Ministry announced an increase of the peacekeeping contingent in Abkhazia from roughly 1,500 to 3,000 men. An airborne battalion was moved close to the border of Abkhazia with Georgia—the Inguri River.[30]

Russia deployed up to 15,000 troops in Abkhazia in total. The Abkhazian regular army, led by Russian officers, was also mobilized for armed action; it included up to 10,000 soldiers and several hundred pieces of armor and guns. The overall number of Russian troops moved into Georgia in August 2008 amounted to 25,000–30,000, supported by more than 1,200 pieces of armor and heavy artillery. Also involved in the action were up to 200 aircraft and 40 helicopters.[31] Together with crews of the Black Sea Fleet deployed for action, Air Force and logistics military personnel who took part in the fray but were not actually moved into Georgia, the overall number of Russian troops taking part in the war may be estimated to have been 40,000. In addition to this, 10,000 to 15,000 separatist militias and fighters acted as auxiliary forces.

The Georgians were falling back from Tskhinvali under Russian pressure and had neither ready forces nor prepared defensive positions to counter the imminent threat of a second invasion into western Georgia. On August 10, Lomaia announced that Georgia would observe a unilateral cease-fire and would move its forces out of South Ossetia.[32] Georgian troops attempted to establish defenses outside South Ossetia; the last serious battle of the war took place in the Georgian village of Nikozi on August 10. However, Russian troops did not stop at the old cease-fire line in South Ossetia but instead pushed southward to the city of Gori.

On August 10, a Russian armored column crossed the Inguri River from Abkhazia into western Georgia. The local Georgian authorities and police offered no resistance, while the Georgian military withdrew ahead of the Russian advance. Over several days the Russian forces spread out without meeting any resistance, occupying Zugdidi, the port of Poti (the main base of the Georgian navy), and a large Georgian military base in Senaki. The Russian forces captured stockpiles of Georgian military equipment and destroyed the Senaki base.

On the eve of the August war, the Georgian navy had been small, armed with old ships which were not ready for serious action. Kutelia told this author in November 2008 that, at the start of the invasion, all seaworthy Georgian naval vessels were moved from Poti south to Batumi to be out of harm's way. The Russian Navy announced it sunk a Georgian "missile ship" during a naval encounter after the latter attempted to attack the Black Sea flotilla.[33] Kutelia asserts the Georgian Defense Ministry knows nothing of such an encounter. Georgia did have two small guided missile ships, one being an old Soviet craft called *Tbilisi* and the other an even older French-built ship, the *Dioskuria*. Both were left stranded in Poti and were sunk in port by the occupying Russian army. In the spring of 2009 the wrecks of the ships were auctioned off as scrap metal for $61,000 in order to clear Poti harbor.[34] The naval encounter reported by the Russian navy in August

2008 was either a propaganda ploy or an illusion. After the war in August, Georgia disbanded its navy and handed over its surviving small ships to the local coast guard.

In August 2008, the Kodori Gorge was apparently the only well-fortified part of Georgian territory. It was also the only part of Abkhazia controlled by the Georgians. Since 2006 Abkhaz leaders in Sukhumi, together with Moscow, were demanding a Georgian withdrawal from this critical area. According to Merabishvili, "About 300–400 Interior Ministry troops were deployed in Kodori," but there were no army troops on the spot. From August 9–12, Abkhaz and Russian forces bombed and shelled the Kodori Gorge but, according to Merabishvili, the Georgian troops there were well entrenched and suffered no casualties. At the same time as the Russian troops were occupying western Georgia without resistance, they were moving forward to cut the only road connecting the Kodori Gorge with the rest of Georgia. Merabishvili ordered his troops and the local population to evacuate Kodori.[35]

Retreat to Mtskheta: The Last Stand

On August 10, the Georgian forces began retreating from South Ossetia and on August 11 began an overall retreat on all fronts, concentrating forces for a last stand to defend the capital, Tbilisi. At the same time, they continued to observe their unilateral cease-fire in the hope that the West would press Moscow to cease its advance. On August 11, the Georgians abandoned Gori. Most regular army units retreated in an orderly fashion but elements of the ragtag National Guard fled from Gori in panic.

As the Russian troops rolled in on the heels of the retreating Georgians, their commanders, fearing further losses of manned aircraft, used SS-21 and SS-26 ballistic missiles to hit targets deep in Georgia. According to Merabishvili, some 60 SS-21 and SS-26 missiles were fired. Eyewitnesses reported that by August 12 the SS-21 ballistic missile batteries of the 58th Army Rocket Brigade were moved through the Roki tunnel into South Ossetia close to Tskhinvali from where they could hit targets in and around Tbilisi.[36]

As the Russians captured Gori, they spread out in all directions, pursuing the retreating Georgians. There were reports that Russian helicopters fire-bombed forests in Borjomi National Park south-west of Gori. These attacks led Saakashvili to publicly accuse the Russian forces of "ecocide."[37] The exact reason for the alleged fire-bombing is not clear, but most likely had to do with other, more practical reasons than attempts to ignite bush fires per se. The Russian helicopters patrolling the Borjomi valley could have used flares to deflect possible heat-seeking anti-aircraft missile attacks. The flares could have hit the dry wooded steep slopes of the Borjomi valley, causing fires that were subsequently controlled by the locals. Merabishvili told the parliamentary commission that after the cease-fire, Georgian tanks were hidden from the advancing Russians in Borjomi and also in Imereti in western Georgia. "The local residents knew where our tanks were hidden, but did not tell the Russians," stated Merabishvili.[38] The Russian attack helicopters may have been seeking the hidden Georgian armor that disappeared in the Borjomi valley and could have actually used missiles to attack suspected hidden targets in the local woods, causing fires.

General Nogovitsyn denounced as "disinformation" reports that Tochka-U (SS-21) missiles had been moved into South Ossetia and, likewise, accusations that Iskander (SS-26) missiles were actually used.[39] The Dutch Foreign Ministry nevertheless announced after an investigation that Dutch cameraman Stan Storimans and four other people were killed in Gori on August 12 (just before a cease-fire was announced) by an Iskander SS-26 missile armed with a cluster warhead.[40] The Russian Foreign Ministry replied that the evidence gathered by the Dutch was inconclusive.[41] Apparently, the Russian command had been aiming at a Georgian military base near Gori but had missed and hit a residential area instead.

Central Georgia—from Tskhinvali to Gori and from there to Tbilisi—is mainly an open plain with scattered hills. It is good country for tanks and the Georgians had no chance of stopping the Russian advance, which was supported by air power. Several kilometers northwest of Tbilisi the road from Gori passes through Mtskheta—the ancient Georgian capital. At Mtskheta, the road to Tbilisi passes through a steep gorge surrounded by high mountains—a good natural defense position at which a determined force may stop an advancing superior foe. By August 12, the Georgian command had gathered most of its regular army and Interior Ministry forces at Mtskheta and in Tbilisi for a last desperate stand.

Kutelia informed this author in November 2008 that there existed no prewar prepared plan for the defense of Tbilisi or Mtskheta in August, and there were no prepared defensive positions or bunkers to shelter troops from Russian air attack. As they retreated in the face of the Russian offensive, the Georgians managed to withdraw most of their more modern heavy equipment. Kutelia said that while 42 tanks were lost in action—a quarter of the overall tank force—this included only two Israeli-modernized T-72s that were abandoned to the Russians in Senaki. Under orders from their superiors, the Georgian forces dutifully fell back, but the retreat rattled the troops. It is not clear whether at this critical moment in the 2008 war they would have been able, under a relentless Russian attack, to hold their ground at Mtskheta, or if they would have caved in, exposing the capital of Tbilisi to occupation.

In any case, the battle of Mtskheta never took place. On August 12, Medvedev in Moscow announced the acceptance of a cease-fire plan brokered by French President Nicholas Sarkozy. At 3.00 P.M. on August 12, Russian troops were ordered to halt military activities.[42] To be sure, even after this announcement Russian military columns continued to advance, to occupy more territory, and to plunder Georgia. While Russian forces turned a blind eye, Ossetian militias marauded and ethnically cleansed Georgian towns and villages inside South Ossetia and between Tskhinvali and Gori. But the march on Tbilisi was called off.

Instead Russian forces established so-called "buffer security zones" in Georgia around the territories of breakaway Abkhazia and South Ossetia, claiming that this was allowed under preexisting cease-fire agreements. On September 2, 2008, Putin announced: "There are no Russian troops left in Georgia - only peacekeepers." Putin further stated, "There are no Russian troops in the Georgian port city of Poti – only peacekeepers nearby." Putin insisted that "Russian peacekeepers" will stay in the "security zones" in Georgia and that on top of that Russia retained the right to impose "additional security measures" it has not yet used. Putin blasted the U.S. for sending humanitarian aid to the port city of Batumi in the south of Georgia on the Turkish border using armed naval ships. Putin stated: "We will surely answer, but in a way you'll know later."[43]

During the occupation of the "buffer security zones" Russian troops captured or destroyed Georgian military equipment and munitions at bases in Poti, Senaki, and Gori. In Senaki the Georgian military had a center for modernizing Soviet-made T-72 tanks—installing Israeli-made night-vision and other modern electronic equipment. According to Kutelia, two T-72 tanks that were in the process of modernization and could not be moved were captured by Russian troops and taken back to Russia. Kutelia expressed the hope that since the computer displays of the captured modernized tanks used the Georgian alphabet, the Russians would not fully figure out how they worked.

In Poti, a week after Moscow accepted the cease-fire, Russian soldiers took about 20 Georgian troops prisoner and commandeered U.S. Army Humvees that were awaiting shipment back to the United States after taking part in anti-terrorist exercises with Georgian troops in July 2008. The deputy chief of Russia's general staff, General Anatoly Nogovitsyn, who acted as Russia's main military spokesman during and after the war, announced the U.S. Army Humvees were military trophies and that the Russian military were investigating the Humvees "very interesting" electronic equipment.[44] The Georgian soldiers captured in Poti were handed back to the Georgians in exchange for the release of Georgian General Roman Dumbadze, who in 2004 openly supported the pro-Russian separatist leadership in the Georgian autonomous republic of Adjara against the Saakashvili government. In 2006 Dumbadze was sentenced to seventeen years in prison for treason by a Georgian court.[45] Aslan Abashidze—the warlord who ruled Adjara from 1992 to 2004—is at present in exile in Moscow. Dumbadze and Abashidze may in the future be used by Moscow to create another center of separatism in Adjara in addition to Abkhazia and South Ossetia.

The main task of the Russian invasion was to bring about state failure and fully destroy the Georgian army and centralized police force. A failed Georgian state, torn apart by political rivalry and regional warlords, cannot ever become a NATO member and could be easier to control from Moscow. A General Staff military official told this author in Moscow after the August war that: "We had plans to capture large numbers of Georgian soldiers after pushing them out of Tskhinvali, but they retreated too fast."

In addition to collecting "trophies" and destroying Georgian military bases and infrastructure, the occupation of the "buffer security zones" gave Russia control of the strategically important road and rail link, as well as gas and oil pipelines that connect the oil and gas rich Caspian region with the Black and Mediterranean Seas. The large Senaki airbase provided a direct air transport link with Russia proper, especially important since South Ossetia does not have a single airstrip and the airbases in Abkhazia are far from the Georgian border. The Russian troops occupied the Akhalgori district that was inhabited by Georgians, but under Communist rule was officially part of South Ossetia. The Georgian population fled Akhalgory and the Russian troops established an important base only several miles from Mtskheta. But there was a serious logistic problem—there was no road directly connecting Tskhinvali and Akhalgory—the only way was through Georgian territory proper, using the "buffer security zone."

The buffer zone around South Ossetia became a lawless area looted and ravaged by the Ossetian militia, while thousands of Georgian civilians fled in panic. In accordance with the EU-brokered cease-fire and under diplomatic pressure from the West, the Russians eventually withdrew from the buffer zones around the territories of Abkhazia and South Ossetia in October 2008 as unarmed EU observers moved in. Before the withdrawal, Russian troops built a makeshift mountain road from Tskhinvali to Akhalgori, but there were problems using it during the winter. As bad weather hampered the use of Russian airpower and snow covered the mountains between October and November of 2008, the Russian military could not continue large-scale military operations in 2008 and withdrew to consolidate their positions and establish military bases inside Abkhazia and South Ossetia. According to the Georgian Defense Ministry, 170 soldiers were killed and 1,198 were wounded. Of the 170 killed, ten bodies are still not identified and are considered "missing in action."[46] One hundred and eighty-eight Georgian civilians, meanwhile, have been reported killed.[47] Merabishvili stated that fourteen Interior Ministry servicemen were killed during the war and 227 wounded.[48] Nogovitsyn announced that the Russian military had 74 dead, 19 missing, and 171 wounded.[49] The official Russian casualty figures were later changed to 71 dead and 340 wounded.[50] As time passed, the official Russian casualty figures continued to fluctuate without any official explanation. The latest available figure is 48 servicemen killed, which includes ten peacekeepers.[51] Russia is known to be a nation with an unpredictably changing past.

Acting deliberately after the cease-fire, Ossetians took vengeance on Georgian villages north of Tskhinvali, razing them to the ground and forcibly expelling their population.[52] Tens of thousands of refugees from South Ossetia have been resettled in newly-build makeshift houses in new settlements near the main road from Gori to Mtskheta. Claims by Russian and Ossetian officials that the Georgians committed "genocide" and killed some 2,000 civilians in Tskhinvali were never substantiated. After months of work, Russia's prosecutor-general's office that was investigating alleged "Georgian war crimes in South Ossetia" confirmed the death of 162 civilians during the war with Georgia in all of South Ossetian territory.[53] South Ossetia is today a barren, sparsely populated land, isolated from both Russia and Georgia, with the local Ossetians and occupying Russian troops surviving the 2008–9 winter under terrible conditions.[54]

Why Did the Kremlin Stop the Advance on Tbilisi?

On August 12, when Medvedev accepted the French-brokered cease-fire and halted the advance on Tbilisi, high-ranking Kremlin insider and spin doctor Gleb Pavlovsky told the radio station Ekho Moskvy that at an "important meeting" on the same day there had been calls not to accept a cease-fire but to march on to Tbilisi and "maybe further than Tbilisi." Pavlovsky insisted that an influential group within the Russian leadership wanted to press on to Tbilisi in order to permanently ruin Russia's relations with so-called "civilized nations" and wreck Medvedev's announced plans to modernize and westernize Russia.[55]

Pavlovsky seems to be right in claiming that even after the war, there remained elements within the Russian leadership that believed the job had not been finished in August 2008. Russian leaders Medvedev and Putin genuinely hate Saakashvili. After the war in August, Medvedev declared in an interview with Italian RAI TV, "For us, president Saakashvili does not exist, he is a political corpse."[56] In March 2009 Medvedev reiterated: "We love and value the Georgian people. I do not want to have any relations with Saakashvili and will not communicate with him. But if, as a result of democratic processes, power in Georgia changes, we are ready for discussions."[57]

If Saakashvili were to be removed from power, a squabble between multiple opposition leaders would be inevitable, and the Georgian state could weaken or disintegrate, allowing Russia to gain more influence in Georgia and restore its dominance in the South Caucasus. And a permanently unstable Georgia would never become a member of NATO.

The cease-fire in August 2008 left the strategically important Russian force in Armenia cut off, with no transit connections by land to Russia. The number of Russian soldiers in Armenia is limited to some 4,000, but during 2006 and 2007 large amounts of heavy weapons and supplies were moved into the country from Russian bases that were being closed in Batumi and Akhalkalaki. At present, there are some 200 Russian tanks, over 300 combat armored vehicles, 250 heavy guns, and other military equipment in Armenia—enough to fully arm a battle force of over 20,000 soldiers.[58] Furthermore, forces in Armenia can be rapidly expanded by bringing in manpower by air from Russia. Spare parts to maintain the armaments may also be transported by air, but if a credible land military transit link is not established in a year or two, there will be no possibility to modernize or replace old equipment. The forces would thus deteriorate, thereby undermining Russia's commitment to defending its ally Armenia and its ambition to reestablish dominance in the South Caucasus.

After the war in August, the Russian military staged its largest military exercises since the end of the Cold War, called Stability-2008. Maneuvers of units on land, sea, and air in Russia and on the high seas began on September 1, lasted over 2 months, and involved some 50,000 soldiers.[59] The scenario of Stability-2008 outlined a local conflict escalating into an all-out air, sea, and land war between Russia and the West which, in turn, escalates into a global nuclear conflict with the U.S. Shortly after the war with

Georgia, Medvedev explained that "we have seen how an absolutely real war can erupt suddenly and how simmering local conflicts, which are sometimes even called 'frozen,' can turn into a true military firestorm."[60]

As the Russian military staffs made preparations for the planned August 2008 invasion of Georgia under the cover of the military exercises Kavkaz-2008, additional strategic reinforcements were mobilized for a possible escalation of hostilities in the eventuality that Washington would offer Tbilisi assistance and get directly involved in the fray. In August 2008 Moscow calculated that Saakashvili was fatally undermined, "a political corpse" who was destined to fall. Hence there seemed to be no need to risk an escalating confrontation with the West by pushing on to Tbilisi.

In August 2008 the Russian forward troops near Gori found themselves at a distance of hundreds of kilometers, over very bad roads, from their supply bases. They were thinly spread out, and experienced severe logistical problems. They were forced to employ undisciplined Ossetian militias as auxiliary infantry as the Georgian regular forces concentrated to defend Tbilisi. Russia could have suffered a humiliating defeat at Mtskheta while, if victorious, marauding militias and hungry Russian soldiers would have plundered Tbilisi, inflicting lasting political damage.

There were therefore ample material and political reasons to take an operational pause and stop short of Tbilisi and full victory. In 2009, however, all these reasons began to evaporate: the overall Western reaction turned out to be meek and the risk of a direct military confrontation between Russia and the U.S. or Europe nonexistent. Saakashvili managed to survive in power, while the need for an offensive pause to supply forward units vanished as Russia established forward bases in Abkhazia and South Ossetia. The Russian troops did not go to Tbilisi in August 2008, but this does not imply that they will never do so.

10

Defining Victory and Defeat: The Information War Between Russia and Georgia

Paul A. Goble

Even before the guns fell silent after the Russian invasion of Georgia, a Soviet-era anecdote began making the rounds in the Russian blogosphere. According to the story, Adolf Hitler comes back from the dead and arrives in Moscow in time for the annual May Day parade. After watching the Soviet military parade, its tanks and missiles, for some time, the Nazi leader begins to smile. A Russian comes up to him and says, "I bet you are thinking that if you had had those weapons you wouldn't have lost the war." No, the late Nazi dictator responds, "I was just thinking that if I had had a newspaper like your *Pravda*, no one would have ever found out that I did."

That story calls attention to three important aspects of the Russia–Georgia conflict. First, both Russian and Georgian leaders were convinced that the way in which the media treated the war was just as important as what took place on the battlefield in determining the winners and the losers. Second, both assumed they could control the media coverage far more effectively than in fact proved to be the case—not only because of the media operations by the other side, but because of the increasing multiplicity of channels, including the blogosphere where this old Soviet anecdote surfaced. And third, neither fully recognized the way in which the facts on the ground, for that reason as well as others, would overwhelm their information strategies both in the short term and especially over time.

However that may be, both the Russian Federation and Georgia engaged in an intensive information war before, during, and after the fighting raged, in order to define for their own peoples, their opponents, and the international community not only who won and who lost but, more to the point, who was the aggressor, and thus deserves blame, and who was the victim, and thus thereby earns sympathy. Because of the various asymmetries of the participants and because of it was part of a larger international conflict, the Russia–Georgia war of August 2008 was and remains first and foremost an information war, in which the victories and defeats in that sphere were in many ways more important and fateful than those which took place on the ground.

Let us first define the nature of information war, and then focus on three aspects of the conflict in Georgia: the new media environment in which it took place; some of the key ways in which it was conducted before, during, and after the "conventional" conflict occurred; and what each side concluded about information war as a result. Findings on this last point will help explain the reading others will give to the Russia-Georgia information war and might also affect how other governments engage in this kind of conflict in the future.

The Changing Nature of Information War

From as far back as human history is recorded, information has been a key weapon in war, and thus it is entirely appropriate to speak of information war as coterminous with the human experience. But if it has always been an aspect of conflict, information has become an increasingly important weapon as the number of people affected by conflicts and whose attitudes can affect outcomes has increased and as the media have developed especially over the last half-century. Consequently, no leader of any country involved in any conflict today can ignore its information dimension, and no history of such a conflict can avoid addressing the particular features of each information war.

Historically, leaders of countries engaged in conflict have sought to send messages to the enemy either to deceive or undermine, to the allies of the enemy to convince them to back away from the participant, to their own populations in order to generate support for the military effort, to their own allies to justify their backing or at least neutrality, and to all other actors on the international scene whose judgments and actions may affect the country or countries involved. Sometimes such information wars have involved attempts at denial through the closure of one or another channel of communication, but most often they revolve around the definition and delivery of particular messages.

As the number of channels has grown, from radio to television to the internet to twitter, and as the number of audiences has increased, the calculations involved in conducting information wars have increased exponentially. This is the case not only because of the difficulties of ensuring that messages reach their intended audiences, but also in order to make sure that these same messages do not have an impact on others to whom they are *not* addressed. Meeting that challenge has become ever more difficult, as the recent conflict between Russia and Georgia shows.

Because it is ever more difficult to shut off the flow of information—after all, individuals and groups can always shift from one channel to another—information war is less about preventing messages from getting out than about delivering messages. Consequently, in the following pages the focus will be mainly on the information content of the war rather than on the various efforts to censor or deny information.

Moscow's Information War and Georgia's Defense

Both Moscow and Georgia engaged in information war before, during, and after the conflict on the ground, but because the capacities of their respective states were so different, the Russian side was in most cases on the offensive and the Georgians on the defensive. Indeed, the only times when that was not true was when Russian missteps or miscalculations allowed others, including the Georgians, to turn their efforts against them or when the Georgians, exploiting the sympathy of many third parties and of many Russians who were appalled by the actions and duplicity of their own government, were able to go over to the attack. Tracing all the ins and outs of that process is beyond the scope of this paper, but it is possible to list here the basic themes each side presented, the ways in which the other side sought to counter the themes advanced by the other, and the intended and unintended consequences of each side's actions.

Each side developed three key themes. For Moscow, these themes were, first and above all, that Georgian President Saakashvili in particular and Georgia more generally was the aggressor; second, that Moscow had been left with no choice but to intervene in the defense of its citizens and their human rights and thus deserved the unqualified support of the international community; and third, that the United States and the West had no basis for criticizing Russian actions because of NATO's earlier actions in Kosovo and elsewhere.

For Georgia, in contrast, the three key messages of its information war were responses to the Russian arguments. First of all, Tbilisi insisted that Russia had violated international law by invading a sovereign country. Moreover, Georgian sources argued that Tbilisi's introduction of troops into the breakaway region of South Ossetia was legitimate and could not be a *casus belli*. And finally, Saakashvili and his government maintained that the situation in Georgia was fundamentally different than the situation in the former Yugoslavia and that Moscow's effort to draw an analogy between them was both self-serving and potentially counter-productive to Russia's own interests. That is because, as the Georgians repeatedly pointed out, if Moscow recognized Abkhazia, why shouldn't the West recognize Chechnya?

Not surprisingly, Moscow and Tbilisi each sought to counter the other, sometimes with careful arguments but quite often by simple denial. Responding to Moscow's representations, Tbilisi argued that regardless of whether one thought it was a good idea or not, Saakashvili's movement of troops into South Ossetia did not constitute a violation of international law, whereas Moscow's invasion of Georgia was a clear violation. Moreover, Georgia insisted that Moscow's argument that it had to intervene to defend its own citizens was utterly false, and based solely on the Russian government's illegal action in handing out passports to people who in no way qualified for them. Finally, Tbilisi argued that the United States and the West had since 1992 committed themselves to championing the stability of borders in the post-Soviet space, regardless of what Western governments had done in the Balkans.

Moscow for its part responded to Georgia's arguments by insisting that Georgia had acted first and hence provoked the conflict. As a result, the Russian government argued both during and after the war that Moscow was not the aggressor; it was "the defender" and by intervening was merely upholding international law. In addition, Moscow argued that Georgia had violated international law by introducing its forces into South Ossetia, a move Moscow said Tbilisi had committed itself not to do under the earlier CIS-sponsored peacekeeping arrangements. And finally, the Russian authorities argued that the right of nations to self-determination took precedence in this case over any claims concerning territorial integrity. Given that Western governments generally support both at the level of principle if not always in practice, Russian spokesmen said, they had little choice but to support what Moscow was doing in support of the Abkhazians and South Ossetians.

Moscow's insistence during and, even more, after the conflict that it had acted defensively in response to Georgian aggression was not only the Russian government's central theme but also its greatest success in the information war. Despite the fact that Tbilisi did not move troops across an international boundary and thus did not violate international law while Russia did precisely that and was the aggressor, even those who supported Georgia, including many Western governments, felt compelled either to criticize Saakashvili for rashness or provocative behavior or to engage in lengthy investigations of the "causes" of the Russia–Georgia war, or both. Such criticism and such investigations, many of which continue, worked to Moscow's advantage and to the detriment of Tbilisi, even when the criticism was made by Georgia's friends and the investigations concluded that Russia, not Georgia, had acted aggressively.

Some European governments, Germany's most prominently, accepted the Russian argument. While they did so almost certainly out of concern for continued access to Russian gas and other economic interests, their arguments in favor of backing Moscow's position have proved influential in the European Union and elsewhere. Reduced to the simplest terms, they are the following: Georgia had agreed to peacekeeping arrangements in South Ossetia that precluded Tbilisi from introducing troops there. By doing so, the Georgian government violated its undertakings, and consequently, Moscow as another signatory was legally justified in using force to expel the Georgian "invaders." Indeed, Germany's Deputy Foreign Minister Gernot Erler was the most outspoken official on this issue, not only stating that Georgia broke international law by "launching military action to reclaim South Ossetia" and by "attacking Russian peacekeepers," but that he had "understanding for Russia's reaction."[1]

There are three problems with the German position, as many European commentators have pointed out. First, the earlier agreement did not deprive Georgia of its sovereignty over South Ossetia, and consequently, Georgia retained the right to act as a sovereign on its territory. Russia did not have that right. Second, the German argument ignores the succession of provocative actions that the Russian side had taken, including but not limited to, military maneuvers just north of South Ossetia in the two weeks preceding the invasion. And third, however that might be, Moscow sent its forces deep into Georgia, far beyond the borders of South Ossetia, something that no agreement had ever sanctioned. Consequently, by accepting Moscow's legalisms on the question of who began the conflict, Berlin, following Moscow, ignored or at least obscured the Russian act of aggression, a violation of international law under any conceivable reading.

In fact, even the discussion of this issue long after the fact works to Russia's advantage because it has the effect of casting doubt on Georgia's position even if it concludes that Russia did act as the aggressor. Because the author of these lines believes that Saakashvili acted foolishly but not criminally in moving Georgian troops from one part of his country to another, he will say no more, convinced as he is that Moscow's "argument" that it was acting defensively deserves no more credence than earlier and immediately dismissed suggestions by Nazi Germany that it had been attacked by Poland in September 1939.

Among the reasons Moscow achieved success in this area was its enormous relative power advantage not only compared to Georgia but, via gas and other resources, over some Western countries. Moreover, it was able to rely not only on its powerful state-controlled media and government apparatus more generally, but also on the presence in Moscow of most of the journalists who would cover the war. Thus, Russia began with enormous advantages in the information war: it had more channels, more money, and more influence with those reporting on the conflict. However, as will be seen below, Moscow not only failed to use these to good advantage but quite frequently behaved in ways that undercut its own message, created problems for itself, and undermined much that Russia was trying to achieve in this sphere of the conflict as well as others.

Georgia, by contrast, had a vastly smaller media and few Western journalists present, at least at the outset. As a result, Tbilisi tended to play defense at least initially, blocking Russian media and the Russian portion of the Internet, steps that both helped it to mobilize the Georgian population and called into question Tbilisi's desired image as an open and democratic society. Indeed, just as many observers have suggested that Vladimir Putin used the Georgian war, as he had used the Chechen conflict before, to tighten the screws in Russia, many people, especially in the Georgian opposition, have since argued that Saakashvili used the conflict with Russia to do the same in his country.

Earlier chapters in this volume indicate that Moscow planned its campaign in Georgia well in advance, with some observers tracing the planning back half a dozen years and others focusing more on the spring of 2008. Be that as it may, Moscow clearly went into intensive planning by the spring of 2008, and many of the declarations it prepared suggest that the Russian authorities expected the war to begin in Abkhazia rather than in South Ossetia.[2]

One of the clearest indications of the importance Moscow attached to the information war in Georgia, and also of the ways in which its actions in that campaign backfired on the Russian authorities, was symbolized by the Russian government's pre-positioning of journalists in Tskhinvali prior to the start of hostilities. The day before Georgia introduced forces into its breakaway region of South Ossetia, there were at least forty-eight Russian journalists there—and only two accredited to foreign outlets—one of the clearest indications that Moscow not only knew that Tbilisi was going to introduce its troops into that breakaway region but had planned its own military response and wanted to ensure both events were extensively covered.[3]

In a related development, also reflecting information war planning, Moscow's state-controlled media were "extremely well-prepared to cover the outbreak of armed conflict in Georgia," with the main television channels immediately putting up "elaborate graphics" and "news anchors and commentators [sticking] to disciplined talking points accusing Georgian President Mikheil Saakashvili of aggression and the Georgian armed forces of genocide and ethnic cleansing," according to RFE/RL's Brian Whitmore.[4]

Moscow's media assault on Georgia before, during, and after the war had unintended and, from the Russian government's perspective, unwanted consequences. Russian television, for example, broadcast such distorted accounts of the war that Russians who wanted to know what was really happening were forced to turn to the Internet or, as during the Cold War, to Western broadcasters such as Radio Liberty. As one St. Petersburg media critic put it, "facts, especially in our days, do not exist on the television screen 'in a pure form,' separate from interpretation and commentary."[5]

What was most striking, this critic suggested, was how unoriginal Russian television was in its themes: "The way in which leading television channels in Russia have covered military actions in South Ossetia [recalled] the work of TV journalists during the second Chechen campaign and the seizure of the school in Beslan." The only difference was that "this time in the role of enemies of Russia and all progressive humanity appear not Chechen militants or abstract 'international terrorists' but Georgian soldiers and President Saakashvili personally, who has been transformed by the efforts of the domestic propaganda machine into something between Hitler and Pinochet."[6]

Russia's military correspondents were generally given high marks by Moscow commentators, but those sitting in Moscow offices understood, such analysts wrote, that "on the basis of one and the same data, contemporary television can create two totally opposite 'texts.'" If necessary, "Georgian forces in the blink of an eye can become angels" or the equivalents of the "punitive agencies of the SS." These commentators suggested that "From the very beginning, Russian media occupied a radically anti-Georgian position," one that was no less striking in light of the fact that Moscow media had never been pro-Georgian. Moreover, Russian TV did everything it could to present Georgian forces as "Hitlerites" and Saakashvili as "a hysterical Fuehrer."

Because the distortions of Russian television were so obvious to anyone who cared to reflect, as Zoya Svetova and Dar'ya Okunyeva of *Novyye Izvestiya* argued, thoughtful Russians quickly recognized that the only place in the Russian media where there could be a serious discussion was the Internet.[7] The "information deficit is in part being filled by the Internet," they wrote. "There are sharp arguments in the blogosphere, communities of opponents and supporters of continuing military operations are forming." And indeed many extremely interesting and valuable pieces of reporting were contained in these online discussions.

Having noted that "pacifist attitudes" had predominated Internet discussions, Svetova and Okunyeva pointed out that "net surfers, who in [Russia] do not represent more than twenty-five percent of the population, do not set the tone." And they suggested that "in the near future one should expect not anti-war but patriotic and pro-Russian statements" to predominate there as well. Nonetheless, many of the articles posted online provide remarkable details about the situation in Georgia and the background of the current crisis. One of the more interesting offerings in this regard was by Dmitry Tayevsky, an analyst at the Siberian news agency Babr.ru.[8] Among other things, he addressed the issue of the number of Russian passport holders in South Ossetia, a number that Russian officials from Dmitry Medvedev and Vladimir Putin on down have made central to their claims that this region must remain under Russian control. Tayevsky noted that South Ossetia is famed for continuing to use Soviet-era postage stamps—something that has attracted the interest of philatelists. He then went on to observe that "it is curious that South Ossetia, which is one of the world leaders in the production of counterfeit dollars, also treats the production of [false] Russian passports in the republic with a great deal of humor." As early as two years ago, Tayevsky says, "the entire Caucasus world laughed over the reliable but humorous report of an unknown Ossetian author who wrote that [South Ossetian] President Kokoity, having received a freshly printed passport with the number "2" on it (number one had been sent as a gift to Putin) discovered in it not his own photograph but a portrait of Abraham Lincoln taken from a one-hundred dollar bill."

There was yet another source to which Russians who wanted to find out what was going on increasingly turned. Experts on the post-Soviet space at Moscow State University who wanted to keep track of Georgian developments reported that they listened not to Russian media but to the broadcasts of U.S.-funded Radio Liberty, thereby undermining the very control Moscow hoped to impose on one of its key audiences.[9] Tragically, instead of helping Russians who increasingly cannot learn the facts from their own media, all too many Western governments—including Washington—have been cutting back on such broadcasts, thereby unintentionally helping Putin and Medvedev to distort the "reality" that is offered on Russian television.

That struggle over what constituted "reality" in this conflict reached the highest levels of the Russian state. At one point, Vladimir Putin lashed out at what he described as the anti-Russian attitudes animating Western media coverage of Moscow's moves in Georgia. He made this charge at the same time his government was using its rapidly expanding control of the Russian media to intensify its ongoing disinformation campaign against the West. At the Valdai discussion club meeting just after the conflict, Putin was asked why Russian forces had gone beyond the borders of Abkhazia and South Ossetia. His response underscored his conviction that Moscow would win the information war.[10] Instead of directly answering the question, he responded that the query did not surprise him: "What surprises me," Putin said, "is something else: just how powerful the propaganda machine of the West is." He said he "congratulate[d]" its organizers. "It is remarkable work! But the results are poor. And they always will be because this work is dishonest and amoral."And then he added that as far as Russia's advance into Georgia was concerned, everyone should "remember how the Second World War began. On September 1, fascist Germany attacked Poland. Then they attacked the Soviet Union. Were we supposed to go back only to the [pre-war] borders and stop there?"

"Moreover," Putin continued, "Soviet forces were not the only ones to enter Berlin—there were Americans, French, and British." The armies of these countries did not stop at their borders because it was necessary not only to repel the invader but to ensure that "an aggressor must be punished." Putin's argument was, to say the least, tendentious. He conveniently failed to mention that Hitler invaded Poland after concluding a pact with Stalin that allowed Soviet forces to move into that country as well. Besides this and his tired invocation of the defeat of Nazism, which for Moscow is a moral solvent in which all Soviet crimes dissolve, there are two other aspects of his remarks that warrant notice.

On the one hand, Putin's comments throw into high relief a critical distinction in information wars: namely, between misinformation, on the one hand, and disinformation, on the other. Misinformation, the spread of completely false reports, is the less serious threat. Typically, reportage that is completely false is not only easily identified but quickly challenged. But disinformation is another matter. As the West's best students of the subject, Natalie Grant and Vladimir Volkoff, have pointed out, disinformation almost always involves the careful mixing of obvious truths with falsehoods in a way that many will either find plausible or, at the very least, impossible to check.[11]

As a result, disinformation, especially if its dissemination begins in what is considered a more or less reliable media outlet, quickly gets picked up by other sources that use it in good faith, which in turn adds credibility to the disinformation.

Throughout the conflict in Georgia, Moscow was confronted with a problem it clearly had not expected: some of the messages it was sending to one group of people were received by a different one, and the latter acted on them in ways that the Russian government clearly did not want. An obvious case was the Russian government's continuing expression of concern that its support for the independence of Abkhazia and South Ossetia might have a spillover effect in the Russian Federation itself. Such fears were something the Georgian government and many in the West did everything they could to promote, seeing it as a potential restraining factor on Russian behavior.

But on the other hand, the Russian government faced blowback in a number of other ways: for example, its officials floated the idea of breaking up Georgia into various pieces and then recombining them, which pleased neither the Abkhazians nor the South Ossetians.[12] In another case, Moscow put out the story that the Georgians were plotting to launch terrorist attacks against Russian cities, a clear effort to whip up Russian anger against Tbilisi but one that led many Russians to ask whether Moscow was doing the right thing.[13] Also, the Russian government put out stories that Israelis were involved on the Georgian side, stories that groups like the notoriously racist Movement Against Illegal Immigration (DPNI) picked up on to promote their anti-Semitic and xenophobic agendas. In some cases, these groups attacked Jews and others as a result, giving Moscow an unintended and unwelcome loss in the information war.[14]

A second category of problems Moscow faced in this information war arose from the fact that as the war continued, the Russian government—or at least its various parts—kept coming up with new explanations for what was happening and why. In part, that reflected the emergence of a 24/7 news cycle, but it had the effect of undermining Russia's credibility, leading many to question whether any of the explanations Moscow was offering were true. In short, the waging of the information war undermined Moscow's broader credibility not only with many of its own people but also with Western governments, even when one or the other was not the target of a particular message.[15]

But the third set of consequences had the most negative consequences from Moscow's point of view. From at least the period since the NATO Budapest summit, when Saakashvili received apparently unqualified backing from Washington, it had been obvious that Vladimir Putin hated the Georgian leader personally and wanted him out. The Russian leader declared that Moscow would never talk to Saakashvili, a position Dmitry Medvedev has maintained and that some see as an implicit call for the overthrow of the leader of the Rose Revolution. But Russian statements in that regard, coupled of course with Russian actions on the ground, had, and to a certain extent continue to have, exactly the opposite effect in Georgia. Indeed, they have generated far more support for Saakashvili than he might otherwise have had. Moreover, they have restrained his opponents who have been concerned that overthrowing him would be read in some quarters as a Russian "victory" in Georgia.[16]

Because it lacked the resources that Moscow had, Tbilisi conducted its information war in a very different way. On the one hand, it sought to restrict the flow of Russian messages into the country by blocking Russian Internet sites[17] and television.[18] And on the other, the Georgian government generally, and Saakashvili personally, sought to exploit the many friends Georgia had in Western capitals to put out its messages for it. Each of these deserves further comment. The Russian government and its allied hackers engineered "denial of service" (DOS) on Georgian government sites throughout the conflict, something Tbilisi got around by shifting the hosting of these sites to other countries and or transforming them into blogs. And Russia's attacks in this sphere had the unintended consequence of making the Georgian blogosphere far more important than it had ever been. The number of Georgian blogs increased, and ever more of them focused on political rather than personal topics.

Giga Paitchadze, one of Georgia's leading bloggers, argued that as a result of the explosive growth of the Georgian blogosphere, even Russians "admit[ted] they [were] losing in this sector of the information war," with Russian bloggers frequently conceding that their Georgian counterparts had "present[ed] their arguments more effectively."[19] This claim may be exaggerated. But if the experience of Georgia's neighbors Armenia and Azerbaijan is any guide, the experiences of Georgian bloggers during the conflict with Russia are certain to have an impact on Georgian life and politics long after the guns have quieted down.

As a result of this and of Russian missteps, Georgia came out better in the information war while the conflict was going on than anyone could have expected, although its victory in that sphere was undercut by Moscow's relentless diplomatic and media efforts after the war to reinforce its messages, efforts that Tbilisi could not and in large measure did not match because of its defeat on the war's other battlefields and because of anger within Georgia and abroad about Tbilisi's actions, justified or not.

Why Both Sides Decided They Lost the Information War

What is remarkable about the Russia–Georgia information war is that, in sharp contrast to the situation on the ground, both sides quickly decided they had lost, either because they had failed to understand the emerging media environment, had sent the wrong messages at the wrong time, or, in the Georgians' case, they could not sustain the information war long enough to win when the conditions on the ground were so much against Tbilisi.

Critics of the Putin-Medvedev regime were merciless in their attacks on Russia's information war effort. The Moscow commentator Lev Rubinshtein argued, shortly after the end of the conflict on the ground, that Russia's invasion of Georgia had highlighted the fundamental difference between Moscow's propaganda now and Soviet propaganda in the past. In Soviet times, he said, the regime sought to convince everyone of the truth of its lies, whereas now, the Kremlin propaganda effort had become so transparent that it was deceiving only those who wanted to be deceived.[20] The Georgian war showed, he continued, that the Russian government's propagandists, "clearly recognizing the new information-technology situation in the country and in the world, count only on deceiving those who are glad to be deceived. Such people, to the great joy [of the current Russian government] are extremely numerous." What about those who "do not believe" the official line? Well, said Rubinshtein, "They do not believe and it is not necessary that they do—let them sit at home and not come to our circus."

During the course of Russia's military advance into Georgia, the Russian government offered a smorgasbord of "varied and contradictory" explanations for what it was doing, some of which were so much at odds that no one who was paying attention could be expected to accept them, unless, of course, he or she wanted to accept whatever the Kremlin was saying. There are two extreme examples of this, the Grani.ru analyst wrote. One is the "official one" which claimed that Moscow attacked in order to defend its citizens. No one, in Russia or abroad, could object lest Moscow bring charges of double standards: "You can, and we cannot?"

Rubinshtein suggested that "generally speaking, [people are] pleased when a strong and just state defends the life, health, rights, and dignity of its citizens, wherever they are located. But in this case, it is precisely 'wherever they are located' which is the key aspect of the case, if one is not to call it the fatal one." That is because the Russian government is quite prepared to defend the rights of its citizens—but only if they live outside the borders of the Russian state, and only if defending them serves other purposes as well. And of course, from the point of view of the Kremlin, it is quite irrelevant whether the Russian citizens involved have asked for such a defense.

The second explanation the Kremlin offered, the Grani analyst pointed out, was very different: Moscow took the measures it did, the regime's spokesmen implied, because it could get away with it. That logic reflects the values of a criminal band rather than a state, he said, but it appeals to those who want to strike out against someone—anyone—to demonstrate how powerful and important they are. Because of the nature of the media, however, anyone who wants to think for himself or herself will quickly see that the Kremlin's propagandists were willing during this conflict to say anything in the hopes of attracting support, even if they have to act in ways that reveal their methods and even their genuine goals.

Another Moscow commentator argued that in the Georgian war Russia suffered a propaganda defeat analogous to the military one in 1941, and he wondered aloud whether Moscow could at any point in the future achieve a Stalingrad-like triumph the next time around.[21] And a third Russian analyst suggested that the Kremlin, unlike the West, does not understand the new media technologies at all.[22] According to this blogger, the war produced a particularly embarrassing propaganda fiasco on the website of the Russian Ministry of Defense; at the start of the war the site posted an article which directly contradicted Moscow's line and then had to take it down quickly in the hope that no one would have noticed.[23]

Criticism from such quarters is not as striking or as important as the criticism the Russian government received from two senior Moscow security analysts. In a remarkable article devoted to the information war with Georgia, Anatoly Tsyganok argued that Russia must face up to the sad reality that it "lost" the information war with Georgia and that it must take immediate steps to correct the situation. Such measures must include the creation of specialized administrative and analytic centers within the government as a whole and the creation of a new Information Forces structure within the Russian armed forces themselves.[24]

An even more important critique of Moscow's performance in information wars was provided by Igor Panarin, the influential dean of international relations at the Diplomatic Academy of the Russian Ministry of Foreign

Affairs. According to this writer, who gained fame in 2009 for predicting the breakup of the United States, Moscow must now recognize its shortcomings and gear up to fight information wars, an aspect of conflict which, he argued, will form an ever greater part of all geopolitical conflicts.[25] Panarin, who has been pushing for more attention to this area since the publication of his 2003 book *Information War and the Third Rome* argued that Moscow must "immediately" move to create "a mechanism" to ensure that the Russian media reflect Moscow's interests.

Such an institution, he suggested, would allow the Russian government to repulse information attacks from abroad and would involve the creation of a Russian public media council; the appointment of a special advisor to the president on information and propaganda; the establishment of a foreign policy government media corporation to "restore the potential of the [Soviet-era] mechanism of foreign political propaganda which was completely destroyed in the 1990s"; to use satellite television to spread Moscow's message across the entire world; and the creation of an analogous institution for the Internet which would oversee "the production of books, video films, video games and other materials for active distribution via the Internet."

In addition, Panarin proposed creating a special service to counter "the information operations of the geopolitical opponents of Russia." This group would work through "a network of Russian NGOs operating on the territories of the CIS, the European Union and the United States," copied from what he described as "the American model" of organizing and supporting NGOs on the territory of the Russian Federation. Finally, he proposed the establishment of a special governmental center to train cadres in the arts of information warfare.[26]

Because of the political turmoil in Georgia since the war and because it is so obvious that Tbilisi lost the war on the ground, that country has produced fewer discussions about this issue. But Georgian commentators have not ignored broader questions of information warfare. First, in contrast to the Russians, Georgians have focused more on the technical issues of information transfer rather than on content, where they believe they won the war. This is not surprising given that they were victims of DOS attacks and given their experience with rapid shifts in the blogosphere. Second, again a reflection of their more limited means, Georgian officials have highlighted the role of Georgian missions abroad in making sure that Tbilisi's position will reach the largest possible audience. And third, despite his political problems, Saakashvili had continued to make use of interviews in the international print and electronic media to press his country's case, especially given his greater proficiency in English than that of most Russian leaders.

Lessons for Future Information Wars

The Russia–Georgia information war offers at least five general lessons for countries that may find themselves engaged in similar struggles in the future.

- First, defining who is the winner and who is the loser in any conflict is likely to depend far more on the information struggle than on the one involving conventional arms. If a country loses on the ground, it may still win in the information sphere, and vice versa.
- Second, clarity and consistency are clearly more important than ever despite the temptations to micromanage messages in a 24/7 news cycle. Those who try to come up with new messages on a continuing basis are likely to find that no one believes any of the ones they are trying to deliver.
- Third, even as the rise of low-intensity and asymmetrical conflict makes the distinction between war and peace less meaningful, so too the difference between public diplomacy in "normal" times and "war" times is declining.
- Fourth, facts on the ground matter, but they matter because they create limits to what can be reasonably claimed, and not because they directly define how any one "winner" or "loser" will see events.
- And fifth, there is a chance that the explosive growth of personal media—websites, blogs, cell phones, and now tweeter—may make the control of any message almost impossible, thus making the conduct of information wars in the future far more difficult but equally far more important.

11

The Implications of the Russia-Georgia War for European Security

James Sherr

Well before the outbreak of the Russia–Georgia conflict of August 2008, it had become increasingly obvious that the West's entire post-Cold War and largely post-modern schéma of security had done nothing to avert, and perhaps much to abet, the revival of a classically modern, Realpolitik culture of security in Russia. Nevertheless, the suggestion that the motif of partnership, which guided the West's relations with Russia in the 1990s, be replaced by a motif of realism has encountered strong intellectual and political resistance. Still greater resistance has been generated by the inescapable corollary of this suggestion: that the tools, as well as the expectations of engagement, with Russia require reassessment and modification.

Even those who believe that "partnership and engagement" should not be replaced by hostility and containment hoped that the conflict would serve as a tipping point in this discussion. It has not. But it has, to alter the metaphor, shifted tectonic plates below the surface and produced several seismic jolts above it. Earlier tremors—the Russia-Ukraine gas crisis of January 2006, and President Putin's Munich speech of February 2007—produced nothing approaching the same shock and awe.

NATO and the EU are not the same as they were before the Georgian war, which constituted the first hostile deployment of Russian armed forces across an interstate border since the Soviet invasion of Afghanistan in 1979.[1] These institutions are profoundly troubled by what occurred, but they are no longer in denial. Moreover, the divisions that have become synonymous with their existence are now qualitatively different from what they were even a short time ago. Consensus about Russia has not only broken down between member states, but within them, notably inside Germany. Even the sanitized language of *communiqués* demonstrates that these are now communities of shared worries, mixed interests, and sharply divergent approaches to addressing "common concerns." They are also communities fragmented over priorities and over how, on the basis of diminishing resources, to rank, sequence, and address them. The existence of priorities greater than Russia—the global economic crisis, Afghanistan, nuclear proliferation, and the threats posed by virulently anti-Western and anti-modern movements and states—is denied by only a minority. But such agreement as exists begs two questions. If Russia is a second priority, should it not be treated with the seriousness it deserves, as a focus of policy and action in its own right, or should it be treated as a variable—as a co-optable instrument in helping us manage greater priorities? Second, could a significant part of the post-Cold War settlement—the independence of Russia's post-Soviet neighbors—be jeopardized without jeopardizing the whole? And would this not reorder our priorities irrespective of our means or will?

Were NATO and the EU engaged in a purely intellectual exercise, these questions and others would be far easier to address than they are in practice. In reality, rationality is strongly conditioned by sentiment, interest, and habit. All three are embedded in institutions. The "habits of cooperation" that characterize institutions such as NATO can readily become habits of inertia. To stimulate change, the stimulus needs to be dramatic, convincing, and sustained. The collapse of the Soviet Union and the Warsaw Pact provided such a stimulus. Even so, post-Cold War habits of thought and behavior did not emerge easily, uniformly, or quickly; but they did emerge. Changing them will not be a quick or easy process, and it is arguable, even according to a strictly rational calculus, how many should now be modified or jettisoned. If we are to measure the desirable against the possible, we must first understand the force of the orthodoxies that have fallen into place since the Cold War officially came to an end: orthodoxies which, ten years later, were reinforced by another dramatic stimulus, the events of 9/11.

Habits of Bureaucracy and of Mind

Those who argued that the end of the Cold War would bring about the return of traditional patterns of untidiness, uncertainty, and complexity in international relations—and not the "end of history"—were not making Western policy in the immediate aftermath of the Cold War, but criticizing it. Their apprehensions were borne out, some relatively swiftly, so that by the mid-1990s Western policy reflected an uneasy interplay between triumphalist, post-modern, and realist influences. But in this amalgam, two apprehensions were largely absent: the possibility that a pre-Cold War pattern of Great Power rivalry would emerge alongside the new post-Cold War realities and that the Russian Federation, the state which at the outset of these changes saw itself "doomed to be a Great Power," would once again acquire the purpose and capacity to act like one.[2]

Nevertheless, in most other respects, NATO accurately grasped what had changed in Europe and addressed these changes with confidence. The European Union addressed them with ambivalence, yet in time with less parochialism and with greater effect. For the former, the Russia–Georgia conflict is the last in a series of relatively recent reverses that have damaged expectations, self-confidence, and cohesion. For the latter, the conflict has reinforced wariness, but it has also widened horizons and, with that, awareness of the security dimension of its own activity and interests.

NATO has good reason not to jettison everything it learnt in the 1990s: the challenges posed by newly independent states and immature democracies, the re-emergence of nationalities, ethnicities, and religious communities long repressed, the progressive disintegration of the institutions and infrastructure of the Soviet superpower (and, co-terminously, the Yugoslav federation), and the planned and unplanned privatization of its economic and a good many of its military and security assets. Bringing security policies, threat assessments, and force requirements into conformity with these conditions was an arduous challenge which, under the catalyzing influence of the Balkan conflicts, some Allies undertook seriously and many more simply paid lip service to whilst cutting resources to the bone. But by the mid-1990s a new lexicon of threat was replacing the old in mindsets and policies: ethnic and religious antagonism; state incapacity, disintegration, and failure; illegal migration, the proliferation of dangerous weapons and technologies, terrorism and, not least, the swiftly growing scope of transnational organized crime. In establishments where thinking had gone furthest (e.g. the British Army's Directorate of Development and Doctrine), the greatest apprehension was that the demarcation lines prerequisite to political order—internal vs. foreign, military vs. civil, economic vs. political, state vs. criminal—were eroding across Eurasia. Perhaps the most convincing demonstration of the pertinence of these concerns was Ukraine's first (1997) National Security Concept, which applied the same framework to a specifically Ukrainian (and Ukraine-Russia) context.

These were the concerns, not classically geopolitical ones, that stimulated the formation of Partnership for Peace (PfP), which was originally devised to *deflect* pressure for enlargement and, after the 1997 Madrid summit (when that pressure no longer could be deflected), NATO enlargement itself. It was these "new security challenges"—in other words, dread of anarchy and, more specifically, fears about "renationalization" of defense and security in Central Europe—in other words, the return of the brittle arrangements of interwar Europe—which explain why Germany, the key European architect of the post-Cold War partnership with Russia, was also an architect of the first wave of enlargement.

Yet enlargement was also the product of two other impulses. The first of these was a transcendental determination on the part of former Warsaw Pact countries to avoid any return to the "grey zone," and an equal determination to be integrated into a structure that would put the ghosts of Germany's *Drang nach Osten* to rest. Overcoming these legacies mattered as much to the internal security of these countries—and the irreversibility of political change –as to their external security. These were *a priori* propositions, tenaciously held, and they outweighed any concern about the revival of Russian ambition and power. The second was the fear, entertained in equal measure by the Clinton administration and European governments, that U.S. interest in NATO would atrophy if the challenges of enlargement were ignored. In short, the motive behind enlargement was not to protect the West from Russia but to protect the West from itself.

East of the Niemen, Bug, and Prut, NATO understood that it was in different territory, not only because of the Russia factor but because the combined effects of the pre-Soviet heritage, the Soviet legacy, and the Communist war against civil society were more brutal and thorough than they had been in Central Europe. But this did not hinder NATO from using PfP as an instrument to foster internal change and elements of de facto integration between these countries and the Alliance. In Ukraine and Georgia, as in Poland and the Czech Republic, this relationship was demand-driven. For the mainstream of Ukraine's political elite, Partnership for Peace was not an anti-Russian instrument, but a pillar of the country's multi-vector policy. It was also, in the words of Minister of Defense Oleksandr Kuzmuk, a means to "advance defense reform in the country." For Georgia (which joined PfP in March 1994, one month after Ukraine) it was a more explicit instrument of protection, urgently required once President Eduard Shevardnadze discovered that the removal of Zviad Gamsakhurdia from power had done nothing to stem Russia's assault upon Georgia's territorial integrity and cohesion. For its part, NATO had persuaded itself that there was nothing anti-Russian about these relationships. They would, as a matter of principle, develop not in accordance with NATO-Russia partnership, but in response to the receptivity and capacity of the countries concerned.

Thus, NATO at fifty was an alliance in renewal. It was content with its success in "projecting stability and security" beyond its traditional borders, and despite an increasingly problematic relationship with Russia, it saw no reason why this enterprise should not continue. On September 11, 2001, it was handed a formidable reason. But this was not so evident at the time, for 9/11 revived hopes of partnership with Russia. Moreover, the Rose and Orange Revolutions of 2003–5 reinforced convictions, not to say complacencies, that the Alliance would remain, in the words of Ukraine's 2008 State Program of Cooperation with NATO, "the most effective structure of collective security in Europe."

Yet for its part, the EU could not decide whether it was more important to be a magnet or a barrier to the newly independent states of East-Central Europe. Indeed, it is not entirely able to do so today. Whereas NATO developed Partnership for Peace as a mechanism to minimize the possibility that enlargement would create "new dividing lines in Europe," the EU's first priority was not to minimize the divide between members and non-members, but to deepen the integration of its members. As an entity historically focused on defense and security, NATO could define integration in relatively limited and permissive terms. But as an entity focused on economics, harmonization, and "ever closer Union," the EU was unable to do so. Not surprisingly, when preparing for enlargement in the late 1990s, the first concern of EU member states was to preserve the integrity of the single market and maintain the Union's defenses against the very challenges that were drawing NATO more deeply into the affairs of East-Central Europe. Yet to the latter states, the EU's defenses –symbolized dramatically by the Schengen Agreement on frontiers—were not only protectionist; they represented the very "new dividing lines" they dreaded most. Thus, countries passionate about the possibility of joining the EU nevertheless feared that EU enlargement would become a process of moving barriers east.

Nevertheless, by the late 1990s, the EU was becoming obliged to take into account the security implications of its own enlargement. Alongside its other objectives, the establishment of the European Security and Defense Policy (ESDP) reflected an overdue recognition that enlargement was a profoundly complex security issue and that the EU must be as concerned with security in the future as it has been with economics in the past. In the words of NATO's then Assistant Secretary-General Klaus-Peter Klaiber, "the old formula, NATO does security and the EU does economics, is no longer viable."[3] By 2000, there was increasingly open recognition that NATO and EU enlargements needed to be harmonized. A key area of harmonization, albeit still underdeveloped, became EU involvement in security sector reform within its New Neighborhood. By the middle of the current decade, the bottle was becoming half full. As a case in point, the establishment of the EU Border and Assistance Mission to Moldova and Ukraine (EUBAM) in November 2005 would have been difficult to conceive of five years earlier and inconceivable in the 1990s.

Even in retrospect, the respective approaches of NATO and the EU to the post-Cold War challenges displayed considerable realism. Yet realism was also hobbled by post-modern assumptions which, to this day, exert a powerful influence on mindsets, discourse, and tools of policy. Amongst these are:

- The systematic devaluation of nation and state—the building blocks of the modern world—and an overestimation of transnational forces: an unfortunate starting point for understanding Russia and other countries of the region;
- A predisposition to view "interdependence," by definition, as a progressive phenomenon: a factor which, to this day, limits understanding of the malign forces at play in the former USSR – inter alia, those driving Russian energy policy—as well as the tensions and barriers erected by divergent business cultures in Europe;
- The hope, bordering on faith, that all countries in the region were, with variations, fits, and starts, embarked upon the broad path of democratization, market liberalization, and "reform": a teleological perspective not seriously questioned until the YU-KOS affair of 2003;
- The all but sacred conviction that there were now "no enemies" and that new threats were generic and common to all: a conviction that led to the near evisceration of "area studies" and, in official domains, the attrition of expertise and collective memory about Russia;
- In all of these respects, a systematic, if often unconscious, devaluation of the political variable, whether in security cooperation, defense and security sector reform, or commerce.

These post-modern assumptions, whilst now unsettled, are still a powerful subliminal force and, in some quarters, dogma. They sit uneasily alongside the sentiments of states in a region where preoccupations are emphatically modern: for Ukraine and Georgia, the recovery of nation, state, and historical memory; for Russia, the recovery of collective self-respect, great power status, and the "strict promotion of national interests." They are also uncommonly difficult to reconcile with the views now common even to mainstream, centrist Russian figures who simply do not accept that any meaningful transformation of NATO has taken place:

> *Preserving itself with almost no changes*, notwithstanding declarations to the contrary after the 'cold war', NATO has predictably revived its spectre in Europe [emphasis added].[4]

The Illusion of Convergence

Russian bitterness about the post-Cold War policies of the West is not new. It was not President Putin at the 2007 Munich conference, but Boris Yeltsin in April 1994 who warned (in a speech to senior echelons of Russia's Foreign Intelligence Service) that "ideological confrontation is being replaced by a struggle for spheres of influence in geopolitics" and added that "forces abroad" wanted to keep Russia in a state of "controllable paralysis."[5] These statements, along with several others, marked the "end of the era of romanticism between Russia and the West."[6] The close of that era coincided with the end of the West's "Russia first" policy and its discovery of the newly independent states as actors in their own right. It also coincided with NATO's first intervention in Balkan conflicts. Likewise, it was not in 2004 but 1994 (at the start of NATO's *UN sanctioned* bombing campaign in Bosnia) that we first heard that "the era of romanticism between Russia and the West has ended" and that "Russian interests will no longer dissolve in the interests of European diplomacy."[7] These statements and reactions brought to the surface several premises that are much in evidence today: a geopolitically driven (and, by implication, zero-sum) view of Russian security interests and the threats that others pose to them; the view that successful interventions in conflict zones outside the former Soviet Union might enhance the propensity of the United States and NATO to intervene inside it;[8] and the belief that instability on Russia's periphery and in the Russian Federation itself serves U.S. and NATO interests. Well before the end of Yeltsin's presidency, Russians were replacing a Cold War mindset with a pre-Cold War mindset that any pre-1914 European leader would have understood.

Remarkably early, Russia's requirement for long-term security cooperation also emerged, that is, recognition by its presumed partners that the former USSR be a zone of Russian "special interests." The first foreign ministry report on the subject in September 1992 defined such integration as a "vital interest" to be pursued by "all legitimate means," including "divide and influence policies" in the newly independent states.[9] As late as February 1993, when Yeltsin called upon the United Nations and other international bodies to "grant Russia special powers as guarantor of peace and stability" in the former Soviet Union, there was still hope that the West would support his efforts—efforts which by then were being backed by force in Georgia and Moldova.

In the West, most people who took note of these views thought they would recede rather than harden. Policy-makers profoundly underestimated the depth of support for the proposition that Russia was entitled to primacy in the former Soviet Union and an "equal" role (i.e., veto) over wider security arrangements in Europe. Yet the assumption was that these ideas were confined to "nationalists" and that Russia would continue to accommodate and "adjust." Russia's self-styled liberals helped to feed this illusion. So did the edifice of the NATO-Russia partnership, exemplified by the May 1997 NATO-Russia Founding Act and NATO-Russia Permanent Joint Council.

Yet to the Russian military establishment and by now the overwhelming majority of the political establishment, NATO was and remains an anti-Russian military alliance. Claims that it has become a political-military alliance dedicated to strengthening common security are regarded as risible and insulting. These views have three sources. The first is the geopolitical determinism of the military establishment which, thanks to the popularization of the works of Russia's traditional and neo-geopolitical theorists, has acquired influence well beyond this narrow milieu. In the Russian understanding, *geopolitika* refers not only to "struggle" between powers, but *ethnoses* (civilizations). With its Darwinian resonances, its emphasis on the "who-whom" of politics, and its "scientific" categories and idiom, geopolitics has filled much of the intellectual vacuum created by the collapse of Marxism-Leninism. Whereas Western security elites define threat in terms of intention and capability, Russia's official Concept(s) of National Security and Military Doctrine(s) define it by the "presence" of foreign forces in areas in the vicinity of Russian territory—whatever their ostensible purpose and irrespective of whether the host countries have invited them or not. Within this schéma, the Russian defense perimeter includes the "former Soviet space," whether or not the countries that inhabit this "space" agree. It is indicative of this way of thinking that at the time of the Bosnian and Kosovo conflicts, the former Yugoslavia was described as being "in the vicinity" of Russia's borders despite the fact that Novorossisk, the nearest Russian city to Belgrade, is over 1,000 miles away.

The second source is the surprisingly swift disintegration of the USSR (which most Russians believe the West abetted) and the perceived "humiliation" of the Russian Federation at a time of ostensible partnership with the West. After both the "era of romanticism" and the Yeltsin era passed, this partnership came to be seen as the fruit of a malign collusion between actors, internal and foreign, who ruined people's lives as well as the state. The fact that most critical Western commentary about "Russia's retreat from democracy" coincided with Russia's recovery—when incomes were growing and pensions paid—has reinforced this impression, persuading ordinary Russians as well as decision-makers that the West simply preferred their country's weakness to its strength.

The third and final source is NATO policies, well or ill-judged, that have hardened Russian perceptions about its aims and character. The 1999 Kosovo conflict was a turning point.[10] Even in the eyes of Russian democrats, it removed any pretense that NATO was a strictly defensive alliance. To the Kremlin, the humanitarian dimension of the conflict was of no interest at all (although Russia's media convincingly presented it as a humanitarian catastrophe for the Serb population). To the Armed Forces, it was clear that "[t]oday they are bombing Yugoslavia but are aiming at Russia."[11] The conflict was (and is) viewed as a dress rehearsal for what NATO would subsequently do in the South Caucasus: a view that, in the wake of the Russia–Georgia conflict, they believe has been vindicated.

Yet the greatest ire has been reserved for NATO enlargement. Russia's indictment is tautological. Because NATO is deemed to be an anti-Russian alliance, its expansion proves that it is aggressive in character. For this reason, it is invariably futile to explain that the issues addressed by NATO's programs of cooperation with Georgia and Ukraine—civil-democratic control of defense and security structures, professionalization, transparency in budgeting, control of dangerous technologies and weapons stocks, border management—would have an intrinsic importance even if Russia did not exist. The fact that the expansion of NATO's "zone" has come at the invitation of others—and that Ukraine and Georgia have no wish to be part of Russia's "zone of special interests"—is seen as immaterial. The fact that NATO's model of defense reform in new member states has not emphasized territorial defense—to Georgia's visible detriment—but expeditionary capabilities far from Europe has hardly been noticed. Anything done near Russia is done against Russia.

Vladimir Putin introduced four new elements into the equation. First, he restored the state. In contrast to Gorbachev and Yeltsin—leaders who sought to create the international conditions necessary, in Shevardnadze's words, "to bring about change *inside* the country"—Putin reverted to an older pattern established by Stalin: restoring the "vertical of power" as a way of returning Russia to its rightful position on the world stage. Under Yeltsin, Russia functioned less as a state than as an arena upon which powerful interests competed for power and wealth, often at Russia's expense. In contrast, Putin was determined that centers of power—the security services, the armed forces, the defense-industrial complex, and the energy sector—should become instruments of national power rather than laws unto themselves.

Second, he established a strong geo-economic impulse to policy and, with the restoration of the "administrative vertical" in Russia, politically usable economic power. The *Energy Strategy of Russia to 2020* (published in 2003, before the rise of global energy prices caused general trepidation) stated that Russia's "mighty energy sector" is "an instrument for the conduct of internal and external policy" and that "the role of the country in world energy markets to a large extent determines its geopolitical influence."[12] When Gazprom's CEO Alexei Miller vaunted the attributes of Gazprom's model to EU ambassadors—"the regulation from a single center of regimes of extraction, transport, underground storage, and sales"— the implication was that this model should be extended "across the entire value chain" in Europe and Eurasia.[13]

Third, he restored national pride on the basis of a selective, but potent fusion between pre-Soviet, Soviet, and post-Soviet values. Russian nationalism, and alongside that, a feeling of *obida* (injury) at perceived humiliation by the West, became foundations of policy that have become at least as potent as Soviet ideology had been, and these sentiments evoke far deeper resonances in what remains a largely illiberal country with a strongly traditional sense of its own identity and "distinctiveness." These themes, in good part stimulated by the Bush administration's "democratic messianism," also exposed the flaws in it, along with the West's broader failure to cope with the emergence of capitalist, prosperous, and illiberal states not only in Russia, but elsewhere. "Globalization" was no longer the West's project. Indeed, in the words of Foreign Minister Sergey Lavrov, "the West [was] losing its monopoly over the globalization process."[14]

Fourth, he freed Russia from its helplessness. As Putin said at Munich in February 2007, "we have a realistic sense of our own opportunities and potential." By then, Western governments had become well aware of this potential in the sphere of energy. But most of them continued to discount the steady expansion of Russian power projection capabilities for regional (intra-CIS) contingencies, including a 25 percent per annum growth in nominal (15 percent in real) defense budgets between 2002–5. This was the case because of the prevalence of complacencies generated by the evident deficiencies of Russia's armed forces measured against Cold War templates.[15] Indicative of this complacency was the critical and highly effective role in the war with Georgia played by Russia's Black Sea Fleet, whose operational capabilities were, at the time, all but dismissed in the West. Even before that conflict, the risk, as this author warned in January 2008, was "not that Russia's Armed Forces repeat the follies of the 1990s but that Russia's neighbors and NATO find themselves surprised."[16]

Initially, it appeared that the colored revolutions in Georgia and Ukraine would jeopardize all of these efforts. But in Russian eyes, the perceived shortcomings (and with respect to Ukraine, the perceived failure) of the revolutions reinvigorated these efforts. To the Kremlin, these were Western "special operations" from beginning to end. After the post-9/11 partnership and years of cultivating the EU, they were seen as nothing short of betrayal. When this author wrote in September 2004, that "the worst scenario for Ukraine is not that Yushchenko loses the election [but that] he wins and then fails," it was out of apprehension that a sense of betrayal becomes dangerous when combined with a sense of vindication. Worse, as pointed out by several Russian analysts, the balance between Putin's characteristic cold bloodedness and passion had tipped. "Since Beslan and Ukraine...emotions have triumphed....Putin has come unhinged."[17] By the time of NATO's Bucharest summit in April 2008, the sense of obida and vindication were pushed to the danger point by the perfectly cold-blooded realization that the U.S. and its allies had become globally overextended, that NATO's "programs of cooperation" in Russia's "near abroad" lacked teeth, that the weaknesses of NATO's partners were chronic, and that NATO itself had become profoundly divided about its future course.

"On Our Terms"

The opinion of part of the Western expert community that the causes of the Russia–Georgia conflict are to be found in the dynamics of the Russia–Georgia relationship is at odds with another center of opinion: the Russian leadership. In his meeting with the Valdai Club on September 12, 2008, President Medvedev used the conflict to warn the assembled Western experts that after years of telling the West that it "does not belong" in a region defined by a "shared, common history" and the "affinity of our souls," Russia was "no longer weak and defenseless" and would "no longer tolerate" the West's "unfair and humiliating" policy in its neighborhood. He also stated that President Saakashvili's "reckless and unprovoked aggression" was not his own doing, but carried out "at the instigation of forces abroad."[18] In his April 2009 article for *The World Today*, Russia's Ambassador to NATO, Dmitry Rogozin, stated:

> We came out of the crisis stronger, our Western partners now regard Russia as a partner they cannot wipe their feet on. We are restoring cooperation and on our terms.[19]

The inventory of official statements, declarations, and initiatives between the time of the April 2008 Bucharest Summit and August 8 may not suggest conclusively that the Russian leadership, or all parts of it, sought a conflict with Georgia or instigated it. But they leave little room for doubt that the Russian leadership views the outbreak of conflict in the context of wider issues in "traditional areas of interest" and wider relationships with "Western partners." This inventory includes:

- President Putin's April 4 speech at the NATO-Russia Council, in which he enumerated the factors that could bring Ukraine's statehood "into question";
- Foreign Minister Lavrov's statement to Ekho Moskvy on April 8 that Russia would take "all possible measures" to prevent Ukraine and Georgia from joining NATO;
- Chief of General Staff Yuri Baluyevsky's statement on April 11 that if Ukraine and Georgia joined NATO, Russia would "take measures with the aim of securing its interests in the close vicinity of its state borders. These will be not only be strictly military measures. They will be measures of different nature";[20]
- President Medvedev's Berlin speech of June 5, setting out hopes for a "new, legally binding European security treaty" and warning that, if NATO's globalization and enlargement agendas proceeded, its relations with Russia would be "fundamentally spoilt for a very long time."[21]
- The Foreign Policy Concept of July 12, with its heavy emphasis on compatriots abroad, steps to "promote and propagate, in foreign states, the Russian language and Russian people's culture"—and its jarring statement: "[s]hould our partners be unprepared for joint efforts, Russia, in order to protect its national interests, will have to act unilaterally but always on the basis of international law."[22]

After the August events, it swiftly became apparent that the conflict would be used to change these relationships. A juxtaposition of two key statements points not only to the intended directions of change, but to revealing contradictions, perilous ambiguities, and significant differences between rhetoric and substance.

The first of these is President Medvedev's August 31 interview to NTV. In response to the question, "The entire system of earlier understandings is seriously changing before our eyes....How do you see the future of the world, the international order and the place of our country in it?" Medvedev stated that Russia would base its policy on five positions. These were first, the "supremacy of international law, which defines relations between *civilized* peoples [emphasis added]"; second, "the world must be multipolar"; third, "Russia does not wish confrontation [but] will not 'isolate itself'"; fourth, the "unquestioned priority...to defend the rights and dignity of our citizens wherever they live"; and fifth, the right for Russia to maintain ("like other countries in the world") regions of "privileged interests," i.e., "with our close neighbors."

The second is Medvedev's October 8 speech at the World Policy Conference in Evian, which followed on the June Berlin initiative, but in more hard-hitting form.[23] In it, he condemns the "NATO-centric approach" and presents his hopes for a new European security treaty. Yet in apparent contradiction to his emphasis on "multipolarity" and overt contradiction to claims of "privileged interests," Medvedev speaks of a system "equal for all states...without zones with different levels of security." About Russia's right to defend "the rights and dignity" of its citizens in foreign countries, the Evian speech is silent. But Medvedev's injunction to confine future relations to "hard security" would rule out any discussion of what these rights might be and how they are to be asserted or defended. Indeed, under this constraint, the new treaty would exclude any examination of Russia's employment of the "civilizational factor" and other forms of soft power in the former USSR. The proposed treaty's affirmation of the "basic principles" of "sovereignty, territorial integrity, and political independence" stands in evident contradiction to Russia's "decision and motivation" in the Caucasus, which, according to Medvedev, should be "clear for all." It is therefore not surprising, given the prosecution of internal wars on Russia's territory, that Medvedev offers no clue as to whether another principle set out in the speech, "the inadmissibility of the use of force," should apply within sovereign states, between them, or simply within some of them and between some of them.

As these declarations and others suggest, the Russian government views the conflict with Georgia as a defining moment in its realization of a revisionist agenda. The undisguised premise behind the call for "equality" is that it does not yet exist. For it to emerge, the "strengthening of the positions of the Russian Federation in international affairs" must be accepted (in short its role must be enhanced), whilst other actors must not overstep their "legitimate" interests and scope of activity (in short their role must be diminished).[24] The United States must adhere strictly to international law and accept the reality of a "polycentric international system" not "ruled from a single capital." However, it must decline calls for assistance from other national capitals.[25] NATO must halt its "mechanical enlargement," even when it occurs by invitation, and confine itself to issues of "hard security" within the "geographical limits of the alliance"—even if, within these geographical limits, no issues of hard security exist.[26] The EU and OSCE must eschew "double standards, respecting the national and historical peculiarities of each state"; but must raise no objection when Russia fails to respect them in the former USSR.[27] Gazprom must (pace Alexei Miller) be recognized as a "global energy leader," and the EU has no right to use anti-monopoly regulations to block its "legitimate ambitions" (even where laws impose "actual limitation of deliveries of Russian gas to the market of Europe.")[28] Finally, Russia's "privileged interests" in the former Soviet Union must be accepted by those who reside there and by those who do not.

In the aftermath of the Russia–Georgia war, three questions are pertinent. First, have the West's responses to the conflict encouraged the pursuit of this agenda or given Russia's leaders grounds to reconsider it? Second, is the global financial crisis giving them grounds to do so, or is it providing vindication and fresh inducement? By "pressing the reset button," will the new U.S. administration be able to identify and address genuine common interests, and will it also be able to influence and restrain Russia's conduct?

One Step Forward, Two Steps Back

On August 12, more than four days after hostilities began, NATO convened an extraordinary meeting of Allied ambassadors and, on August 19, a special foreign ministerial session of the North Atlantic Council (NAC). That was its first mistake. Given NATO's 14-year investment in Georgia, to protocol-conscious Russians, a ministerial meeting could only be read as a weak signal of NATO's purpose, suggesting that any adverse consequences would be temporary. Even if the Foreign Ministers had read out a declaration of war, Moscow would have downplayed the gravity of the message. A more appropriate sequence would have been to convene the NAC at the highest level, if only symbolically, and only then convene Foreign Ministers to agree a plan of action.

At the August 19 ministerial session, NATO placed meetings of the NATO-Russia Council (NRC) "on hold until Russia adhered to the cease-fire" negotiated with the French presidency of the European Council. That was the second mistake. It strengthened the dominance of the EU, whose role as a mediator could not have been performed by NATO. But it strengthened it too much. Military conflict between Russia and a key PfP Partner was NATO's core business, and communication was required at every level. The suspension also provided Russia with an added incentive to delay implementing the cease-fire provisions (still not fully implemented) and allow divisions inside NATO to ripen. Worse still, it not only allowed those divisions to ripen, but channeled them in a demeaning direction. "Should we talk to the Russians?" is not an issue that should detain NATO governments or even leader writers of the *Financial Times*. Given those divisions, the battle is bound to be lost sooner or later—and more likely sooner, to the embarrassment of NATO. The issues that matter are—"what should we say?" and "what should we do?"

Not surprisingly, the NRC suspension became grist to Moscow's mill. Much was made of NATO's rebuff to Russia's request to convene the NRC on August 8. But why August 8, when the danger of war was obvious to everyone from late July? The request was, in Russian parlance, a provocation. The more serious question is why, despite expectations to the contrary, the subject of the grotesquely misnamed "frozen conflicts" was not put on the agenda of the NRC on May 15 or at any time since the Bucharest summit, when a crisis was developing under everyone's noses.

The answer is that the NRC was on its way to becoming a virtual institution well before this point, as was the NATO-Russia relationship. This long-standing Russian criticism has more than some validity. NATO has tried to focus the Council's work on practical cooperation (e.g. terrorism, maritime security and, so it thought until recently, missile defense). As a result, areas of agreement have received more attention than areas of disagreement, which when they have been discussed (as in the case of CFE), tend to reiterate differences rather than narrow them. The formalistic, methodical, and programmatic approach of the NATO bureaucracy—defining objectives and monitoring their fulfillment—has not helped. In fact, it has imparted an artificially technical character to intrinsically political questions. The tendency to assess NATO-Russia cooperation in terms of the number of "activities" planned and implemented has added a layer of virtual reality to the relationship, persuading some until recently that relations were considerably better than they actually were. As a case in point, the trust developed between technical experts in the joint working group on missile defense left NATO poorly prepared for the Russian leadership's vehement opposition to the U.S. deployment decision. It will be interesting to see what NATO has learnt from these mistakes when the Council reconvenes.

Mistakes aside, NATO has made important decisions. The establishment of the NATO-Georgia Commission (long overdue) and the commitments by NATO to "assess the state of the Georgian Ministry of Defense and Armed Forces," and by the United States to rebuild the latter, demonstrates that the game is not over. Whereas the U.S. Sustainment and Stability Operations Program provided training for unit level (as opposed to combined arms) "crisis response operations" in multi-national peacekeeping operations rather than territorial defense, that emphasis is bound to change. Moreover, the decision to enhance the two NATO offices in Kyiv and the NATO-Ukraine Defense Ministers meeting at Tallinn in November 2008 provided two indications that the regional implications of the conflict were not lost on the Alliance. Both steps, in addition to those taken with respect to Georgia, reflect a clear attempt to shift discussion away from Membership Action Plans, membership itself, and timetables towards concrete and sustainable measures to strengthen Georgian and Ukrainian security and self-confidence in practical terms. The Alliance is also asking more radical questions about the applicability of Article 5 and its adaptation to new conditions, including cyber-attack, exploitation of seabed hydrocarbons in the legally contested waters of the high north and, inter alia, then President Putin's October 2006 claim that Russia's Baltic Fleet will play the leading role in the construction, protection, and environmental security of the Nord Stream pipeline.[29]

Of possibly even greater import, the EU is now playing a proactive role. But its most conspicuous foray in the region, the French-sponsored ceasefire agreements, was also its least illustrious. Russia negotiated with the EU on the basis of two of its most traditional diplomatic principles: "words have a meaning" (as French President Nicholas Sarkozy said himself), and that which is not stated does not bind.

In the six-point agreement of August 12, Sarkozy, as President of the European Council, made two questionable concessions. The more perilous one—that "awaiting an international mechanism, Russian peacekeepers shall implement additional security measures" (point 5)—gave Russia an unintended license to establish its 8-km "security zone" below the administrative borders of South Ossetia and Abkhazia.

If there were lessons to be drawn from this exercise in casual drafting, they were not. Out of apprehension that this security zone could become permanent, Sarkozy and Medvedev then concluded a three-point agreement on September 8 mandating the "complete withdrawal" of Russian "peacekeeping forces" from the security zone by October 10, as well as the deployment of "at least 200" EU observers in "the zones adjoining South Ossetia and Abkhazia." Yet the EU High Representative, Javier Solana, stated that the contingent "will be deployed with the spirit that it can deploy everywhere," and the French Ministry of Foreign Affairs agreed. On the basis of what? Far from accepting this "spirit," on September 9, Russia's Minister of Defense, Anatoly Serdyukov, announced that Russia would base two contingents of troops, 3,800 each, in the two territories. To pre-empt any charge that Russia was violating what had just been concluded, Foreign Minister Sergey Lavrov stated, "[t]hey are not peacekeepers. They are military contingents."

More promising was the September 9 commitment to conclude an Association Agreement with Ukraine in 2009. That pursuit will now take place within the framework of the Eastern Partnership, the initiative launched by Poland and Sweden in May 2008, but given impetus and momentum by the war in Georgia and, latterly, the January 2009 Russia-Ukraine gas dispute. The Partnership will provide six neighbors of "strategic importance" with support to "upgrade the level of political engagement," facilitate legal "approximation," "good governance," and "enhanced energy security arrangements"—and thereby enhance their integration in tangible ways: visa facilitation, deep and comprehensive free trade areas, and Energy Community membership for Ukraine and Moldova. Although very modestly financed, it is regarded by Russia with trepidation. The MFA has termed it a bid to create a "sphere of influence" at Russia's expense and bring its immediate neighbors into the EU's "normative and juridical space." It is further illustration, were it needed, of the potential of ostensibly technical mechanisms to achieve deep and far-reaching political changes. If the EU does not shy away from this potential, the Eastern Partnership will be the clearest indication that the Georgia conflict has served as a rite of passage in the European Union's perception of itself.

Economics and Geo-Economics

The global economic crisis is the latest development that should draw attention to the differences between Western perceptions of Russia and Russia's perception of itself. Of course, there is more than one Russia, and there are Russian experts and advisers well known in the West who have voiced apprehension and criticism of the Russian leadership's understanding of these events. But whilst the West needs to be mindful of this discussion, it dare not be less mindful of the perspective of those who press buttons and make things happen. That perspective points to divergences between and within each "camp" of the tandem that runs Russia, but not on a scale that can be termed fundamental. There is thus far little evidence to substantiate the *ex cathedra* conviction that the crisis will moderate the country's course. In Russia's immediate neighborhood, some of the evidence suggests the opposite.

Since the Russian stock market collapse in the summer of 2008, there have been three waves of official reaction in Moscow. The first was denial, smugness about the foreign origins of the crisis, and a public front, based on a sanctimonious wish, that Russia would be an "island of stability" and "safe haven." At the World Policy Conference at Evian in October 2008, Medvedev blamed the crisis on the "unipolar economic model," "economic egoism," and the refusal of other countries to respond to warnings by Russian experts about the "increasing negative trends" in the world economy. This reaction entirely ignored the domestic sources of Russia's crisis and warnings issued by the IMF and World Bank to Russia from the beginning of 2008.[30] The second wave, starting in the autumn, was a behind-the-scenes panic, as the real economy started sliding rapidly downhill and questions about political stability in the worst-affected regions began to surface (in the starkest form in an article by presidential adviser Evgeniy Gontmacher, "The Novocherkassk Scenario—2009").[31] In February special Interior Troops were flown in from Moscow to quell demonstrations in Vladivostok. Yet by the spring of 2009 these waves appeared to have subsided into a relative calm. Behind it were three factors. First, in contrast to the situation in 1991–92 and 1998, the population knows that the crisis is world-wide and despite rallies against "Putler," it is not on the whole inclined to blame the leadership. Second, whilst it is most unlikely that the oil price will recover to its former levels in the foreseeable future, it appears to have hit bottom and has begun to rise. Third, there is still a hefty cushion—half of the financial reserves (which stood at $600 billion before the crisis started)—and a sense that the government is adopting more realistic policies. Although the high level of external corporate debt ($35 billion *per quarter)* remains a wild card in this equation, there has been a steadying of nerves and expectations. Taken in the round, this steadying is likely to sustain two beliefs present when the crisis began: that the underlying economic model is sound, and that the regime's core task is to weather the slump's short-to-mid term effects. These conclusions make it unlikely that two deep-seated problems will be addressed.

The first is the rise of monopolization and anti-competitive practices in the economy, along with their two inescapable corollaries: unprecedented levels of corruption and rising costs. Despite the economic downturn, inflation stands at 13 percent. The cost of Moscow mayor Yury Luzhkov's planned fourth ring road in Moscow is €511 million *per kilometer*. Obtaining the necessary paperwork for construction in Moscow now costs $1,600 per square meter of real estate.[32] The second problem is low investment in the domestic energy sector (virtually stagnant from 2006–8), as opposed to external pipeline projects and non-energy acquisitions, Indeed, only 43 percent of Gazprom's investments go into its primary business. To this is added gargantuan energy inefficiency, with two-thirds of gas production going to the internal Russian market, a volume equal to the consumption of Japan, India, the UK, and Italy combined.[33]

Instead, as has been clear since the Russia-Ukraine gas crisis of 2006, answers to Russia's problems are being sought abroad. The financial crisis, whose impact on Ukraine is dire, has sharpened comparative advantages in Russia's favor and a determination to exploit them. Like the Russia–Georgia conflict, the gas crisis with Ukraine of January 2009 was a case of the inevitable provoking surprise. Once the crisis began, Europe saw it as a replay of the 2006 crisis, but with a significant exception: this time, Ukraine was to blame. But as the EU realized on January 7, when Russia cut the gas supply to all of its European customers, that perception was only half true, and the characterization of the crisis as a "commercial dispute" to be resolved by "the parties concerned" was not even as true as that. In actuality, the crisis was the first product of the malign synthesis between the Georgia conflict and the global financial crisis. Three factors distinguished it from the events of 2006.

The first of these was pressure to secure comparative advantages before they were lost. "Market pricing" (in practice, European pricing according to the Baumgarten formula relating gas and oil prices) would soon cease to operate in Russia's favor. In January 2008 oil prices fell from $147 per barrel to $48. At the next bi-annual pricing review, gas prices would fall accordingly. Russia's end of year terms included an apparently generous offer of $250 per thousand cubic meters (tcm)—compared to the notional European average of $418—but this only applied to gas sourced in Russia and left open the question of what Ukraine would be expected to pay for the considerably higher volume of gas that Gazprom buys from Turkmenistan and then resells to the controversial intermediary structure, RosUkrEnergo. When Ukraine's President, in a flagrant demonstration of the ineptness to which he is congenitally prone, broke off negotiations in December, Russia reacted with fury. It annulled its earlier staged pricing agreement of October and set a take-it-or-leave-it price of $418 (which swiftly became $450). The final agreement, which reflected the EU's belated intervention, does not meet these aims, but it preserves the non-transparent arrangements that allow Russia to reopen disputes and interpose political issues more or less at will.

The second factor was Russia's anticipated loss of leverage in European markets. Gazprom, which had to be bailed out by the state after the value of its shares declined 76 percent, is far harder pressed to find capital for Nord Stream and South Stream than would otherwise be the case. If it cannot directly control Ukraine's gas transit system, which supplies Europe with 80 percent of the gas it imports from the former USSR, then it has become increasingly urgent to do so indirectly by means of a European consortium established with its preferred partners. Under these terms, Ukraine would lose the ability to repeat its one stroke of brilliance during the crisis: its reversal of the flow of the main East-West trunk-line in order to transfer gas from its own storage facilities to eastern and southern Ukraine. Ukraine's indebtedness, which is almost certain to increase, could provide Gazprom with the leverage sought.

The third difference is that Russia was far stronger in the region than it was in 2006. For the foreseeable future, NATO enlargement is dead in the water. By autumn 2008, it appeared that the EU's undoubted apprehensions about Russia made it more inclined to conciliate than confront it. Ukraine's infirmities were substantially greater than they were in 2006. Its political crises were arising at ever shorter intervals, its economic crisis was assuming perilous proportions, and the EU had steadily lost patience with a leaderless country whose vulnerabilities seemed largely self-induced. For the EU's part, despite the European Commission's "Energy Policy for Europe" and the European Council's "Action Plan," anyone could see that much has been said and next to nothing done. Finally, the United States was preoccupied with itself, between presidents and far away.

Apart from the Russia-Ukraine crisis, there have been other illustrations of this malign synthesis. On March 30, Surgutneftegaz, Russia's fourth largest oil producer, acquired a 21 percent stake in the private Hungarian energy company MOL, which owns the best refining facilities in Central Europe and, through a subsidiary, controls Hungary's gas transit system. That system forms a key part of the overdue project, critical to European energy security, designed to interconnect the energy transit systems of Central and Southeastern Europe. MOL is also the dominant shareholder of Croatia's oil and gas company INA, and a partner in a planned LNG terminal on Croatia's Krk island in the Adriatic which, it is also hoped, will diminish dependence on Russian supply networks.[34] Although Surgutneftegaz is registered as a private company, "24 per cent of its shares are traded on Russian exchanges," according to the *Financial Times*, while the remaining 76 per cent are held through a complicated web of cross-shareholdings.' According to the Hungarian website *Magyar Hirlap*, this scheme includes a partial merger with state-owned Rosneft, whose chairman, Deputy Prime Minister Igor Sechin, is as assiduous and unrelenting a proponent of the state's energy interests as Putin himself.[35] According to Valeriy Nesterov at *Troika Dialog*, "it looks like Surgut has been pushed into this by the Kremlin."[36] But the step also complements the industrial logic of Gazprom and other vertically integrated Russian companies that seek control of the "entire value chain" of production, refining, and distribution. Although its stake in MOL represents its first foreign holding, Surgut now states that "we are very interested in Eastern Europe."[37] Until recently, Gazprom sought a "friendly merger" with MOL for similar reasons by means of its stake in Austria's OMV, and it is OMG's block of shares that Surgut has acquired. The transaction suggests that Russia's "civilized" system of relations between business and the state might provide ingenious ways of using the strength of one player to compensate for the weakness of another. It also suggests that Gazprom's current infirmities will not be allowed to disrupt the commercial and geo-economic logic of Russia's energy policy.

The radical question is whether the EU is ready to challenge that logic itself. The potential of the Eastern Partnership to do so has not been lost on Moscow, much as it might be derided inside the EU. Neither has Moscow failed to note that the formal launch of the Partnership virtually coincided with the publication of a joint declaration on March 23 by Ukraine, the EU, the World Bank, and a group of investors to commit €2.4 billion designed to modernize and reform Ukraine's grotesquely derelict and opaquely managed gas transit system. Through this initiative, the EU representatives conveyed their understanding that this system plays a strategic role in Europe's energy security, that it must not be held hostage to political interests in Russia or Ukraine, and that the most effective way of avoiding this will be to integrate Ukraine's energy sector into its emerging Energy Community and (in the language of Russia's MFA) its "normative and juridical space." Moscow was, for once, taken completely by surprise and threatened, in Putin's words, "to start re-examining the principles of relations with our partners."[38]

There is no doubt that the initiative can be rendered stillborn either by malign interests in Ukraine or the irresolution of the EU. Igor Sechin is correct in his assertion that the initiators of the declaration constitute a well-known group of officials who can be outmaneuvered. To prove the point, on the morrow of the declaration, he secured the backing of Paolo Scaroni, Chief Executive of Italy's ENI, in his insistence that Russia play a full part in any such arrangement. The fact remains that the EU is being ineluctably drawn into a geopolitical game and that the number of insiders willing to rise to the challenge is increasing.

But is the EU finally drawing connections between the various crises on Russia's periphery? The political events in Moldova are possibly the third example of the synthesis between geopolitics and financial pressure. The first reflex of the EU High Representative for the Common Foreign and Security Policy, Javier Solana, was to treat the outbreak of protests in Chisinau on April 7 as a straightforward, if ugly, dispute about election results. Those conditioned to accept the world of appearances have difficulty grasping that, east of the Prut, it is artificial to compartmentalize issues in this way. The geopolitical dimension of Moldova's electoral crisis, if not immediately apparent when President Vladimir Voronin branded the country's opposition leaders "putchists," should have become plain the next day when he linked Romania to the protests, expelled the country's ambassador, and imposed a visa regime that effectively sealed the border. Horizons should have widened further when, that very day, the Russian State Duma, as if by telepathy, passed a resolution echoing Voronin's accusations. These in turn were reinforced in a blunt interview given by Foreign Minister Lavrov on April 9.

Here as elsewhere when problems arise in the former USSR, it is useful to ask, *komu eto vygodno?* (who stands to gain?) The post-electoral condition of Moldova is attractive to Russia in five ways. It strengthens the hand of its clients in Transnistria, deepens the dependency of the Moldovan leadership upon Moscow, and drives wedges between Romania and its EU partners. No less significantly, it strikes a pre-emptive blow at the EU's Eastern Partnership, which to be effective requires willing and capable local partners. Perhaps most significantly, by invoking the Romanian question—and luring President Basescu into incautious calls for the mass distribution of Romanian passports to Moldovan nationals—it plays right into the hands of Russia's "privileged" claims in the former USSR. If Romania is entitled to protect its "co-nationals" in Moldova, how can Russia be denied similar rights in its "near abroad"? As with the efforts to provoke Mikheil Saakashvili after Bucharest and capitalize on the divisions inside Ukraine's political system, the Russians have judged their opponents well and in each case appear to have exercised an element of "reflexive control."[39]

Thus, from the summer of 2008 to the spring of 2009, three separate crises have broken out in the "post-Soviet space" with varying degrees of Russian instigation and exploitation. All three have strikingly local attributes and qualities, all of them touch upon issues that could stand alone in their intrinsic importance, and all of them would be inexplicable without a multiplicity of actors seeking to advance fluid, flawed, and deeply subjective agendas. Yet each of them shed light upon Russia and its sense of purpose. They also shed light on a methodology, by now ingrained, to achieve objectives by means of "divide and influence,"[40] the realization of "understandings" with local elites who "feel insufficiently self-confident,"[41] and "control of an opponent's decision."[42] All three techniques serve to build one's own security on the weakness of others. There is no contradiction between anxiety, uncertainty, and a sense of purpose bordering on aggressiveness. In his magisterial 1939 study of what became the Pacific war, historian Geoffrey Hudson stated that "nothing leads more ineluctably to war than a steady decline of relative power."[43] It would not be out of keeping with that insight to say that nothing leads to imprudence and provocation more ineluctably than the fear that today's relative power will be lost. Russian fears, Russian power, and Russian imprudence demarcate the problem we face.

Resetting Relations and Paradigms

The paradigms that defined debate about Russia before the war in Georgia are the ones that define it now. The war has shifted the occupants about, but left the paradigms intact. Each has its purists and dogmatists, but each leaves room for ambivalence, for points of commonality and for those who believe that no single lens on reality will cure myopia. In debating halls, there are always two paradigms. It is usually wiser to have three. With respect to Russia, three are well in place.

The first paradigm, in keeping with the perspective set out in this chapter, is defined by skepticism. Its adherents doubt the likelihood of finding a proper meeting of minds or broad convergence of interests with Russia in the foreseeable future. After the Cold War, these adherents were a small and scattered minority, even on the right of the political spectrum. This is not because they refused to accept that "the Cold War is over." It is because they were mindful of Joseph de Maistre's warning that "we do not invent ourselves" and because they believed that ideologies change more swiftly than ways of thinking and ways of life. Their view about Russia's post-Cold War policies was not that they were fraudulent but that they would not last: not only because those justly dubbed "romantics" would be outflanked by their critics, but because most of them would cure themselves when they found Western advice *obidno* (demeaning) and realized that their most basic demands—a seat at every top table and "special rights" in the post-Soviet "space"—would be opposed by their neighbors and by Western partners who had begun to see these neighbors in their own terms and not as little Russias. Some of the paradigm's adherents believe that "the Cold War is back," but some do not. Even after the war in Georgia, relatively few believe that "containment" and "deterrence" offer remedies to the problems we face, and very few believe they will be sufficient. Quite a few have criticized the West for displaying a condescending, arrogant, and all too casual approach to Russia. Most believe that Russia's interests, out of prudence if not principle, must be treated with respect. What they all have in common is a refusal to subordinate the more reasonable interests of Russia's neighbors to the less reasonable interests of Russia— or allow demands for "inclusion" to compromise the integrity of institutions, like NATO and the EU, that embody values and standards as much as interests. All of them believe that the war in Georgia makes it imperative to sustain the independence, welfare, and recovery of that country.

The second paradigm is defined by globalism and a belief that Russia and the former Soviet Union should not be allowed to distract the West from graver international challenges. Eight years after 9/11 and the start of combat operations in Afghanistan, this point of view is well established. But its adherents defined themselves years before the events of 9/11, as many in Washington turned their attention to an emerging inventory of global threats, whilst in Europe defense establishments began to think about demographic explosions and imbalances, resource scarcity, instability in the Maghreb and sub-Saharan Africa and, on an incipient scale, climate change. We easily forget that the administration of George W. Bush came to office with clearer views about nuclear proliferation, missile defense, and Taiwan than about Russia. If there was an implicit enemy in the Pentagon's first net assessment, it was China. NATO enlargement expressed the U.S. administration's commitment to expand freedom everywhere, rather than contain Russia. It was not until the post-YUKOS and pre-color revolution period that the latter came into focus. Even so, the decision to site components of the global missile defense network in Central Europe was not taken by neo-cold warriors, but by people who, as far as Russia was concerned, were literally thoughtless.

Like the globalists, most supporters of the first paradigm believe that Western interests face greater threats than those that might be posed by Russia. For this reason, the globalists argue, there is no need to make Russia and its neighbors priority concerns or "rebuild expertise about Russia across government."[44] Yet, this conclusion is far from axiomatic. As this author has noted elsewhere;

> If the dangers of radical Islam took us by surprise after the Cold War, they did so because those intrepid enough to worry about these issues during the Cold War itself got no plaudits and no promotions.[45]

A second priority is still a priority. If for the sake of global security, relations with Russia must be well managed, not to say improved, we need to devote the resources required to manage it. For this reason alone, we cannot agree to treat Russia, in the words of a former senior British official, as "the variable": an issue to be considered only in the context of bigger issues in other domains. The very propinquity of Russia, the Caucasus, the Black Sea region, and the Caspian to these domains, not to say their role in the production and supply of hydrocarbons, argues for a different approach. For the same reasons, we cannot accept that "Partnership for Peace, the Membership Action Plan and wider association agreements…are essentially marginal to NATO's core rationale." For the globalists, the Russia–Georgia conflict demonstrates that we were insufficiently "cautious about taking on new commitments."[46] It could also be said that it demonstrates the perils of neglecting commitments undertaken. That conflict, which developed under our noses, is a flagrant example of the consequences of inattentiveness. Between the Bucharest summit and August 8, the only subjects deemed worthy of high-level coordination by the Bush White House were Afghanistan and Iraq.[47] Those who attach importance to Russia, the Black Sea region, and the Caucasus are not to blame for that.

The third paradigm is defined by conciliation. Until the election of Barack Obama, this paradigm was most conspicuous in Europe, notably in Germany. Yet the war in Georgia, in Chancellor Merkel's words, marked a "caesura" in Germany's relations in Russia. It is paradoxical that just as the EU was coming to the conclusion that "partnership and engagement" are not enough and consensus over "strategic partnership" with Russia was breaking down in Germany itself, the new American administration decided that it is time to resurrect it.

"Pressing the reset button" is short-hand for a high-level, comprehensive effort to return to fundamentals and resurrect the U.S.-Russia partnership on the basis of "common challenges," many of which, it must be said, are indistinguishable from those of the globalists. The effort is informally backed and supported by commissions, projects, and reports bringing together some of the most senior American experts and officials associated with the last three administrations. These experts rightly warn that "common challenges...are not the same as common interests"[48]; they acknowledge the risk of disappointment ("Moscow will likely be a difficult partner at best")[49]; and anticipate "inevitable competition" in the former USSR, where "Ukraine poses perhaps the most formidable challenge."[50]

Like the proponents of the first paradigm, the authors of this effort take Russia seriously and emphasize the importance of giving a special coordinating role to a "senior official...capable of speaking authoritatively across the administration's foreign policy agenda."[51] But it is not clear whether they would accord similar attention to the post-Soviet region as a whole. Despite asserting, in terms consistent with Vice President Joseph Biden's speech at Munich in February 2009, that "no American administration could, or should, concede a Russian sphere of influence in the region,"[52] the states of the former USSR for the most part appear in these reports as obstacles, problems, and cautionary tales in the errors of provoking Russia rather than as countries to be cultivated, strengthened, and valued. It is, perhaps, sub-consciously indicative that in the introductory list of eight recommendations by the Commission on U.S. Policy Toward Russia, the one reference to new NATO member states arises in a negative context (missile defense) and the reference to Ukraine and Georgia *first* states that they are not "ready for NATO membership" and *then* affirms a "commitment to their sovereignty." The tone could not be different from that of Constanze Stelzenmüller, a leading exemplar of the new generation in Germany, who asserts that the "most immediate aim" of a new *Ostpolitik* must be the "stabilization and democratization of the nations along Europe's eastern boundary, from Belarus to Georgia."[53] From these reports, one would be hard put to recognize the contribution that NATO and EU enlargement have made to the "liberal, democratic and relatively secure system that exists in Europe today."[54] Instead, the reiteration of the Kremlin's refrain that "there will be no enduring security in Europe without Russia's inclusion" implies that its inclusion is our challenge rather than Russia's and that, in Russia's absence, other accomplishments have no intrinsic value.[55]

It must also be said that many proponents of the first paradigm would agree with much of the narrative that these authorities put forward about "what went wrong" in the 1990s and the role that Western triumphalism, ignorance, and "democratic messianism" played in the process. But it bears reiterating that just as it was culturally arrogant to suppose we could have "transformed" Russia, it is self-indulgent to blame ourselves for "losing" it. The authors of these reports do not ignore the influence of Russia's harmful mythologies and legacies in this drama, let alone the influence of "objective factors," such as the swiftness of the Soviet collapse, but it is necessary to assign more weight than they do to the instincts and habits of mind that the crucible of disillusionment has brought to the fore: a Darwinian view of the world, a conspiratorial view of politics, distrust of outsiders, and the belief that every disagreeable thing they do is really aimed at Russia, contempt for weakness, a reverence of power, and the prevalence of a mode of behavior, in business as well as politics, that unsettles partners, alienates competitors, and polarizes opinion. Furthermore, less attention should be paid to the architecture of relations and more attention to what Sir Andrew Wood has called "Russia's conversation with itself."[56]

Many skeptics would, as much as the conciliators, be willing to tease the substance and value out of President Medvedev's decidedly vague European security initiative. But one should not put one's faith in a "shared concept of security that incorporates Russian perspectives"[57] until those perspectives are shared. Even more venturesome is the suggestion that if a "security architecture based on...the United States, the European Union and Russia...leads to the subsuming of NATO into a larger structure over the long term, we should be prepared to accept that."[58] Why? How would a more inclusive structure overcome the divisions that are present in a more intimate one? Is inclusiveness synonymous with security, or is the point of a security structure to provide its members with protection and combine capacity and purpose in a convincing manner? The League of Nations "experiment" should have answered that question definitively. The time to "subsume" NATO or abolish it will arise when its members no longer see a use for it. We might reach that point, but it is more likely to lead to a fragmentation and diminution of security than an expansion and enhancement of it. The focus on security "concepts" rather than security interests belies the realism that many of these authors profess.

Perhaps the most unsettling aspect of this commentary is its distinctly twentieth-century approach to European security, the instruments of sustaining it, and the methods and techniques of undermining it. The issue of NATO is discussed almost exclusively in terms of security guarantees and membership. There is no discussion of the role that NATO has played in transforming security and defense cultures in East-Central Europe. Thanks to fifteen years of NATO-Ukraine cooperation, a substantial proportion of younger generation Ukrainian officers has more in common with their counterparts in NATO countries than with the same generation of military officers in Russia. The Orange Revolution triumphed in part because the beneficiaries of this system disobeyed illegal orders to crush it. When the Soviet Union fell apart, Ukraine had 1.7 million service personnel under arms, not including police. What would have happened had NATO not performed this role? What will happen if NATO membership is taken off the table and a "finlandization" of Ukraine "to ease Russian concerns" takes its place?[59] Why should Russia not behave with its customary confidence? For Russia, after all, the issue in Ukraine is not simply NATO membership, but NATO's presence.

Equally dated is the treatment in these reports of economic relations and energy security ("We do not fear Russian downstream investment in the United States or Europe").[60] Little awareness is shown of the aggressive uses of Russian economic power and its intelligence presence, not only in the former Soviet Union but, with increasing confidence and guile, in the new EU member states of Central and Southeastern Europe. It is Russia's novel modes of engagement, not "Cold War stereotypes," that explain why *shreyderizatsia* (Schröderization) has become part of the region's vocabulary. Well before the latest Russia-Ukraine energy dispute, Frank-Walter Steinmeier, Germany's supposedly pro-Russian Foreign Minister, concluded that energy diversification had become an imperative for the country. Will the United States help in this evolution if it launches a grandiose initiative for energy cooperation with Russia just at a time when the European Commission's *Energy Policy for Europe,* the European Energy Community, and the Eastern Partnership are establishing a realistic basis for European solidarity?

The Obama administration's resetting of relations might or might not prove to be a challenge for Russia. It will almost certainly prove to be a challenge for Europe. Today, some in Washington believe the United States "should pursue more active consultations with our European allies" in order to "ease European concerns."[61] That is not why consultations are needed. They are needed in order to avoid mistakes and protect long-term

Western interests. With all of its divisions, it is Europe, not the United States, that best understands what has changed in the syntax and grammar of European security. Europe is also best placed to understand what has changed and what has regressed in Russia. Russia today is a power pursuing classical nineteenth century aims with twenty-first century tools: intelligence and covert penetration, commerce and joint ventures, "lobbying structures" and litigation, energy and downstream investment and, in the former USSR, Russian diasporas and other "civilizational" forms of soft power. From Riga to Sofia, not to say Brussels and Berlin, these tools have raised concerns about the integrity of executive institutions, regulatory mechanisms, and the political process itself. Thus far, Russian policy has not inspired Europe to find its voice. It remains to be seen whether U.S.-Russia cooperation will do so.

Notes

Unless otherwise indicated, internet links were accessible on 10 May 2009.

Notes to Chapter 3 (Gordadze)

1. Jaba Ioseliani, *Sami Ganzomileba* (Tbilisi: Azri, 1999). Later Kitovani initiated war in Abkhazia, when despite an order coming from President Shevardnadze to deploy troops only along the roads, his battle units entered the town of Sukhumi. In 1995 Kitovani, together with a colonel of the Russian army, attempted another march on Abkhazia. He was arrested on his way to Abkhazia by the Georgian police. After his release in 1998, Kitovani moved to Russia and lived under the protection of the FSB. He periodically appeared in pro-Kremlin Russian media as an "expert" on Georgian affairs.

2. In the quest for a providential leader who would have been acceptable for the majority of Georgian society, non-Zviadist nationalists first tried to convince the representative of the Georgian royal family living in Spain—Jorje Bagration Y Mukhrani—to come back to the country. After the refusal of the latter, they had to support Shevardnadze's candidacy.

3. For example, the only serious factor that played in the process of elaboration of the American position in the war between Armenia and Azerbaijan, were the efforts deployed by the Armenian Diaspora, which through its lobby in Congress obtained the adoption of amendment 907, which banned American public economic and military aid to Azerbaijan.

4. There is much evidence of the direct involvement of the regular Russian armed forces in fighting against the Georgian army, such as the Russian military plane downed in Sukhumi in winter 1993, or the capture of several acting officers of the Russian army by the Georgians as prisoners of war.

5. A few days after the fall of Sukhumi, Shevardnadze, sharply criticized in the Georgian Parliament, declared that the capture of Sukhumi by rebels was planned and elaborated by the Russian officers stationed in Gudauta military base.

6. Through the 1990s, Shevardnadze and other Georgian officials were used to opposing "democratic and reactionary Russias." Georgia was officially at war with the "reactionary Russia," whereas the "democratic Russia" was supposed to be supportive of Georgia. This dual nature of the Russian elite was partly a fiction of Georgian politicians who wanted to see a part of the Russian establishment in their camp. Unfortu-

nately for Georgia, Russian liberals had no word in Moscow's policies towards the "near abroad," with the topic being more or less consciously abandoned to the hawkish conservatives.

7. Kevin Fedarko et al., "In Russia's shadow," *Time*, 11 October 1993, www.time.com/time/magazine/article/0,9171,979366,00.html

8. In 1994, Russia had received $12 billion in direct financial aid from the IMF and the World Bank.

9. In his desperate address, Shevardnadze also called on his Armenian and Azerbaijani counterparts to secure Georgia's main transit roads.

10. The Council of the Heads of States of the CIS responded positively to the joint appeal, demanding that CIS member states send their troops to Abkhazia. In the meantime, Russian troops stationed in Abkhazia (troops that actually participated in fighting against the Georgian army) received the status of the CIS Peace-Keeping Force in Abkhazia.

11. Russia's Ministry of Foreign Affairs even suggested to the UN in the summer of 1994 that it allocate funds for financing its mission in Abkhazia.

12. Nadibaidze did not even speak Georgian properly and was clearly not a person who could build-up a modern-style Georgian national army from scratch. While serving at ZAKVO, he was in charge of supplies.

13. The same awkwardness characterized Georgian attempts to capitalize on perceived emotional attachments, recalling that Yevgeny Primakov had spent his childhood in Tbilisi; that Sergey Kirienko (Russian prime minister after Chernomyrdin) was born in Sukhumi; and that Igor Ivanov had a Georgian mother.

14. *Argumenty I Fakty*, 2 July 2005.

15. Thus Giorgi Chanturia, the leader of the National Democratic Party, and Soliko Khabeishvili—Shevardnadze's close friend and the president of his foundation—were the two most famous examples of assassinated politicians. Giorgi Karkarashvili, a former defence minister, was also targeted, but he miraculously survived his injuries.

16. In 1995, according to a close collaborator of Shevardnadze, Igor Giorgadze had already alerted Russia that Georgian secret services were on the brink of being totally controlled by the Americans.

17. Shevardnadze, TV interview, 29 August 1995.

18. The president survived again, and while all fingers again pointed at Russia, Primakov publicly made ironical remarks about the assassination attempt.

19. For example, he backed the Russian company Industriya to buy Georgian Manganese mines in Chiaturia. The memorandum was signed but the company failed to pay the determined amount.

20. As a result, 40,000 Georgian returnees to Gali became refugees for the second time and more than 100 people were killed.

21. At the end of 2001, Igor Ivanov, based on dubious information from a supposed driver of the leader of Al-Qaeda, declared that Osama Bin Laden was possibly hiding in the Pankisi Gorge in Georgia. Half-mockingly, Shevardnadze launched a surveillance operation in the valley, starting from the house of Ivanov's family (the latter's mother is originally from Pankisi).

22. Russia sent a paratrooper division to the Itum-Kale district of Chechnya in the winter of 2000, which took control of the border with Georgia. The paratroopers occupied the Georgian hamlet of Pitchvni where they established their post.

23. See Thornike Gordadze, "Géorgie : l'Irak du pauvre" (Georgia : the Poor Man's Iraq), *Le Figaro*, 21 October 2002.

24. The American contribution was the most important. In 1999, Georgia received several combat helicopters from the U.S. The amount of American aid to this department attained $50 million. This was the first case of successful cooperation between the two countries in the military domain.

25. Russia decided to choose the Vaziani and Gudauta bases for tactical reasons. Vaziani was a military air base close to Tbilisi and during the Soviet period, it was designed for control of the southern airspace (in the direction of Turkey and the Middle East). It had no strategic importance for the control of Georgia. Gudauta was in Abkhazia and the Georgians had no possibility to verify if the base was really closed; and, in fact, despite Russia's commitment, the Gudauta base was never dismantled. It continues to be used in 2009. Batumi and Akhalkalaki bases were of no significant military importance either, but they were situated in more "sensitive" regions of Georgia (Adjara and Javakheti), where in case of need they could have been used to destabilize Georgia. Moreover, these two bases were closed in 2007 with little resistance from Russia, because seeing Abashidze ousted from power in Adjara and state control reinforced in Javakheti, keeping them was becoming an unaffordable luxury.

26. Some groundless rumours about the probable opening of Turkish military bases in Armenian-populated regions of Georgia were spread by some "trustworthy sources," provoking the indignation and protest of local Armenians. By the same token, Abkhaz children and women were suggested to lie down on the railway close to Gudauta, in order to prevent the evacuation of the Russian base.

27. This possibility was raised by William Cohen during his visit to the South Caucasus in July 1999.

28. Sergey Ivanov is famous for his sharp phrases on Georgia. As a symptomatic illustration of this tendency one could quote his (at that time already Russian Minister of Defense) comment on Georgia's desire to join NATO: "Georgia can join any international organisation it wants, even the league of Sexual minorities," see *Vremya Novostej*, 20 September 2002.

29. The former ambassador reiterated his vision in a recent interview to the radio station Ekho Moskvy on 25 April 2009.

30. Stanevski stated many times that Russia was the greatest supplier of financial aid to Georgia, introducing a rather strange approach and definition of "economic aid": he proposed categorizing as aid the money that Georgians working in Russia sent annually back to Georgia.

31. See interview of Sergey Ivanov to *Vlast,* 18 January 2002.

32. Initially, some Georgian analysts and politicians talked about the possible positive consequences of the Russian decision. They naively believed that the residents of Abkhazia and Tskhinvali Region would have been obliged to come to Tbilisi to obtain Russian visas and that move would have had an unexpectedly positive effect on the reintegration of the separatist provinces.

33. Even the tiny and almost totally controlled Abkhazia defied in 2004 a unilateral and blunt attempt of Moscow to impose a KGB officer as a de facto president of the breakaway region against the more popular, and supposedly more independent-minded, Sergey Bagapsh.

Notes to Chapter 4 (Illarionov)

1. "Georgia near Exit from CIS," *Eurasia Daily Monitor* 3 (92), 11 May 2006, www.jamestown.org/single/?no_cache=1&tx_ttnews%5Btt_news%5D=31670

2. "Russians Send a Message to Georgians: Toe the Line," *New York Times*, 21 December 2000, www.nytimes.com/2000/12/21/world/russians-send-a-message-to-georgians-toe-the-line.html?n=Top/Reference/Times%20Topics/Subjects/T/Travel%20and%20Vacations

3. "Fighting Terrorism in Another Failed State," Center for Defense Information, 22 March 2002, www.cdi.org/terrorism/georgia.cfm

4. "Georgia Protests about Russian Citizenship Law Amendments," Rustavi-2 Television, 1600 GMT, 10 June 2002, in BBC Monitoring.

5. Jaba Devdariani, "Georgia's Turmoil Heightens Tensions in Separatist Regions," *Eurasia Insight*, 15 October 2002, www.eurasianet.org/departments/insight/articles/eav101502.shtml

6. Irakly Areshidze and Irakly Chkhenkely, "Georgian Diplomats, Blaming Russia, Invite Important Questions," *Eurasia Insight*, 27 November 2002, www.eurasianet.org/departments/insight/articles/eav112702.shtml

7. "Russian Defense Minister Denies Pankisi Bombings, Offers Probe," *Interfax*, 26 August 2002, in BBC Monitoring.

8. "Breakaway States Get Together," Institute for War and Peace Reporting, *Caucasus Reporting Service* no. 146, 12 September 2002.

9. "Putin Accuses Georgia in Letter to UN," *The Russia Journal*, 12 September 2002, www.russiajournal.com/node/11993

10. "Putin Considers Strike on Georgia," *Moscow Times*, 12 September 2002, www.moscowtimes.ru/article/850/49/243668.htm

11. "Shevardnadze Officially Requests Invitation to Join NATO," *RFE/RL*, 22 November 2002, www.rferl.org/Content/Article/1101463.html

12. "Kurieri," Rustavi-2 Television 17:00 GMT, 26 December 2002, in BBC Monitoring.

13. Information from Dmitry Sanakoyev, who then, in capacity of high-ranking South Ossetian official, was in charge of receiving those tanks. "South Ossetian Leader Denies Georgian Reports on Deployment of Tanks," *Prime News Agency*, Tbilisi, 28 February 2003, in BBC Monitoring,

14. "US calls for International Monitoring of Roki Tunnel," *Civil Georgia*, 2 March 2006, www.civil.ge/eng/article.php?id=11972

15. "Khugaev disavowed the Baden document," visit-telekom.ru, 4 August 2003, www.vist-telecom.ru/item/35/10739

16. "Russia: Voyeninform military news bulletin for October 03," Voyeninform news agency of the Russian Ministry of Defense, 11 December 2003, in BBC Monitoring.

17. "Georgia protests over Russian visa move," Rustavi-2 TV, 9 December 2003, in BBC Monitoring.

18. In official testimony to the parliamentary inquiry held by the Georgian Parliament into the August 2008 war, Saakashvili testified as follows: "He told us that our security minister – Valery Khaburdzania – was his friend and asked us to take care of him and not to touch him [meaning not to sack him]. I have nothing against Valery Khaburdzania, but the fact is that Putin, the leader of the state, which was bombing us, told me that our security minister was their friend." "Alasania Resigns with Politics in Mind," *Civil Georgia*, 6 December 2008, www.civil.ge/eng/article.php?id=20086

19. Saakashvili met with members of the Parliament Bureau on 24 August 2008, www.president.gov.ge/?1=E&m=0&sm=1&st=0&id=2721Your

20. "Yuzhnaya Osetiya rasschityvaet, chto ee budut zashishat russkie soldaty?" (Does South Ossetia assume that it will be defended by Russian soldiers?), *Natsionalnye interesy*, 12 December 2006, www.niros.ru/news/13708.html

21. "South Ossetia urges Russian Parliament to recognize its Independence," Rustavi-2 TV, 7 June 2004, in BBC Monitoring.

22. Kokoshin stated that "Russian citizens constitute a large share of population living on the territory of South Ossetia and Abkhazia. Russia must protect their lives, health, property, honour and dignity by all available means, like the USA and other

Western nations are doing." See "Russia must use all means to protect compatriots in Georgia, says senior MP," *Interfax-AVN Military News Agency*, 1 June 2004, in BBC Monitoring.

23. "Arms Seizure Flares Tensions in South Ossetia, Causes Controversy in Georgian Cabinet," *Civil Georgia,* 7 July 2004, www.civil.ge/eng/article.php?id=7280

24. "Tbilisi says 'No' to the Use of Force, Despite Attacks on Georgia Checkpoints in South Ossetia," *Civil Georgia,* 8 July 2004, www.civil.ge/eng/article.php?id=7353

25. "Georgian village comes under fire in Georgian-Ossetian conflict zone," *Interfax*, 10 July 2004, in BBC Monitoring.

26. Russian Television ORT, 11 July 2004.

27. "Georgia gives 'last chance for Peace' in South Ossetia," *Civil Georgia,* 19 August 2004, www.civil.ge/eng/article.php?id=7658

28. Ibid., "People Stuck at Border, Journalists – in Vladikavkaz," 7 September 2004, www.civil.ge/eng/article.php?id=7762

29. Ibid., "Timeline-2004," 3 January 2005, www.civil.ge/eng/article.php? id=8712 &search=2004%20timeline

30. Ibid., "Saakashvili says Energy 'Saboteurs Destroyed,'" 21 October 2004, www.civil.ge/eng/article.php?id=8129&search=october%202004%20saakashvili; "Temporary (AD HOC) Parliamentary Commission on investigation of the military aggression and other actions of the Russian Federation undertaken against the territorial integrity of Georgia," Parliament of Georgia, 7 January 2009, www.parliament.ge/index.php?lang_id=ENG&sec_id=1315&info_id=22617; "Emergency Statement by President Saakashvili," President of Georgia Homepage, 22 January 2006, www.president.gov.ge/?l=E&m=0&sm=3&st=130&id=1365

31. "Both Abkhaz presidential candidates in Moscow for negotiations," *ITAR-TASS,* 2 November 2004, in BBC Monitoring.

32. "Georgia: Abkhaz presidential candidate names key ally as future premier," Apsnypress news agency, Sukhumi, 8 December 2004, in BBC Monitoring.

33. Ibid., "Georgia: Top defense posts filled in breakaway Abkhazia," 23 March 2005, in BBC Monitoring.

34. "Georgia: New interior minister appointed in South Ossetia," Kavkasia-Press news agency, Tbilisi, 26 April 2005, in BBC Monitoring.

35. "Georgian interior minister proud of 'high precision' work on Gori blast case," Imedi TV, Tbilisi, 27 July 2005, in BBC Monitoring; "Georgian minister says Russia not helping with car bomb probe," Radio 1, Tbilisi, 10 November 2005, in BBC Monitoring; "Georgian TV shows documentary on Gori car bombing," Rustavi-2 TV, Tbilisi, 1 February 2006, in BBC Monitoring

36. "Georgia Orders Megafon to Pay Fine," *St. Petersburg Times*, 24 June 2008, www.sptimes.ru/index.php?story_id=26358&action_id=2

37. Calculations by the IEA in the forthcoming *Russia-Georgia War* (Moscow, 2009).

38. David Kezerashvili's speech to the Temporary Parliamentary Commission on 27 October 2008, www.parliament.ge/index.php?lang_id=ENG&sec_id=1329&info_id=21926

39. Mikheil Saakashvili's Speech to the members of the Parliament on 24 August 2008, *Civil Georgia*, August 25 2008, www.civil.ge/rus/_print.php?id=17462

40. The Military Balance (London: The International Institute for Strategic Studies, 2003–2009); "Yuzhnaja Osetija rasschityvaet, chto ee budut zashishat russkie soldaty?" (Whether South Ossetia assumes that it will be defended by the Russian soldiers?), Natcionalnye interesy, 12 December 2006, www.niros.ru/news/13708.html; Zaur Alborov, "Boevoj opyt vojny v Osetii" (Military Experience of War in Ossetia), Segodnya, 8 September 2008, osinform.ru/analitic/8556-boevojj-opyt-vojjny-v-osetii.html

41. "Georgia dismisses South Ossetian unification appeal to Russia," Prime-News, Tbilisi, 22 March 2006, in BBC Monitoring.

42. "Georgian leader accuses Russia of "major act of sabotage," Rustavi-2 TV, Tbilisi, 22 January 2006.

43. "Russian public health boss requests ban on wine imports from Moldova, Georgia," *Interfax,* Moscow, 27 March 2006 in BBC Monitoring.

44. "Another Georgian bottled water brand faces ban in Russia," RTR Russia TV, Moscow, 6 May 2006, in BBC Monitoring.

45. *RFE/RL,* 12 July 2006.

46. "Putin urges 'universal principles' to deal with ethnic disputes," RTR Russia TV, Moscow, 31 January 2006, BBC Monitoring.

47. "Russian PM's aide says incorporation of Georgia's South Ossetia decided – paper," *Vedomosti*, Moscow, 23 March 2006, in BBC Monitoring.

48. "Unrecognized republics within Georgia and Moldova plan increased cooperation," Radio Ekho Moskvy, 14 June 2006, in BBC Monitoring.

49. Sergey Blagov, "Putin to Tbilisi: Our Peacekeepers are Staying Put," *Eurasia Insight,* 27 June 2006, www.eurasianet.org/departments/insight/articles/eav062706.shtml

50. "Russian upper house gives president powers to use forces abroad," *ITAR-TASS,* Moscow, 7 July 2006, in BBC Monitoring.

51. "Russia Caught in Web of Espionage," *Kommersant*, 28 September 2006, www.kommersant.com/page.asp?idr=530&id=708235

52. "Russian defence minister accuses Georgia of banditry," ITAR-TASS, 28 September 2006, in BBC Monitoring.

53. "Russian Spies to Appear in Court", *RFE/RL*, 29 September 2006, www.rferl.org/content/article/1071683.html

54. "First Emergencies Ministry plane to evacuate Russians lands in Tbilisi," *Interfax*, 29 September 2006.

55. "Russia deports Georgians amid rising diplomatic tensions," *Voice of America*, 6 October 2006.

56. "Russia suspends all transport, postal links with Georgia," *USA Today*, 3 October 2006.

57. Masha Lipman, "'Enemy' Schoolchildren in Moscow," *Washington Post*, 20 October 2006.

58. "Russia is Generously Making New Laws for Georgians," *Kommersant*, 5 October 2006.

59. Maria Danilova, "Moscow asks schools for names of children with Georgian surnames," *Associated Press*, 7 October 2006.

60. "Measures towards Georgians in Russia not excessive – Chaika," *Interfax*, 6 October 2006, in BBC Monitoring.

61. "Georgian deportee dies in Moscow," *BBC News*, 17 October 2006.

62. "Russian navy violating Georgian waters, impeding shipping – Georgian minister, "*AFX Europe*, 18 October 2006, in Europe Intelligence Wire.

63. "Chechen 'volunteers' could support Abkhazia, South Ossetia – Alkhanov," *Interfax-AVN*, 20 October 2006.

64. "Two referendums and two 'presidents' in South Ossetia," *Caucaz.com*, 20 November 2006.

65. "Georgia opposed to Russian discussion of South Ossetia referendum," *Xinhua*, 7 December 2006.

66. "South Ossetian leader replaces defence minister," South Ossetian Press and Information Committee, 11 December 2006, in BBC Monitoring.

67. "War with Georgia 'practically inevitable' after Putin's remarks, says pundit," Radio Ekho Moskvy, 2 October 2006, in BBC Monitoring.

68. Ibid., "Georgia says Kodori shelled," 12 March 2007.

69. "Russian paper links shift in Georgian leader's rhetoric to US Senate's NATO vote," *Nezavisimaya Gazeta*, 20 March 2007, in BBC Monitoring; "U.S. House of Reps. Approves NATO entry for Georgia and Ukraine," *RIA Novosti*, 7 March 2007.

70. "Traffic stopped in Georgian-South Ossetian conflict zone," *RIA Novosti*, 11 May 2007.

71. See Svante E. Cornell, David J. Smith, and S. Frederick Starr, *The August 6 Bombing Incident in Georgia: Implications for the Euro-Atlantic Region* (Washington D.C. and Stockholm: CACI & SRSP Silk Road Paper, October 2007).

72. "Georgia: Separatists deny Russians violated airspace," *Interfax*, 25 August 2007, in BBC Monitoring.

73. "Russia to withdraw troops from Georgia ahead of schedule," NTV Mir, 10 November 2007, in BBC Monitoring.

74. "Peacekeeper rotation under way in Georgia's Abkhazia," Mze TV, 7 December 2007, in BBC Monitoring.

75. Mikhail Saakashvili's speech to the members of the Parliamentary Bureau on 24 August 2008, www.civil.ge/rus/_print.php?id=17462

76. "Georgian pundits comment on results of Putin-Saakashvili meeting," *24 Saati,* 28 February 2008, in BBC Monitoring.

77. Marina Perevozkina, "Polet na Operezhenie," *Nezavisimaya Gazeta,* 17 July 2008, www.ng.ru/cis/2008-07-14/1_abhazia.html

78. "Paper Mulls Official Ties with Abkhazia, S. Ossetia," *Georgian Daily,* 14 April 2008, georgiandaily.com/index.php?option=com_content&task=view&id=1027& Itemid=133

79. Marina Perevozkina, "Moskva otvetit NATO Abkhaziey" (Moscow Will Respond to NATO with Abkhazia), *Nezavisimaya Gazeta,* 14 April 2008, www.ng.ru/prin ted/209407; Svante E. Cornell and David J. Smith, "Moscow Moves to De Facto Annexation of Georgian Breakaway Regions", *Central Asia-Caucasus Analyst,* 16 April 2008, www.cacianalyst.org/?q=node/4839

80. "Political commentator ridicules Putin's instructions on Abkhazia, South Ossetia," *Novaya Gazeta,* 27 April 2008, in BBC Monitoring.

81. "Georgian Speaker slams Putin for liaising with separatist leaders," Mze TV, 4 April 2008, in BBC Monitoring.

82. "Moscow to Prevent Ukraine, Georgia's NATO Admission," *RIA Novosti,* 8 April 2008, en.rian.ru/russia/20080408/104105506.html

83. Vladimir Socor, "Russia Moves toward open annexation of Abkhazia, South Ossetia," *Eurasia Daily Monitor* 5 (74), 18 April 2008, www.jamestown.org/single/?no _cache=1&tx_ttnews%5Btt_news%5D=33560

84. "Russia criticized over Abkhazia," *BBC News,* 24 April 2008.

85. Vladimir Socor "UN mission confirms Georgia, rejects Russian version of air clash," *Eurasia Daily Monitor* 5 (100), 27 May 2008, www.jamestown.org/single/ ?no_cache=1&tx_ttnews%5Btt_news%5D=33665

86. David Kezerashvili's comments to the Temporarily Parliamentary Commission on 27 October 2008, www.parliament.ge/index.php?lang_id=ENG&sec_id=1329&info _id=21926.

87. "Russian General to Georgia: Russian peacekeepers' patience running out," *International Herald Tribune,* 19 June 2008.

88. "Abkhazians warn to capture Kutaisi," Kavkaz-Center, 4 May 2008, www.kav kazcenter.com/eng/content/2008/05/04/9551.shtml

89. Ibid., "Moscow to launch war operations against Georgia in late August," 5 July 2008, www.kavkazcenter.com/eng/content/2008/07/05/9984.shtml

90. Anatoly Baranov, "Rossiya stoit na grani bolshoy kavkazskoy voyny" (Russia is at the edge of a Big Caucasian War), forum.msk.ru/print.html?id=496351

91. "Russian peacekeepers in Abkhazia enhance combat readiness," ITAR-TASS, 7 July 2008, in BBC Monitoring; Konstantin Timerman, "Our fellows died not so that we would give up," *Izvestia*, 2 October 2008, www.izvestia.ru/russia/article3121131/.

92. Alexander Dugin, "Ossetians are waiting for war. Alexander Dugin on the situation in South Ossetia," geopolitica.ru, 8 July 2008, geopolitica.ru/Video/7/

93. "Russia confirms its aircraft intruded into Georgia," *Civil Georgia,* 10 July 2008, www.civilgeorgia.ge/eng/article.php?id=18748.

94. "Caucasus 2008," Russian Defense Ministry website, 15 July 2008, www.mil.ru/eng/1866/12078/details/index.shtml?id=47629

95. *Nezavisimaya Gazeta,* 26 July 2008.

96. "Russia deploys more military hardware in Abkhazia, Georgia says," Rustavi-2 TV, 6 July 2008, in BBC Monitoring.

97. Pavel Sheremet, "Abkhazia: ni mira, ni voyny, ni otdykha" (Abkhazia: no peace, no war, no rest), *Ogonyok*, no. 31, 2008, www.ogoniok.com/5057/18/

98. "Georgia reports shootout in S. Ossetia," *Civil Georgia,* 29 July 2008, www.civil.ge/eng/article.php?id=18854

99. Brian Whitmore, "Scene At Russia-Georgia Border Hinted At Scripted Affair," *RFE/RL,* 23 August 2008, www.rferl.org/content/Russia_Georgian_Scripted_Affair/1193319.html

100. "58-aya armiya RF gotova voyti v Tskhinvali" (58th Russian Army is ready to enter Tskhinvali), apsny.ge, 3 August 2008, www.apsny.ge/news/1217792861.php

101. Victor Vodolatskiy: "Kazaki odnimi iz pervykh vstali na zashchitu naroda kavkaza" (Cosacks stood up first to defend the peoples of the Caucasus), *Vesti,* 10 September 2008, skavkaz.rfn.ru/region/rnews.html?id=150137&rid=1051

102. Yegor Sazoev, "Rossiyskaya armiya podozhla k granitse yuxhnoy osetii" (The Russian Army approached the South Ossetian border), Life.ru, 4 August 2008, life.ru/news/27624

103. David Kezerashvili's comments to the Temporary Parliamentary Commission on 27 October 2008, www.parliament.ge/index.php?lang_id=ENG&sec_id=1329&info_id=21926

104. osradio.ru/news/all//11656.html (page no longer available as of 12 May 2009).

105. "Volunteers from neighboring regions rush to help Georgia's separatist region," *Interfax*, 7 August 2008, in BBC Monitoring.

106. Kezerashvili's comments to the Temporarily Parliamentary Commission.

107. "Yuzhnaya Osetiya moxhet predyavit Gruzii territorialnye pretenzii" (South Ossetia might claim territories in Georgia," *Rosbalt,* 6 August 2008, www.rosbalt.ru/2008/08/06/510922.html.

108. Marina Perevozkina, "Abkhazia gotova otkrit vtoroy front" (Abkhazia is ready to open a second front), *Nezavisimaya Gazeta,* 5 August 2008, www.ng.ru/cis/2008-08-05/1_abhazia.html

109. Kezerashvili's comments to the Temporary Parliamentary Commission.

110. www.izvestia.ru/world/article3119222/; osradio.ru/news/all/41.html

111. "Osvobozhdenye ot upryamstva," Radio Ekho Moskvy, www.echo.msk.ru/blog/buntman/539523-echo/comments/new?comment[parent_id]=270307;   ugo-osetia.ru/9_19+20/9_19+20-10. html

112. "Voyna vsyo spishet" (War is escalating), apn.ru, 12 August 2008, www.apn.ru/column/article206 35.htm

113. Marina Perevozkina, "Eto ni konflikt – eto voyna" (This is not a conflict, this is a war), *Nezavisimaya Gazeta,* 8 August 2008, www.ng.ru/politics/2008-08-08/1_war.html

114. Information provided by the Office of the Georgian President.

Notes to Chapter 5 (Nilsson)

1. Ghia Nodia and Alvaro Pinto Scholtbach, *The Political Landscape of Georgia* (Delft: Eburon, 2006), p. 13.

2. Charles H. Fairbanks, "Georgia's Rose Revolution," *Journal of Democracy* 15, no. 2 (April 2004): 112–115.

3. Nodia and Scholtbach, *The Political Landscape of Georgia,* pp. 18–20.

4. Valerie Bunce and Sharon Wolchik, "Youth and Electoral Revolutions in Slovakia, Serbia, and Georgia," *SAIS Review* 26, no. 2 (Summer-Fall 2006): 61–63.

5. Fairbanks, "Georgia's Rose Revolution," 113; Nodia and Scholtbach, *The Political Landscape of Georgia,* p. 19.

6. Fairbanks, "Georgia's Rose Revolution," 14.

7. OSCE/ODIHR Election Observation Mission Report Part 1, Georgia Parliamentary Elections, 2 November 2003.

8. See Dan Sershen, "Chaotic Election Day in Georgia Produces Contradictory Results," *EurasiaNet,* 3 November 2003, www.eurasianet.org/departments/insight/articles/eav110303.shtml

9. Nodia and Scholtbach, *The Political Landscape of Georgia,* p. 19.

10. "Revival Receives 95% of Adjara Votes," *Civil Georgia,* 6 November 2003, www.civil.ge/eng/article.php?id=5425&search=Revival%20Receives%2095%%20of%20Adjara%20Votes

11. Fairbanks, "Georgia's Rose Revolution," 116.

12. Giorgi Sepashvili, "Strange Game of the New Allies," *Civil Georgia*, 12 November 2003, www.civil.ge/eng/article.php?id=5486&search=Strange%20Game%20of%20the%20New%20Allies

13. OSCE/ODIHR Election Observation Mission Final Report, Georgia Extraordinary Presidential Election, 4 January 2004.

14. OSCE/ODIHR Election Observation Mission Report Part 2, Georgia Partial Repeat Parliamentary Elections, 28 March 2004.

15. The World Bank, Georgia, Country Brief 2009, web.worldbank.org/WBSITE/EXTERNAL/COUNTRIES/ECAEXT/GEORGIAEXTN/0,,menuPK:301755~pagePK:141132~piPK:141107~theSitePK:301746,00.html

16. Transparency International, Georgia, www.transparency.ge/index.php?lang_id=ENG&sec_id=142

17. See Vladimer Papava, "The Political Economy of Georgia's Rose Revolution," *Orbis* 50, issue 4 (Autumn 2006): 661–663.

18. Miriam Lanskoy and Giorgi Areshidze, "Georgia's Year of Turmoil," *Journal of Democracy* 19, no. 4 (October 2008): 160–161.

19. "Abashidze Flees Georgia," *Civil Georgia*, 6 May 2004, www.civil.ge/eng/article.php?id=6880

20. Louise Shelley, Erik R. Scott, and Anthony Latta, ed., *Organized Crime and Corruption in Georgia* (London: Routledge, 2007); Svante E. Cornell, "The Growing Threat of Transnational Crime," in *The South Caucasus: A Challenge for the EU*, ed. Dov Lynch (Paris: EU Institute of Security Studies, 2004).

21. See International Crisis Group, "Georgia: Avoiding War in South Ossetia," *Europe Report*, no. 159, 26 November 2004, www.crisisgroup.org/home/index.cfm?l=1&id=3128

22. See Niklas Nilsson, "Tbilisi Withdraws from the Joint Control Commission: Proposes New Format for South Ossetia," *Central Asia–Caucasus Analyst*, 19 March 2008, available at www.cacianalyst.org/

23. Molly Corso, "Georgia Promotes South Ossetia Peace Plan," *Eurasianet*, 12 July 2005, www.eurasianet.org/departments/insight/articles/eav071205.shtml; John Mackedon and Molly Corso, "Little Optimism for Georgia's Abkhazia Peace Plan," *Eurasianet*, 20 January 2005, www.eurasianet.org/departments/insight/articles/eav012005.shtml

24. See Liz Fuller, "Abkhazia Certain to Reject New 'Peace Plan'," *RFE/RL*, 13 April 2007, www.rferl.org/content/article/1075857.html

25. See International Crisis Group, "Georgia's South Ossetia Conflict: Make Haste Slowly," *Europe Report*, no. 183, 7 June 2007, www.alertnet.org/thenews/newsdesk/ICG/f1e68999963124126bde07bd4d6de41b.htm

26. See, for example, International Crisis Group, "Georgia: Sliding Towards Authoritarianism?" *Europe Report,* no. 189, 19 December 2007, www.crisisgroup.org/home/index.cfm?id=5233&l=1

27. See Niklas Nilsson and Svante E. Cornell, *Georgia's May 2008 Parliamentary Elections: Setting Sail in a Storm* (Washington D.C. and Stockholm: CACI & SRSP Policy Paper, May 2008).

28. See Svante E. Cornell, Johanna Popjanevski, and Niklas Nilsson, *Learning from Georgia's Crisis: Implications and Recommendations* (Washington D.C. and Stockholm: CACI & SRSP Policy Paper, December 2007).

29. OSCE/ODIHR, Final Report, Georgia: Extraordinary Presidential Election, 5 January 2008.

30. Lanskoy and Areshidze, "Georgia's Year of Turmoil," 163.

31. OSCE/ODIHR, Final Report, Georgia: Parliamentary Elections, 21 May 2008.

32. Nodia and Scholtbach, *The Political Landscape of Georgia,* pp. 34–35.

33. National Security Concept of Georgia, article 5.4.1. Membership of the North Atlantic Treaty Organization.

34. National Security Concept of Georgia, article 5.4.2. Integration into the European Union.

35. Nodia and Scholtbach, *The Political Landscape of Georgia,* pp. 37–42.

36. See Graeme P. Herd, "Colorful Revolutions and the CIS: 'Manufactured' vs. 'Managed' Democracy?" *Problems of Post-Communism* 52, no. 2 (March/April 2005): 3–18.

Notes to Chapter 6 (Blank)

* The views expressed in this chapter do not represent those of the U.S. Army, Defense Department, or the U.S. Government.

1. Stephen Blank, "America and the Russo-Georgian War," forthcoming in *Journal of Small Wars and Insurgencies*; Lt. Col. Robert Hamilton, *After August: Causes, Means, and Policy Implications of the Russo-Georgian War*, Strategy Research Project, U.S. Army War College, 2009; Col. George T. Donovan, *Russian Operational Art in the Russo-German War of 2008*, Student Research Paper, U.S. Army War College, 2009.

2. C.J. Chivers, "Russia Keeps Troops in Georgia, Defying Deal," *New York Times,* 2 April 2009, www.nytimes.com/2009/04/03/world/europe/03georgia.html

3. Steven Erlanger and Helene Cooper, "Europeans Offer Few New Troops For Afghanistan," *New York Times*, 4 April 2009, www.nytimes.com/2009/04/05/world/europe/05prexy.html?ref=us; Joshua Chaffin, Scheherazade Daneishku, and Chris Bryant,

"Obama Urges EU To Welcome Turkey," *Financial Times*, 5 April 2009, www.ft.com/cms/s/0/a4a1d6a8-2201-11de-8380-00144feabdc0,s01=1.html

4. Colin Gray, *National Security Dilemmas: Challenges & Opportunities*, Foreword by General Paul Van Riper (USMC) Ret. (Washington, D.C.: Potomac Books, 2009), p. 6.

5. Sergey Markedonov, "Geneva Talks: From Ideological Confrontation to Diplomatic Routine," Moscow, politkom.ru [in Russian], 19 December 2008, Open Source Center, Foreign Broadcast Information Service, Central Eurasia, (hereafter *FBIS SOV*), 27 December 2008.

6. Brian Whitmore, "U.S.-Georgian Security Pact Said To Be In The Works," Imedi TV [in Georgian], *FBIS SOV*, 28 December 2008.

7. "Problems and Recommendations," in *The Caucasus Crisis: International Perceptions and Policy Implications for Germany and Europe*, ed. Hans-Henning Schröder, Stiftung Wissenschaft und Politik (Berlin: German Institute of International and Security Affairs, 2008), p. 5.

8. Robert Legvold, "Introduction: Outlining the Challenge," in *Statehood and Security: Georgia After the Rose Revolution*, ed. Bruno Coppieters and Robert Legvold (Cambridge, MA, and London: MIT Press, 2005), p. 29; Stephen Blank, "Russia and Europe in the Caucasus," *European Security* 4, no. 4 (Winter 1995): 622–645.

9. Dmitry Trenin, "Russia's Security Interests and Policies in the Caucasus Region," in *Contested Borders in the Caucasus*, ed. Bruno Coppieters (Brussels: Vrije Universiteit Brussels Press, 1996), p. 101.

10. Coppieters, "Introduction," in *Contested Borders in the Caucasus*, ed. Coppieters, p. 9.

11. Vilnius, Delfi Internet [in Lithuanian], *FBIS SOV,* 3 May 2006.

12. Moscow, *Interfax* [in English], *FBIS SOV,* 5 June 2006.

13. Eugene B. Rumer and Jeffrey Simon, *Toward a Euro-Atlantic Strategy For the Black Sea Region* (Institute for National Strategic Studies, National Defense University, Ft. Lesley McNair, Washington, D.C., Occasional Papers, no. 3, 2006) p. 16.

14. Vladimir Socor, "Democratize, Decriminalize, Demilitarize: A Strategy For Ending Post-Soviet Separatist conflicts," *Wall Street Journal Europe*, 14–16 May 2004, available at www.wsj.com; interview with Temuri Yakobashvili, "Tbilisi Akhali Versia, in Georgian, Open Source Center, Foreign Broadcast Information Service, Central Eurasia, *FBIS SOV,* 19 January 2004.

15. Fiona Hill and Omer Taspinar, "Turkey and Russia: An Axis of the Excluded," *Survival* 48, no. 1 (Spring 2006): 81–92; Idem., "Russia and Turkey in the Caucasus: Moving Together to Preserve the Status Quo," *Russie.Nei. Visions,* no. 8, IFRI, Paris, 2006.

16. Elin Suleymanov, "The South Caucasus: Where the U.S. and Turkey Succeeded Together," *Turkish Policy Quarterly* (Spring 2005): 120.

17. Trenin, "Russia's Security Interests and Policies in the Caucasus Region," pp. 98–100; Alexei Zverev, "Ethnic Conflicts in the Caucasus, 1988–1994," in *Contested Borders in the Caucasus*, ed. Coppieters, pp. 51–55.

18. Leslie H. Gelb, "Foreign Affairs; Yeltsin as Monroe," *New York Times*, 7 March 1993, www.nytimes.com/1993/03/07/opinion/foreign-affairs-yeltsin-as-monroe.html

19. Stephen Blank, "Is Russia a Democracy and Does It Matter?" *World Affairs*, MCLVII, no. 3 (Winter 2005): 125–136.

20. Abram Chayes and Antonia Handler Chayes, "Transition and Conflict: Russian and American Perspectives On the Former Soviet Union," in *Managing Conflict in the Former Soviet Union: Russian and American Perspectives* ed. Alexei Arbatov, Abram Chayes, Antonia Handler Chayes, and Lara Olson (Cambridge, MA: MIT Press, 1997), p. 15.

21. Hannes Adomeit and Heidi Reisinger, *Russia's Role in Post-Soviet Territory: Decline of Military Power and Political Influence.* Forsvarstudier 2002: 4 (Oslo: Norwegian Institute for Defence Studies, 2002), p. 5.

22. Vladimir Mukhin, "The Redivision of Eurasia," *Nezavisimaya Gazeta*, 4 December 2006, pp. 1–2, retrieved from Lexis-Nexis.

23. Alexander Cooley and Lincoln A. Mitchell, "No Way To Treat Our Friends: Recasting Recent U.S.-Georgian Relations," *The Washington Quarterly* 32, no. 1 (January 2009): 27–41; Lincoln Mitchell, *Uncertain Democracy: U.S. Foreign Policy and Georgia's Rose Revolution* (Philadelphia: University of Pennsylvania Press, 2008).

24. Douglas M. Gibler and Jamil A. Sewell, "External threat and Democracy: The Role of NATO Revisited," *Journal of Peace Research* 63, no. 4 (2006): 413–431.

25. Ibid., esp. pp. 416–417.

26. Ibid., p. 423.

27. Dov Lynch, *Why Georgia Matters*, Chaillot Paper, no. 86, 2006, pp. 7–11, www.eu-iss.org.

28. Svante E. Cornell, Mamuka Tsereteli, and Vladimir Socor, "Geostrategic Implications of the Baku-Tbilisi-Ceyhan Pipeline," in *The Baku-Tbilisi-Ceyhan Pipeline: Oil Window To the West,* ed. S. Frederick Starr and Svante E. Cornell (Washington, D.C. and Stockholm: CACI-SRSP, 2007), p. 27.

29. Lord George Robertson, "The Future of NATO: A New Organization for New Threats,?" *Harvard International Review* 26, no. 3 (Fall 2004): 47.

30. Victor D. Bojkov, "Conflicting Discourse of International Society in Europe: the Balkans in the Process of EU Enlargement," in *Post-Communist Transition in Europe and its Broader International Implications,* ed. Mario Zucconi (Ravenna: Longo Editore, 2004), p. 219.

31. Pamela Jawad, *Europe's New Neighborhood On the Verge of War: What Role for the EU in Georgia?* (Peace Research Institute Frankfurt, Report, no. 74, 2005) p. 14.

32. Ibid., p. 28 (quotes are cited there).

33. Lynch, *Why Georgia Matters*, pp. 14–15; author's conversations with Georgian officials, Washington, D.C., May, 2008; Nicu Popescu, "Georgia and the EU—an overview of current relations," npopescu.yam.ro/2008/07/02/georgia-and-the-eu—-an-overview-of-current-relations/; Nicu Popescu, Mark Leonard, and Andrew Wilson, *Can the EU Win the Peace In Georgia?* European Council on Foreign Relations, *ECFR Policy Brief,* 25 August 2008, www.ecfr.eu; Mikheil Saakashvili, "The Way Forward: Georgia's Democratic Vision For the Future," *Harvard International Review* (Spring, 2006): 68–73; *RFE/RL Newsline,* 20 April 2007. All the above offer examples of the overestimation of Georgia's readiness to join European security organizations and those organizations' readiness to accept it.

34. Paris, AFP Domestic Service [in French], *FBIS SOV,* 13 November 2008; "Sarkozy Scorns Bush Over Georgia," *BBC News,* 13 November 2008; Medvedev's Speech at U.S. Council on Foreign Relations, 15 November 2008, www.youtube.com/watch?v= 0ss_LzlxjUA, and www.cfr.org/publication/17775

35. "Sarkozy: Russia 'Largely Implemented' Ceasefire Terms," Tbilisi, *Civil Georgia,* 14 November 2008, www.civil.ge/eng/article.php?id=19961&search=sarkozy%20 novemner%2014

36. John R. Bolton, "After Russia's Invasion of Georgia, What Now For the West?" *Daily Telegraph,* 15 August 2008, www.telegraph.co.uk/news/worldnews/europe/geor gia/2563260/John-Bolton-After-Russias-invasion-of-Georgia-what-now-for-the-West. html

37. Moscow, *RIA Novosti* [in Russian], *FBIS SOV, 4* May 2005.

38. Michael Schwirtz, "Georgia To Revise Peacekeeping Agreement," *New York Times,* 10 August 2006, query.nytimes.com/gst/fullpage.html?res= 9C0DE6DB163 EF933A2575BC0A9609C8B63; "GUAM Wants UN To Take Up 'Frozen' Conflicts In CIS," *Interfax,* 1 September 2006; Moscow, *Agentstvo Voyennykh Novostey* [in English], *FBIS SOV,* 15 February 2006; Tbilisi, *Kavkaz-Press* [in Georgian], *FBIS SOV,* 17 January 2006; Richard Weitz, "Russia and the United States For Control of the OSCE agenda," *Eurasia Insight,* 8 January 2007, www.eurasianet.org/departments/insight/ articles/eav010807a.shtml; Vladimir Socor, "Russia Rejects Wider OSCE Role in South Ossetia," *Eurasia Daily Monitor,* 3 August 2004; "U.S., Russian Diplomats Clash At OSCE Meeting," *RFE/RL,* 4 December 2006.

39. Jawad, *Europe's New Neighborhood On the Verge of War*, p. 23, based on interviews with members of the European Commission that she held in May 2006.

40. Ibid., p. 23.

41. Pierre Jolicoeur, *The Frozen Conflicts of the Wider Black Sea Region*, Occasional Papers no. 62 (Kingston, Ontario, Canada: Centre for International Relations, Queen's University, 2008), p. 13.

42. Bruno Coppieters, "Georgia in Europe: The Idea of a Periphery in International Relations," in *Commonwealth and Independence in Post-Soviet Eurasia* ed. Bruno Coppieters, Alexei Zverev, and Dmitry Trenin (London: Frank Cass Publishers, 1998), p. 65.

43. Jawad, *Europe's New Neighborhood On the Verge of War*, p. 28 (quotes are cited there).

44. Ibid., pp. 30–31.

45. Ibid.; Lynch, *Why Georgia Matters,* pp. 73–81.

46. *A Secure Europe In a Better World: European Security Strategy* (Brussels: European Union, 2003), www.ue.eu.int/uedocs/cmsUpload/78367.pdf

47. Arkady Moshes, "Prospects For EU-Russia Foreign and Security Policy Cooperation," *The EU-Russia Review*, no. 2 (November 2006): 24.

48. Alvaro de Vasconcelos and Marcin Zaborowski, eds., *The EU and the World in 2009, European Perspective On the New American Foreign Policy Agenda*, ISS Report, no. 4, 2009, European Union Institute for Security Studies, Paris, p. 23.

49. Stephen Blank, "Security and Democracy in the Black Sea Basin," *Insight Turkey* 7, no. 1 (January-March 2005): 108–117.

50. Joanna Kaminska, "Battle of Influences Or a Partnership? The EU, Russia, and the Shared Neighborhood," paper presented to the annual convention of the International Studies Association, New York, 2009, p. 11.

51. Stephen Blank, "Germany and Turkey Keep Nabucco On the Rocks," *Central Asia-Caucasus Analyst,* 25 March 2009.

52. "Caspian Basin: Does EU Move Mean the Bell Tolls For Nabucco?" *Eurasia Insight*, 19 March 2009, www.eurasianet.org/departments/news/articles/eav031909.shtml; "Nabucco Project Not in EU Pipeline," Istanbul, *Hurriyet* [in English], *FBIS SOV*, 18 March 2009.

53. Kaminska, "Battle of Influences Or a Partnership?" p. 11.

54. Anita Orban, *Power, Energy, and the New Russian Imperialism* (PSI Reports) (Westport, Connecticut: Praeger Security International, 2008); Janusz Bugaski, *Expanding Eurasia: Russia's European Ambitions* (Washington, D.C.: Center for Strategic and International Studies, 2008); Edward Lucas, *The New Cold War: Putin's Russia and the Threat to the West*, Second, Revised, and Updated Edition (New York: Palgrave Macmillan, 2009); and for earlier works see, Robert Larsson, *Nord Stream, Sweden and Baltic Sea Security* (Stockholm: Swedish Defense Research Agency, 2007); Robert Larsson; *Russia's Energy Policy: Security Dimensions and Russia's Reliability as an Energy Supplier* (Stockholm: Swedish Defense Research Agency, 2006); Janusz Bu-

gajski, *Cold Peace: Russia's New Imperialism* (Washington, D.C.: Praeger in cooperation with the Center for Strategic and International Studies, 2004), passim; Richard J. Krickus, *Iron Troikas: The New Threat from the East* (Carlisle Barracks, PA: Strategic Studies Institute of the U.S. Army War College, 2006); Keith C. Smith, *Russian Energy Politics in the Baltics, Poland, and the Ukraine: A New Stealth Imperialism?* (Washington, D.C.: Center for Strategic and International Studies, 2004).

55. Yannis Valinakis, *The Black Sea Region: Challenges and Opportunities for Europe*, Chaillot Paper, no. 38 (Paris: European Union Institute for Security Studies and Defense, 1999); Oleksandr Pavliuk and Ivanna Klympusah-Tsintsadze, ed., *The Black Sea Region: Cooperation and Security Building* (Armonk, NY: M.E. Sharpe, 2004); Robert E. Hunter, "NATO and Mediterranean Security," in *Strategic Yearbook 2003: Euro-Mediterranean Security and the Barcelona Process,* ed. Bo Huldt, Mats Engman, and Elisabeth Davidson (Stockholm: Swedish National Defense College, 2002); Mustafa Aydin, *Europe's Next Shore: the Black Sea Region After EU Enlargement,* Occasional Paper of the European Union Institute for Security Studies and Defense, no. 53, 2004; Ronald D. Asmus, ed., *Next Steps in Forging a Euroatlantic Strategy for the Wider Black Sea*, German Marshall Fund, 2006; Svante E. Cornell et al., *The Wider Black Sea Region: An Emerging Hub of European Security* (Washington D.C. and Stockholm: CACI-SRSP Silk Road Paper, 2006); and the series of Xenophon Papers published by the International Center for Black Sea Studies are only a few of the many studies reports, etc. on this region

56. See, for example, Alvaro Vasconcelos, ed., *The European Security Strategy 2003–2008: Building On Common Interests* (Paris: European Union Institute for Security Studies, 2009), esp. p. 47.

57. Alvaro de Vasconcelos, "Multilateralizing Multipolarity," in *Partnerships for Effective Multilateralism: EU Relations with Brazil, China, India, and Russia,* ed. Giovanni Grevi and Alvaro de Vasconcelos, Chaillot Paper, no. 109 (Paris: Institute for Security Studies of the European Union, 2008), p. 25.

58. Lynch, *Why Georgia Matters*, pp. 51–53; Mitchell, *Uncertain Democracy*, passim.

59. Lynch, *Why Georgia Matters,* p. 53.

60. Cited in Cathy Young, "From Russia With Loathing," *New York Times*, 21 November 2008, www.nytimes.com/2008/11/21/opinion/21young.html

61. Secretary of State Condoleezza Rice, "Interview With Sylvie Lanteaume, Lachlan Carmichael, and Jordi Zamora Barceló of Agence France-Presse," 22 December 2008, www.state.gov/secretary/rm/2008/12/113437.htm (henceforth Rice interview).

62. Ibid.

63. Alexander Cooley and Lincoln A. Mitchell, "No Way To Treat Our Friends: Recasting Recent U.S.-Georgian Relations," *The Washington Quarterly* 32, no. 1 (January 2009): 27–28.

64. Ibid., pp. 27–41.

65. Jan Cienski, "Tbilisi Admits Misjudging Russia," 21 August 2008, www.ft.com/cms/s/0/0d8beefe-6fad-11dd-986f-0000779fd18c.html?nclick_check=1; "Georgia's Saakashvili Defends Ossetia Assault," *RFE/RL*, 28 November 2008.

66. Author's conversations with Georgian officials, May 2008, and with U.S. experts, November 2008.

67. Testimony of Daniel Fried, Assistant Secretary of State for European and Eurasian Affairs before the House Committee on Foreign Affairs, 9 September 2008, "U.S.-Russia Relations in the Aftermath of the Georgia Crisis," www.foreignaffairs.house.gov/110/fri090908.pdf

68. Tbilisi's frustration with the West is illustrated by numerous media reports and conversations of Western experts with Georgian officials during spring 2008. In May, President Saakashvili observed that "Georgia is not going and is not able to have a war with Russia. We do not even have so many combat army units and NATO will not help us in this." See "Russian Agencies: Saakashvili Says Threat of War Remains," *Civil Georgia*, 8 May 2008, www.civil.ge/eng/article.php?id=17792#. On 12 May, following Russia's first admitted overflights of Georgian territory, speaking in the presence of five visiting European foreign ministers, Saakashvili alluded to the events of 1921, when Georgia was occupied by Soviet Russia, and stated that "Europe left Georgia alone at that time [in 1921], Europe did not even speak out." See "Saakashvili Urges for EU's Help," *Civil Georgia*, 12 May 2008, www.civil.ge/eng/article.php?id=17812&search=Saakashvili%20Urges%20for%20EU's%20Help

69. Ref. Svante Cornell's conversations with President Saakashvili, Tbilisi, May 2008, personal communication to author.

70. Conversations with U.S. officials, Washington, D.C., December 2008.

71. Though the literature on intelligence failures is immense and there was one in this case, it is clear that the failure was not only in failing to deploy sufficient intelligence assets in this area, but also in failing to grasp what was happening and its importance.

72. Jim Hoagland, "Rice's Not-Quite-Shining Moment," *Washington Post*, 24 August 2008, p. B7, retrieved from Lexis-Nexis.

73. Ibid.

74. Rice interview.

75. For a discussion of strategic shocks and surprises and the distinction between them, see Nathan Freier, *Known Unknowns: Unconventional "Strategic Shocks" in*

Defense Strategy Development (Carlisle Barracks, PA: Strategic Studies Institute and Peacekeeping and Stability Operations Institute, U.S. Army War College, 2008).

76. Heather Maher, "U.S. and Ukraine Strengthen Ties With New Security Agreement," *RFE/RL*, 20 December 2008; Molly Corso, "Georgia: Washington And Tbilisi Sign Strategic Pact Sure To Irk the Kremlin," *Eurasia Insight*, 9 January 2009, www.eurasianet.org/departments/insightb/articles/eav010909b.shtml; Andrew F. Tully, "Georgian Foreign Minister Hopeful About Accord With U.S.," *RFE/RL*, 10 January 2009.

77. "Can the EU Ensure Europe's Security? *Bergedorf Round Table,* no. 138, *Warsaw,* 28-30 September 2007 (Hamburg: Körber-Stiftung, 2008), p. 55; Lolita C. Baldor, "Gates' Visit Shows U.S. Support for Ukraine, Baltics," 11 November 2008, available at www.usatoday.com/news/washington/2008-11-11-1610694587_x.htm

78. M.K. Bhadrakumar, "China Seeks Caucasian Crisis Windfall," *Asia Times Online*, 19 August 2008, www.atimes.com/atimes/Central_Asia/JH19Ag01.html

79. Ahto Lobjaskas, "NATO Attempts Balancing Act Over Georgia-Russia Conflict," *RFE/RL*, 18 August 2008; Janusz Bugajski and Ilona Teleki, *Atlantic Bridges: America's New Allies* (Lanham, MD.: Rowman & Littlefield, 2007), pp. 10–13, 54–56.

80. Gray, *National Security Dilemmas,* p. 6.

81. Dmitry Danilov, "Russia's Search For an International Mandate in the Caucasus," in Coppieters, ed., *Contested Borders in the Caucasus*, pp. 137–152.

82. Gray, *National Security Dilemmas,* p. 5.

Notes to Chapter 7 (Smith)

1. Dorothy Parker, "The Artist's Reward," *New Yorker,* 30 November 1929, pp. 28-31.

2. Although Thomas Kuhn confined his study of paradigms to the physical sciences, the concept is useful in the social sciences as well. Governments, particularly diplomatic services, hold paradigms—sets of intellectual assumptions, modes of logic and even terminology—that channel their thinking and analysis. See Thomas S. Kuhn, *The Structure of Scientific Revolutions* (Chicago: University of Chicago Press, 1962).

3. Deservedly or not, Georgia was roundly criticized by the international community for the way it handled closure of the smugglers' market near the South Ossetian town of Ergneti, interception of a Russian arms cache, and subsequent violent flare-ups. The incidents sparked government in-fighting, particularly between State Minister for Conflict Resolution Goga Khaindrava, now an opposition leader, and Interior Minister Irakli Okruashvili. See, for example, "Arms Seizure Flares Tensions in South Ossetia, Causes Controversy in Georgian Cabinet," *Civil Georgia,* 7 July 2004, www.civil.ge/eng/article.php?id=7280&search=khaindrava. Okruashvili went on to distinguish himself

with rash statements such as, "I was in Abkhazia several days ago, together with several soldiers. I stayed there for several days. I was sleeping in the forest there. And I vowed, while being there, that none of us will walk on our territory as partisans anymore." Zaal Anjaparidze, "Tbilisi Returns to Saber-Rattling in Abkhaz Policy," *Eurasia Daily Monitor* 2 (174), 20 September 2005, www.jamestown.org/programs/edm/single/ ?tx_ttnews%5Btt_news%5D=30877&tx_ttnews%5BbackPid%5D=176&no_cache=1. Okruashvili famously declared in 2006 that he would celebrate the New Year (2007) in Tskhinvali. Zaal Anjaparidze, "South Ossetia Peace Plans Smell of Gunpowder," *Eurasia Daily Monitor* 3 (120), 21 June 2006, www.jamestown.org/single/?no_cache=1& tx_ttnews%5Btt_news%5D=31799. Finally, The Georgian police were subjected to Western criticism for their use of tear gas and rubber bullets to quell a November 7, 2007 anti-government riot.

4. Tony Halpin, "Russia accused of looking for a fight over Georgia and Ukraine," *Times,* 29 May 2008, www.timesonline.co.uk/tol/news/world/europe/article4023082. ece

5. The *Threat Assessment Document* is classified; however, an unclassified summary appears in Ministry of Defense of Georgia, *Strategic Defence Review,* 2007, p. 67, which was published in January 2008. It is available at: www.mod.gov.ge/2007/ downloads/The_Strategic_Defence_Review(www.mod.gov.ge).pdf. For a brief account of the *Strategic Defence Review,* see David J. Smith, "Three Cheers for Georgia's Strategic Defense Review!" *24 Saati,* 28 January 2008, p. 1, www.gfsis.org/gsac/eng/public ations/24Saati_SDR.pdf

6. In an earlier time, Halford Mackinder pointed out that to the British free trade was a desirable normal condition. Otto von Bismarck rejoined, "Free trade is the policy of the strong." Halford J. Mackinder, *Democratic Ideals and Reality,* ed. Anthony J. Pierce (New York: Norton Library, 1962), p. 141.

7. The point is not to denigrate the reports or the people who write them, but that the international community wallows in details and painstaking even-handedness to dodge concrete action on what it knows to be true. For the reports on the Russian bombing of Tsitelubani, see Svante E. Cornell, David J. Smith, and S. Frederick Starr, *The August 6 Bombing Incident in Georgia: Implications for the Euro-Atlantic Region* (Washington D.C. and Stockholm: CACI-SRSP Silk Road Paper, October 2006), www.isdp.eu/files/ publications/srp/07/sc07georgiabombing.pdf. For the report on the March 2007 Russian helicopter attack on the Kodori Gorge, see David J. Smith, "Russian Attack on Georgia: Time to Speak Out," *24 Saati,* 7 July 2007, available at: embassy.mfa.gov.ge/index.php ?lang_id=GEO&sec_id=45&info_id=2773

8. "EU, U.S. Say Kosovo Unique Case," *Civil Georgia,* 19 February 2008, www.civil.ge/eng/article.php?id=17146

9. "Kosovo independence to spark chain reaction in Caucasus?" *Russia Today,* 27 December 2007, www.russiatoday.ru/Top_News/2007-12-27/Kosovo_independence_to_spark_chain_reaction_in_Caucasus.html/print

10. "Russian NATO Envoy Warns Tbilisi of S. Ossetia, Abkhazia Secession," *Civil Georgia,* 11 March 2008, www.civil.ge/eng/article.php?id=17325&search=

11. John Erickson, "Russia Will not be Trifled With: Geopolitical Facts and Fantasies," in *Geopolitics: Geography and Strategy,* ed. Colin S. Gray and Geoffrey Sloan (London: Frank Cass Publishers, 1999), p. 260.

12. Michele Kelemen, "Bush Calls for NATO Expansion at His Last Summit," 2 April 2008, *NPR,* www.npr.org/templates/story/story.php?storyId=89300373

13. "Merkel Against NATO Membership of States with Conflicts," *Civil Georgia,* 10 March 2008, www.civil.ge/eng/article.php?id=17321&search=

14. NATO, *Bucharest Summit Declaration,* 3 April 2008, www.nato.int/cps/en/nato live/official_texts_8443.htm?selectedLocale=en

15. Adrian Blomfield and James Kirkup, "Stay away, Vladimir Putin tells NATO," *Daily Telegraph,* 7 April 2008, www.telegraph.co.uk/news/worldnews/1584027/Stay-away-Vladimir-Putin-tells-Nato.html

16. "Moscow to prevent Ukraine, Georgia's NATO admission – Lavrov," *RIA Novosti,* 8 April 2008, en.rian.ru/russia/20080408/104105506.html

17. For more on Russian positions and a thorough refutation of the analogy between Kosovo and the Georgian territories, see David J. Smith, "Kosovo no Precedent for Abkhazia," *24 Saati,* 13 February 2006, p. 1; "Beyond Kosovo: Time for International Engagement in Abkhazia," *24 Saati,* 5 February 2007, p. 1; and "Kosovo: A Hash in the Balkans?" *24 Saati,* 7 February 2008, p.1.

18. For immediate Georgian reaction to Kosovan independence, see "Georgia Will not Recognize Kosovo: Foreign Minister," *Civil Georgia,* 19 February 2008, www. civil.ge/eng/article.php?id=17147&search=; "Burjanadze Comments on Kosovo," 18 February 2008, www.civil.ge/eng/article.php?id=17141&search=; "Senior MP: Georgia Should not Recognize Kosovo," 18 February 2008, www.civil.ge/eng/article.php?id=17138&search=; "'Georgia Will not Recognize Kosovo' – Senior MP," 18 February 2008, www.civil.ge/eng/article.php?id=17144&search=

19. Ibid., "Saakashvili warns against Kosovo Precedent," 18 February 2008, www.civil.ge/eng/article.php?id=17143&search=

20. Ibid., "Georgian, Russian Ministers on Putin-Saakashvili Talks," 21 February 2008, www.civil.ge/eng/article.php?id=17169&search=georgian%20russian%20ministers%20on%20putin-saakashvili%20talks

21. Ibid., "Georgia Withdraws Troops from Kosovo," 15 April 2008, www.civil.ge/eng/article.php?id=17580&search=georgia%20troops%20kosovo

22. Ibid., "Georgia to Send at Least 350 Troops to Afghanistan," 31 March 2008, www.civil.ge/eng/article.php?id=17490&search=; "Georgia Extends Troop Deployment in Iraq," 21 March 2008, www.civil.ge/eng/article.php?id=17411&search=

23. Ibid., "Georgian UN Envoy Slams Russia for Lifting Abkhaz Sanctions," 12 March 2008, www.civil.ge/eng/article.php?id=17331&search=zalmay%20alasania%20sanction

24. Ibid., "Tbilisi Says Lifting Abkhaz Sanctions 'Dangerous,'" 6 March 2008, www.civil.ge/eng/article.php?id=17281&search=

25. Ibid.,"Georgia MFA Statement Against Lifting Abkhazia Sanctions," 7 March 2008, www.civil.ge/eng/article.php?id=17286

26. Ibid., "Zero Tolerance to Abkhazia 'Militarization' – Saakashvili," 7 March 2008, www.civil.ge/eng/article.php?id=17292

27. Ibid., "MP Hints on Scrapping Russian Peacekeeping," 7 March 2008, www.civil.ge/eng/article.php?id=17288&search=

28. Khatuna Salukvadze, "Russia Out of Peacekeeping? Georgia Challenges the Status Quo," *Cental Asia–Caucasus Analyst,* 19 October 2005, www.cacianalyst.org/?q=node/3478; Jean-Christophe Peuch, "Georgia: Parliament Votes Russian Troops Out of South Ossetia," *RFE/RL,* 15 February 2006, www.rferl.org/content/article/1065805.html

29. "Tbilisi Waits for EU, U.S. Engagement before Demanding Peacekeepers' Withdrawal," *Civil Georgia,* 23 June 2008, www.civil.ge/eng/article.php?id=18603&search=lomaia%20peacekeepers

30. Ibid., "Tbilisi Proposes New Negotiating Format for S. Ossetia," 1 March 2008, www.civil.ge/eng/article.php?id=17244&search=. For an explanation why the JCC did not work and how 2+2+2 could have worked, see David J. Smith, "2+2+2=Progress in South Ossetia," *24 Saati,* 17 March 2008, p. 1, www.gfsis.org/gsac/eng/publications/2+2+2_Progress_South_Ossetia.pdf

31. "Georgian, Russian Negotiators Discuss S. Ossetia," *Civil Georgia,* 6 March 2008, www.civil.ge/eng/article.php?id=17277&search=2+2+2

32. Ibid.,"Saakashvili's Statement on Tbilisi's Proposals to Abkhazia," 28 March 2008, www.civil.ge/eng/article.php?id=17475&search=

33. Ibid., "Sokhumi Rejects Tbilisi's Proposal as 'PR Stunt,'" 29 March 2008, www.civil.ge/eng/article.php?id=17476&search=

34. Ministry of Foreign Affairs of Georgia, *Statement of the Ministry of Foreign Affairs of Georgia,* 8 April 2008, www.mfa.gov.ge/index.php?lang_id=ENG&sec_id=36&info_id=6280

35. Essentially, Russia used Abkhazia and South Ossetia as bridgeheads or, more precisely, lodgments on the southern slope of the Caucasus Mountains from which to conduct military operations against Georgia. Although Russia had—and has—instant

access to these two Georgian territories, the Sochi-Gagra Road into Abkhazia and the Roki Tunnel into South Ossetia are narrow defiles, constricting the throughput of military equipment and forces. Russia would not have been able to fight the war that it fought in August 2008 without several months of buildup in Abkhazia and South Ossetia. However one analyzes events of the first days of that war, the fact that Russia long and well planned the war is unassailable.

36. Mike Eckel, "Russia Sounds Warning to Georgia over Breakaway regions," *Associated Press,* 25 April 2008, www.blnz.com/news/2008/04/22/Russia_sounds_warning_Georgia_over_2644.html. Hereafter cited as Eckel, "Russia Sounds Warning." "Moscow's Move to Bolster Peacekeepers Anders Tbilisi, Worries EU," *RFE/RL,* 30 April 2008, www.rferl.org/content/article/1109659.html. Hereafter cited as RFE/RL, "Moscow's Move."

37. Georgian Armed Forces, Joint Staff, informal paper, *Trainings of Georgian Armed Forces Units,* informal paper, provided to the author 1 May 2009.

38. "Saakashvili Hails 'Historic' NATO Summit Results," *Civil Georgia,* 3 April 2008, www.civil.ge/eng/article.php?id=17517&search=bakradze%20nato%20summit

39. Ibid., "Saakashvili Tells Ministers to Work on Abkhaz Peace Plan," 12 April 2008, www.civil.ge/eng/article.php?id=17569&search=saakashvili%20abkhazia

40. Ibid., "Bagapsh Again Rejects Tbilisi's Proposals," 13 April 2008, www.civil.ge/eng/article.php?id=17571&search=saakashvili%20abkhazia

41. Ibid., "Saakashvili Hails Free Economic Zone in Poti," 15 April 2008, www.civil.ge/eng/article.php?id=17582&search=poti

42. For development of this concept, see David J. Smith, "Zugdidi, Ochamchire, Gali + 2," *24 Saati,* 30 April 2008, p. 1.

43. "UN General Assembly Backs Tbilisi's Abkhaz Resolution," *Civil Georgia,* 16 May 2008, www.civil.ge/eng/article.php?id=17843&search=idp

44. Ministry of Foreign Affairs of Georgia, *Statement of the Ministry of Foreign Affairs of Georgia,* 17 April 2008, www.mfa.gov.ge/index.php?lang_id=ENG&sec_id=59&info_id=6316

45. "'Revise Decision' – Saakashvili Tells Moscow," *Civil Georgia,* 17 April 2008, www.civil.ge/eng/article.php?id=17609

46. Once again, Tbilisi demurred on this matter.

47. Ibid., "Tbilisi Renews Anti-Russian Peacekeeping Push," 24 April 2008, www.civil.ge/eng/article.php?id=17684&search=

48. Ibid., "Saakashvili Calls on Abkhazians, Ossetians to Jointly Resist External Force," 29 April 2008, www.civil.ge/eng/article.php?id=17722&search=

49. "Russian MIG 29 fighter shot down UAV above Georgia," YouTube, 20 April 2008, www.youtube.com/watch?v=U49n1JuWAmc

50. United Nations Observer Mission in Georgia (UNOMIG), *Report of UNOMIG on the Incident of 20 April Involving the Downing of a Georgian Unmanned Aerial Vehicle Over the Zone of Conflict,* 26 May 2008, www.unomig.org/data/other/ 080526_unomig_report.pdf. See also David J. Smith, "UN: Russia Downed Georgian Aircraft!" *24 Saati,* 2 June, 2008, p. 1, www.gfsis.org/gsac/ eng/publications/Russia_Do wned_Georgian_Aircraft.pdf

51. "Drone Downing Discussed at UN Security Council," *Civil Georgia,* 30 May 2008, www.civil.ge/eng/article.php?id=18441&search=

52. For analysis of the significance of the Railroad Troops, see David J. Smith, "I've Been Working on the Railroad," *24 Saati,* 9 June 2008, www.gfsis.org/gsac/eng/publi cations/Ive_Been_Working_Railroad_090608.pdf

53. "MIA Releases Drone Footage of Russian Military in Abkhazia," *Civil Georgia,* 12 May 2008, www.civil.ge/eng/article.php?id=17814&search=

54. Ibid., "State Minister: Georgia 'Very Close' to War," 30 April 2008, www. civil.ge/eng/article.php?id=17775&search=

55. See *Statement(s) of the Ministry of Foreign Affairs,* 2 May 2008, www.mfa.gov. ge/index.php?lang_id=ENG&sec_id=59&info_id=6557

56. "Tbilisi Condemns Russian 'Railway Troops' in Abkhazia," *Civil Georgia,* 31 May 2008. www.civil.ge/eng/article.php?id=18445&search=

57. Ibid., "Saakashvili Calls Europe to Deter Russia's Moves," 2 May 2008, www. civil.ge/eng/article.php?id=17745&search=

58. Ibid., "Russian Agencies: Saakashvili Says Threat of War Remains," 8 May 2008, www.civil.ge/eng/article.php?id=17792&search=

59. Ibid., "Saakashvili Urges for EU's Help," 12 May 2008, www.civil.ge/eng/arti cle.php?id=17812&search=

60. Ibid., "Saakashvili Says Russia's Moves Triggered 'Serious Crisis'," 14 May 2008, www.civil.ge/eng/article.php?id=17832&search=

61. Ibid., "Saakashvili Lays Out Priorities Ahead of Talks with Medvedev," 27 May 2008, www.civil.ge/eng/article.php?id=18411&search=

62. Ibid., "No Breakthrough on Key Issues with Russia – FM," 7 June 2008, www. civil.ge/eng/article.php?id=18492&search=

63. Ibid., "Lavrov on Saakashvili-Medvedev Talks," 6 June 2008, www.civil.ge/en g/article.php?id=18486&search=

64. Ibid., "No Medvedev-Saakashvili Talks in Near Future – Lavrov," 9 June 2008, www.civil.ge/eng/article.php?id=18507&search=

65. Ibid., "Moscow Accuses Tbilisi of 'Open Aggression' in S.Ossetia," 4 July 2008, www.civil.ge/eng/article.php?id=18686&search=

66. Ibid., "Saakashvili, Medvedev Meet in Astana," 6 July 2008, www.civil.ge/eng/ article.php?id=18701&search=

67. Ibid., "NATO Expansion 'Red Line' in Russo-U.S. Ties – Kremlin Official," 6 July 2008, www.civil.ge/eng/article.php?id=18700&search=

68. Ibid., "Rice: Russian Moves Increase Tensions," 8 July 2008, www.civil.ge/eng/article.php?id=18720&search=

69. Ibid. "Russia Confirms its Aircraft Intruded into Georgia," 10 July 2008, www.civil.ge/eng/article.php?id=18748&search=

70. Incongruously, the International Crisis Group published a report on 5 June 2008 that said "Hawks in Tbilisi are seriously considering a military option." It cryptically continued, "A number of powerful advisers and structures around President Mikheil Saakashvili appear increasingly convinced a military option in Abkhazia is feasible." The report appears to have been based upon "Crisis Group interviews" with unnamed sources and "senior diplomats" who confirmed that the Senaki Georgian Armed Forces Base was on "alert." Without corroborating evidence or further information, it is impossible to weigh the import of this report. International Crisis Group, "Georgia and Russia: Clashing Over Abkhazia," *Europe Report,* no. 193, 5 June 2008, www.crisis group.org/home/index.cfm?id=5469

Notes to Chapter 8 (Popjanevski)

1. See statements by Georgian Minister for Reintegration Temuri Yakobashvili, "New State Minister Speaks on Conflict Resolution," *Civil Georgia,* 4 February 2008, www.civil.ge/eng/article.php?id=17048

2. Established in 1992, the JCC consists of four parties: Georgia, the South Ossetia de facto authorities, Russia, and the Republic of North Ossetia. The OSCE holds an informal seat in the Committee, but has no role in negotiations. For more on Georgia's withdrawal from the JCC, see e.g. Niklas Nilsson, "Tbilisi withdraws from the Joint Control Commission; proposes new format for South Ossetia", *Central Asia–Caucasus Analyst,* 19 March 2008, www.cacianalyst.org/?q=node/4816

3. The provisional South Ossetian administration was established in May 2006 as part of Tbilisi's campaign for the hearts and minds of the South Ossetian people. Its head, ethnic Ossetian Dmitry Sanakoyev, a former separatist fighter, supports reintegration of South Ossetia with the rest of Georgia.

4. See e.g., "Russia lifts Abkhazia sanctions," *BBC News*, 6 March 2008, news.bbc.co.uk/2/hi/europe/7282201.stm

5. The plan also offered the Abkhaz government veto-power in relation to decisions concerning the constitutional status of Abkhazia; and also security guarantees in the conflict zone, including gradual merger of the Abkhaz and Georgian law enforcement authorities. See the website of the President of Georgia at: www.president.gov.ge/?l=E&m=0&sm=1&st=130&id=2569.

6. At the 3 April 2008 summit in Bucharest, Georgia aspired to, but was denied, a NATO Membership Action Plan (MAP). Georgia and Ukraine were, however, assured they will be offered membership at an undefined time in the future. See point 23 of the NATO Bucharest Summit Declaration at: www.nato.int/cps/en/natolive/official_texts_8443.htm?selectedLocale=en.

7. The Group of Friends, comprising Russia, the UK, France, Germany, and the U.S., was established in 1993 to lead the multilateral mediation process in relation to the Abkhaz conflict.

8. See Group of Friends Press Statement of 20 June 2008, georgia.usembassy.gov/pr-06202008.html

9. See "Report of UNOMIG on the Incident of April 20 Involving the Downing of a Georgian Unmanned Aerial Vehicle Over the Zone of Conflict," www.smr.gov.ge/uploads /file/080526_unomig_report.pdf

10. See UNOMIG Press Release, "Russian Military Threatens to Boost Force," 8 May 2008, www.unomig.org/media/headlines/?id=10589&y=2008&m=5&d=8

11. International Crisis Group "Georgia and Russia: Clashing over Abkhazia," *Europe Report* No.193, 5 June 2008, www.crisisgroup.org/home/index.cfm?id= 5469

12. The resolution emphasized the urgent need for a timetable to ensure the prompt voluntary return of IDPs to their homes and underlined the importance of preserving the property rights of IDPs "including victims of reported 'ethnic cleansing.'" See General Assembly Draft Resolution on "Status of Internally Displaced Persons and Refugees from Abkhazia, Georgia," 12 May 2008, www.un.org/ga/search/view_doc.asp?symbol= A/62/ L.45&Lang=E

13. Fourteen states voted in favor of the resolution (among those: the U.S., Sweden, Slovakia, Azerbaijan, and the Baltic states) and 11 states voted against (among those: Russia, Serbia, and Armenia). 105 countries abstained from voting (among those: France, Germany, and the UK), see "General Assembly adopts Resolution Recognition Right of Return by Refugees, Internally Displaced Persons to Abkhazia, Georgia," 15 May 2008, www.un.org/News/Press/docs/2008/ga10708.doc.htm

14. See statements by the then Deputy Minister of Foreign Affairs of Georgia Grigol Vashadze, "Tbilisi Condemns Russian 'Railway Troops' in Abkhazia," *Civil Georgia*, 31 May 2008, www.civil.ge/eng/article.php?id=18445&search="Tbilisi%20Condemns%20Russian%20'Railway%20Troops'%20in%20Abkhazia,"

15. Ibid., "Nato tells Russia to withdraw Railway Forces from Abkhazia," 4 June 2008, www.civil.ge/eng/article.php?id=18463&search="Nato%20tells%20Russia%20to%20withdraw%20Railway%20Forces%20from%20Abkhazia,"

16. See "European Parliament Resolution of 5 June 2008 on the situation in Georgia," www.europarl.europa.eu/sides/getDoc.do?pubRef=-//EP//TEXT+TA+P6-TA-2008-0253+0+DOC+XML+V0//EN

17. According to Georgian intelligence sources, the military bases in Sukhumi, Gudauta, Ochamchire, and Okhurei were in the same period provided with new anti-tank missiles, howitzers, Grad systems, air defense systems, and MI-24 helicopters. On 6 June, Georgian intelligence sources reported also on detecting several SU-25 and SU-27 combat-ready fighter planes at the military base in Gudauta in Abkhazia.

18. See *Civil Georgia* archive, 17 June 2008.

19. "Moscow to launch war operations against Georgia in late August," *Kavkaz Center,* 5 July 2008, www.kavkazcenter.com/eng/content/2008/07/05/ 9984.shtml

20. "Tbilisi Calls for Joint Police Force in Gali, Ochamchire," *Civil Georgia,* 7 July 2008, www.civil.ge/eng/article.php?id=18715

21. See "Statement by the Presidency of the Council of The European Union on the Explosion on 6 July in Abkhazia (Georgia)," 8 July 2008, www.delgeo.ec.europa.eu/en/press/8July2008-2.html

22. See, for example, "US attacks Russia over Georgia tension" *Kavkaz Center,* 8 July 2008, www.kavkazcenter.com/eng/content/2008/07/08/9967.shtml

23. Three Georgian police men were injured in the attack. The incident was followed by a shoot-out between Sankoyev's bodyguards and unknown gunmen firing from the south Ossetian villages of Kokhati and Sarabuki. See e.g. Nina Akhmeteli, "Explosion from Abkhazia to South Ossetia," *Georgian Daily,* 4 July 2008.

24. See e.g. Vladimir Socor, "'De-Recognition' of Georgia's Territorial Integrity Disqualifies Russia as 'peacekeeper,'" *Eurasia Daily Monitor,* 11 July 2008, www.jamestown.org/single/?no_cache=1&tx_ttnews%5Btt_news%5D=33792

25. See e.g. "Georgia Protests Russian Military Drills in North Caucasus," *RIA Novosti,* 16 July 2009, en.rian.ru/world/20080716/114126411.html

26. For background, see *Civil Georgia* archive, July 2008.

27. Villages attacked included Ergneti, Nuli, and Kvemo Nikozi. See "Six die in South Ossetia Shootout," *Civil Georgia,* 2 August 2008, www.civil.ge/eng/article.php?id=18871

28. See e.g. UNOMIG Latest Headlines, "South Ossetia Shootout Leaves 6 Killed, 22 Injured – Report," UNOMIG Latest Headlines, 4 August 2008, www.unomig.org/media/headlines/?id=11093& y= 2008&m=08&d=04

29. See statement by Minister for Reintegration Temuri Yakobashvili, quoted by *Civil Georgia* in "Russia Tries to Create 'Illusion of War' – Tbilisi Says," 4 August 2008, www.civil.ge/eng/article.php?id=18886&search=Russia%20Tries%20to%20Create%20'Illusion%20of%20War

30. See Brian Whitmore, "Scene At Russia–Georgia Border Hinted At Scripted Affair," *RFE/RL,* 23 August 2008, www.rferl.org/content/Russia_Georgian_Scripted_Affair/1193319.html

31. See UNOMIG Latest Headlines, "South Ossetia Shootout."

32. See Spot Report by the OSCE Mission to Georgia, "Update on the Situation in the Zone of the Georgian-Ossetian Conflict," 7 August 2008, www.parliament.ge/files/1329_22127_732854_danarti_13.pdf

33. "Parties Confirm S.Ossetia talks arranged," *Civil Georgia,* 6 August 2008, www.civil.ge/eng/article.php?id=18904

34. Casualties were reported in the South Ossetian-controlled villages of Khetaguro-vo, Dmenisi, Sarabuki, and Ubait, see *Civil Georgia* reporting on 6 August 2008.

35. See Andrei Illarianov at: aillarionov.livejournal.com.

36. State Minister Yakobashvili's visit in Tskhinvali is described in a number of articles, e.g., "Georgia Report: How a Flat Tyre Took Georgia to War," *Daily Telegraph* 17 August 2008.

37. State Minister Yakobashvili's press conference was broadcasted live at 6.40 P.M. local time on 7 August 2008.

38. Rossiya TV, Moscow, in Russian 16:00 GMT, 7 August 2008, reported in BBC Summary of World Broadcast. Up until late April 2009, Bagapsh's statement [in Russian] was also available at www.vesti.ru/doc.html?=id=199443.

39. Including the villages of Prisi, Avnevi, and Tamarasheni, see *Civil Georgia* reporting on 7 August 2008.

40. Ibid., "Hundreds' of Fighters Infiltrate into S.Ossetia from Russia – Georgia Says," 8 August 2008, www.civil.ge/eng/article.php?id=18943&search=

41. The attacks targeted the three military bases Vaziniani, Marneuli, and Bolsini, all located in the vicinity of the Georgian capital of Tbilisi. Attacks were also carried out against villages in the Gori area, including the villages of Variani and Kareli and against the radar-station in Shavshvebi, see timeline by Georgian State Ministry for Reintegration, smr.gov.ge/uploads/file/A_Summary_of_Russian_Attack.pdf. See also "Russian jets attack Georgian town," *BBC News,* 9 August 2008, news.bbc.co.uk/2/hi/europe/7550804.stm; and Human Rights Watch, "Russia–Georgia: Militias attack Civilians in Gori Region," *UNHCR Refworld,* 17 August 2008, available at: www.unhcr.org/refworld/docid/48a930671a.html

42. A detailed account of Russian attacks on Georgian targets is provided at the website of the Ministry of Foreign Affairs of Georgia, www.mfa.gov.ge/index.php?sec_id=552&lang_id=ENG.

43. In a meeting between French President Nicolas Sarkozy Russian President Dmitry Medvedev in Moscow on 12 August, Russia signed an EU-brokered 6-point peace-plan. Later the same evening, Georgian President Saakashvili accepted the plan, albeit refusing a provision calling for international talks on the future status of Abkhazia and South Ossetia.

44. Churkin's statement was made at the 5954th (closed meeting) of the Security Council on 11 August. See Global Security, "South Ossetia-Daily Chronology," 11 August 2008, www.globalsecurity.org/military/world/war/south-ossetia-10.htm.

45. See e.g., Human Rights Watch, "Georgia/Russia: Update on Casualties and Displaced Civilians," 10 August 2008, hrw.org/english/docs/2008/08/10/georgi19581.htm.

46. "Russia Scales Down Georgia Toll," *BBC News,* 20 August 2008, news.bbc.co.uk/2/hi/europe/7572635.stm.

47. Several researchers contributing to this volume have made this argument, most prominently Pavel Felgenhauer and Andrei Illarionov. Others include Hoover Institution scholar John Dunlop.

48. Available at: lenta.ru/articles/2008/08/08/ossetia.

49. International Crisis Group, "Georgia vs. Russia: The Fallout," *Europe Report,* no. 195, 22 August 2008, www.crisisgroup.org/home/index.cfm?id=5636

50. Including an article by Peter Finn, "A Two-Sided Descent into Full-Scale War," *Washington Post,* 17 August 2008.

51. In a mobile phone conversation between a supervisor at the South Ossetian border guard headquarters and a guard stationed at the Roki tunnel, the guard was asked whether the armor had arrived. The guard confirmed, stating: "the armor and people," and added when asked if they had gone through: "Yes, 20 minutes ago." See C.J. Chivers, "Georgia offers fresh evidence on war's start," *New York Times,* 15 September 2008, www.nytimes.com/2008/09/16/world/europe/16georgia.html; and also "Phone taps 'prove Georgia's case,'" *BBC News,* 16 September 2008, news.bbc. co.uk/2/hi/europe/7619275.stm

52. According to the GoG, the recordings went missing when the Georgian surveillance team moved from Tbilisi to Gori during the war, but was retrieved again in early September. Copies of the recordings were sent to U.S. officials and to the *New York Times,* who after independent translations deemed them as credible, if not conclusive.

53. Chivers, "Georgia Offers Fresh Evidence on War's Start."

54. Media digest provided by the Georgian Ministry for Reintegration.

55. Brian Whitmore, "Georgia argues its case to OSCE, seeks to lay blame on Russia," *RFE/RL,* 26 September 2008, www.rferl.org/content/article/1291882.html

56. See e.g. Niklas Nilsson, "New Evidence Emerges on Start of Georgian-Russian War," *Central Asia–Caucasus Analyst,* 17 September 2008, www.cacianalyst.org/?q=node/4943

57. For background on the right to anticipatory self-defense (as an exemption to the prohibition of use of force, as laid down in the Charter of the United Nations), see e.g. Peter Malanczuk, *Akehurst's Modern Introduction to International Law* (London: Routledge, 1997), with further reference to D.W. Bowett, *Self-Defence in International Law* (New York: Praeger, 1958), chapters 5–6.

58. In its report from 2001, The International Commission on Intervention and State Sovereignty lays down four precautionary principles that limit the application of the "Responsibility to Protect" concept, namely; right authority; right intention; last resort; proportional means and; reasonable prospects. For more information see Report of the ICISS, "Responsibility to Protect," December 2001, www.iciss-ciise.gc.ca/pdf/Comm ission-Report.pdf.

59. Ibid.

60. For background on the court case "Application of the International Convention on the Elimination of All forms of Racial Discrimination (Georgia v. the Russian Federation)," see the website of the ICJ at: www.icj-cij.org.

Notes to Chapter 9 (Felgenhauer)

1. "Chief of Staff Testifies Before War Commission," *Civil Georgia*, 29 October 2008, www.civil.ge/eng/article.php?id=19851

2. "Voinstvuyushchie Mirotvortsy" (Militant peacekeepers), *Nezavisimaya Gazeta*, 18 July 2008, www.ng.ru/regions/2008-07-18/1_peacemakers.html

3. "National Security Council Chief Testifies Before War Commission," *Civil Georgia,* 28 October 2008, www.civil.ge/eng/article.php?id=19845

4. Ibid., "Intelligence Chief Testifies Before War Commission," 25 October 2008, www.civil.ge/eng/article.php?id=19829

5. Ibid.

6. "Abkhazia rasstavila goryachie tochki" (Abkhazia put full stop over hot spots), *Kommersant*, 5 May 2008, www.kommersant.ru/doc.aspx?fromsearch=431827be-6331-4c6e-b40a-561530e2a17a&docsid=889057

7. "Defense Minister Testifies Before war Commission," *Civil Georgia*, 27 November 2008, www.civil.ge/eng/article.php?id=20036

8. "Interview with Russian television channels," kremlin.ru, 24 December 2008, www.kremlin.ru/eng/speeches/2008/12/24/1916_type82916_210970.shtml

9. *Interfax*, 30 December 2008.

10. "Pyatidnevnaya voyna" (Five-Day War), *Kommersant*, 18 August 2008, www. kommersant.ru/doc.aspx?fromsearch=9bc89bfa-e09a-425f-b46b-1447e207dc7f&   docsid=1011909

11. *Interfax*, 30 December 2008.

12. *RIA Novosti*, 13 September 2008.

13. "Chief of Staff Testifies Before War Comission," *Civil Georgia*, 29 October 2008, www.civil.ge/eng/article.php?id=19851

14. Ibid., "Chief of Staff Testifies Before War Comission," 29 October 2008, www. civil.ge/eng/article.php?id=19851

15. Ibid., "Interior Minister Testifies Before War Commission," 27 November 2008, www.civil.ge/eng/article.php?id=20032

16. *Moscow Defense Brief*, 13 September 2008.

17. *Voenno-Promyshlennyi Kurer*, 29 April 2009.

18. Radio Ekho Moskvy, 28 March 2009.

19. "Gruzinskie 'Buky' popali ne v te globalnye seti" (Georgian "Buks" went to the wrong global network), *Vlast,* 13 April 2009, www.kommersant.ru/doc.aspx?fromse arch=6dc6ccdd-90d7-42af-ab83-67547be1d44e&docsid=1147486

20. "Russia Confirms Spy Drone Deal with Israel," *RIA Novosti*, 10 April 2009, en.rian.ru/russia/20090410/121045416.html

21. "National Security Council Chief Testifies Before War Commission," *Civil Georgia*, 28 October 2008, www.civil.ge/eng/article.php?id=19845

22. "SMI: rossiyskie voyska voshli b yuzhnuyu osetiu eshe do nachala boyevykh deystviy" (SMI: Russian Forces entered South Ossetia even before the beginning of military operations), *newsru.com*, 11 September 2008, newsru.com/russia/11sep2008/ voshli.html

23. Ministry of Foreign Affairs of Georgia, "Timeline of Russian Aggression in Georgia," 25 August 2008, www.mfa.gov.ge/index.php?lang_id=ENG& sec_id=556

24. "Interior Minister Testifies before War Commission," *Civil Georgia*, 27 November 2008, www.civil.ge/eng/article.php?id=20032

25. Ibid.

26. "Russia Confirms Spy Drone Deal with Israel," *RIA Novosti*, 10 April 2009, en.rian.ru/russia/20090410/121045416.html

27. "Pyatidnevnaya voyna" (Five-Day War), *Vlast*, 18 August 2008, www.kommer sant.ru/doc.aspx?fromsearch=9bc89bfa-e09a-425f-b46b-1447e207dc7f&docsid=101 1909

28. "Russian Troops Inaugurate Railroad in Abkhazia," *RIA Novosti*, 30 July 2008, en.rian.ru/world/20080730/115249475.html

29. "Russia Warns of Harsh Response to Georgian Provocations-3," *RIA Novosti*, 29 April 2008, en.rian.ru/russia/20080429/106214189.html

30. Ministry of Foreign Affairs of Russian Federation, "Press Release: Concerning Situation in Georgia-Abkhaz Zone of Conflict," mid.ru, 4 May 2008, www.mid.ru/brp_ 4.nsf/e78a48070f128a7b43256999005bcbb3/94fd44a99f85dff7c32574400037e98f?Ope nDocument

31. "Pyatidnevnaya voyna" *Vlast*, 18 August 2008.

32. *Interfax*, 10 August 2008.

33. Ibid.

34. Ibid., 3 April 2009.

35. "Interior Minister Testifies Before War Commission," *Civil Georgia*, 27 November 2008, www.civil.ge/eng/article.php?id=20032

36. "It was no Spontaneous, but Planned War," *Novaya Gazeta*, 14 August 2008, en.novayagazeta.ru/data/2008/59/01.html

37. "Saakashvili speaks of "Second Rose Revolution," *Civil Georgia*, 24 September 2008, www.civil.ge/eng/article.php?id=19587

38. Ibid., "Defense Minister Testifies Before war Commission," 27 November 2008, www.civil.ge/eng/article.php?id=20036

39. *RIA Novosti*, 18 August 2008.

40. Ibid., 20 October 2008.

41. Ministry of Foreign Affairs of Russian Federation, "Response by the Russian Foreign Ministry's Spokesman to a Media Question about the Death in Gori, Georgia, of a Netherlands Citizen in August 2008," mid.ru, 23 October 2008, www.mid.ru/brp_4.nsf/e78a48070f128a7b43256999005bcbb3/33bcaba43279f37fc3257523003f9ec7?OpenDocument

42. "Georgian Leader Signs Document agreed by Medvedev, Sarkozy," *Interfax*, 12 August 2008, in BBC Monitoring.

43. www.government.ru, 2 September 2008.

44. *Interfax*, 26 August 2008.

45. Ibid., 28 August 2008.

46. "Saakashvili on Army's "Combative Spirit," *Civil Georgia*, 20 April 2009, www.civil.ge/eng/article.php?id=20759

47. Ibid., "MoD Releases Names of Fallen, Missing Soldiers", 29 September 2008, www.civil.ge/eng/article.php?id=19624&search=

48. "Interior Minister Testifies before War Commission," *Civil Georgia*, 27 November 2008, www.civil.ge/eng/article.php?id=20032

49. *Interfax*, 13 August 2008.

50. Interfax, 3 September 2008.

51. *RIA Novosti,* 22 April 2009.

52. Ibid., 14 August 2008.

53. Ibid., 22 April 2009.

54. "Yuzhnaya Osetiya ne vosstanavlivayetsya dostignutom" (South Ossetia has not been rebuilt so far), *Kommersant*, 16 March 2009, www.kommersant.ru/doc.aspx?fromsearch=419df8a0-b750-4a6b-8f95-9b35d5923b78&docsid=1138793

55. Radio Ekho Moskvy, 12 August 2008.

56. "Interview with Italian Television Channel RAI," kremlin.ru, 2 September 2008, www.kremlin.ru/eng/speeches/2008/09/02/2216_type82916_206091.shtml

57. www.kremlin.ru, 29 March 2009.

58. *Nezavisimoye Voyennoye obozrenie*, 20 August 2004.

59. *RIA Novosti,* 26 September 2008.

60. "Opening Address at a Meeting with Commanders of Military Districts," kremlin.ru, 26 September 2008, www.kremlin.ru/eng/speeches/2008/09/26/2019_type82912 type84779_206970.shtml

Notes to Chapter 10 (Goble)

1. "German minister says Georgia breaking international law," *Deutsche Presse-Agentur,* 9 August 2008; "SPD kritisiert Georgien" (SPD criticizes Georgia) N-tv.de, 9 August 2008, www.n-tv.de/1006442.html

2. "Voinu s Gruzeyei podgotovila Rossia, i sama zhe ee nachala," (War against Georgia was prepared by Russia and launched by Russia itself), *Nasha Abkhazia,* 29 September 2008, www.abkhazeti.info/news/1222739236.php

3. Brian Whitmore, "Scene at Russia–Georgia Border Hinted At Scripted Affair," *RFE/RL,* 23 August 2008, www.rferl.org/content/Russia_Georgian_Scripted_Affair/ 1193319.html

4. Ibid.

5. "Idyot voyna – informatsionnaya" (The information war is going on), fontanka.ru, 12 august 2008, www.fontanka.ru/2008/08/12/033/

6. Infamously, but without confirmation that their actions were the result of Russian government information war policy, Russian hackers broke into the site of Georgian President Mikheil Saakashvili and posted pictures of Adolf Hitler.

7. "Voyennaya pautina" (a web war), *Novoye Izvestiya,* 12 August 2008, www. newizv.ru/news/2008-08-12/95814/

8. "Otkuda u parnya rossiyskaya grust" (Where does the Russian sadness, that the guy feels, come from?), babr.ru, 12 August 2008, www.babr.ru/?pt=news&event=v1& IDE=46993

9. "Situatsiya v Gruzii v voskresenie" (The situation in Georgia on Sunday), informatsionniy-analitichskiy tsentr, 10 August 2008, www.ia-centr.ru/expert/1942/

10. "Putin: 'Zapadnie SMI, eto bylo khoroshaya rabota. Ya vas pozdravlyayu! Tolko rezultat plokhoy'" (Putin: "Western media, it was a good job. I congratulate you! Yet, the result was bad"), polit.ru, 12 September 2008, www.polit.ru/news/2008/09/12/valda. html

11. Natalie Grant, "Deception on a Grand Scale," *International Journal of Intelligence and Counterintelligence,* 1:4 (1986): 51-77; and Vladimir Volkoff, *Petite histoire de la désinformation: Du Cheval de Troie à Internet* (The Short Story of Disinformation: from the Trojan horse to the Internet) (Paris: Rocher, 1999).

12. "Kavkazu gotovili novuyu federatsiyu" (Caucasians were preparing a new Federation), *Argumenty nedeli,* no. 8, 26 February.

13. Dmitry Vladimirov, "'Patrioty Gruzii' gotovyat terakty v Moskve?" ("Georgian Patriots" preparing terrorist acts in Moscow?), *Izvestiya*, 15 October 2008, www. izvestia.ru/investigation/article3121603

14. "Rossiyskim SMI napomnili neobkhodimosti izbegat' vozbuzhdenya natsionalnoy I religioznoy rozin pri osbeshchenii sobytiy v Osetii" (Russian media was warned about the necessity of avoiding inter-ethnic and religious intolerance while covering the events in South Ossetia) *Interfax*, 11 August 2008, www.interfax-religion.ru/?act=news &div=25973

15. For a discussion of this, see www.kavkaz-uzel.ru/newstext/news/id/1232291. html, www.contrtv.ru/common/2911/, and www.contrtv.ru/common/2916/

16. Irina Baramidze, "'Ostanovis,' Rossiya" ("Stop," Russia) *Novoye Izvestiya*, 12 August 2008, www.newizv.ru/news/2008-08-12/95817/

17. "Gruzinskiye vlasti razblokirovali rossiyskie sayty" (Georgian authorities have blocked Russian websites), *Interfax,* 21 October 2008, www.interfax.ru/news.asp?id= 40597

18. "Rossiyskiye telekanali v Gruziya ostayutsya zablokirovannymi" (Russian Television Channels will remain blocked in Georgia), vlasti.net, 22 October 2008, www. vlasti.net/news/26367

19. Onnik Kriokrian, "Georgia: Blogging the War", *Global Voices*, 28 August 2008, globalvoicesonline.org/2008/08/28/georgia-blogging-the-war/

20. Lev Rubinshtein, "Obnazheniye priyema" (Disclosing the method), grani.ru, 11 September 2008, www.grani.ru/Society/Media/m.141302.html

21. "Spravitelniy analiz strategiy informatsionnykh kampaniy rossii i gruzii," (Comparative analysis of strategies of Russian and Georgian news and information agencies), informatsionniy-analitichskiy tsentr, 15 September 2008, www.ia-centr.ru/ expert/2312/

22. "Gruzino-yugoosetinskiy konflikt pokazal shto rossiyskiye SMI poka ne gotovy rabotat' v novom informatsionnom pole" (Georgian-South Ossetian conflict has demonstrated that the Russian media is not yet ready to work in a new informational environment), informatsionniy-analitichskiy tsentr, 15 September 2008, www.ia-centr.ru/ expert/2237

23. On that particular propaganda failure, see "S Sayta gazety minoborony propala skandalnaya statya, oprvergayushchaya zayavleniya vedomstsva" (A scandalous article has disappeared from the website of the Ministry of Defense of Russia), sobkor.ru, 15 September 2009, www.sobkorr.ru/news/48CDF323AD99B.html. The article taken down but cached was available for a time at: www.209.85.135.104/search?q=cache: b4aQl4aVFbkJ:www.redstar.ru/2008/09/03_09/2_03.html+www.redstar.ru/2008/09/03_09/2_03.html&hl=ru&ct=clnk&cd=1&gl=ru

24. Anatoly Tsyganok, "Informatsionnaya voyna – real'nost geopolitiki," (Information war – realities of geopolitics), *FSK Forum*, October 29 2008, www.fondsk.ru/article.php?id=1714

25. Igor Panarin, "Sistema informatsionnogo protivoborstva" (System of information rivalry), *Voenno-promyshlenniy kur'yer*, no. 41 (15–21 October 2008), www.vpk-news.ru/article.asp?pr_sign=archive.2008.257.articles.conception_01

26. For discussions on these ideas see, for example, "Eksperty: V Rossii natchalsya novy etap informatsionnykh voin" (Experts: in Russia a new stage of informational war has started), *APN*, 15 April 2009.

Notes to Chapter 11 (Sherr)

1. This is not to overlook the involvement of these forces in, and their arguable instigation of, conflicts on territories where they had already been stationed when the USSR collapsed, including Abkhazia and South Ossetia. Neither is it to deny, up to the final stage of the Cold War itself, the relationship, even dependency of "fraternal" forces on Soviet military (and KGB) advisory groups, the infrastructure of the Soviet Ministry of Defense and the command-and-control organs of the Soviet General Staff.

2. Andrey Kozyrev, *Preobrazheniye* (Moscow: Mezhdunarodniye Otnosheniya, 1999), pp. 38–39.

3. Michael Winfrey, "New Europe Needs New EU-NATO Relationship –Klaiber," *Reuters,* 11 May 2001.

4. Sergey Karaganov, "Nuzhna li nam NATO?" (Do We Really Need NATO?), *Russia in Global Affairs*, 11-12 August 2008. The previous sentence reads, "Thanks to the continual expansion of its own activity, NATO has become the basic cause of the revival of apprehension [*nedoveriya*] in Europe, in any case in relation to Russia."

5. At a closed address on 27 April 1994, excerpted (and partially paraphrased) by ITAR-TASS.

6. Vyacheslav Kostikov, *Trud*, 22 February 1994. Kostikov had only just retired as Yeltsin's press secretary.

7. Ibid. For good measure Kostikov added, "Russia increasingly sees itself as a Great Power, and it has started saying this loudly."

8. Hence the verdict of *Krasnaya Zvezda* (Red Star) during the 1999 Kosovo conflict (27 March 1999): "Today they are bombing Yugoslavia, but are aiming at Russia." The article goes on to say that "tomorrow they will bomb Russia because of Chechnya, Ukraine because of Crimea, Moldova because of Trans-Dnestria and Georgia because of Abkhazia and South Osetia." Along similar lines, Lieutenant General Leonid Ivashov, Head of the MOD's International Cooperation Directorate, told NTV: "If the world community swallows this large-scale aggression, this barbarity, then it is today

difficult to say who will be next, but there will be a state that is going to be next in line without fail."

9. Fedor Shelov-Kovedyayev, "Strategiya i taktika vneshney politiki Rossii v novom zarubezh'ye" (Strategy and tactics of Russian foreign policy in the new abroad) (September 1992). Or, as another self-described liberal put it at the same time, "Russian domination [in the former USSR] is an inevitability. The whole question is at what price. One can't become a great power using the methods of the Tsarist or Communist regimes…We need to learn civilised and neo-colonialist ways of influencing others…The biological uniformity—the strong subordinate the weak—is still valid in world politics with the inexorability of universal gravitational laws." M. Shmelev, "*Za nashu i vashu metropoliyu*" (For our and your metropolis), *Moskovskiye Novosti,* no. 4 (1992), p. 8. In a similar vein, the Foreign Ministry's December 1992 "Concepts" document stipulated the interest of "the leading democratic states" in the "provision of stability" on the former Soviet "geopolitical space" and warned that this would depend "on our ability to uphold with conviction, *and in extreme cases with the use of means of force*, the principles of international law, including human rights, and to achieve firm good neighbourliness," *Kontseptsiya Vneshney Politiki Rossiyskoy Federatsii* (Foreign policy concepts of the Russian Federation), December 1992 (emphasis added).

10. As this author and a colleague wrote in April 1999, "[t]he most serious consequence of the Kosovo crisis is likely to be the legitimisation of anti-Western perspectives which Russia's moderates have thus far kept under control.… In the worst, but far from implausible case that an anti-Western leadership comes to power [after Yeltsin], four axes of breakout would arouse interest: (1) 'reviving Russia' by a 'strong', regulated economic policy and by a stronger and larger 'Slavic core' (to Ukraine's possible peril); (2) a serious long-term commitment to revive Russia's military power; (3) the Balkans, where 'intelligence struggle' will be enlisted to undermine Western allies and clients; (4) a search for 'strategic partnerships' with India, China and possibly Arab countries and Iran." James Sherr and Dr. Steven Main, *Russian and Ukrainian Perceptions of Events in Yugoslavia* (Surrey, UK: RMA Sandhurst, Conflict Studies Research Centre, 1999).

11. *Krasnaya Zvezda*, April 1999.

12. *Energeticheskaya strategiya rossii na period do 2020* (Energy Strategy of Russia to 2020), Government of the Russian Federation, 28 August 2003, no. 1234-g.

13. Text of Alexei Miller's address to EU ambassadors, "Rasshirovka viystupleniya Predsedatelya Pravleniya OAO <Gazprom> Alekseya Millera na vstreche s poslami stran Evropeyskogo Soiuza v rezidentsii posla Avstrii," Moscow, 18 April 2006, p. 1.

14. Sergey Lavrov, "The Present and Future of Global Politics," *Russia in Global Affairs*, no. 2 (April–June 2007).

15. To which one must also add the budgets of military forces outside the subordination of the Ministry of Defense, which perform a number of highly critical roles. In 2003 Putin trebled the budget of the Federal Security Service. Whereas the defense (MOD) budget is officially 2.8 percent of the whole (higher than NATO's 1.8 percent average, but only 13 percent of the U.S. budget in absolute terms), independent Russian experts estimate the burden at 10–30 percent of GDP, depending on whether or not non-MOD structures are included. See Jan Leijonhielm, Jan T. Knopf, Robert L. Larsson, Ingmar Oldberg, Wilhelm Unge, Carolina Vendil Pallin, *Russian Military Capability in a Ten-Year Perspective: Problems and Trends in 2005,* FOI Memo 1396 (Stockholm: Swedish Defense Research Agency (FOI), Division for Defense Analysis, 2005), pp. 7, 11.

16. James Sherr, *Russia and the West: A Reassessment*, The Shrivenham Papers, no. 6, January 2008, p. 27 (henceforth *Shrivenham*).

17. Sergey Blagov, "Russian Leaders Mull Geopolitical Moves in 2005," *Eurasianet,* 4 January 2005, www.eurasianet.org/departments/insight/articles/eav010405.shtml

18. President Medvedev's lunch with the Valdai Club on 12 September 2008 at which the author was present.

19. Dmitry Rogozin, "NATO At Sixty: On Our Terms," *The World Today* 65, no. 4 (April 2009), www.chathamhouse.org.uk/publications/twt/archive/view/-/id/1889/

20. Interview with news channel *Vesti,* republished in English by BBC Summary of World Broadcasts (hereafter SWB).

21. Yet this speech, one month into his presidency, strengthens suspicions that Medvedev was out of the planning loop in the Caucasus. The next sentence begins with the words, "[c]learly, there will be no confrontation." Unlike Putin and Lavrov, Medvedev gives very little attention to NATO enlargement and makes no mention of Georgia. No less revealing, this is the only speech by a senior Russian figure that praises aspects of the Bucharest summit: the agreement "on transit of non-military cargos by land through the territory of the Russian Federation." The contrast between the hopeful, unthreatening tone of this address, two months before the conflict, and Medvedev's pugnacious and alarming statements in the immediate aftermath of it gives the impression of a titular president desperate to move into the centre stage after being sidelined by the de facto leader of the country—much as Stalin in the 1930s effectively sidelined Litvinov and allowed him to present a policy abroad that was being undermined at home (complete text in *Vesti,* 5 June and in SWB).

22. *The Foreign Policy Concept of the Russian Federation,* 12 July 2008, p. 5, SWB, 12 July (henceforth *Concept*).

23. Dmitry Medvedev, "Viystuplenie na Konferentsii po mirovoy politike" (Speech at the conference on international politics, Evian), 5 October 2008, published in Russian and English on Presidential website, www.kremlin.ru

24. *Concept.*

25. Dmitry Medvedev, "Poslanie Federal'nomy Sobraniu Rossiyskoy Federatsii" (Address to the Federal Assembly of the Russian Federation)', 5 November 2008, Presidential website and in English in *SWB.*

26. Rogozin, "NATO At Sixty."

27. *Concept.*

28. Miller, Address.

29. Robert L. Larsson, *Nord Stream, Sweden and Baltic Sea Security* (Stockholm: Swedish Defense Research Agency (FOI), March 2007), p. 36.

30. Julian Cooper, "Russia and the Economic Crisis: No Safe Haven," *The World Today* 64, no. 11 (November 2008).

31. Evgeniy Gontmacher, "Stsenariy: Novocherkassk-2009" (The Novocherkassk Scenario–2009), *Vedomosti,* 6 November 2008.

32. Vladislav Inozemtsev, "The 'Resource Curse' and Russia's Economic Crisis," presentation at Chatham House, 10 March 2009.

33. Ibid.

34. Vladimir Socor, "The Strategic Implications of Russia's Move against Hungary's MOL," *Eurasia Daily Monitor* 6, issue 77 (22 April 2009).

35. *Magyar Hirlap* website, 3 April 2009, cited in SWB.

36. Catherine Belton, Haig Simonian, and Thomas Escritt, "Surgut drills into its deep cash reserves," *Financial Times,* 30 March 2009, www.ft.com/cms/s/0/ 25e5386e-1d51-11de-9eb3-00144feabdc0.html

37. As quoted by the *Financial Times*, "We [*Surgut*] would like to expand our activity as a vertically integrated company....We have large-scale production but are less balanced on the refining and distribution side. We are very interested in eastern Europe."

38. Joshua Chaffin and Roman Olearchyk, "Russia Postpones Ukraine Gas Talks," *Financial Times*, 23 March 2009, available at www.ft.com/cms/s/0/e6e6cdc2-17e6-11de-8c9d-0000779fd2ac,dwp_uuid=81c13626-53d0-11db-8a2a-0000779e2340.html

39. For a discussion of reflexive control in the Georgian context, see C. W. Blandy, "Provocation, Deception, Entrapment: The Russo-Georgian Five Day War," Advanced Research and Assessment Group, UK Defense Academy, Shrivenham, March 2009.

40. Shelov-Kovedyayev, "Strategiya i taktika vneshney politiki Rossii v novom zarubezh'ye."

41. Dmitry Trenin, *Proyekt SNG'– noviy prioritet rossiyskoy vneshney politiki?* (The CIS Project—The New Priority of Russian Foreign Policy?), February 2004 (author's copy).

42. V.A. Lefebvre and G. L. Smolyan, *Algebra Konflikta* (Moscow 1968); V. A. Le-febvre, *Konflikhtuyshchiye Struktury* (Moscow: Soviet Radio Publishing House, 1973), cited in Blandy, "Provocation, Deception, Entrapment," p. 2.

43. G.F. Hudson, *The Far East in World Politics* (Oxford: Oxford University Press, 1939).

44. "We must rebuild expertise in Russia across government, not just in traditional domains—foreign ministries, defense ministries and intelligence and security estab-lishments—but in areas relevant to the new currency of Russian influence: regulatory authorities, departments of trade, customs, immigration and police. Horizontal integra-tion between departments and experts is also needed in order to be able to relate the parts to the whole." Sherr, *Shrivenham*, p. 33.

45. Ibid.

46. Michael Clarke, "NATO at Sixty: Unhappy Returns," *The World Today* 65, no. 4 (April 2009), www.chathamhouse.org.uk/publications/twt/archive/view/-/id/1886/. In the same article, largely focused on Afghanistan, the author nevertheless states that "[t]he most important issue is, as it always was, for NATO to link North America to European security and through that to have a stable relationship with Russia." But there is no discussion of what this link is or how it is to be forged. By saying that "[e]nlargement has burnished NATO's exterior but has not strengthened it," does the author mean to imply that if NATO keeps out of Russia's way, security east of the Niemen, not to say the Neisse, will sort itself out? If not, then what?

47. James Sherr, "Russia and Georgia: Culpabilities and Consequences," *Chatham House Briefing Note,* September 2008. For additional discussion of the issues leading to and emerging from the conflict, see the other five Briefing Notes in the Chatham House *Perspectives on the Georgia Conflict* series by Philip Hanson, Neil Macfarlane, Arkady Moshes, James Nixey, and Lilia Shevtsova, www.chathamhouse.org.uk/research/russia _eurasia/papers

48. Thomas Graham, *U.S.-Russia Relations: Facing Reality Pragmatically* (Wash-ington: CSIS & IFRI, 2008), p. 6.

49. *The Right Direction for U.S. Policy toward Russia: A Report from the Commis-sion on U.S. Policy toward Russia* (Washington: Nixon Center and Belfer Center for Science and International Affairs, Harvard Kennedy School, March 2009), p. iii (hereaf-ter, *Commission*).

50. Thomas Graham, *Resurgent Russia and U.S. Purposes* (New York: The Century Foundation, April 2009), p. 25 (hereafter Graham, *Century*)

51. Ibid., p. 19.

52. Ibid., p. 27.

53. Constanze Stelzenmüller, "Germany's Russia Question," *Foreign Affairs* 88, no. 2 (March/April 2009): 99.

54. Sherr, *Shrivenham*, p. 36.

55. Graham, *Century*, p. 24.

56. As he notes, Russia has been "very much the main actor here, and Western policies towards the country have been a contributory rather than a principal factor in determining what has happened." Sir Andrew Wood, "Reflections on Russia and the West," *REP Programme Paper,* 1/08 (November 2008), www.chathamhouse.org.uk/files/12710_1108russia_west

57. *Commission*, p. 4.

58. Graham, *Century*, p. 24.

59. Ibid., p. 25.

60. *Commission*, p. 12.

61. Graham, *Century*, p. 24.

Contributors

Stephen J. Blank is Professor of Russian National Security Studies at the Strategic Studies Institute of the U.S. Army War College in Pennsylvania. He is the author of over 600 articles and monographs on Soviet/Russian, U.S., Asian, and European military and foreign policies. He has published or edited 15 books focusing on Russian foreign, energy, and military policies and on International Security in Eurasia. His most recent book is *Russo-Chinese Energy Relations: Politics in Command*, London: Global Markets Briefing, 2006. He has also published *Natural Allies?: Regional Security in Asia and Prospects for Indo-American Strategic Cooperation*, Carlisle Barracks, PA: Strategic Studies Institute, US Army War College, 2005. Earlier, Blank was Associate Professor for Soviet Studies at the Center for Aerospace Doctrine, Research, and Education of Air University at Maxwell Air Force Base, and Assistant Professor of Russian History at the University of Texas, San Antonio. He holds M.A. and Ph.D. degrees from the University of Chicago and a B.A. from the University of Pennsylvania.

Svante E. Cornell is Research Director of the Central Asia-Caucasus Institute & Silk Road Studies Program, a Joint Research and Policy Center affiliated with Johns Hopkins University-SAIS, Washington D.C., and the Stockholm-based Institute for Security and Development Policy (ISDP). He is a co-founder and Director of ISDP. He is also the Editor of the Joint Center's biweekly *Central Asia-Caucasus Analyst* (www.cacianalyst.org). Cornell was educated at the Middle East Technical University, Ankara, and received his Ph.D. in Peace and Conflict Studies from Uppsala University. He was awarded an honorary doctoral degree by the Azerbaijani Academy of Sciences in 1999. Cornell has academic affiliations as Associate Research Professor at SAIS, and as part-time Associate Professor of Government at Uppsala University. He served as Course Chair for the Caucasus at the Foreign Service Institute in 2002–3. His main areas of expertise are security issues, broadly defined, and state-building in the Caucasus, Turkey, and Central Asia. He is the author of four books, including *Small Nations and Great Powers*, the first comprehensive study of the post-Soviet Caucasus, and numerous academic and policy articles.

Pavel E. Felgenhauer is a Moscow-based defense analyst and columnist in *Novaya Gazeta*. He graduated from Moscow State University in 1975, served as researcher and senior research officer in the Soviet Academy of Sciences in Moscow, where he received a Ph.D. in 1988. Felgenhauer is the author of numerous articles on topics dealing with Russian foreign and defense policies, military doctrine, arms trade, military-industrial complex, etc. He was associated with *Nezavisimaya Gazeta* as Defense Analyst and Correspondent in 1991–93, and then from 1993 to 1999 served as member of the editorial board and Chief Defense Correspondent for the Moscow daily *Segodnya*. From 1994 to 2005, Felgenhauer published a regular column on defense issues in the English language *Moscow Times*. In July 2006, he joined the staff of *Novaya Gazeta*, and continues to provide regular comments on Russia's defense-related problems to many other local and international media organizations and is a weekly contributor to the Jamestown Foundation's *Eurasia Daily Monitor*.

Paul Goble is a longtime specialist on ethnic and religious affairs in the former Soviet space. After serving in the U.S. government, U.S. international broadcasting, and various American think tanks, he has taught in Estonia and Azerbaijan. He is the editor of five volumes on developments in the region and currently prepares reports on it for his blog, Window on Eurasia. (http://windowoneurasia.blogspot.com/)

Thornike Gordadze is a Research Fellow at the French Institute of Anatolian Studies (IFEA) in Istanbul, directing the Institute's Caucasus department. He obtained his Ph.D. in 2005 at the Paris Institute of Political Studies (Sciences-Po) with a thesis entitled "The Socio-historical Formation of the Georgian Nation: The Legacy of Pre-modern Identities, Nationalist Actors and Ideologies." Gordadze received a fellowship with the Yale Center for International and Area Studies, Yale University, in 2002–3. From 2000 to 2006 he taught various courses at the Paris Institute of Political Studies, especially relating to the questions of ethnicity, nationalism, and the historical sociology of state formation. From 2004 to 2005, he worked as a consultant on Caucasus issues to the Center for Analysis and Prediction of the French Ministry of Foreign Affairs. He is also an associate researcher with the Centre for International Studies and Research (CERI) in Paris, since February 2007, and a research fellow and founding member with the Foundation for the Analysis of Political Societies (FASOPO). His current research interests include the study of imperial legacies in the Caucasus, Soviet nationality policy, Stalinism and destalinization, and the political economy of the de facto states and their relations to their external sponsors.

Thomas Goltz is an author, academic, and adventurer, currently serving as adjunct professor of Political Science at Montana State University, Bozeman. He spent some twenty years in the field as a print and electronic journalist. He has written news, features, and op-eds for most leading U.S. publications, including the *New York Times,* the *Los Angeles Times,* the *Wall Street Journal,* and the *Washington Post.* His 1998 book *Azerbaijan Diary* has been hailed as "essential reading for all post-Sovietologists." His second book on the post-Soviet Caucasus, *Chechnya Diary*, appeared in 2003, and in Turkish in 2005. The third, *Georgia Diary*, was first published in hardback in 2006, and re-issued with an extended update as paperback in 2009. A memoir about Africa in the 1970s, *Assassinating Shakespeare*, was issued in 2006, and published also in Hungarian in 2007. Goltz has lectured at most leading U.S. universities and foreign policy-related institutes in Azerbaijan, Canada, Georgia, the United Kingdom, and the United States.

Andrei Illarionov is a Senior Fellow with the Cato Institute's Center for Global Liberty and Prosperity in Washington D.C., and the President of the Institute of Economic Analysis, an independent economic think tank in Moscow, Russia. Until December 27, 2005, he was an Economic Adviser to the President of the Russian Federation. Illarionov conducted undergraduate and doctoral studies at the Department of Economics of St. Petersburg State University, and served as an Assistant Professor for International Economics at SPSU from 1983 to 1990. He also studied economics in Austria, the United Kingdom, and the United States. After brief service in government in 1993–94, he founded the Institute of Economic Analysis (IEA) and became its director. Since then, the IEA has become one of the leading Russian liberal economic research centers. From April 2000, Illarionov served as Chief Economic Advisor to newly-elected Russian President Vladimir Putin, and as his Personal Representative to the Group of Eight (G-8). He was the driving force behind the adoption of a 13 percent flat income tax, the creation of a Stabilization Fund for windfall oil revenues, and the early repayment of Russia's foreign debt. He resigned from these positions in 2005, as a result of the negative transformations in Russian politics. Illarionov holds honorary degrees from St. Petersburg State University, the Financial Academy in Moscow, the Kyrgyz Slavonic University in Bishkek, and the Ryskulov Academy of Economics in Almaty.

Niklas Nilsson is a Research Fellow with the Central Asia-Caucasus Institute & Silk Road Studies Program, a Joint Research and Policy Center affiliated with Johns Hopkins University-SAIS, Washington D.C., and the Stockholm-based Institute for Security and Development Policy (ISDP). He is also a Ph.D. Candidate in Political Science at Uppsala University/Södertörn University College, where he specializes in security politics in the EU's Eastern Neighborhood. He has authored or co-authored several articles and monographs on politics, security, conflict, and energy issues in the South Caucasus and Caspian regions. His articles and commentaries have appeared in international scholarly journals as well as in the European and U.S daily press. He is the Associate Editor of the biweekly analytic online journal *Central Asia-Caucasus Analyst.*

Johanna Popjanevski is Deputy Director of the Central Asia-Caucasus Institute & Silk Road Studies Program, a Joint Research and Policy Center affiliated with Johns Hopkins University-SAIS, Washington D.C., and the Stockholm-based Institute for Security and Development Policy (ISDP). Her specialization is in development and security issues in the South Caucasus region, primarily in Georgia. In 2005–6, she was a visiting researcher at the Georgian Foundation for Strategic and International Studies in Tbilisi. Ms. Popjanevski holds an LL.M. degree from Lund University, specialized in Public International Law. She is the author and co-author of several publications and numerous commentaries on Georgian affairs. She frequently visits Georgia to conduct field-research, and was present on the ground before and during the August 2008 war, immediately prior to which she had been on a field visit to Abkhazia.

James Sherr is Head of the Russia and Eurasia Programme at the Royal Institute of International Affairs (Chatham House) in London. Between 1995 and May 2008, he was a Fellow of the Advanced Research and Assessment Group (formerly Conflict Studies Research Centre) of the Defence Academy. He is also a member of the Faculty of Social Studies of Oxford University. For over ten years, Mr. Sherr has been NATO's principal external consultant on Ukraine and a key adviser to the UK and other Western governments on Russia and the Black Sea region, where he collaborates closely with official bodies and NGOs. He is also a prolific writer. James Sherr was born in New York City and holds British and U.S. citizenship.

David J. Smith is Director of the Georgian Security Analysis Center, Assistant Professor of International Relations at the University of Georgia, and a columnist for *24 Saati*. He is also Senior Fellow at the Potomac Institute for Policy Studies in Washington, D.C. Ambassador Smith holds degrees from the University of Arizona, London School of Economics, and Harvard University. From 2002 to 2006 he was the U.S. Member of the International Security Advisory Board for Georgia (ISAB). Earlier, he was U.S. Chief Negotiator for Defense and Space, Chief of Staff for Arizona Congressman Jon Kyl, Assistant for Strategic Policy and Arms Control to Senate Republican Leader Bob Dole, Professional Staff Member for the U.S. Senate Foreign Relations Committee, and a member of U.S. delegations to negotiations on conventional forces and chemical weapons. He was a Major in the U.S. Air Force.

S. Frederick Starr is Chairman of the Central Asia-Caucasus Institute & Silk Road Studies Program, a Joint Research and Policy Center affiliated with Johns Hopkins University-SAIS, Washington D.C., and the Stockholm-based Institute for Security and Development Policy (ISDP). He is a Research Professor at the Paul H. Nitze School of Advanced International Studies, Johns Hopkins University. His research, which has resulted in twenty books and 200 published articles, focuses on the rise of pluralistic and voluntary elements in modern societies, the interplay between foreign and domestic policy, and the relation of politics and culture. Starr holds a Ph.D. in History from Princeton University, an MA from King's College, Cambridge University, and a BA from Yale University. He is also the holder of honorary degrees from Middlebury College, Olivet College, Marietta College, and Loyola University. Prior to Founding the Central Asia-Caucasus Institute, Starr served as founding Director of the Kennan Institute for Advanced Russian Studies in 1974–79; as Vice-President for Academic Affairs at Tulane University in 1979–82; as Scholar-in-Residence of the Historical New Orleans Foundation in 1982–83. He served as President of Oberlin College between 1983 and 1994. In 1994–96, he served as President of the Aspen Institute. He served as an advisor on Soviet Affairs to President Reagan in 1985–86 and to President George H.W. Bush in 1990–1992.

Index